COLLECTED ESSAYS IN LAW

Meaning, Mind and Law

Collected Essays in Law Series
General Editor: Tom D. Campbell

The Great Juristic Bazaar:
Jurists' Texts and Lawyers' Stories

William Twining

ISBN: 978 0 7546 2211 6

Legal Rules and Legal Reasoning

Larry Alexander

ISBN: 978 0 7546 2004 4

Dispute Processing and Conflict Resolution

Carrie Menkel-Meadow

ISBN: 978 0 7546 2305 2

Objectivity in Ethics and Law

Michael Moore

ISBN: 978 0 7546 2329 8

Crime, Compliance and Control

Doreen McBarnet

ISBN: 978 0 7546 2349 6

Democracy Through Law

Johan Steyn

ISBN: 978 0 7546 2404 2

Legal Reasoning, Legal Theory and Rights

Martin P. Golding

ISBN: 978 0 7546 2669 5

Meaning, Mind and Law

Dennis Patterson

ISBN: 978 0 7546 2749 4

Dennis Patterson

Meaning, Mind and Law

Routledge
Taylor & Francis Group
LONDON AND NEW YORK

First published 2008 by Ashgate Publishing

2 Park Square, Milton Park, Abingdon, Oxfordshire OX14 4RN
711 Third Avenue, New York, NY 10017

Routledge is an imprint of the Taylor & Francis Group, an informa business

First issued in paperback 2018

British Library Cataloguing in Publication Data
Patterson, Dennis
Meaning, mind and law. - (Collected essays in law)
1. Law - Philosophy 2. Jurisprudence
I. Title
340.1

Library of Congress Cataloging-in-Publication Data
Meaning, mind and law / edited by Dennis Patterson.
p. cm. – (Collected essays in law)
Includes bibliographical references and index.
ISBN 978-0-7546-2749 4
1. Law–Philosophy. 2. Jurisprudence. I. Patterson, Dennis M. (Dennis Michael), 1955-

K235.M43 2008
340'.1–dc22

2007031499

ISBN 978-0-7546-2749-4 (hbk)
ISBN 978-1-138-38355-5 (pbk)

Contents

Acknowledgements

The editor and publisher wish to thank the following for permission to use copyrighted material.

Canadian Journal of Law and Jurisprudence for the essay: (1989) Realist Semantics and Legal Theory, *Canadian Journal of Law and Jurisprudence,* **2**, pp. 175–9.

Columbia Law Review for the essays: (1990) Law's Practice (Review of The Case Law System in America by Karl Llewellyn), *Columbia Law Review*, **90**, pp. 575–600; (1993) Conscience and the Constitution (Review of Constitutional Interpretation by Philip Bobbitt), *Columbia Law Review,* **93**, pp. 270–307.

Northwestern University Law Review for the essay: (1995) Langdell's Legacy, *Northwestern University Law Review*, **196**, pp. 196–203.

Oxford Journal of Legal Studies for the essay: (2006) Dworkin on the Semantics of Legal and Political Concepts, *Oxford Journal of Legal Studies*, **26**, pp. 545–57.

Oxford University Press for the essays: (2007) Moral Evaluation and Conceptual Analysis in Jurisprudential Methodology (with John Oberdiek), in Michael Freeman and Ross Harrison (ed.) *Law and Philosophy*, Oxford: Oxford University Press, pp. 60–75; (2006) Notes on the Methodology Debate in Contemporary Jurisprudence: Why Sociologists might be Interested, in Michael Freeman (ed.) *Law and Sociology*, Oxford: Oxford University Press, pp. 254–8.

Blackwell Publishing for the essay: (2006) Wittgenstein on Understanding and Interpretation (Comments on the work of Thomas Morawetz), *Philosophical Investigations*, **29**, pp. 129–39. Copyright © 2006 Blackwell Publishing.

San Diego Law Review for the essay: (2005) Interpretation in Law, *San Diego Law Review*, **42**, pp. 685–709. Copyright © 2005 *San Diego Law Review.*

Southern Methodist University Law Review for the essay: (1999) Explicating The Internal Point of View, *Southern Methodist University Law Review*, **52**, pp. 67–74.

Texas Law Review for the essays: (1994) Wittgenstein and Constitutional Theory, *Texas Law Review*, **72**, pp. 1837–55. (2003) Fashionable Nonsense, *Texas Law Review*, **81**, pp. 841–94.

Villanova Law Review for the essay: (1984) Interpretation in Law: Toward A Reconstruction of the Current Debate, *Villanova Law Review*, **29**, pp. 671–94.

Virginia Law Review for the essay: (1990) Law's Pragmatism: Law as Practice and Narrative, *Virginia Law Review*, **76**, pp. 937–96.

William and Mary Law Review for the essay: (2001) Normativity and Objectivity in Law, *William and Mary Law Review*, **43**, pp. 325–63.

Series Editor's Preface

Collected Essays in Law makes available some of the most important work of scholars who have made a major contribution to the study of law. Each volume brings together a selection of writings by a leading authority on a particular subject. The series gives authors an opportunity to present and comment on what they regard as their most important work in a specific area. Within their chosen subject area, the collections aim to give a comprehensive coverage of the authors' research. Care is taken to include essays and articles which are less readily accessible and to give the reader a picture of the development of the authors' work and an indication of research in progress.

Dennis Patterson

Preface

The essays collected in this volume are the product of twenty-plus years reflection on the relationship of law to philosophy. Like any work in legal philosophy, my jurisprudential point-of-view is informed by a distinct approach to philosophy and its relationship to legal theory. As these essays show, my philosophical views are grounded in the work of Wittgenstein, especially that of the *Philosophical Investigations* and subsequent work. As an argumentative practice, law is especially suited to the methodology evinced in Wittgenstein's work. From rule-following to the concepts of mind and thought, Wittgenstein's work has never been more relevant to legal philosophy. I hope the essays collected here are of value to scholars in both law and philosophy.

Over the course of the last twenty years, I have had the pleasure of working with many scholars in the United States, the UK, and continental Europe. I wish to acknowledge the many kindnesses shown to me by my friends and colleagues alike. I dedicate this work to my family and to three special friends who were especially supportive of me during my darkest hour, when I was stricken with cancer in 2001. During the many months it took me to wrest back control of my life from this dreaded curse, I received constant support from my family and my friends, who all made it possible for me to endure a very difficult time. In gratitude, I dedicate this work to them.

Dedication

To

Barbara, Sarah, and Graham

and

Three Special Friends:

Philip Bobbitt

Barry Stern

&

Jefferson White

Introduction

The task of general jurisprudence is to provide an account of law that, at least in part, identifies its principal features and explains what it is about the practice of law that gives it unity and coherence. As I see it, different schools of jurisprudence distinguish themselves from one another by virtue of the different answers each gives to the question of the distinctiveness of law. John Austin provides a clear example of this with his claim that law is the command of a sovereign. Similarly, Hart's Rule of Recognition and Kelsen's *Grundnorm* are each, in their way, distinct answers to the question of the essential features of law. As Gerald Postema has pointed out, even so great a critic of positivism as Ronald Dworkin shares the view that the nature of law is best explained in terms of the "ground rules" for identifying true propositions of law. Insightfully, Postema points out that despite his criticisms of positivism, Dworkin shares the positivist view that "the unity and coherence of law . . . depend on some formal constitutive structure."[1]

In *Law and Truth*,[2] I advanced the argument that debates in contemporary analytic jurisprudence are centered around the question of what it is that makes legal propositions true. I argued against the premise of the question, that is, that the task of general jurisprudence was identifying the "something" in virtue of which propositions of law are true. My argument was that law is a complex practice of reason-giving, one that is not best explained by the reductive accounts I saw on offer from the principal participants in contemporary debates. I retain my belief both in my critique of contemporary debates and in the alternative picture of law that I developed in *Law and Truth*. The essays in this volume take the project of *Law and Truth* further. In this brief Introduction, I shall outline the general orientation for these essays and explain what work remains to provide a full alternative approach to the issues.

It is sometimes said that the claim that "law is a practice" is a platitude. Platitude or not, I believe the question is now becoming a central focus of much work in analytic jurisprudence. Even if everyone agrees that law is a certain type of practice, that agreement will not answer the question of what sort of practice law is or how best to give an account of law. As I said, I think the question of how best to explain law as a practice is becoming the question of the day. In my opinion, the best answers to this question will proceed from a more general account of the nature of practices, accounts of meaning and

1 Gerald Postema, "'Protestant' Interpretation and Social Practices," 6 *Law and Philosophy* 283, 317 (1987).

2 Dennis Patterson, *Law and Truth* (1996).

the important role of epistemology and metaphysics in the course of any explanation of the nature of law and legal practice.

My jurisprudential perspective is directly informed by the so-called "later" work of Wittgenstein, that is, the work produced after 1929.[3] Of course, there are many perspectives on Wittgenstein's work. Some have recently taken disagreement over the proper reading of the Wittgenstein corpus to curious levels of intensity and argument.[4] For my part, the later work of Wittgenstein provides the most formidable point of reference for illumination of solutions to jurisprudential issues. But there is a further point to be made in locating this point of view and explicating its details.

I take what might broadly be characterized as "social view" of the nature of meaning and normativity.[5] As I see it, normativity and meaning are the products of social practices. An explication of the normativity of practices is a useful preliminary to explication of legal practice. Thus, Wittgenstein's account of meaning, mind and practices provides much of what is needed to ground and develop a jurisprudence that proceeds from the assumption that law is a special sort of conventional, social practice. Let me start with the most salient of Wittgenstein's many examples of his views, that of rule-following.

Wittgenstein's discussion of rule-following[6] comes after his discussion of a variety of other topics that all devolve to the point that the meaning of our actions are best understood not from the point-of-view of the Cartesian inner theater but from the perspective of our collective interactions with others. It is the ineliminable social dimension of meaning that grounds Wittgenstein's treatment of meaning and its relationship to rule-following. As I show throughout the essays collected in this volume, it is the social character of linguistic meaning that provides us with the tools we need for a proper account of law and legal practice.

The social view of the nature of meaning begins with the rejection of all "realist" accounts of the nature of linguistic meaning, rule-following and understanding. As I argue in various of the papers collected here, even if there is some "thing" in virtue of which are meanings are grounded, we are still

3 Especially Ludwig Wittgenstein, *Philosophical Investigations* (G.E.M. Anscombe trans., 3d ed. 1958) (hereafter "PI").

4 I have in mind those "new Wittgensteinians" who think the best way to read Wittgenstein is from the point of view of a certain reading of the *Tractatus*. For a critique, see P.M.S. Hacker, "Was He Trying to Whistle It?," in *Wittgenstein: Connections and Controversies* 98–140 (2001).

5 The most insightful commentary on this aspect of Wittgenstein's thought is Meredith Williams, *Wittgenstein, Mind and Meaning* (1999).

6 The passages from 198 to 206 of the *Investigations* are sufficient to make my point but sections 143–242 are generally regarded as containing the entire discussion of meaning and understanding.

not free of the burden of establishing how that "thing" is to be taken and used to parse correct and incorrect applications of concepts and rules. There is no standard of correctness that comes with instructions for its own use. Even the Standard Metre requires a practice to establish its status *as* a standard, one capable of generating a norm of correctness. The point is that the norm of correctness is not to be found in the thing (e.g., the Standard Metre) but in the way in which the thing is used. Correctness and incorrectness can, of course, be quite firm. But the question is whence that hardness of (judgments of) measurement comes? What is it that makes the Standard Metre of the rule (or a rule) "firm"? The practice does that.

The problem of rule-following (i.e., what does it mean to "follow" a rule?) is bound up with the question of interpretation. An extremely popular view of rule-following is that when it comes to correctness and incorrectness, the matter is best explained as a question of "interpretation." In other words, the question whether or not one is following a rule or not is a matter of one's having "interpreted" the rule (or the norms of correctness) properly. Notwithstanding decades of debate over this question, fundamental differences remain over how best to understand Wittgenstein's position.[7]

Wittgenstein explodes the hermeneutic claim that "all understanding is interpretation" with his Infinite Regress and Paradox of Interpretation Arguments.[8] If the way to understand a rule is with an interpretation, there is no reason to stop at the first interpretation. All interpretations are just re-expressions of the rule in question, each requiring their own "interpretation" (the infinite regress argument). As Wittgenstein says, "Interpretations by themselves do not determine meaning."[9] Likewise, if every course of action can somehow be "interpreted" to fit the rule, then interpretations do not tell us anything (the paradox of interpretation argument). What to do?

It is at this juncture that skepticism gains a foothold. Having undermined the realist view of rule-following, one is pushed to the conclusion that nothing grounds meaning and rules and that skepticism about meaning is the only proper course. This was Kripke's view, famously.[10] But Wittgenstein has a different answer: he rejects both objectified meaning and the skepticism entailed by the rejection of objectified meaning.

Wittgenstein remarks: "there is a way of grasping a rule which is *not* an *interpretation*, but which is exhibited in what we call 'obeying the rule' and

7 These differences are discussed in my treatment of the work of Thomas Morawetz in "Wittgenstein on Understanding and Interpretation (Comments on the work of Thomas Morawetz)."

8 See "Normativity and Objectivity in Law."

9 PI, § 198.

10 See Saul A. Kripke, *Wittgenstein on Rules and Private Language* (1982).

'going against it' in actual cases."[11] Constraints on rule-following – the ground of correct and incorrect – arise from our actual uses of rules. Correctness and incorrectness are inculcated in the course of training. Through training, our reactions to rules are calibrated with those of others. The necessity of "agreement in judgments"[12] is the ground of normativity in that the effectiveness of rules as norms is possible only when the socialization of initiates into rule-following practices yields a collective understanding of the norms of application.

I said that Wittgenstein's account of rule-following is grounded in his account of the distinction between understanding and interpretation. Wittgenstein locates normativity in action: action is the the nerve of the distinction between understanding and interpretation ("*Im Anfang war die Tat*"). The lesson of Wittgenstein's example of the signpost in PI 85[13] is that only *action* can provide the ground for correct and incorrect judgment. Without a practice of following it – a way of acting – the signpost by itself provides us no clue as to its proper use. There are as many potential ways of "following" the signpost as there are possible conventions for determining how it is to be used and what counts as following it. But once a convention for following signposts evolves, a background of understanding evolves; for it is against this background that the need for interpretation arises.

As an account of correct and incorrect action in a practice (be it law, arithmetic, or measurement), interpretation is a non-starter because interpretation draws our attention away from the techniques that make understanding possible. Correct and incorrect forms of action are immanent in practices. Thus, correct forms of action cannot be imposed on a practice, by interpretation or otherwise. It is only when we master the techniques employed by participants in a practice that we can grasp the distinction between correct and incorrect action (e.g., in law-assertion).

The immanent nature of norms of correctness in practices provides a singularly unique focus for law. If Wittgenstein is right about practices, then his claims about the social character of normativity lead to the conclusion that

11 PI, § 201.

12 PI § 242.

13 PI § 85:

> A rule stands there like a sign-post.—Does the sign post leave no doubt open about the way I have to go? Does it shew which direction I am to take when I have passed it; whether along the road or footpath or cross-country? But where is it said which way I am to follow it; whether in the direction of its finger or (e.g.) in the opposite one?—And if there were, not a single sign-post, but a chain of adjacent ones or of chalk marks on the ground – is there only *one* way of interpreting them?—So I can say, the sign-post does after all leave no room for doubt? Or rather: it sometimes leaves room for doubt and sometimes not. And now this is no longer a philosophical proposition, but an empirical one.

the task of general jurisprudence is clarification and elucidation of the norms of correctness immanent in the practice of law. I believe the best work in this regard is Philip Bobbitt's account of the modalities of legal argument.[14] Bobbitt identifies the grammar of legal argument with such clarity that his descriptive categories are now part of the conventional account of constitutional argument. While enormously helpful, I think Bobbitt's account of legal argument is incomplete.

To complete the project of a jurisprudence informed by the later work of Wittgenstein, we need an account of interpretation in law. In this volume, I have a chapter on this topic but more needs to be done. At the moment, I am working on a completely fresh account of a jurisprudence that proceeds from the later work of Wittgenstein. A complete account of the role of interpretation in such a jurisprudence is a central feature of the project. The essays collected here are each, in their way, a preliminary effort at a synoptic account of law from the Wittgensteinian perspective. I look forward to sharing that larger work.

Dennis Patterson
Voorhees, New Jersey
July, 2007

14 See Philip Bobbitt, *Constitutional Interpretation* (1991). For my critique of Bobbitt's position, see Chapter 7 of *Law and Truth* and "Wittgenstein and Constitutional Theory" in this volume.

[1]
Moral Evaluation and Conceptual Analysis in Jurisprudential Methodology
(with John Oberdiek)

Analytic general jurisprudence has become increasingly attentive to its own methodology in recent years. No longer content with its traditional first-order questions revolving around the varieties, commitments, and defensibility of legal positivism, the discipline of jurisprudence has turned inward, asking the second-order question, How should one do jurisprudence?[1] This second-order methodological question is not unrelated to jurisprudence's traditional first-order concerns, to be sure, as the role of evaluation, and indeed the role of moral theorizing more specifically, figures prominently in the methodological inquiry much as it does in the first-order debate among positivists, interpretivists, and natural law theorists about the role that morality plays or can play as criteria of legality. But the methodology debate has a cast all its own—it is not a mere proxy war between rival positivists and their mutual foes. In the first instance, second-order methodological positions on the role of moral evaluation in jurisprudence do not correspond directly to first-order positions regarding the relationship between legality and morality. Furthermore, the methodology debate focuses on one of the few planks in nearly all of the contenders' platforms, forcing legal philosophers to justify or jettison their shared commitment to conceptual analysis. It is the purpose of this discussion to introduce the methodology debate, draw attention to the merits and shortcomings of various positions already staked out, and to contribute to the debate by, albeit briefly, defending the claims that moral evaluation has (at least) a modest role in analysing the concept of law and that conceptual analysis, or rather, many of its incarnations, is defensible and indeed inescapable in jurisprudence.

[1] See, for example, L Green, 'General Jurisprudence: A 25th Anniversary Essay' (2005) 25 OJLS 4, 575; J Dickson, 'Methodology in Jurisprudence: A Critical Survey' (2004) 10 Legal Theory 117, 117–56; J Dickson, *Evaluation in Legal Theory* (Oxford, 2001); as well as Jules Coleman, *The Practice of Principle* (New York, 2001) 179–217, which is substantially reproduced as 'Methodology,' in J Coleman and S Shapiro (eds), *The Oxford Handbook of Jurisprudence and Philosophy of Law* (New York, 2002) 311–51.

I. A Brief History of the Debate

In his seminal 1961 book, *The Concept of Law*, HLA Hart advanced a powerful case for legal positivism, which he characterized as 'descriptive jurisprudence.'[2] A central feature of Hart's project was the clarification of legal practice through a perspicuous description of its principal features. Chief among these elements, in his view, was the conjunction of primary and secondary rules, where primary rules apply directly to citizens while secondary rules regard the identification, interpretation, and modification of primary rules. The keystone in Hart's scheme was a particular secondary rule, namely, the Rule of Recognition. The Rule of Recognition was the master rule within Hart's system because it alone provided the criteria determining whether a given rule was valid or not. Thus, by appeal to the Rule of Recognition, lawyers and non-lawyers alike could identify legal norms as legal norms and, in that way, decide what the law is on any given question.[3]

Ronald Dworkin, the most persistent critic of legal positivism, has consistently contested the possibility of the descriptive jurisprudence that Hart envisioned. One of Dworkin's central claims—advanced most systematically in his magisterial 1986 book *Law's Empire*[4]—is that 'law' is what Dworkin terms 'an interpretive concept'. Law is an interpretive concept because to understand the concept, one needs to grasp its point or purpose.[5] In Dworkin's view, one of the key dimensions of law is its coerciveness, and consequently, any explication of the concept of law must be able to explain and justify this important aspect of state action.[6] For Dworkin, justifying state coercion is a (if not *the*) fundamental task of jurisprudence. More importantly, it is an enterprise that is inescapably normative and not, *pace* Hart, merely descriptive.

The second edition of *The Concept of Law*, published posthumously in 1994, contained a rich and controversial *Postscript*, wherein Hart maintained that he and Dworkin were engaged in different philosophical enterprises, and that both enterprises were legitimate methodologies for jurisprudence. In reply, Dworkin remained unpersuaded, maintaining that his was the only appropriate methodology for jurisprudence.[7]

Thus, the debate within analytic general jurisprudence has turned increasingly to methodology, asking not 'What is law?', but, more self-consciously, 'How should one do philosophy of law?' As noted above, this second-order debate is related to the older first-order debate about the nature of law in that the methodology

[2] HLA Hart, *The Concept of Law* (2nd edn, Oxford, 1994) preface, i.

[3] See Hart, ibid 94–9 (describing the Rule of Recognition).

[4] R Dworkin, *Law's Empire* (Cambridge, MA, 1986).

[5] Dworkin, ibid 190 ('A conception of law must explain how what it takes to be law provides a general justification for the exercise of coercive power by the state. . .').

[6] Dworkin, ibid 94.

[7] R Dworkin, 'Hart's Postscript and the Character of Political Philosophy' (2004) 24 OJLS 1. This essay is reprinted in R Dworkin, *Justice in Robes* (Cambridge, MA, 2006) 140–186.

debate began with the question of whether purely descriptive jurisprudence is possible, or whether it instead must presuppose normative and specifically moral commitments.[8] Hart, and positivists generally, have argued that description of the law without justification of the law was possible. Dworkin, as well as John Finnis[9] and Stephen Perry,[10] have insisted that jurisprudence must engage in moral justification. Perry's work on this topic is widely considered to be the clearest starting point of the new methodology debate, and it is worth elucidating his central claims.

Perry has argued that Hart's own jurisprudential methodology, though avowedly purely descriptive, in fact incorporated both descriptive and normative elements.[11] It was descriptive insofar as Hart attempted simply to describe the concept of law, but it was unavoidably normative, his own self-understanding notwithstanding, insofar as Hart sought to describe it from the perspective of those over whom the law claims authority. Hart could not carry out a purely descriptive enterprise, according to Perry, because law itself is inherently normative, in that it purports to provide its subjects with overriding normative reason to do that which they otherwise would lack reason to do. To the extent that the phenomenon to be described is normative in this way, Perry argued, its hermeneutic, internal description must also be normative. Put roughly, in order to explain why those subject to legal authority should *respect* that legal authority, as is necessary if one seeks to describe the concept of law from the perspective of those over whom the law claims authority, then it is necessary to explain what is *respectable* about that legal authority. Showing what is respectable about a legal authority in turn involves (at least partially) justifying that legal authority. Accordingly, Perry concluded that, in light of the inherent normativity of law—the object of description—Hart's pure descriptivism could not stand.

Hart's most thorough defender on this score has been Julie Dickson, who has argued not only that Hart's methodology is not nearly as unstable as Perry makes it appear, but that Hart's is in fact jurisprudence's proper methodology.[12] Dickson accepts that Hart seeks to describe the concept of law and that doing so requires taking up the internal perspective of those working with and subject to law, but she steadfastly denies Perry's claim that describing the law from the internal perspective requires justifying law. While accepting that some form of evaluation is necessary in describing law, Dickson distinguishes between moral evaluation of the kind that marks a justification, on the one hand, and non-moral evaluation,

[8] For a clear and concise account of the debate thus far, see Dickson, 'Methodology in Jurisprudence: A Critical Survey' n 1 above.

[9] See J Finnis, *Natural Law and Natural Rights* (Oxford, 1984) 4.

[10] See especially, SR Perry, 'Hart's Methodological Positivism' in J Coleman (ed), *Hart's Postscript* (New York, 2001).

[11] In addition to the above article, see, Perry, 'Interpretation and Methodology in Legal Theory' in A Marmor (ed), *Law and Interpretation* (Oxford, 1995); and Perry, 'Holmes v Hart: The Bad Man in Legal Theory' in S Burton (ed), *'The Path of Law' and its Influence* (New York, 2000).

[12] See Dickson, *Evaluation in Legal Theory* n 1 above.

on the other. It is Dickson's view that legal theorists certainly do evaluate the data that they are trying to explicate, insofar as they are trying to explicate the significant and important data about law, and not extraneous data. Dickson moreover contends that the legal theorist's evaluations must be attuned to what those persons who create, administer, and are subject to the law take to be significant and important about law. The systematization and clarification of the concept of law relies on just such theoretical evaluation. But Dickson is resolute in maintaining that evaluation of this kind is a far cry from the outright moral evaluation that Perry argues is necessary. Dickson's is an evaluative-but-not-morally-evaluative, or what she terms 'indirectly evaluative', jurisprudence.[13]

If Perry and Dickson have each staked out clear alternative positions in the methodology debate, Brian Leiter has significantly widened it by relating the debate to important developments in metaphysics and epistemology. Traditionally, jurisprudence has been concerned with a single animating question, namely, the nature of law. Until Leiter's foray into the methodology debate, no one in the field questioned jurisprudence's fundamental animating premise, namely, that 'law' had a nature capable of explication. Adverting to WVO Quine's famous 1951 paper, 'Two Dogmas of Empiricism',[14] and the robust empiricism that it ushered in, Leiter maintains that the idea that concepts have a nature or necessary structure or content is mistaken, and that *a priori* inquiry into the concept of law—the task that jurisprudence has traditionally set for itself—is therefore fundamentally misguided. What jurisprudence must undergo, according to Leiter, is a naturalistic revolution, abandoning the traditional mission of conceptual analysis of 'law' and instead employing empirical methods to understand law. As Quine's naturalized epistemology is Leiter's model, reviewing Quine's central claims motivates and sheds light on Leiter's position.

Since Plato, philosophers have endeavoured to develop accounts of concepts—concepts like mind, knowledge, or justice—that unpack their content in terms of necessary and sufficient conditions discernable *a priori*. According to the so-called 'Classical Theory of Concepts', most concepts are 'structured mental representations that encode a set of necessary and sufficient conditions for their application …'.[15] While a single theory cannot be continuously identified from Plato on, it is not an overstatement to say that something like the Classical Theory was a significant element in philosophy from antiquity to the middle of the 20th century.[16] The reason for the longevity of the Classical Theory is not

[13] Similarly, Jules Coleman argues, '[i]t is one thing to claim that normative considerations figure in the project of identifying the features of law the theory of the concept must account for; quite another to claim that the norms to which one must appeal are those of political morality.' Coleman, *The Practice of Principle* n 1 above, 199.

[14] WVO Quine 'Two Dogmas of Empiricism' (1951) 60 *Philosophical Review* 20, reprinted in his *From a Logical Point of View* (Cambridge, MA, 1953) 20–46.

[15] S Laurence and E Margolis, 'Concepts and Cognitive Science' in E Margolis and S Laurence (eds), *Concepts: Core Readings* (Cambridge, MA, 1999) 18.

[16] Frank Jackson is the most vigorous, contemporary defender of conceptual analysis. See F Jackson, *From Metaphysics to Ethics: A Defence of Conceptual Analysis* (Oxford, 1998).

hard to see: it holds the promise of tremendous explanatory power, 'offering unified accounts of concept acquisition, categorization, epistemic justification, analytic entailment and reference determination, all of which flow directly from its basic commitments.'[17]

One or another version of the Classical Theory held sway until 1951, when Quine published the paper, 'Two Dogmas of Empiricism'.[18] Of the several theses Quine advanced in that landmark paper, the most important one for present purposes was his denial of what is known as the analytic/synthetic distinction.[19] Analytic statements are true in virtue of the meaning of the constituent terms. The most famous example is the proposition 'All bachelors are unmarried males'. Synthetic judgments, on the other hand, are claims of contingent fact. So, the proposition 'it is raining outside' is true not just in virtue of the meaning of any of the constituent terms but in virtue of facts in the real world. Quine argued, among other things,[20] that the analytic/synthetic distinction was indefensible because all statements are revisable, as he says, 'in the light of experience.' In other words, repudiating the analytic/synthetic distinction entails repudiating the distinction between necessary and contingent truths, a distinction upon which conceptual analysis depends.[21]

[17] ibid.

[18] Quine, 'Two Dogmas of Empiricism' n 14 above, 20–46.

[19] Here is the famous passage that sums up Quine's position:

> The totality of our so-called knowledge or beliefs, from the most casual matters of geography and history to the profoundest laws of atomic physics or even of pure mathematics and logic, is a man-made fabric which impinges on experience only along the edges. Or, to change the figure, total science is like a field of force whose boundary conditions are experience. A conflict with experience at the periphery occasions readjustments in the interior of the field. Truth values have to be redistributed over some of our statements. Re-evaluation of some statements entails re-evaluation of others, because of their logical interconnections-the logical laws being in turn simply certain further statements of the system, certain further elements of the field. Having re-evaluated one statement we must re-evaluate some others, whether they be statements logically connected with the first or whether they be the statements of logical connections themselves. But the total field is so undetermined by its boundary conditions, experience, that there is much latitude of choice as to what statements to reevaluate in the light of any single contrary experience. No particular experiences are linked with any particular statements in the interior of the field, except indirectly through considerations of equilibrium affecting the field as a whole.
>
> If this view is right, it is misleading to speak of the empirical content of an individual statement-especially if it be a statement at all remote from the experiential periphery of the field. Furthermore it becomes folly to seek a boundary between synthetic statements, which hold contingently on experience, and analytic statements, which hold come what may. Any statement can be held true what may, if we make drastic enough adjustments elsewhere in the system.

Quine, ibid 39–40.

[20] For a detailed explication of Quine's arguments in 'Two Dogmas of Empiricism', see S Soames, *Philosophical Analysis in the Twentieth Century* (Princeton, 2003) 351–405. For an assessment of the long-term influence of Quine's position, see PMS Hacker, *Wittgenstein's Place in Twentieth Century Philosophy* (Oxford, 1996) 183–227.

[21] In fact, it is doubtful that there is such a thing as 'the' analytic/synthetic distinction. For discussion, see PMS Hacker, 'Passing By the Naturalistic Turn: On Quine's *Cul-De-Sac*,' (2006) 81 *Philosophy* 231, 233–34 (pointing out that the limited Quine's target was Carnap's account of the analytic/synthetic distinction and enumerating a variety of other accounts of the distinction).

Even if Quine is right, how do his arguments matter to analytic general jurisprudence? Dworkin, recall, maintains that law's coercive power is essential to law and that it is that power that must be justified in any explication of the concept of law. This project assumes the defensibility of some form of conceptual analysis; indeed, Dworkin couches his project in precisely those terms.[22] Legal positivists, too, engage in conceptual analysis. Joseph Raz, the tradition's leading living exponent, writes:

> In as much as a general theory of law is about the nature of law it strives to elucidate law's essential features, i.e., those features which are possessed by every legal system just in virtue of its being legal, by every legislative institution in virtue of its being legislative, by every practice of legal reasoning in virtue of its being a practice of legal reasoning, and so on. A claim to necessity is in the nature of the enterprise.[23]

If Quine is right,[24] it would seem that neither Dworkin nor Raz (to take two prominent examples) can be right about methodology in legal theory. The reason is that claims to be describing the 'essential features' of law depend for their efficacy on the analytic/synthetic distinction. If the analytic/synthetic distinction is untenable, as Quine maintains, then it would seem to follow that no project of conceptual analysis, whether Dworkinian or positivist, gets off the ground. This is, in broad brush, Leiter's negative claim. More constructively, Leiter wants to fill the gap that he believes Quine creates by importing Quine's naturalism into legal theory.[25] Just as science replaces philosophy in Quine's naturalized epistemology,[26] Leiter maintains that social science must replace concept-driven legal philosophy as the best explanatory methodology for law. Instead of conceptual analysis, philosophers should be engaged in social scientific empirical research.[27]

In light of his thoroughly naturalized jurisprudence, Leiter stakes out a position distinct from both Perry's and Dickson's. Like Dickson, Leiter believes that jurisprudence is a largely descriptive enterprise and is evaluative only to the extent that it must be responsive to the normative understanding of the law

[22] Dworkin writes, '[e]ach conception [of law] furnishes connected answers to three questions posed by the concept. First, is the supposed link between law and coercion justified at all? Is there any point in requiring public force to be used only in ways conforming to rights and responsibilities that "flow from" past political decisions? Second, if there is such a point, what is it? Third, what reading of "flow from"—what notion of consistency with past decisions best serves it?' Dworkin, *Law's Empire* n 4 above, 94.

[23] J Raz, 'On the Nature of Law' (1996) 82 *Archiv für Rechts- und Sozialphilosophie* 1, 2. It is worth noting that Raz explicitly states, 'I will leave the question of the kind of necessity involved unexplored.' ibid.

[24] But see P Grice and PF Strawson, 'In Defense of a Dogma' (1956) 65 *Philosophical Review* 141–58, reprinted in Paul Grice, *Studies in the Way of Words* (Cambridge, MA, 1989) 196–212.

[25] See B Leiter, 'Beyond the Hart/Dworkin Debate: The Methodology Problem in Jurisprudence' (2003) 48 American Journal of Jurisprudence 17.

[26] See B Leiter, 'Naturalism in Legal Philosophy' in *Stanford Encyclopedia of Philosophy* (2002), available at <http://plato.stanford.edu/entries/lawphil-naturalism/>.

[27] See Leiter, 'Beyond the Hart/Dworkin Debate' n 24 above, 48–52.

held by those subject to law. However, Leiter also believes that all that is needed is the meta-theoretic evaluation that is part of any theorizing—no theory can be entirely 'value free'—involving evaluative judgments of explanatory power, coherence, simplicity, and so forth. Indeed, while Leiter joins the consensus that jurisprudence should respond to the internal point of view of those subject to law, he parts with Dickson in maintaining that jurisprudence should do without any mediating evaluative judgments about the relevance of certain understandings of law.[28] In Leiter's view, it is not for the legal philosopher to determine which internal understandings are sufficiently important and which are confused. It is all just indistinguishable factual data, the simple collection and systematization of which is the legal philosopher's task. This is naturalistic jurisprudence in that it eschews any aspiration to capture law's conceptual essence apart from what can be gleaned from empirical data on what people think law is and the role that they accord to it in their self-understanding. Leiter thus seems to accept a more modest role for evaluation in jurisprudence than even Dickson.

The thumbnail sketch of the recent history and current state of play in the methodology debate is, of course, simplified. There are many more players and theses than those just discussed. At the same time, the positions staked out by Perry, Dickson, and Leiter mark clear poles in the debate, and the framework provided by their positions is therefore a useful one. As currently structured, the methodology debate within analytic jurisprudence (finally) joins wider debates in the philosophy of language, epistemology and metaphysics. In what follows, we take up the different facets of this debate under two broad headings: Part II discusses the role of moral evaluation in jurisprudence and Part III takes up the role of conceptual analysis.

II. Moral Evaluation in Jurisprudence

In this section, we attempt to explore further Perry's claim that the explication of the concept of law requires moral evaluation and that jurisprudence is in that sense normative. It is common ground that *some* evaluation is required to unpack the content of the concept of law; what is controversial is whether the evaluation must be moral in nature. The line to be explored here is that every legal system in fact possesses a morally attractive property, deriving from its adherence to the rule of law, and that moral premises must therefore be relied upon to understand the nature of law. The argument does not countenance an inference from legality to moral legitimacy. Laws and legal systems can of course be morally illegitimate. But one can reject the inference from legality to moral *legitimacy* while maintaining that law *qua* law has some moral *value*. Moral value, on this view, is not an

[28] This is Dickson's interpretation of Leiter's position, advanced while correcting what she regards as Leiter's misinterpretation of her position. See Dickson, 'Methodology in Jurisprudence: A Critical Survey' n 1 above, 133–39.

all-things-considered judgment, but a claim about one feature of law. In this respect, the moral value that we are suggesting inheres in law is defeasible, such that the moral worth of a legal system can be undermined by morally illegitimate laws, while retaining some moral value simply in virtue of its adherence to the rule of law.

Our argument is brought into relief most clearly by attending to an argument dismissed by Jules Coleman.[29] Coleman suggests that 'law' functions as a 'predicate of weak commendation', that any account of law must explain why we valorize legal governance as we do, and that the case for so-called 'normative jurisprudence' might succeed if 'the best explanation of how it is that law plays this role in our normative discourse is that law has a moral property adequate to warrant "law's" linguistic role.'[30] Coleman connects the dots as follows:

> If law has such a property, an analysis of the concept of law should specify what this property M is—and in so doing, the analysis must appeal to moral argument in two ways: in specifying the content of M, the analysis must reveal how or why that property is morally attractive; and the overall analysis must be such that it picks out only things that have the property M.[31]

Coleman, to repeat, denies that this argument is sound. And he does so in two steps. First, he argues that the best explanation of the weak commendation role of law is the *potential* possessed by legal systems for good governance; second, that law has the potential or capacity to facilitate good governance does not, according to Coleman, entail that this capacity is part of the concept of law.[32] In Coleman's view, the potential to facilitate good government, that instrumental value, is a feature of law that any plausible analysis of the concept of law must account for, to be sure, but it is not a central feature, any more than the capacity to be used as a paperweight is a central feature of the concept of a hammer.

Let us grant for the sake of argument that Coleman is correct that if law can only be commended in virtue of its potential, moral considerations need not be invoked to unpack the concept of law. It remains an open question, however, whether the commendation of law is elicited or warranted *solely* in virtue of law's potential for facilitating good government. More specifically, the value of *the rule of law* does not depend on the contingent content of the law, but rather on features of law itself, and thus if it is the rule of law that (at least in part) elicits or warrants law's commendation, and the rule of law is central to the concept of law, it follows that a case can be made for normative jurisprudence that escapes any criticism focused on law's mere potential.

Now, the first question is whether the rule of law is central to the concept of law. If it is not central, after all, then adducing the moral value inherent in the rule of law will do nothing to establish that moral argument is required to

29 See Coleman, *The Practice of Principle* n. 1 above, 190–5.
30 ibid 191.
31 ibid.
32 ibid 192–4.

explicate the concept of law. How central, then, is the rule of law to the concept of law? There is some reason to think that it is *not* central. Raz, for example, holds that '[t]he rule of law is a political ideal which a legal system may lack or may possess to a greater or lesser degree.'[33] If so, if a legal system can remain a legal system even in the absence of upholding the rule of law, then it would seem to follow that the rule of law cannot be a central feature of the concept of law.

But this is perhaps the wrong way to read Raz. In discussing Lon Fuller's claim that the rule of law is essential to the existence of law, Raz admits that the principles of the rule of law—that laws should be open, clear, accessible, and stable, for example—'cannot be violated altogether by any legal system.'[34] This suggests, contrary to the import of his earlier claim, that there could be no legal system that failed utterly to adhere to the rule of law. It suggests, that is, that some degree of fidelity to the rule of law, some degree of formal fairness, is a necessary feature of any legal system, and so of the concept of law. Coleman, too, appears to accept this proposition. He maintains, '[t]o be sure, a legal system need not be effective in constraining the exercise of the ruler's power, and may even stipulate that the law imposes no such constraints; but in so far as a ruler exercises purely arbitrary power, he or she does not govern by law.'[35] Coleman argues that the exercise of 'purely arbitrary power' cannot be lawful, which of course entails that power must be constrained in some way or to some degree in order to be lawful. And while Coleman nowhere mentions 'the rule of law', the idea that arbitrary power is to be curtailed just is the idea of the rule of law.[36]

There is much more to be said on this score, but let us proceed on the assumption, which we have provided some reason to endorse, that the rule of law is central to the concept of law. The question now is whether the commendation of law is elicited or warranted by a feature of the rule of law itself or whether instead the commendation is due merely to the capacity or potential law has for good governance. Raz is again instructive. According to him, the rule of law cannot depend entirely for its value on the content of whatever laws are adopted. As Raz points out, '[i]f the rule of law is the rule of the good law then to explain its nature is to propound a complete social philosophy. But if so the term lacks any useful function.'[37] And again, 'conformity to the rule of law is an inherent value of laws, indeed it is their most important inherent value.'[38] At the same time, however, Raz maintains,

> Clearly, the extent to which generality, clarity, prospectivity, etc. are essential to the law is minimal and is consistent with gross violations of the rule of law. But are not

[33] J Raz, 'The Rule of Law and its Virtue' in *The Authority of Law* (Oxford, 1979) 211.

[34] ibid 223. Summarizing his point, Raz maintains, 'at least some of the rules of recognition and of adjudication of every system must be general and prospective.'

[35] Coleman, *The Practice of Principle* n 1 above, 192–3.

[36] As Raz puts it, 'certainly many of the more common manifestations of arbitrary power run foul of the rule of law.' Raz n 33 above, 219.

[37] ibid 211.

[38] ibid 225.

considerations of the kind mentioned sufficient to establish that there is necessarily at least some moral value in every legal system? I think not. The rule of law is essentially a negative value.... [C]onformity to it does not cause good except through avoiding evil and the evil which is avoided is evil which could only have been caused by the law itself.[39]

The value of the rule of law is not, in Raz's estimation, sufficient to endow any legal system with any moral value, however minimal. Raz's argument in support of that conclusion is highly compressed and it is worth briefly unpacking it.

Raz illustrates his claim about the rule of law's purely negative value by analogizing the rule of law to honesty: just as one who cannot communicate or thus deceive deserves no credit for being honest, the fact 'that the law cannot sanction arbitrary force or violations of freedom and dignity through total absence of generality, prospectivity, or clarity is no moral credit to the law.'[40] Indeed, Raz goes so far as to liken the conceptual inability of law to instantiate the evil of arbitrary rule to its inability to murder—and no one finds it a moral virtue of the law that it cannot itself murder anyone. Raz rejects the claim that there is any merit in refraining from doing that which is conceptually impossible. He thus concludes that insofar as the rule of law is conceptually incompatible with completely arbitrarily-directed power, the fact that law cannot be guilty of that evil is not to its credit.

This argument is much too quick. One can concede that the rule of law is a negative virtue and yet find its negative virtue to be an authentic commendation feature, in Coleman's words, and so find grounds for commending governance under law. One can see what more can be said on behalf of the rule of law's negative virtue if one considers other forms of governance in assessing the value of the rule of law.

Societies can take any number of different forms, and specifically, they need not incorporate a legal system. This is uncontroversial. We can, moreover, imagine a society without a legal system that is prosperous and just. Clearly, such a society would be superior to a society that possessed a legal system, and thus the rule of law, but which was neither prosperous nor just. This is also uncontroversial. But now compare a society without a legal system that is prosperous and just with one that has a legal system and that is also prosperous and just; when that comparison is made, it is hard to deny that the society with the rule of law is superior to the society lacking the rule of law. And this has everything to do with the rule of law's negative virtues, enumerated by Raz. Neil MacCormick captures the point nicely in maintaining, 'There is always something to be said for treating people with formal fairness, that is, in a rational and predictable way, setting public standards for citizens' conduct and officials' responses thereto.'[41] The rule of law always adds something of value to the societies that possess it. And it is for this reason that if one were in a position to choose which of these two societies to live in, both of

[39] ibid 224.

[40] ibid 224.

[41] N MacCormick, 'Natural Law and the Separation of Law and Morals' in Robert George (ed), *Natural Law Theory* (New York, 1995) 123. MacCormick goes on to claim, 'That indeed is what we mean by the Rule of Law.' ibid.

which were prosperous and just but only one of which abided by the rule of law, one would have reason to live in the society with the rule of law, precisely because of its negative virtues. Even if a society achieves prosperity and distributes goods and resources justly, failing to do so according to the rule of law constitutes a moral demerit. That prosperity and justice should be pursued in an open, predictable, and rule-governed manner is an undeniable moral good. In this way, the moral value of the rule of law, while negative, is nonetheless additive; societies which are otherwise good and just are better if they also have a legal system formalizing norms that underwrite their prosperity and justice.

None of this should be construed to suggest that societies that possess the rule of law are morally superior to any society that lacks it. There is no question that a prosperous and just society lacking the rule of law is morally better than one that possesses the rule of law but which has substantively immoral laws. Yet this consideration raises what might be thought to be a problem for the claim advanced here, that legality is inherently morally valuable. The potentially troubling thought is this: persons living in a thoroughly morally bankrupt society with the rule of law might in fact be better off without the rule of law, if that would mean that some who would otherwise be subject to morally indefensible laws would be spared from them, precisely because such exceptions would run contrary to the rule of law's strictures concerning generality, prospectivity, and formally equal treatment. If this is true, the thought goes, then the rule of law by itself cannot always be morally valuable.[42] Instead, the rule of law would have value only when the legal system giving effect to the rule of law was substantively just, which is to say that the rule of law would have merely potential value.

It is important to recognize that this objection misses its mark. If one were living in a deeply unjust society, whose injustice was codified in law, then one's interests, characterized along one dimension, could indeed be served if the rule of law were abandoned insofar as one would at least have a chance of escaping consistent application of substantively repellant laws. But there is more to one's interests than what will or does happen to one. One also has an interest in having a certain moral status, that is, in being *owed* treatment of a certain kind. Having a certain moral status is reasonably conceived as among one's interests because it makes one *worthy* of respect, regardless of whether, as a matter of fact, one is respected.[43]

Conceived along the dimension of moral status, one's interests would not be served, at least not entirely, by dismantling the rule of law. MacCormick is right to claim that '[t]here is always something to be said for treating people with formal fairness', and the reason is that the formal fairness demanded by the rule of law expresses a view about the moral status of people, namely, that persons are

[42] We thank William Edmundson for raising this point.

[43] See FM Kamm, 'Inviolability' in PA French, TE Uehling Jr and HK Wettstein (eds), *Midwest Studies in Philosophy* vol XX (University of Notre Dame Press, 1996) 165–75. For more expansive treatment of moral status so conceived, see Kamm, *Morality, Mortality: Rights, Duties, and Status* (New York, 1996) Pt III.

worthy of being treated in non-arbitrary ways. The rule of law, quite apart from the content of particular laws, responds to the status of those subject to it as being owed treatment of a certain kind. In fact, nothing about the content of the laws whose application is formally fair can diminish the value of their formally fair application in accordance with the rule of law.

People are of course owed much more than formally fair, non-arbitrary treatment—substance and not just form matters. But to the extent that people are owed non-arbitrary treatment, form does matter. It is true that fewer people might have substantive injustice visited upon them if a morally bankrupt society abandoned the rule of law, since some would be excepted from substantively unfair treatment, but if that came to pass, it would follow that the society no longer embraced the formal respect for persons that the rule of law entails. And that would constitute a moral loss. Perhaps that loss should be sustained in some cases—that multiple dimensions of value constitute one's interests does not entail that trade-offs are not possible across those dimensions. In all cases, though, such a trade-off would remain a moral loss. That the rule of law's value is defeasible does not entail that it is not always valuable.

Returning to the line of argument for normative jurisprudence that Coleman hypothesizes only to reject, we conclude that he is mistaken to construe law's commendation feature as purely instrumental, being based only on the law's potential or capacity for good governance. Law surely has such a commendation feature, but it also has the non-instrumental commendation feature of instantiating the rule of law and all of its virtues. It is in this sense that we submit that the concept of law may be inescapably normative, requiring moral argument to explicate its content.

III. Conceptual Analysis in Jurisprudence

Quine's thesis regarding analyticity, which he described as the first of two dogmas of modern empiricism,[44] was a denial of what he referred to as 'some fundamental cleavage' between truths which are analytic (true in virtue of meaning) and truths which are synthetic (true in virtue of facts). Quine's claim[45] was that there is no principled way to distinguish analyticity from mere co-extensionality. Quine's argument was quickly met with a rebuttal by Grice and Strawson.[46] Grice and Strawson argued that if talk of synonymy is meaningless then so too must be talk about the meaning of a sentence. They pressed their point this way:

> Is all talk of correct and incorrect *translation* of sentences of one language into sentences of another language meaningless? It is hard to believe that it is. But if we do successfully

[44] Quine, 'Two Dogmas of Empiricism' n 14 above, 20.
[45] ibid 27–32.
[46] Grice and Strawson n 24 above.

make the effort to believe it, we have still harder renunciations before us. If talk of sentence-synonymy is meaningless, then it seems that talk of sentences having a meaning at all must be meaningless too. For if it made sense to talk of a sentence having a meaning, or meaning something, then presumably it would make sense to ask 'What does it mean?' and if it made sense to ask 'What does it mean?' of a sentence, then sentence synonymy could be roughly defined as follows: Two sentences are synonymous only if the true answer to the question 'what does it mean?' Asked of one of them, is a true answer to the question, asked of the other.[47]

Quine, it seems, thought that Grice and Strawson were right for, as Scott Soames describes, 'four years after this criticism appeared, he published *Word and Object*, in which he does advocate … giving up meaning and translation entirely.'[48]

Quine does, in fact, give up on meaning. Quinean naturalism mandates that talk of 'meaning' and cognate terms (eg 'synonymy' and 'analyticity') be jettisoned in favour of tabulations of correct and incorrect responses to stimuli. All talk of 'meaning' can be replaced with a naturalistic account given by way of behavioural stimuli. As Quine puts it: 'The stimulus meaning of a sentence for a subject sums up his disposition to assent to or dissent from the sentence in response to the present stimulation.'[49]

So, let us return to legal philosophy and ask what all of this means for the methodology debate. Leiter argues that Quine's supposed demolition of the analytic/synthetic distinction makes way for naturalism in legal philosophy, for like philosophy generally, legal philosophy must go empirical and be absorbed into science, social science included. On the outside looking in, according to Leiter, is conceptual analysis, analytic general jurisprudence's traditional method of inquiry: '… if analytic statements are gone, then so too is conceptual analysis: since any claim of conceptual analysis is vulnerable to the demands of a posteriori (ie empirical) theory construction, philosophy must proceed in tandem with empirical science, not as the arbiter of its claims, but as a reflective attempt at synoptic clarity about the state of empirical knowledge.'[50] Leiter's claim depends, of course, on eliminating the distinction between conceptual and empirical questions. But what is conceptual analysis, and is it really vulnerable to Quine's attack, and in his wake, Leiter's?

In our view, the key mistake that Quine and, by extension, Leiter make is to treat conceptual analysis as one particular type of philosophical work, and one, moreover, that depends upon a robust conception of the analytic/synthetic distinction. But there are at least four distinct, overlapping methods of conceptual analysis that are not challenged in any serious way by Quinean naturalism, and it is worth considering them each, if briefly, in order to assess whether anything more than what they offer is needed for jurisprudence as traditionally practised.

[47] ibid 201.
[48] S Soames, *Philosophical Analysis in the 20th Century* (Princeton, 2003) 377.
[49] WVO Quine, *Word and Object* (Cambridge, MA, 1960) 40.
[50] Leiter, 'Beyond the Hart/Dworkin Debate' n 25 above, 45.

On one prominent conception of the enterprise, 'conceptual analysis is the very business of addressing when and whether a story told in one vocabulary is made true by one told in some more fundamental vocabulary.'[51] The point of this modest form of analysis is to show whether and how one set of terms is reducible to another, or what to say about a posit in an old theory when a new theory comes along. Frank Jackson and Philip Pettit explain this approach as follows:

> Take the new theory to have the truth of the matter—or at least more of it than the old theory. The question of the fate of a particular posit of the old theory is then decided by considering how the posit was conceived in the old theory and seeing whether something satisfying that conception nearly enough is to be found in the new theory. If the answer is yes ... the old posit survives; if the answer is no, as it is for impetus, phlogiston, caloric fluid, et al., the old posit is eliminated.[52]

Jackson suggests that this method is in fact quite close in practice—even if not in theory—to Quinean 'paraphrasing', where '[t]he objective would not be synonomy, but just approximate fulfillment of likely purposes of the original sentences ...'.[53]

A second type of conceptual analysis is what we might call 'therapeutic'. In this endeavour, the philosophical task is to identify and eliminate claims or assertions that lack sense. Take the claim 'to understand a legal text, one must interpret it.' This claim expresses the familiar position within the Hermeneutic tradition that 'all understanding is interpretation', such that when we read a text, or hear an utterance, we achieve understanding by taking the text or utterance and translating it into something meaningful. We can conceptually analyse the claim 'all understanding is interpretation' therapeutically by noting that it leads to an infinite regress: if every 'text' requires interpretation before its meaning can be gleaned, then why stop at the initial text?[54] The 'interpretation' of the text will itself require interpretation before its meaning can be discerned, and so on infinitely. Hence, there must be something wrong with the idea that 'all understanding is interpretation.'[55] And in facilitating interrogation of the claim, it is conceptual analysis that illuminates this problem.

A third form of conceptual analysis is what might be termed 'conceptual theorizing'. Kenneth Himma provides a good account:

> Conceptual analysis attempts to theorize ... intuitions or core conventions by identifying deeper metaphysical commitments that are either implied or presupposed by these

[51] Jackson, *From Metaphysics to Ethics: A Defence of Conceptual Analysis* n 16 above, 28.

[52] F Jackson and P Pettit, 'In Defence of Folk Psychology' in F Jackson, P Pettit, and M Smith, *Mind, Morality, and Explanation* (Oxford, 2004) 33.

[53] WVO Quine, *Word and Object* n 49 above, § 46. See Jackson n 16 above, 45.

[54] See L Wittgenstein, *Philosophical Investigations* § 198 (GEM Anscombe (trans), 2nd edn, Oxford, 1967), '"But how can a rule shew me what I have to do at this point? Whatever I do is, on some interpretation, in accord with the rule."—That is not what we ought to say, but rather: any interpretation still hangs in the air along with what it interprets, and cannot give it any support. Interpretations by themselves do not determine meaning.'

[55] For detailed discussion, see Dennis Patterson, *Law and Truth* (New York, 1996) 71–127.

intuitions, as well as more general principles that would explain these intuitions or conventions. While this might or might not be a distinctively philosophical enterprise, it goes well beyond the empirical task of identifying shared intuitions or core conventions.[56]

Now, there are two ways of doing the kind of conceptual analysis Himma imagines. The difference is marked by the word 'metaphysical'. Leaving that word in this passage, on a traditional approach, the activity is classic, reductive metaphysics—reducing one set of terms to another. The metaphysical aspect is filled in by commitment to some set of necessities that underlie the terms in questions. But there is another way to do this form of conceptual analysis, one that does not require the invocation of metaphysical commitments.

In this 'lite' version of conceptual analysis, the task is not metaphysical reduction but the identification of presupposition through redescription. Consider, in this regard, Raz's 'service conception' of authority, in which the law plays a mediating role between right reason and persons, serving those on whom legal authority bears by claiming to guide them better than they could guide themselves. Raz offers this conception of authority as a way of identifying one distinguishing feature of legal norms. Raz does not claim, nor need he, that the service conception of authority is 'metaphysically necessary'. All he need do is claim, as he does, that this conception of authority is presupposed by 'our' concept of law.[57]

A fourth and final version of conceptual analysis untouched by Quine's critique is closely related to this third, 'lite' version, and consists, as Coleman puts it, in 'uncovering the most salient features of the concept: those that figure most prominently in an explanation of the kind of thing it is the concept of—that are central to our understanding and appreciation of it.'[58] The goal here is not to find analytic truths, or essential features of concepts, but to discern what in the concept under consideration warrants picking out the concept as the concept that we do.[59] This form of conceptual analysis is, in many respects, continuous with Quinean naturalism—indeed Coleman attributes his approach in part to Quine.[60] Its roots notwithstanding, this method of inquiry is plausibly understood as conceptual analysis. Discerning which features of a concept warrant according the concept its particular role in our discourse must consist in analysing that concept.

What this very brief overview of forms of conceptual analysis illustrates is, first, of course, that there is no one form of conceptual analysis but that, second, conceptual analysis need not take any form in practice that conflicts with Quine's arguments in 'Two Dogmas'. Our earlier points about the possibility of truth in virtue of meaning alone suggests that Quine's arguments do not establish—or

[56] KE Himma, ch 1 above.
[57] See Raz, 'On the Nature of Law' n 23 above, 1–12.
[58] Coleman, *The Practice of Principle* n 1 above, 179.
[59] See also B Zipursky, 'Pragmatic Conceptualism' (2000) 6 Legal Theory 457.
[60] See Coleman n 1 above, at 6 and 9.

rather, undermine—all that they claim to. The present synopsis of forms of conceptual analysis strongly suggests that, even if Quine's arguments are sound, they do not put conceptual analysis out of business, but rather merely one particularly strong version of it. This overview implies a third point as well, and that is that it is simply not clear that one can get by without relying in some degree on one of these forms of conceptual analysis in understanding law.

Indeed, Coleman has noted that Leiter himself must do a good deal of conceptual analysis even to frame his own position. As Coleman puts it, 'the naturalized project can proceed only after a good deal of philosophical spadework.'[61] Focusing more specifically on Leiter's work on adjudication, Coleman argues that '[t]he very idea of an adjudicatory function operating on authoritative legal standards presupposes that we have criteria for determining what the authoritative legal standards are. Thus, the naturalist is committed as a conceptual matter to the existence of a test of legality.'[62] Similarly, Leiter's own commitment to exclusive legal positivism,[63] and his claims of its compatibility with American-style legal realism, are conceptual claims.[64] The point here is that a naturalistic account of law cannot *replace* but in fact *presupposes* a conceptual understanding of law.

It is just not clear, at the end of the day, whether Leiter recognizes that there are more forms of conceptual analysis than that which Quine had in his cross-hairs. Nor is it clear whether Leiter recognizes that, at least in the main, little in jurisprudence depends upon Quine being mistaken. Of course, in light of his own conceptual presuppositions about law, noted above, Leiter would seem to be committed to there being at least one 'acceptable' form of conceptual analysis. But Leiter exegesis is not our goal.[65] What is important to establish, by our lights, is that there are many forms of conceptual analysis besides that which Quine argues is bankrupt, and that jurisprudence as traditionally conceived can, and in fact, always has, helped itself primarily to those secure conceptual resources.[66]

[61] Coleman n 1 above, 213.

[62] ibid 213–4.

[63] B Leiter, 'Legal Realism and Legal Positivism Reconsidered' (January 2001) *Ethics* 286.

[64] See H Oberdiek, 'Legal Realism: What Does Quine Have to Do With it?' unpublished manuscript 26.

[65] For thorough discussion of Leiter's work on naturalism in jurisprudence, see H Oberdiek ibid.

[66] In his new book, *Naturalizing Jurisprudence* (Oxford, 2007) 196, n 49, Brian Leiter comments on a draft of this article, with specific attention to the four forms of conceptual analysis we deem invulnerable to the Quinean critique of Carnap's distinction between analytic and synthetic propositions. Leiter asserts that we 'somewhat bizzarely' claim that two of our four methods are impervious to the Quinean critiqiue. He further asserts that two of the methods are 'obviously vulnerable granting the soundness of Quinean naturalism'. It is, unfortunately, impossible to assess Leiter's claims as he provides no arguments to support them. It is perhaps worth noting for the interested reader, in addition, that in referring to the four methods by number and not substance, Leiter appears to confuse them with one another.

[2]
Dworkin on the Semantics of Legal and Political Concepts

Abstract—In a recent comment on H.L.A. Hart's 'Postscript' to *The Concept of Law*, Ronald Dworkin claims that the meaning of legal and political concepts may be understood by analogy to the meaning of natural kind concepts like 'tiger', 'gold' and 'water'. This article questions the efficacy of Dworkin's claims by challenging the use of natural kinds as the basis for a semantic theory of legal and political concepts. Additionally, in matters of value there is no methodological equivalent to the scientific method. Thus, there is little hope of finding hidden essences to explain the meaning of legal and political concepts. Finally, even if there are natural kinds, Dworkin's arguments for their efficacy in jurisprudence are problematic and unpersuasive. The problem for Dworkin is that his embrace of natural kinds undermines the 'fit' side of the fit/justification model of adjudication that lies at the heart of his theory of law.

> 'Even the debate about the nature of law, which has dominated legal philosophy for some decades, is, at bottom, a debate within the philosophy of language and metaphysics.' Ronald Dworkin[1]

The relationship between problems in legal theory and the philosophy of language has been a leitmotif in analytic jurisprudence for the better part of the last half-century.[2] From the influence of Wittgenstein's and Austin's thought on Hart in *The Concept of Law*[3] to Ronald Dworkin's claim that his

* Distinguished Professor of Law (Camden) and Philosophy (New Brunswick) and Co-Director of the Rutgers (Camden) Institute for Law and Philosophy. Email: dpatters@camden.rutgers.edu. My thanks to Brian Bix, Curtis Bridgeman, John Dupré, Kim Ferzan, Hanjo Glock, P.M.S. Hacker, Andrew Halpin, Ken Himma, George Letsas, Patrick S. O'Donnell, Hans Oberdiek, John Oberdiek, Ralf Poscher, Danny Priel, Joseph Raz, Larry Solum, Nicos Stavropoulos, Brian Tamanaha and Jefferson White for comments on a draft of this article. Special thanks to Matt Adler and Claire Finkelstein for the opportunity to discuss this article at the University of Pennsylvania Law School Legal Theory Workshop. Work on this article was completed while the author was the holder of the Fulbright Distinguished Chair in Law at Trento, Italy, 2005.

[1] Ronald Dworkin, 'Introduction' in *The Philosophy of Law* 1 (Ronald Dworkin ed., 1977).

[2] Of course, when Hart wrote *The Concept of Law*, 'philosophy of language' was conceived of as 'philosophical logic'. While Hart paid some attention to questions of meaning, it is only recently that issues of reference, meaning and truth have become central in analytic jurisprudence. For doubts about the role of ordinary language philosophy in Hart's jurisprudence, see Les Green 'The Concept of Law Revisited', 94 *Michigan L Rev* 1687 (1996).

[3] H.L.A. Hart, *The Concept of Law* (2nd edn, 1994) at 297 (referencing and endorsing Wittgenstein's rule-following discussion). See also P.M.S. Hacker, *Wittgenstein's Place in Twentieth-Century Analytic Philosophy* (1996) at 156 ('[Hart] applied lessons learnt from contemporary reflections in the philosophy of language, in particular from Austin, Wisdom . . . Wittgenstein and Waismann, to jurisprudential questions').

dispute with positivism is best seen as a local version of the global realism/anti-realism debate in the philosophy of language,[4] legal philosophers have often acknowledged that progress in jurisprudence can be enhanced by approaching problems in legal theory from the vantage point of philosophy of language.[5]

In a recent commentary on Hart's *Postscript* to *The Concept of Law,*[6] Dworkin once again brings the philosophy of language to bear on jurisprudence. By way of analogy with so-called 'natural kind' terms, Dworkin argues that the meaning of many of our most cherished political concepts—e.g. justice—are not a matter of shared criteria of application (as Hart thought, according to Dworkin), but a function of what Dworkin calls 'a deep structure'.[7]

I will argue that Dworkin's incorporation of natural kinds semantics into his jurisprudence is problematic for three reasons. First, I attack the fundamental premise of Dworkin's argument; to wit, the claim that the meaning of natural kind terms such as 'gold', 'tiger', and 'water' is a function of the deep structure of the things to which these terms refer. Proponents of natural kinds make two claims. Metaphysically, natural kinds are identical with their underlying natures. Semantically, natural kinds are directly referential; that is, the meaning of natural kind terms is a function of direct reference cashed out in terms of microstructure. I grant, *arguendo*, the metaphysical thesis but deny the semantic thesis. In short, my claim is that there is no necessary relationship between natural kinds and the *meaning* of natural kind terms. If this argument is successful, then the premise from which Dworkin's argument proceeds necessarily fails.

My second argument grants, *arguendo*, the premise that there are natural kinds. But Dworkin's argument for hidden essences for political and legal kinds fails because, unlike science, in matters of value there is no agreed way to adjudicate disputes over the existence and features of such essences. Without epistemic or methodological confirmation, debates about the 'real' meaning of political and legal concepts will not be resolved by appeals to 'the hidden nature of things'.

My final argument also grants, *arguendo*, that there are natural kinds. But if Dworkin is to be taken at his word about similarities between natural kind and

[4] See Dworkin, 'Introduction', above n 1 at 8 ('I think that many positivists rely, more or less consciously, on an anti-realist theory of meaning').

[5] The usefulness of realist semantics is questioned in Brian Bix 'Can Theories of Meaning and Reference Solve the Problem of Legal Determinacy?', 16 *Ratio Juris* (2003) at 281.

[6] See Ronald Dworkin, 'Hart's Postscript and the Character of Political Philosophy', (2004) 24 *OJLS* 1. This essay is reprinted in Ronald Dworkin, *Justice in Robes* (2006) at 140–86. All citations are to the original essay.

[7] Ibid at 12 (describing political values as 'real' and possessed of a 'deep structure' or 'essence'). Positivists have long rejected Dworkin's view that positivism presupposes a criterial theory of the meaning of law. Dworkin confuses the view that the content of the rule of recognition is determined by shared criteria, which is a positivist view, with the view that the meaning of the word 'law' is determined by shared criteria. The latter is no part of the theory of positivism. For discussion, see Kenneth Einar Himma 'Ambiguously Stung: Dworkin's Semantic Sting Reconfigured', 8 *Legal Theory* (June 2002) 145–84.

legal concepts,[8] then there is a material—indeed, significant — shift in his general jurisprudential position. If legal and political concepts are best understood as akin to natural kinds, then judges should ignore precedents whenever those precedents fail to reflect the judge's sense of the (natural kind) meaning of the term in question. In Dworkin's terminology, the 'fit' side of the fit/justification picture of adjudication becomes superfluous. In short, adjudication would be 'justification all the way down'.[9]

1. *Hart's Archimedean Jurisprudence*

Hart characterized his theory of law as a 'descriptive jurisprudence'. In this, he sought to clarify legal practice through a perspicuous description of its principal features. Chief among these elements are the concepts of primary and secondary rules, the internal point of view, and, most importantly, the Rule of Recognition. Through the use of the Rule of Recognition, lawyers and non-lawyers alike are able to identify legal norms and, in that way, decide what the law is on any given question.[10]

A long-standing critic of positivism, Dworkin renews his objections to the positivist account of the nature of law with the claim that Hart is what Dworkin terms an 'Archimedean'. According to Dworkin, Archimedeans take a practice and divide its discourse into two different sorts of assertions: first and second-order.[11] First-order assertions are substantive claims, such as claims of right.

[8] I am mindful that Dworkin says that there are *'instructive similarities'* (Dworkin, p. 12) to be drawn between natural kind concepts like water, tiger and gold and political concepts like democracy, liberty, and equality. It is difficult to discern just how far Dworkin intends to take this comparison. Michael Green has recently argued that Dworkin commits a 'fallacy' (Green dubs it 'Dworkin's Fallacy') by grounding an interpretive theory of law in an interpretive theory of meaning. See Michael Steven Green 'Dworkin's Fallacy, or What the Philosophy of Language Can't Teach Us About the Law', 89 *Virginia L. Rev.* 1897, 1909–10 (2003). Dworkin describes Green's account of his argument as a 'surprising misreading'. Dworkin, *Justice in Robes*, above n 7 at 226. Additionally, Dworkin states that legal concepts are 'interpretive concepts' and not natural kind concepts. ('I explicitly rejected a natural kind interpretation of any of the concepts of law'. Ibid at 227). One is left to wonder just what Dworkin means when he states there are 'instructive similarities' to be drawn between legal and natural kind concepts. The essence of natural kind concepts is necessity, specifically metaphysical necessity (see the discussion of Kripke below at n 28). If legal and natural kind concepts are not similar in terms of metaphysical necessity, it is rather unclear in just what sense Dworkin thinks they are 'similar'.

[9] I owe this way of making the point to John Oberdiek.

[10] Hart, above n 3 at 94–99 (describing the Rule of Recognition). Jules Coleman argues that the Rule of Recognition need not be epistemic. See Jules Coleman, *The Practice of Principle* (2001) at 132.

[11] Here, Dworkin describes what he takes to be one of the leading examples of Archimedean philosophical thought, meta-ethics: 'The most familiar of these specialist philosophies is so-called 'meta-ethics'. It discusses the logical status of the "value judgments" that ordinary people make when they say, for example, that abortion is morally wrong, or that racial discrimination is wicked or that it is better to betray one's country than one's friends. Some meta-ethical philosophers say that these value judgments are either true or false, and that if they are true then they correctly report some mind-independent moral fact. Others deny this: they say that value judgments are not reports about an independent reality, but are rather expressions of emotion or personal taste, or recommendations for behaviour, or something subjective of that character. But the philosophers in both groups insist that their own theories-the theory that value judgments are objectively true as well as the rival theory that they only express emotion-are not themselves value judgments. Second-order philosophical theories about value judgments, the philosophers insist, are neutral, philosophical and uncommitted. They take no position about the morality of abortion or discrimination or friendship or patriotism. They are conceptual or descriptive, not substantive and engaged'. Dworkin, above n 6, at 2–3.

Second-order assertions concern what it means to 'have a right'. Archimedeans, Dworkin argues, think there is a difference between making a purportedly true claim (e.g. 'I have a right to *x*') and explaining what it would mean for a claim in a given practice to be true (e.g. 'one has a right to *x* just in the case the legislature has acted so as to create such a right'). The first sort of assertion expresses a value judgment; the second describes what it means to assert a true proposition. First-order assertions are 'substantive and engaged'[12] while second-order ones are 'conceptual or descriptive'.[13]

Dworkin denies the distinction embraced by meta-ethicists and positivists alike, that is, that there is a logical distinction between first and second-order assertions. For Dworkin, all assertions are first-order because 'definitions or analyses of the concepts of equality, liberty, law and the rest are as substantive, normative and engaged as any of the contending opinions in the political battles that rage about those ideals'.[14] Thus, no account of law could be as Hart argued, that is, purely descriptive, for all description involves evaluation.

2. *Dworkin on Conceptual Content*

What governs the use of political concepts like 'liberty' and 'law'? One view is that the use of a concept is a matter of 'shared criteria' for its application. 'Artifact concepts'[15] might describe the use of words such as 'paper' or 'book', but the idea of shared criteria 'does not hold . . . for the concept of justice'.[16] For Dworkin, it cannot be the case that a question such as 'whether judicial review imperils democracy' can be answered by the application of criteria. This question requires a different sort of answer.

A second possibility is that 'the correct attribution of [a] concept is fixed by a certain kind of fact about the objects in question, facts that can be the object of very widespread error'.[17] Dworkin argues that 'natural kind' concepts provide the clearest example. Consider the word 'tiger'. It might be that the many animals described by people in using this term may not, in fact, be 'real' tigers. While the animals may look exactly like 'real' tigers, they lack 'the distinctive DNA'[18] that only 'real' tigers possess.[19] The word 'tiger' is properly used only to refer to those animals with 'the distinctive tiger DNA'.[20] To use the word in any other way is to make a mistake.

[12] Ibid at 3.
[13] Ibid.
[14] Ibid at 3.
[15] Ibid at 10.
[16] Ibid.
[17] Ibid.
[18] Ibid at 11.
[19] For a detailed argument for the proposition that 'species' is a dubious natural kind concept, see Joseph Laporte, *Natural Kinds and Conceptual Change* (2004) at 63–91.
[20] Dworkin, above n 6 at 11.

The meaning of words like 'tiger', 'gold', and 'water' is a function not of how these words are used but to what the words refer. This referring relation is the key to meaning and, thus, correct use. Assuming this account of meaning is correct for natural kind terms like tiger, gold and water, can the same be said of legal and political concepts?

While it is true that '[l]iberty has no DNA',[21] Dworkin maintains that political and legal concepts have a 'deep structure'[22] that determines what these terms 'really mean'.[23] We cannot find the deep structure of liberty like we can discover the DNA of a tiger, but we can get at the deep structure of legal and political concepts by employing a different strategy. The reason is simple: '[t]he deep structure of political values is not physical—it is normative'.[24]

Dworkin's argumentative strategy is clear. Like natural kind concepts, political and legal concepts have a 'deep structure'.[25] It is this hidden structure that gives each term its meaning and, more importantly, determines correct and incorrect applications of the term. Thus, debates over the 'true' meaning of legal and political terms turn on identifying the normative equivalent of DNA or chemical composition. There is a right answer to the meaning and truth of our assertions about what law and politics require. The route to true propositions is through discovery of the true meaning of our terms.

3. *Natural Kinds: The Very Idea*

The idea of a natural kind was presaged by Locke's theory of real and nominal essences. The real essence of a thing is that which makes the thing what it is.[26] Nominal essences, by contrast, are the means by which we distinguish things as belonging to a kind.[27] Real essences, which give rise to the properties of a kind, are a feature of microscopic structure and are the real source of the phenomenal properties of a thing. Locke and his contemporaries lacked the tools to access

[21] Ibid.

[22] Ibid at 13. See also ibid at 12 (describing legal and political concepts as having a 'nature or essence').

[23] Ibid at 19.

[24] Ibid at 13. The key paragraph reads: 'The difference between natural kinds and political values that I emphasized of course remains after we have noticed these similarities. The deep structure of natural kinds is physical. The deep structure of political values is not physical - it is normative. But just as a scientist can aim, as a distinct kind of project, to reveal the very nature of a tiger or of gold by exposing the basic physical structure of these entities, so a political philosopher can aim to reveal the very nature of freedom by exposing its normative core. In each case we can describe the enterprise, if we wish, as conceptual. The physicist helps us to see the essence of water; the philosopher helps us to see the essence of liberty. The difference between these projects, so grandly described, and more mundane projects-between discovering the essence of water and discovering the temperature at which it freezes, or between identifying the nature of freedom and deciding whether taxation compromises freedom-is finally only one of degree. But the comprehensiveness and the fundamental character of the more ambitious study-its self-conscious aim at discovering something that is fundamental by way of explanation-justifies reserving the name of conceptual for it. We cannot sensibly claim that a philosophical analysis of a value is conceptual, neutral and disengaged. But we can sensibly claim it to be normative, engaged, and conceptual'. Ibid.

[25] Ibid at 12 ('[P]olitical values have a deep structure that explains their concrete manifestations').

[26] John Locke, *An Essay on Human Understanding* , Vol. II, 26 (1894, 1959) (A.C. Fraser ed., New York: Dover) ('the being of anything whereby it is what it is').

[27] For discussion, see John W. Yolton, *A Locke Dictionary* (1993) at 179–80 (entry for 'Properties').

the microscopic level of things. This meant that when it came to the meaning of words, nominal essences and not natural kinds were all they had to guide them.

All of this has changed. Contemporary natural science affords us full access to the microscopic level of substances of all kinds. These scientific developments have been taken up by philosophers with an interest in marrying advances in scientific knowledge to semantic theory. During the 1960s and 1970s, Saul Kripke[28] and Hilary Putnam[29] developed sophisticated semantic theories that took the idea of a 'natural kind' concept to a new level of refinement. Putnam argues that a natural kind concept has the following four features:

(1) a syntactic marker (in the case of 'water', for example, *mass noun, concrete*);
(2) a semantic marker (*natural kind, liquid*);
(3) a stereotype (*colourless, transparent, tasteless, thirst-quenching, etc.*); and
(4) an extension (H_2O).[30]

The first three items on this list are all features within a normal speaker's linguistic competence. But if Putnam is right, those features do not determine the extension (and thus, meaning) of a natural kind term, for that is a matter of nature. The nerve of the natural kinds argument is the idea that the rigid referential component — a micro-structural property (e.g. DNA or molecular formula)—is dispositive of the meaning of the term to which the rigid designator has attached.[31] In addition, the extension (usually a micro-structural feature) is an *aposteriori* scientific discovery.

If Putnam's account of the semantics of natural kind terms is correct, the following would be the case:

(1) the extension of a natural kind term is determined not by its intension, nominal essence, or sense, but by a possibly unknown [i.e., pending scientific discovery] 'sameness relation' between the microstructural properties of the paradigm and items belonging to the extension;

[28] See Saul A. Kripke, 'Naming and Necessity' in *Semantics of Natural Language* (1972), Donald Davidson and Gilbert Harman (eds). While not directly important for the purposes of this article, there is some relevant history of philosophy that needs to be told. Concepts such as analyticity and necessity played an indisputably central role in philosophy until the publication in 1951 of Quine's seminal article 'Two Dogmas of Empiricism'. The conventional understanding is that with this article, Quine showed that the long-held distinction between analytic and synthetic truths could not be maintained. Quine's view was orthodoxy until 1970, when Saul Kripke gave three lectures at Princeton that became the book *Naming and Necessity*. Kripke, it was believed, showed that propositions like 'Water is H2O' and 'Whales are mammals' are both necessarily true and their truth discovered as a result of scientific investigation. Hence, these propositions are necessary, aposteriori truths. For details, see Scott Soames, *Philosophical Analysis in the 20th Century* (2 volumes, 2003).

[29] Hilary Putnam, 'The Meaning of Meaning' in *Mind, Language and Reality* (1975) at 215–71.

[30] Ibid at 269.

[31] The Kripke/Putnam account of natural kinds is not without its difficulties: 'A paradoxical consequence of this view is that two words may be used in exactly the same way, according to exactly the same criteria, yet differ in meaning because they happen to be applied to things or substances with different essences. For example, people on a different planet may use a word exactly as we use the word 'water': to denote a transparent, tasteless, drinkable liquid that occurs in rivers, lakes and as rain, but their word would have a different meaning if 'water' on their planet was not constituted of H2O. Conversely, if water was discovered to have the same molecular structure as tar, then the words 'water' and 'tar', in spite of their markedly different use, would have the same meaning'. Severin Schroeder, *Wittgenstein* (2006) at 248.

(2) expressions in different languages may share the same syntactic and semantic markers and the same stereotype, yet mean something quite different. Hence a liquid (on an imagined planet called 'twin Earth') with all the properties of water save being constituted of XYZ rather than H_20, despite being called 'water' (by twin-Earthians), would not actually be water.

(3) conversely, expressions which do not share the same stereotype may nevertheless turn out to have the same extension or real essence. For example, a substance with atomic number 79, which possessed none of the overt properties of gold, would none the less be gold (and if so, then the stereotype of gold was wrong).

(4) mastery of the use of an expression falls short of knowing what it really means. Indeed, a linguistic community may use an expression for millennia without finding out what it really means and without realizing that they do not know what it really means.

(5) the ultimate arbiter of what natural kind terms mean is empirical science. It is not that scientific discoveries lead to changes in the meanings of the relevant terms, but rather that they reveal what those terms, unbeknownst to their users, have always meant.[32]

Consider 'Twin Earth', the imaginary planet Putnam devised to illustrate his theory. Twin Earth is identical with our planet in every respect, save one. On Twin Earth, the substance there called 'water' shares all the phenomenal properties of water on our planet and plays precisely the same roles on Twin Earth as it does on Earth. The only difference is that the substance called 'water' on Twin Earth has the chemical composition XYZ and not H_20. Putnam maintains that when we learn the truth about XYZ we will be forced to conclude that it is not 'water' because water is necessarily H_20.[33]

Instead of denying that XYZ is water, would it not be better to view XYZ as simply 'another type of water'? Is this not precisely how we treat so-called 'heavy water' (D_2O) which differs from H_2O in that it is composed of deuterium (an isotope of hydrogen)? Are we to say that this substance is not 'water' because it has a chemical composition other than H_2O? Curiously, a simple request for 'a glass of water' could not be satisfied if the substance came from the kitchen tap

[32] Hacker, above n 3, at 251.

[33] Putnam, above n 28 at 270. There are further difficulties with Putnam's argument, not the least of which is that if Putnam's XYZ example were plausible, much of our scientific knowledge would collapse. Peter Hacker details the problem thus: 'If X, Y and Z are elements, what are their atomic numbers? How can they be accommodated in the periodic table of elements? There is no "room" for them compatible with our knowledge of chemistry. What valencies might they have, and what is the form of the chemical bonding into which they enter in the compound XYZ? What are the properties of pure X (Y and Z), which are such that twin Earth is overtly indistinguishable from Earth? Does XYZ have the same weight as H_20? If so, how is that possible, given the rest of our knowledge of, chemistry and of chemical elements? If not, then it cannot behave in the same way as H_20. If X, Y and Z are not elements, but 'XYZ' merely abbreviates a 'long and complicated formula' (as Putnam suggests), how is it possible, compatibly with established chemical theory, that it have the same overt properties (freezing and boiling points, weight, etc.) as H_20?' Hacker, above n 3, at 329, n 43.

because that substance contains a wide variety of elements that alter its composition.[34]

When we look at other parts of the natural world, the idea of a natural kind is of limited explanatory use. For a variety of reasons, the kinds distinguished by science have an extension not reflected in ordinary language. For example, in normal parlance no one would be persuaded to refer to onions and garlic as lilies, and yet they are part of the family of Liliaceae. Similarly, in non-scientific contexts, one would not classify vultures as hawks or butterflies as a type of moth.[35] By contrast, the term 'tree'—a word widely employed in common parlance—fails to find a place in any scientific taxonomy. Ordinary language and scientific practice often overlap in the meaning assigned to linguistic terms. But just as often, ordinary parlance and science diverge.

Realists (in jurisprudence and elsewhere) dismiss the divergence between science talk and ordinary parlance. Their claim is that as between the world and diction, the world wins every time.[36] But the realist premise (which underwrites Putnam's natural kinds argument) is that scientific classification yields a natural order untouched by human purpose. Given substantial evidence that there are multiple objective ways of organizing features of the natural world,[37] the realist position is not without its challenges. Whatever the shortcomings of realism, the kernel of truth in the natural kinds argument is the recognition that the existence of the world is mind-independent. The problem is that one need not believe in natural kinds semantics to believe this obvious truth.

It is important to be clear about the precise nature of my critique of Dworkin's argument. I do not deny that tigers have DNA or that pure water is composed of hydrogen and oxygen. Rather, I deny that the *meaning* of terms like 'tiger' and 'water' *is a function of* these hidden essences. My argument is a brief against the reductionist view of natural kind theorists and those (like Dworkin[38]) who seek to solve problems in legal theory through the use of arguments drawn from natural kind semantics.

4. *The Achilles' Heel of Realism*

Even if we grant Dworkin's premise—that political, legal and moral kinds have a hidden essence—there is little hope that such kinds will ever be identified in any

[34] These include phosphates, nitrates, sodium, potassium, magnesium, calcium, sulphates, chlorides and hydrogen carbonate. See http://www.iapws.org/faq1/isotope.htm. See Noam Chomsky, 'Language and Nature', *Mind*, 104 (1995) at 22 (whether something is water depends on human interests).

[35] See John Dupré, *The Disorder of Things* (1993) at 28.

[36] See Michael S. Moore, 'A Natural Law Theory of Interpretation' (1985) 58 *S. California L. Rev.* 277–398.

[37] See John Dupré, 'Is "Natural Kind" a Natural Kind Term?' (2002) 85 *The Monist* 29–49 (examples from biology); Philip Kitcher, 'Ghostly Whispers: Mayr, Ghiselin, and the "Philosophers" on the Ontological Status of Species' (1987) 2 *Biology and Philosophy* 184–92 (on the concept of 'species').

[38] See also Nicos Stavropoulos, *Objectivity in Law* (1996); David O. Brink, 'Legal Interpretation, and Judicial Review' (1988) 17 *Philosophy and Public Affairs* 105.

manner comparable to natural science. The reason for this is quite simple: there is no agreed procedure for resolving disagreements in matters of value.

The lack of methodological consensus in morals and politics represents the Achilles' heel of moral realism.[39] When scientists disagree about the truth of a scientific proposition, they employ a variety of methods to settle the question at issue.[40] It is because ethics and politics lack what Thomas Nagel refers to as 'uncontroversial and well-developed methods'[41] for settling disputes that an idea like natural legal and political kinds is so problematic.

The Achilles' heel of moral realism undermines Dworkin's argument for hidden essences to explain the meaning of legal and political concepts. Like water or gold, Dworkin claims, political concepts have a 'deep structure'.[42] With respect to legal and political concepts, it is this mind-independent[43] deep structure 'that explains their concrete manifestations'.[44] The difference from natural kinds is that the essence of political concepts is 'normative' not empirical. But how is the deep structure of political concepts revealed?[45] What is Dworkin's normative analogue to DNA, atomic number and molecular formula?[46]

It would be unfair to say that Dworkin has no answer to this question. However, the answer Dworkin gives[47] is the familiar one of integrity wedded to 'a

[39] Jeremy Waldron, *Law and Disagreement* (1999) at 179 ('[I]n non-moral cases . . . we can supplement the simple epistemology of looking-and-seeing with a whole apparatus on which we agree . . . There is nothing comparable in ethics'.). Dworkin has consistently denied that the failure to demonstrate the truth of legal propositions does not mean there is no truth of the matter. See his essay 'Is There Really No Right Answer in Hard Cases?' in Ronald Dworkin, *A Matter of Principle* (1985) at 137–45 (rejecting the 'non-demonstrability thesis'). My point, following Waldron, is not to deny the claim that there is in fact a right answer. Rather, the claim is that the fact of a right answer does not matter because the failure to identify the right answer as such means that the answer cannot help us in identifying the true state of the law on any given question. Thus, the claim is not that moral realism is false; the claim is that it is superfluous.

[40] Jules Coleman and Ori Simchen argue that 'a perceived lack of agreement among jurisprudents would constitute a key factor as to why the extension of "law" is not fixed by reliance on jurisprudential expertise'. see Jules L. Coleman and Ori Simchen, 'Law' (2003) 9 *Legal Theory* 26. In fact, 'the kind of disagreement that Dworkin emphasizes and no one disputes—undermines the trust necessary for reliance on jurisprudential expertise'. Ibid at 26.

[41] Thomas Nagel, *The Last Word* (2001) at 101. Nagel further argues: 'We can regard our scientific beliefs as objectively true not because the external world causes us to have them but because we are able to arrive at those beliefs by methods that have a good claim to be reliable, by virtue of their success in selecting among rival hypotheses that survive the best criticisms and questions we can throw at them . . . It is mainly because we have no comparably uncontroversial and well-developed methods for thinking about morality that a subjectivist position here is more credible than it is with regard to science.' Ibid at 101–102. (Nagel goes on to argue that, while objectivity in ethics is more difficult to defend than objectivity in science, it can nonetheless be successfully defended). My thanks to John Oberdiek for reminding me of Nagel's discussion.

[42] Dworkin, above n 6 at 12.

[43] Ibid. ('[T]he existence and character of freedom as a value does not depend on anyone's invention or belief or decision'.)

[44] Dworkin, above n 6 at 12.

[45] Dworkin claims that 'just as a scientist can aim . . . to reveal the very nature of a tiger or gold by exposing the basic physical structure of these entities, so a political philosopher can aim to reveal the very nature of freedom by exposing its normative core'. Dworkin, above n 6 at 13.

[46] Of course, a realist might dismiss my objection as a mere epistemic quibble. My point is that even if we grant the realist his metaphysical premises, his account of normativity (i.e. correct and incorrect judgment) is woefully inadequate for the simple reason that without consensus on a standard, appeal to 'the true nature of things' is empty. This is the lesson of Wittgenstein's 'Paradox of Interpretation Argument'. For discussion, see Meredith Williams, *Wittgenstein, Mind and Meaning* (1999) at 160.

[47] See Dworkin, above n 6 at 13 ('the task of the political philosopher is to show justice in its best light').

larger web of conviction'.[48] This answer is fine, as far as it goes. But the entire meta-ethical debate is over the question of what we mean when we say that a proposition of politics or morality is 'true'.[49] By and large (methodologically speaking), science has an answer to the question of the truth of empirical propositions and a widely-shared methodology for settling disputes. Dworkin has no comparable answer or methodology for propositions of morality and politics because he deems such an answer unnecessary.[50]

While Dworkin wants to deny the relevance of meta-ethical approaches to questions of moral and political value, his argument for moral and political kinds has the consequence of confirming the importance of the meta-ethical enterprise he rejects. The logical distinction between the question of the truth of a proposition and the criteria for assessing its truth is a distinction recognized in science as well as ethics. An ironic feature of Dworkin's position is that in denying its importance he shows just how important the distinction really is.

5. *Whither Fit?*

One of the hallmarks of Dworkin's jurisprudence is his long-standing commitment to the methodology of 'constructivism'. Early on, Dworkin endorsed Rawls' method of reflective equilibrium as a model for how to think about adjudication. Dworkin put it this way: 'It [the constructive model] treats intuitions of justice not as clues to the existence of independent principles, but rather as stipulated features of a general theory to be constructed'.[51] Dworkin contrasted the constructive model with another, one he identified as the 'natural model'. This model presupposes 'an objective moral reality [one that is not] created by men or societies but . . . rather discovered by them, as they discover the laws of physics'.[52]

Construction and discovery are two ways of characterizing adjudication. The constructivism of *Taking Rights Seriously* evolved to the interpretivist thesis at the heart of *Law's Empire*. A consistent feature of Dworkin's methodological approach to jurisprudence was his commitment to a constructivist model of adjudication and his rejection of the discovery or 'natural' model. The question now is whether Dworkin's claims regarding natural kind concepts and interpretive concepts like 'law' mark a change in his jurisprudential position.

[48] Dworkin, above n 6 at 14.

[49] See Dennis Patterson, *Law and Truth* (1996) (arguing for a practice theory account of the meaning of 'truth' in law).

[50] While he eschews meta-ethics, Dworkin reaffirms his commitment to the epistemic virtues of holism and Rawlsian reflective equilibrium (Dworkin, above n 6 at 14 and 18).

[51] Ronald Dworkin, *Taking Rights Seriously* (1977) at 160. Dworkin further explained that the 'constructive model does not assume . . . that principles of justice have some fixed, objective existence, so that descriptions of these principles must be true or false in some standard way. It does not assume that the animal it matches to the bones actually exists'. Ibid.

[52] Ibid.

As a semantic theory, natural kinds dictates that the extension (meaning) of a term is a function of a mind-independent reality such as atomic number, DNA, or molecular formula. Does Dworkin mean to suggest that political and legal concepts are 'like' natural kinds in that their essence is similarly mind-independent, hidden from view and unchanging? In the article under discussion, Dworkin says many things that suggest, for him, the truth of propositions of politics and law is a matter of hard fact. Consider:

> Natural kinds . . . are real: neither their existence nor their features depend on anyone's invention or belief or decision.
>
> They have a deep structure—their genetic profile or molecular character that explains the rest of their features, including the surface features through which we recognize them whether or not we are aware of that deep structure.
>
> Political and other values are in almost all those respects like natural kinds.
>
> [P]olitical values, too, are real: the existence and character of freedom as a value does not depend on anyone's invention or belief or decision.
>
> [P]olitical values have a deep structure that explains their concrete manifestations. If progressive taxation is unjust, it is unjust in virtue of some more general, fundamental, property of just institutions that progressive taxation lacks.
>
> The deep structure of natural kinds is physical. The deep structure of political values is not physical: it is normative.
>
> But just as a scientist can aim, as a distinct kind of project, to reveal the very nature of a tiger or of gold by exposing the basic physical structure of these entities, so a political philosopher can aim to reveal the very nature of freedom by exposing its normative core.
>
> The physicist helps us to see the essence of water; the philosopher helps us to see the essence of liberty.[53]

Dworkin makes it clear that he thinks the essences of political and legal concepts (i.e. values) are mind-independent (i.e. their 'existence and character' do not depend on anyone's beliefs). This is a strong, and seemingly realist,[54] characterization of the metaphysical status of political and legal values. Like the scientist, the political philosopher's task is discovery, not construction. The political philosopher does not tell us what she thinks is the best constructive interpretation of our practice. Rather, through the process of interpretation, the political philosopher reveals the content and substance of values the essence of which exist and are waiting to be discovered.[55]

[53] Dworkin, above n 6 at 12–13.

[54] Of course, Dworkin has described himself as a 'realist'. See Ronald Dworkin, 'Objectivity and Truth: You'd Better Believe It' (1996) 25 *Philosophy & Public Affairs* 87, 128 ('My realism . . . knows no bounds').

[55] If Dworkin is *not* shifting his account of adjudication from a constructive to a discovery model, then the point of his argument for 'instructive similarities' between natural kind terms and interpretive concepts like 'law' is opaque. As stated above, if legal (i.e. interpretive) concepts and natural kind concepts are not similar in terms of metaphysical necessity, it is rather unclear in just what sense Dworkin thinks they are similar.

Dworkin's claim that useful analogies can be drawn between natural kind concepts and interpretive concepts serves only to problematize a central feature of his jurisprudence. I refer, of course, to the distinction between fit and justification.[56] Through the use of imaginative examples such as the practice of courtesy[57] and the chain novel,[58] Dworkin has insisted that any interpretation of a practice has to account for a significant part of the past practice of the community. As Dworkin himself has said, the purported justification 'need not fit every aspect or feature of the standing practice, but it must fit enough for the interpreter to be able to see himself as interpreting that practice and not inventing a new one'.[59]

With his argument that legal and political concepts are akin to natural kind concepts, Dworkin seemingly abandons the fit requirement.[60] If the judge's obligation is to find the 'true meaning' of legal and political concepts, why should it matter whether such meaning is consistent with past practice? When marine biologists discover that whales are mammals and not fish, we do not require them to make their discovery 'fit' past practice. If Dworkin is serious about the analogy with natural kind concepts, then he has to be read as saying that the effort to find the 'true' meaning of legal and political concepts should respect past practice not because it is past but only in so far as it gets things right.[61] From this point of view, there is no reason to accommodate and

[56] For an excellent discussion of the distinction between fit and justification, see Lawrence Solum, *Legal Theory Lexicon*: Fit and Justification, http://lsolum.blogspot.com/archives/2005_03_01_lsolum_archive.html#111072607292619611 (March 26, 2006) (revised version) *Legal Theory Lexicon* ('Fit and Justification').

[57] Ronald Dworkin, *Law's Empire* (1986) at 47–9.

[58] Ibid at 229–30.

[59] Ibid at 66 (citation omitted).

[60] Further complicating matters, Dworkin does say that both natural kinds and political values 'have a deep structure that explains their concrete manifestations'. Dworkin, above n 6 at 12. Assume arguendo that this is true, it is not at all clear what difference this makes to the basic question of the meaning of natural kind and political terms. The gravamen of natural kinds analysis is that meaning is a function of microstructure and not stereotype (e.g. 'gold is a yellow metal'). See Putnam, above n 29 at 233: '[O]nce we have discovered the nature of water, nothing counts as a possible world in which water doesn't have that nature. Once we have discovered that water (in the actual world) is H_2O, *nothing counts as a possible world in which water isn't* H_2O. In particular, if a "logically possible" statement is one that holds in some "logically possible world", *it isn't logically possible that water isn't* H_2O'. If Dworkin's argument has merit, that merit cannot come as a result of an analogy with Putnam's position as Putnam's natural kinds analysis draws no necessary connection between microstructure and stereotype.

[61] An initially charitable reading of Dworkin is that in drawing parallels with natural kinds, Dworkin is advancing what Coleman and Simchen describe as 'the pedestal view' defended by Nicos Stavropolous: 'The rough overall claim . . . is that the application of concepts is sensitive to theory. The arguments in the philosophy of language to be considered will support this overall claim, by showing that theory must explain and justify a concept's past application—its use—through substantive claims about what property the concepts picks out, and how that property's nature determines future applications. Theory . . . guides future applications . . . "Theory" here is meant not as a body of formal or abstract reasoning, but rather as a set of substantive claims amenable to argument. Notice that theory will be relevant *whatever* the property picked out by the concept is, whether complex and difficult to identify, or simple and identifiable by everyone. What matters is that *which* property is involved is understood to be a substantive issue.' Coleman and Simchen, above n 40 at 11 n 16 (citing and quoting Nicos Stavropoulos, above n 38 at 15). What is 'charitable' in this reading is that Dworkin avoids identifying the meaning of 'law' solely with a microstructure. But the pedestal view is not without its own problems. According to Coleman and Simchen, '[t]he problem is that such a view attributes to speakers, when using a kind term N, the intention to refer to everything having the same underlying nature as some paradigmatic sample of N quite apart from what any expert doctrine about the nature of N does or would reveal. But speakers cannot be plausibly ascribed any such intention because it requires attributing to them a robust metaphysical notion that is simply not likely to be part of their conceptual repertoire'. Ibid at 36, n 43.

account for past (but mistaken) practice.[62] Instead of producing a decision that 'both fits and justifies what has gone before',[63] a judge should identify the true nature of the concept in question and proceed from there to explain its concrete manifestations.

6. *Conclusion*

In his discussion of similarities between natural kind terms and the terms of political and legal argument, Dworkin is clearly trying to articulate the 'deep structure' of political and legal argument. As we have seen, Dworkin's effort to articulate 'instructive similarities' between natural kind and legal terms is fraught with problems. In the end, it might have been better had Dworkin never mentioned natural kinds.[64]

[62] I appreciate that this reading of Dworkin sees his commitment to metaphysical realism as much stronger than he has previously expressed. While one of his students has argued for the use of the semantic theories of Kripke and Putnam for law (see Stavropoulos, above n 38) Dworkin himself has never endorsed natural kinds as a way of understanding the meaning of legal and political terms (in fact, he explicitly rejects such a view). Nevertheless, taken at his word, Dworkin seems to have moved his jurisprudence much closer to that of Michael Moore, who has criticized Dworkin for his failure to adopt a strong metaphysical position. See Michael Moore, 'Metaphysics, Epistemology and Legality' 60 *Southern California L Rev* 453, 458 (1987) (describing Dworkin as a 'conventionalist'). Needless to say, Dworkin himself makes things no less difficult by failing to mention, let alone discuss, any of the literature on natural kinds. (For example, in his entire article the names 'Kripke' and 'Putnam' (nor anyone else in the literature) are never mentioned). The importance of this matter lies in the fact that the nerve of natural kinds arguments is *metaphysical*. The reason Kripke's work is seen as revolutionary (see Soames, above at n 28) is that it restored necessity to the analytic tradition, thereby rebutting Quine's claim that all essences are nominal. For discussion, see Richard Rorty, 'How Many Grains Make a Heap?' (2005) 27 *London Review of Books* 12–13 (reviewing Soames, above at n 28).

[63] Dworkin, *Law's Empire*, above n 57 at 239.

[64] Dworkin seems to have come to this view himself. See Dworkin, *Justice in Robes*, above n 6 at 224–25. In a previously unpublished chapter (Chapter Six—'The Concepts of Law') in this collection of essays, Dworkin reverts to his long-standing methodological argument for 'constructive interpretation'. Here is his description of how two participants in a practice decide the meaning of 'justice': 'Liberals and conservatives share the concept of justice but they do not agree either about the criteria for judgments about justice or about which institutions are just and which unjust. They participate in a social practice of judging acts and institutions just and unjust and because each has opinions, articulate or inarticulate, about what the most basic assumptions of that practice, its point and purpose, should be taken to be. They draw from those assumptions more concrete opinions about the right way to continue the practice on particular occasions: the right judgments to make and the right behavior in response to those judgments. An illuminating analysis of the concept of justice must be an interpretive theory of just that kind. The analyst must deploy his own sense of the values that the practice should be taken to serve and of the conceptions of the concepts in play that best serve those values. An analysis of a criterial or natural kind concept must be neutral among the various normative controversies in which the concept figures: whether bachelors should be encouraged to marry or whether tigers should be protected as an endangered species. But a useful analysis of an interpretive concept—beyond the bare statement that it is interpretive and a very general account of the practices in which it figures—cannot be neutral. It must join issue in the controversies it hopes to illuminate'. Ibid. This is classic 'fit and justification' Dworkin. The meaning of 'justice' is not fixed by anything other than argument. Judgments about the meaning of interpretive concepts are fashioned not by identifying a normative core but by appeal to the participant's own sense of the point or purpose of the institution in question.

[3]
Wittgenstein on Understanding and Interpretation

It is a great pleasure for me to comment on this fine collection of essays by Tom Morawetz. Over the course of several decades, I have profited from reading Professor Morawetz's work in legal theory. Broadly speaking, we share both an appreciation of the later work of Wittgenstein and we both believe that Wittgenstein's work after 1929 can be useful and important in addressing problems in legal theory.

In commenting on Professor Morawetz's work, I take issue with one aspect of his account of the implications of Wittgenstein's thought for law. I believe Professor Morawetz misconstrues the importance of Wittgenstein's fundamental distinction between understanding and interpretation.[2] I fear that in his effort to highlight the "deliberative" aspects of law, Professor Morawetz embraces

1. Distinguished Professor of Law (Camden) and Philosophy (New Brunswick), Rutgers University. In the course of my remarks, I cite to three texts by Professor Morawetz. References to *Law's Premises, Law's Promise* will be by page number in the body of my comments and, in footnotes, I will use the signal "Morawetz, LPLP at __." There are two sets of remarks by Professor Morawetz. His original remarks at the APA Eastern Division Meeting in December 2004 are indicated as "Morawetz, APA at __." References to Professor Morawetz's remarks published here will be cited as "Morawetz, Comments at __."

2. The bulk of Wittgenstein's comments on the relationship of understanding to interpretation occurs in *Philosophical Investigations*. There are also passages in *Remarks on the Foundations of Mathematics* and elsewhere that should be considered. I can recommend two books that together provide a virtually comprehensive account of the matter. The first is Meredith Williams, *Wittgenstein, Mind and Meaning* (Routledge, 1999) pp. 158–187. This chapter covers not only understanding and interpretation but demonstrates why the (revised in her hands) "community view" of rule-following is correct. The second book is G. P. Baker and P. M. S. Hacker, *Wittgenstein: Rules, Grammar and Necessity* (*Volume 2 of An Analytical Commentary on the Philosophical Investigations*) (Blackwell, 1985) (hereafter cited as "RGN"). Were a reader to consult the pages collected under the index entry for "Interpretation," the rich panoply of Wittgenstein's argument could be seen.

an anti-Wittgensteinian view of practices, one that finds a home in the hermeneutic tradition that runs from Heidegger through Gadamer to Charles Taylor.[3] Of course, the hermeneutic approach to understanding and interpretation has many defenders. But Wittgenstein was not one of them: for him, understanding, not interpretation (i.e. reflection) is primary. This is as true for the practice of law as it is for our use of colour words, arithmetic symbols, road signs and the myriad of practices that comprise the whirl of organism known as the human.

Wittgenstein begins his argument for the primacy of understanding in characteristic fashion: by presenting us with a paradox. He writes:

> This was our paradox: no course of action could be determined by a rule, because every course of action can be made out to accord with the rule. The answer was: if everything can be made out to accord with the rule, then it can also be made out to conflict with it. And so there would be neither accord nor conflict here.[4]

Why does Wittgenstein question the importance of interpretation as an explanation of meaning (i.e. how to explain what it is to grasp the meaning of a rule or what the rule requires by way of correct action)? His point is that if understanding of an utterance or sign were a matter of advancing an interpretation (which is just another utterance or sign), then the interpretation itself would require its own interpretation, and so on, infinitely.[5] This argument – the infinite regress argument – is not designed to, and should not, move us to a point of frustration or failure. Rather, Wittgenstein urges us to

3. As I discuss later, both Dworkin and Fish work within the framework of hermeneutics. For Dworkin, see his discussion of hermeneutics in Ronald Dworkin, *Law's Empire* (Harvard U.P., 1986) p. 419 n. 2. Fish's theory of "Reader Response Criticism" is a radical expression of the hermeneutic claim that the meaning of a text is produced through a process of interpretation. For a legal example of Fish's methodology, see his discussion of *Riggs v. Palmer* in Stanley Fish, *Is There a Text in This Class?* (Harvard University Press, 1980) pp. 278–281. I discuss the hermeneutic dimensions of Dworkin and Fish at length in Dennis Patterson, *Law and Truth* (1996) Chapters 5 and 6.

4. Ludwig Wittgenstein, *Philosophical Investigations* 3rd edition, G. E. M. Anscombe trans. (Blackwell, 1958) §201 (hereafter cited as "PI"). The paradox is that "[g] iven the fact of multiple interpretations, for any action, that action can be characterised both in a way that accords with a given rule and conflicts with it – even if the interpretation of the rule itself were transparent." Williams at 160.

5. PI, §201. ("[W]e ought to restrict the term 'interpretation' to the substitution of one expression of the rule for another.")

rethink the notion that before we can understand an utterance we must first interpret it. As he says, "there is a way of grasping a rule which is not an interpretation . . . ."[6]

Wittgenstein's insight on rule-following – one that breaks the back of the realism/scepticism debate – is that rule-following is not a mental phenomenon. Consistent with his critique of psychologism, Wittgenstein relocates normativity in action, specifically social action. The normativity of rule-following – the ground of correctness and incorrectness – is not to be found in the agreement of others as such. Agreement is a necessary feature of the normativity of our practices, but the "agreement" must be a regularity in reaction to use. In short, when we say there must be "agreement in action" what we are really saying is that there must be harmony in application, over time.[7] This harmony in reaction and application is constitutive of all practices, including legal practice. It is the basis of our legal judgements.

Understanding, Wittgenstein argued, is fundamental to our role as participants in practices. Interpretation, by contrast, is an activity we engage in when our understanding of how to "go on" in a practice breaks down. Morawetz's idea of law as a "deliberative practice" looks a lot like what Wittgenstein refers to as "interpretation." If I am right

---

6. PI, §201.
7. Williams, at 176.

> It is in this sense that community agreement is constitutive of practices, and that agreement must be displayed in action. There are two important features about this account that need to be highlighted. First, it is the social practice that provides the structure within which individual understanding can obtain or individual judgement be made. Central to Wittgenstein's thought is the claim, repeatedly argued for, that no isolated event or behaviour can correctly be described as naming or obeying or understanding. The rule as formula, the standard as chart, or the paradigm as an instance have no normative or representational status in their own right. They have this status only in virtue of the way the formula or the chart or the instance is used. It is the use that creates the structured context within which signposts point, series can be continued, orders be obeyed and paradigms be exemplary. Only then can we see a particular action as embodying or instancing a grammatical structure. In short, the mandatory stage setting is social practice.
>
> Second, community agreement does not constitute a justification for particular judgements. What is indispensable for correct, or appropriate, judgement and action is that there is concord, not that each individual justifies his (or anyone else's) judgement and action by appeal to its harmony with the judgement of others.

about this, then the idea of law as a "deliberative practice" places the emphasis in the wrong place; for it is understanding, not interpretation, that is primary.

Morawetz makes the ideas of a practice and games central to his account of law. But what sort of a practice is law and does the metaphor of games really capture what goes on in law? Morawetz maintains that law is a *deliberative* practice. He rejects the idea of law as a game because judicial behaviour does not fit the metaphor of games (99). Morawetz compares the practice of law to those of driving and swimming and draws the conclusion that deliberation about legal decisions "is more complex . . ." (89) than the practices just mentioned. Much of Morawetz's effort in several of the essays in his collection is in service of the claim that law is a complicated practice, one irreducible to unreflective conduct and action.[8]

According to Professor Morawetz, deliberative practices like law are complicated because those who inhabit law – the space of Hart's "internal point of view"[9] – not only share ways of "going on" with the practice but have individual or idiosyncratic ways of "doing law." It is in this latter aspect of the practice that law as a deliberative practice finds the complexity Morawetz so clearly surveys in his essays. Here is an example:

> Without a framework derived from her own way of interpreting experience and giving value, the judge cannot know where to begin. The process of identifying the law cannot be reduced to rules because it cannot be separated from the judge's distinctive way of conceiving justificatory arguments and using them to work toward a decision. What the judge sees as determinate and indeterminate in the law is colored by her understanding of the justificatory arguments that the law encompasses. (154)

8. Professor Morawetz maintains that Wittgenstein's account of understanding cannot be "an exhaustive account of all practices" because Wittgenstein never addresses the distinction between " 'simple' and 'complex' practices." Morawetz, Comments at 12. Of course, one reason Wittgenstein never addressed such a distinction is because he did not have to. After all, *Philosophical Investigations* explores practices as simple as the language-game of the builders to the speaking of a language. It is difficult to imagine a more complex practice than speaking a language. Hence, there is no need to draw the distinction so important to Professor Morawetz's claims on behalf of law as a "deliberative" practice (i.e. the distinction between "simple" and "complex" practices).

9. H. L. A. Hart, *The Concept of Law* 2nd edition (Clarendon Press, 1994) pp. 55–58.

Morawetz denies that law can be reduced to rules. Fair enough. His explanation for this is that, in law, there are two competing "frameworks," one which judges have in common and, another, which is their own. Judges, Morawetz argues, have their own, individual "distinctive ways" of deciding what is law. Determinacy and indeterminacy are "colored by [the individual judge's] understanding of the justificatory arguments that the law encompasses."[10] I think this is a sound account neither of practices in general nor the particular practice of law. I think Wittgenstein's later work demonstrates why this is so.

The basic problem with Morawetz's approach to the problem of disagreement in law is that he rejects the quotidian dimension of law as a starting point. As a result, the logic of questioning and validation that Morawetz describes turns out to be less a matter of subjective preference or idiosyncracy (Morawetz's "deliberation") than it is an attempt to find agreement against a background of unreflective habits of argument.[11]

I believe that interpretation is a *parasitic* activity in legal practice. In other words, I want to disagree with those (e.g. Dworkin and Fish) who make the case for interpretation as a basic or fundamental feature of law. While interpretation is certainly an important element of legal practice, it is an activity that depends upon existing and widespread agreement among legal practitioners with respect to most features of legal practice. In short, interpretation is not the firmament of law.[12]

As Wittgenstein constantly reminds us, action is the ground of normativity and the nerve of the distinction between understanding and interpretation ("*Im Anfang war die Tat*"). The point of Wittgen-

---

10. Morawetz, LPLP at 154.

11. This, I shall argue below, is Wittgenstein's view. The task of philosophy is to get a clear surview of the grammar of our linguistic practices (PI, §118). The reason for this is that the raising of questions, the need for interpretation and, above all, doubt, all arise against a background of unreflective action already being in place. Wittgenstein's point is that we need a clear view of the everyday uses of words (understanding) so that we might make sense of the extraordinary (interpretation).

12. In his remarks, Professor Morawetz quotes my remarks as follows: "In short, interpretation is not the firmament [sic] of law." Morawetz Comments at 14. Obviously, Professor Morawetz believes I am using the word "firmament" incorrectly. As with many words, there is more than one meaning of "firmament." This is the meaning I intended: "Anything which strengthens or supports; a substratum, a firm support or foundation." *Oxford English Dictionary*, "Firmament" (citations and illustrations omitted).

stein's example of the signpost in PI 85[13] is that only *action* can provide the ground for correct and incorrect judgement.[14] Without a practice of following it – a way of acting – the signpost by itself provides us no clue as to its proper use. There are as many potential ways of "following" the signpost as there are possible conventions for determining how it is to be used and what counts as following it. But once a convention for following signposts takes hold, a background of understanding evolves. It is against this background that the need for interpretation arises.[15] Interpretation is a reflective (deliberative?) *practice* we engage in when understanding breaks down.

Understanding is exhibited in action.[16] For example, we show that we understand the request "Please shut the door" by closing the portal. The need for interpretation arises from a firmament of *praxis*.

13. Wittgenstein, PI §85:

> A rule stands there like a signpost. – Does the signpost leave no doubt open about the way I have to go? Does it shew which direction I am to take when I have passed it; whether along the road or footpath or cross-country? But where is it said which way I am to follow it; whether in the direction of its finger or (e.g.) in the opposite one? – And if there were, not a single signpost, but a chain of adjacent ones or of chalk marks on the ground – is there only *one* way of interpreting them? – So I can say, the signpost does after all leave no room for doubt. Or rather: it sometimes leaves room for doubt and sometimes not. And now this is no longer a philosophical proposition, but an empirical one.

14. See also Robert Brandom, *Making It Explicit* (Harvard University Press, 1996) p. 13 ("To understand or grasp . . . a meaning is to be able to distinguish correct from incorrect uses.")

15. All interpretation presupposes understanding. No one could interpret the following: Nog drik legi xfom. The term first has to be translated or deciphered before interpretation takes place. *Contra* Quine, translation is not interpretation. W.V. Quine, *Ontological Relativity and Other Essays* (Columbia University Press, 1969) pp. 51–55. We interpret an utterance when we choose between different ways of understanding it. Legal interpretation is the activity of deciding which of several ways of understanding a rule given provision is the correct or preferable way of understanding. This is precisely the sort of activity Wittgenstein has in mind when he writes: "we ought to restrict the term 'interpretation' to the substitution of one expression of the rule for another." Wittgenstein, PI at §201.

16. See G. P. Baker and P. M. S. Hacker, *Wittgenstein: Understanding and Meaning* (*Volume 2 of An Analytical Commentary on the Philosophical Investigations*) (Blackwell, 1980) p. 667 ("[G]iving a correct explanation is a criterion of understanding, while the explanation given is a standard for the correct use of the expression explained. Correspondingly, using an expression in accordance with correct explanations of it is a criterion of understanding, while understanding an expression presupposes the ability to explain it.")

That is, interpretation in law arises from established forms of action that all participants recognise and employ whenever they make, appraise and adjudicate claims about the state of the law.[17] Interpretation is grounded in a distinct form of discursive action that we recognise as "legal" in nature.

As an account of correct and incorrect action in a practice (be it law, arithmetic or measurement), interpretation is a non-starter because interpretation draws our attention away from the techniques that make understanding possible. Correct and incorrect forms of action are immanent in practices. Thus, correct forms of action cannot be imposed on a practice, by interpretation or otherwise. It is only when we master the techniques employed by participants in a practice that we can grasp the distinction between correct and incorrect action (e.g. in law – assertion).

We seek return to the quotidian dimension of praxis where the business of making claims about the current state of the law are adjudicated through employment of intersubjectively employed standards of appraisal. Clarification of these standards and the rules for their use is the Wittgensteinian project expressed in jurisprudence. As Wittgenstein says, "It is not interpretation which builds the bridge between the sign and what is signified //meant//. Only practice does that."[18] But how?

For his part, Morawetz does say that "it is [ ] misleading to ignore the ties that bind judges into a shared practice." (193) But Morawetz never really tells us what those ties are. Are they the familiar forms of argument (text, history, structure, prudence and doctrine[19]) or does the explanation lie elsewhere? Is deliberation a form of interpretation? Is law an "interpretive activity?"

As I have said, the answer is that interpretation depends upon understanding already being in place.[20] Interpretation is an activity

17. See Chapter 8 of Dennis Patterson, *Law and Truth* (Oxford University Press, 1996) and Dennis Patterson "Normativity and Objectivity in Law," 43 *William and Mary Law Review* (2001) pp. 325–363.

18. Cited in G. P. Baker and P. M. S. Hacker, *RGN*, at 136.

19. For an account of the relationship between the forms of legal argument and interpretation in legal practice, see Dennis Patterson, "Interpretation in Law," 42 *U. San Diego L. Rev.* (2005) pp. 685–709.

20. See James Tully, "Wittgenstein and Political Philosophy," 17 *Political Theory* (1988) pp. 172, 196:

> [Interpretation] is a practice we engage in when our understanding and use of signs is in some way problematic or in doubt. Here we attempt to

– deliberative, to be sure – that depends upon understanding (which is not an activity; rather it is unreflective action). Interpretation repairs the fabric of understanding. Interpretation enables the practice to go on, as before.

My argument can now be summarised. The task of jurisprudence is to get a clear surview of the practice of law. A clear surview means clarification of the contours of what Hart called the Rule of Recognition. It is the Rule of Recognition that enables us to appraise claims about what is the case as a matter of law. The elements of the Rule of Recognition[21] are themselves neither true nor false: they are the means for assessing the truth and falsity of legal assertions.

One methodological task of jurisprudence is clarifying the relationship between understanding and interpretation and their relationship to grammar and the internal point of view. In this way philosophy will leave law as it is.

In commenting on my critique of his position, Professor Morawetz acknowledges the importance of Wittgenstein's distinction between understanding and interpretation. However, he maintains that Wittgenstein's point was limited to the practices he used to illustrate his point (i.e. colours, mathematics and road signs) and, more importantly, that Wittgenstein's argument "depended on the

---

> come to an understanding of the sign in question by offering various interpretations (expressions) as opposed to different ones, adjudicating rival interpretations, in some cases calling the criteria of adjudication into question, and so on . . . . Interpretation should thus be seen as one important practice of critical reflection among many, resting comfortably in more basic ways of acting with words (self-understanding) that cannot themselves be interpretations.

Tully's original paper has recently been republished in an expanded version in *The Grammar of Politics: Wittgenstein and Political Philosophy*, Cressida J. Heyes (ed.) (Cornell University Press, 2003). Tully uses Wittgenstein's distinction between understanding and interpretation to illustrate fatal weaknesses in the hermeneutic approach to explaining understanding and interpretation in practices. In fact, Tully reports that his argument has even convinced Charles Taylor that he (Taylor) was wrong in his original argument for the priority of interpretation to understanding. (Heyes, p. 228, n. 70).

21. My several references to Hart's conception of a Rule of Recognition is not an endorsement of Hart's positivism. I refer to the Rule of Recognition because it is a familiar jurisprudential concept. Although I have criticised Hart's account of the nature of law (See Dennis Patterson, *Law and Truth*, Chapter 4), I completely agree with his effort to describe the ways in which lawyers decide what the law is (not what "law" means).

simplicity of the examples used to illustrate his (i.e. Wittgenstein's) point."[22] There are good reasons to suggest that neither of these claims is true.

It is important to remember that Wittgenstein advanced the distinction between understanding and interpretation in the specific context of rule-following. Thousands of books and articles have been devoted to rule-following problem.[23] Would all of these pages be written for simple problems of colours, mathematics and road signs? I doubt it. More fundamentally, Wittgenstein's discussion of understanding and interpretation in the context of rule-following[24] is just

---

22. Professor Morawetz contests my characterisation of his view, describing it as "peculiar" and claiming that "no one . . . has ever applied Wittgenstein as narrowly as Patterson thinks I do." Morawetz, Comments at 12. With respect to the first point, I was responding to Professor Morawetz's original set of remarks (delivered at the APA Meeting in Boston). He said:

> In considering Patterson's comments about the relationship of understanding and interpretation, we need to be clear about the scope and limits of Wittgenstein's examples of linguistic practices. The examples of language use that fill *Philosophical Investigations* and *On Certainty* are almost invariably unproblematic and unreflective. For the most part, we describe colors, use numbers, and describe pains in everyday discourse, just as we refer to historical events, use each other's names, and tell jokes. The very existence of the linguistic practices exemplified by these linguistic moves depends on the fact that they are problematic only rarely.

Morawetz, APA at 1–2. I do not think it at all "peculiar" to suggest that Professor Morawetz is here expressing the view that, because Wittgenstein's distinction between understanding and interpretation is unpacked in the contexts of colors, numbers and pain talk, his argument is limited by those examples (this seems consistent with Professor Morawetz's caution that we need to be mindful of "the scope and limits of Wittgenstein's examples of linguistic practices."). Second, Professor Morawetz's claim that "no one has ever advanced such a reading of Wittgenstein" is false. See Scott Hershovitz, "Wittgenstein on Rules: The Phantom Menace," 22 *Oxford Journal of Legal Studies* (2002) pp. 619–640 ("Nothing much can be learned about legal rules or legal interpretation by attending to Wittgenstein's remarks, because they were aimed at wholly different phenomena."). See also Brian Bix, "The Application (and Mis-Application) of Wittgenstein's Rule-Following Considerations to Legal Theory," in *Wittgenstein and Law*, Dennis Patterson (ed.) (Ashgate, 2004) pp. 381–407 (law is a reflective activity quite unlike arithmetic and color talk).

23. Not the least of which is Kripke's infamous (mis)reading of Wittgenstein's argument. See Saul A. Kripke, *Wittgenstein on Rules and Private Language* (Harvard University Press, 1982).

24. Of course, the rule-following discussion begins at PI, §138: "But we *understand* the meaning of a word when we hear or say it; we grasp it in a flash, and what we grasp in this way is surely something different from the "use" which is extended in time!" As Wittgenstein goes on to show, use – and nothing else – accounts for meaning.

one of many examples in the *Investigations* of the still more fundamental point that meaning is a matter of action.

Professor Morawetz joins ranks with Dworkin and Fish in his claim that law is an interpretive practice.[25] There are many people who think that all human practices are best understood as interpretive. Wittgenstein rejected this view and made a convincing case for the proposition that all human practices are grounded in understanding exhibited in action. The merits of Wittgenstein's argument notwithstanding, it is simply not plausible to claim that one is doing jurisprudence "after Wittgenstein" if one is committed to the interpretive approach to law found in the work of Dworkin and Fish.[26]

25. Morawetz, Comments at 16 ("Practices are interpretive . . . ."; "Law is both deliberative and interpretive in its own distinct way.")

26. This is precisely what Professor Morawetz maintains. See Morawetz, LPLP at 154, 187 ("Dworkin's view of judging is compatible with seeing judicial decision making as a deliberative practice."); ("[Fish's] descriptions resonate particularly well with the idea of being situated in a deliberative practice."). When it comes to demonstrating the incoherence of Fish's position as well as the utter incompatibility of Fish and Wittgenstein on meaning, no one can improve on the words of John Ellis. See John Ellis, *Against Deconstruction* (Princeton University Press, 1989) p. 121, n. 6 (emphasis in original) (citation omitted):

> Stanley Fish has long since committed himself to the initial assertions of reader-response criticism and continues to do so but, by changing his position a number of times, has struggled with the kinds of unacceptable consequences of those assertions that I have set out in this chapter. But his latest reformulation (Fish, *Is There a Text in This Class?*), which is offered as if no more than a refinement, amounts in fact to his abandoning its essentials completely. His most recent version, then, involves the postulation of interpretive communities, with assumptions and conventions that guide interpretation; this, in his view, allows communication to take place and so rescues him from the consequences of earlier formulations. Now it is, of course, true that a text means nothing without conventions shared by the speakers of the language concerned, but to acknowledge this fully would, as Fish sees, abolish his reader-response position: if readers are guided by the rules of language, they do not have the freedom envisaged by reader-response theory, and so the text together with its relation to the linguistic system can be the place to which disputes are appealed after all, contrary to the statement by Fish that I cited. In order to continue to cling to his reader-response position, then, Fish continues to deny that it is sharing a language and "knowing the meanings of individual words and the rules for combining them" that is involved in communication but, instead, a "way of thinking, a form of life." But this direct denial that the shared rules of language makes [sic] communication possible is surely bizarre, and the distinction he makes here is certainly untenable. Oddly enough, Fish's language here recalls Wittgenstein's, but in using it Wittgenstein was pointing out precisely that a language with its rules, conventions and agreements is a way of thinking and form of life!

Wittgenstein argued that the meaning of our words lies in their use. *Philosophical Investigations* is an extended defense of the idea that meaning is neither in the head nor a matter of the way the world is, metaphysically or otherwise. Wittgenstein's approach to the puzzles of philosophy is to show how those puzzles result from misunderstandings of how meaning arises in practices. I respectfully disagree with my colleague and friend, Thomas Morawetz, on this important point. But I applaud the intellectual accomplishment represented by this splendid collection of his essays.

School of Law
State University of New Jersey
Rutgers Campus at Camden
217 N. Fifth Street
Camden
New Jersey 08102
USA

[4]

Notes on the Methodology Debate in Contemporary Jurisprudence: Why Sociologists might be Interested

Introduction

In the Continental tradition, legal philosophy and legal sociology are closely aligned, both pedagogically and theoretically. It is not at all unusual (especially in German-speaking countries) to have the same person hold an appointment in legal philosophy and legal sociology. The Anglophone world enjoys no such joining of the conceptual and the social. In fact, I would venture to say that most analytic philosophers of law have little time, or none, for sociology.

While I do not see any grand rapprochement in the immediate future, I do think there is a brewing debate that might bring sociologists and philosophers together. I have in mind the nascent 'methodology' debate. Methodology in any field concerns the 'right way' to conduct the field. In jurisprudence, the issue is 'What questions should we ask'? As philosophers, we are interested in the *kind* of question deemed appropriate. The question is uniquely philosophical.

Philosophers have always been interested in conceptual content. But what does it mean to say that concepts have 'content'? Where does this content come from? And what sort of content is it? The Ancients believed that many concepts had 'necessary and sufficient conditions' for their application. This perceived truth held sway until the middle of the last century. Now, almost no one believes this ancient learning, at least not without substantial qualifications.[2]

The debate over the necessity of conceptual content has reached jurisprudence. Does the concept of 'law' have necessary content? What, if anything, must a system

1 My thanks to John Oberdiek and Jefferson White for comments on a draft of this chapter and to Amanda Lanham for excellent research assistance.

2 An excellent, brief account is found in Jerry Fodor, 'Water's Water Everywhere' (2004) 26 *London Review of Books* 17–19 (reviewing Christopher Hughes, *Kripke: Names, Necessity and Identity* (Oxford, 2004)).

of norms possess if it is to count as 'law'? This is the question at the heart of the methodology debate. In this chapter, I will describe this debate and, apropos of the present occasion, make the case that this debate should be of interest to legal sociologists. If I am right, there may yet be an Anglophone rapprochement between philosophers and sociologists of law.

The Methodology Debate

For better or worse, the last twenty-five years in analytic jurisprudence have been dominated by the so-called 'Hart–Dworkin' debate.[3] In *The Concept of Law*, H.L.A. Hart advanced the case for a 'descriptive jurisprudence'. A central feature of Hart's project was the clarification of legal practice through a perspicuous description of its principal features. Chief among these elements are the concepts of primary and secondary rules, the internal point of view, and, most importantly, the Rule of Recognition. Through the use of the Rule of Recognition, lawyers and non-lawyers alike are able to identify legal norms as such and, in that way, decide what the law is on any given question.[4]

Ronald Dworkin—the most persistent critic of legal positivism—has consistently contested the possibility of a wholly descriptive jurisprudence. Dworkin's central claim—advanced most systematically in *Law's Empire*[5]—is that 'law' is 'an interpretive concept'. Law is an interpretive concept because to understand the concept, one needs to grasp its point or purpose.[6] Because the state exercises its coercive power over citizens, any concept of law must explain and justify this important example of state action. This is the fundamental normative dimension of jurisprudence, one that is evaluative, and necessarily so.

To the degree there has been a 'methodology debate' in jurisprudence, the debate has been over the question whether descriptive jurisprudence is possible.[7] Hart, and positivists generally, made the case that description without evaluation (endorsement) was possible. *Pace* Hart, Dworkin and John Finnis have insisted that evaluation is a necessary element of jurisprudential analysis.

Since Hart's death, the methodology debate has taken a new turn, one that joins it—finally—with important developments in metaphysics and epistemology. Before I describe this turn, a little background is in order.

Since Plato, philosophers have endeavoured to develop accounts of concepts that unpack their content in terms of necessities. According to the so-called

[3] For a polemical account of the debate, see Brian Leiter, 'The End of Empire: Ronald Dworkin and Jurisprudence in the 21st Century' (2004) 36 *Rutgers Law Journal* 165.

[4] See H.L.A. Hart, *The Concept of Law* (Oxford, 1994), 94–9 (describing the Rule of Recognition).

[5] Ronald Dworkin, *Law's Empire* (London, 1986).

[6] *Ibid*, 190 ('A conception of law must explain how what it takes to be law provides a general justification for the exercise of coercive power by the state. . . . ').

[7] For a clear and concise account of the debate thus far, see Julie Dickson, 'Methodology in Jurisprudence: A Critical Survey' (2004) 10 *Legal Theory* 117–56.

'Classical Theory of Concepts', most concepts are 'structured mental representations that encode a set of necessary and sufficient conditions for their application. . .'.[8] While a single theory cannot be continuously identified from Plato on, it is not an overstatement to say that something like the Classical Theory was a significant element in philosophy from antiquity to the middle of the twentieth century.[9] The reason for the longevity of the Classical Theory is not hard to see: it holds the promise of tremendous explanatory power, 'offering unified accounts of concept acquisition, categorization, epistemic justification, analytic entailment and reference determination, all of which flow directly from its basic commitments'.[10]

One or another version of the Classical Theory held sway until 1951, when Willard Van Orman Quine published his paper *Two Dogmas of Empiricism*.[11] Of the several theses Quine advanced in this paper, the most important one for present purposes is his denial of the analytic/synthetic distinction.[12] Here is the famous passage that sums up Quine's position:

> The totality of our so-called knowledge or beliefs, from the most casual matters of geography and history to the profound laws of atomic physics or even of pure mathematics and logic, is a man-made fabric which impinges on experience only along the edges. Or, to change the figure, total science is like a field of force whose boundary conditions are experience. A conflict with experience at the periphery occasions readjustments in the interior of the field. Truth values have to be redistributed over some of our statements. Re-evaluation of some statements entails re-evaluation of others, because of their logical interconnections—the logical laws being in turn simply certain further statements of the system, certain further elements of the field. Having re-evaluated one statement we must re-evaluate some others, which may be statements logically connected with the first or may be the statements of logical connections themselves. But the total field is so underdetermined by its boundary conditions, experience, that there is much latitude of choice as to what statements to reevaluate in the light of any single contrary experience. No particular experiences are linked with any particular statements in the interior of the field, except indirectly through considerations of equilibrium affecting the field as a whole.
>
> If this view is right, it is misleading to speak of the empirical content of an individual statement—especially if it be a statement at all remote from the experiential periphery of the field. Furthermore it becomes folly to seek a boundary between synthetic statements,

[8] Stephen Laurence and Eric Margolis, 'Concepts and Cognitive Science', in: Eric Margolis and Stephen Laurence (eds), *Concepts: Core Readings* (Cambridge, Mass, 1999), 18.

[9] Frank Jackson is the most vigorous, contemporary defender of conceptual analysis. See Frank Jackson, *From Metaphysics to Ethics: A Defense of Conceptual Analysis* (Oxford, 1998).

[10] *Ibid.*

[11] W.V.O. Quine, 'Two Dogmas of Empiricism' (1951) 60 *The Philosophical Review* 20, reprinted in Willard Van Orman Quine, *From a Logical Point of View* (Cambridge, Mass, 1980), 20–46.

[12] Analytic propositions are true in virtue of the meaning of their constituent terms. Synthetic propositions are true in virtue of facts. For discussion, see Georges Rey, 'The Analytic Synthetic Distinction', *Stanford Encyclopedia of Philosophy*, available at http://plato.stanford.edu/entries/analytic-synthetic/.

which hold contingently on experience, and analytic statements, which hold come what may. Any statement can be held true come what may, if we make drastic enough adjustments elsewhere in the system.[13]

There is a great deal in this quotation that merits comment.[14] For our purposes, it is sufficient to note that, if Quine is correct (i.e., if the analytic/synthetic distinction cannot be maintained), then all statements are revisable in the light of experience. In other words, the demise of the analytic/synthetic distinction means that the distinction between necessary and contingent truths disappears.

Why is this important? Even if Quine is right, how does it matter to jurisprudence? Let us return to the Hart/Dworkin debate and the question that animates it, namely: whether description of the current content of law is possible without thereby evaluating (endorsing) it? As I have pointed out, Dworkin, as well as John Finnis,[15] have argued that description without evaluation is not possible. What sort of claim is this? Is it one of logical necessity? In all the debates about the meaning of the word 'law', this is what the critics of Hart (e.g. Dworkin and Finnis) seem to be saying.

But it is not only critics of positivism who have been making claims of logical necessity. Thus, Joseph Raz maintains that:

An interpretation of something is an explanation of its meaning. Many if not all legal philosophers think of themselves as explaining the essential features of legal practices, and explaining the relations between them and related phenomena such as other forms of social organization, other social practices, and morality . . . [Hart himself] was seeking to interpret the complex social institution the law is. If Hart and others did not make as extensive use of 'interpretation' as Dworkin does, this is in part because fashions dictate the use of terms, and because they may well have wished to avoid being associated with theories that, in their eyes, misconstrued the nature of interpretation.[16]

If Quine is right,[17] neither Dworkin and Finnis nor the Exclusive Positivists (such as Raz) can be right about methodology in legal theory. The reason is that claims to be describing 'the essential features of law' depend for their efficacy on the analytic/synthetic distinction. In the wake of Quine's demolition of the analytic/synthetic distinction, no project of 'conceptual analysis' gets off the ground.

[13] Quine, n.11, above, 42–3.

[14] For a detailed explication of Quine's arguments in 'Two Dogmas of Empiricism', see Scott Soames, *Philosophical Analysis in the Twentieth Century* (Princeton, New Jersey, 2003), 351–405. For real understanding of the long-term influence of Quine's position, see Peter M.S. Hacker, *Wittgenstein's Place in Twentieth Century Philosophy* (Oxford, 1996), 183–227.

[15] See John Finnis, *Natural Law and Natural Rights* (Oxford, 1980), 4.

[16] Joseph Raz, 'Two Views of the Nature of the Theory of Law: A Partial Comparison', in Jules Coleman (ed.), *Hart's Postscript* (Oxford, 2001), 1–2.

[17] A well-regarded attack on Quine's argument is that of Paul Grice and Peter Strawson, 'In Defense of a Dogma' (1956) 65 *The Philosophical Review* 141–58, reprinted in Paul Grice, *Studies in the Way of Words* (Cambridge, Mass, 1989), 196–212.

Now what? Brian Leiter wants to fill the gap that Quine creates by importing Quine's naturalism into legal theory.[18] Quine's naturalized epistemology eliminates the conceptual work of philosophy and makes philosophy continuous with science (including social science). In other words, with the demise of the analytic/synthetic distinction, science replaces philosophy[19] (and, of course, normative legal theory) as the best explanatory methodology for law.

I will forgo for another occasion a full evaluation of Quine's argument, and of Leiter's claims about the implications of Quine's analysis for legal theory. Instead, I offer a few thoughts about why sociologists should be interested in this debate, and how they might participate.

Rejection of analyticity is an invitation to sociology. Taking their lead from Quine's demolition of analytic/synthetic distinction and Wittgenstein's remarks on rule-following, 'constructivist' sociologists of knowledge[20] have made the case that 'scientific knowledge' is not a reflection/representation of nature but a communal achievement of scientific communities.[21] In its strong expression, the constructivist view of scientific knowledge replaces natural explanations with social ones. In other words, our knowledge of nature is not the product of sense perception and data but 'interests,' 'practices,' or 'forms of life'.

In his argument for naturalism in law, Leiter wants to embrace Quine while privileging 'nature' as the explanans of legal phenomena. In the context of philosophy of science, this is precisely where the constructivists have dug in and insisted that Quine cannot have it both ways.[22] The demise of the analytic/synthetic distinction means that there is no 'first philosophy': science will not replace philosophy. Rather, science will be a discourse like any other and pragmatism will be the criterion of theory choice.[23]

Conclusion

Analytic jurisprudence is slowly emerging from a long, narrow debate, one that has kept it isolated from virtually all of the interesting debates in epistemology and metaphysics. Quine's controversial naturalism poses a direct threat to projects of conceptual analysis the efficacy of which depend upon the analytic/synthetic distinction. This debate opens the way for sociologists to engage with the discourse in analytic jurisprudence in ways not previously recognized. I hope they accept the invitation.

[18] See Brian Leiter, 'Beyond the Hart/Dworkin Debate: The Methodology Problem in Jurisprudence' (2003) 48 *American Journal of Jurisprudence* 17.

[19] See Brian Leiter, 'Naturalism in Legal Philosophy' (2002) *Stanford Encyclopedia of Philosophy*, available at http://plato.stanford.edu/entries/lawphil-naturalism/.

[20] See, e.g. David Bloor, *Knowledge and Social Imagery*, 2nd edn. (Chicago, 1992).

[21] A classic example of such work is Bruno Latour and Steve Woolgar, *Laboratory Life: The Construction of Scientific Facts*, 2nd edn. (Princeton, New Jersey, 1986).

[22] This point is well developed in Joseph Rouse, *How Scientific Practices Matter* (Cambridge, 2002).

[23] This is Richard Rorty's reading of Quine. See Richard Rorty, *Objectivity, Relativism, and Truth* (Chicago, 1991), 1–17.

[5]
Interpretation in Law

TABLE OF CONTENTS

I. INTRODUCTION

Interpretation is a familiar feature of law and legal practice. For some legal theorists, interpretation is a central—even foundational—aspect of law. Despite many discussions of interpretation, in a variety of legal theoretical contexts, there remains widespread disagreement over the nature of interpretation in law. It may well be that the reason interpretation remains a widely contested aspect of legal theory is that our very conception of what counts as law depends on a proper understanding of the role of interpretation in law.

---

* Distinguished Professor of Law (Camden) and Philosophy (New Brunswick), Rutgers University. My thanks to Kim Ferzan, Peter Hacker, Andrew Halpin, Patrick S. O'Donnell, and Jefferson White for comments on drafts of this Article. Justine Kasznica provided outstanding research assistance. A version of this Article was presented to the Oxford University Legal Theory Discussion Group, Mind and Society (Manchester) and the law faculties at Southampton, Palermo and Luiss (Rome).

I argue that interpretation is a *parasitic* activity in legal practice. In other words, I want to disagree with those who make the case for interpretation as a basic or fundamental feature of law.[1] While

1. *See, e.g.*, RONALD DWORKIN, LAW'S EMPIRE (1986). I anticipate that some will take issue with my characterization of Dworkin's interpretivism. One version of this criticism is that Dworkin is not really making a semantic argument at all. Rather, his claims are normative in nature and, thus, not susceptible to critique in the same manner as, say, Stanley Fish. At a minimum, I think this is a contestable reading of the argument in LAW'S EMPIRE. I will not make a sustained argument here because I have already made the case elsewhere. *See* DENNIS PATTERSON, LAW AND TRUTH 76–98 (1996). I will, however, record my complete agreement with Gerald Postema's characterization of a central problem with Dworkin's argument. *See* Gerald Postema, *"Protestant" Interpretation and Social Practices*, 6 LAW & PHIL. 283, 288–89 (1987) ("[W]hile [Dworkin] regards the activity of the practice [of law] as public and collective, he seems to regard the enterprise of understanding that activity as private and individual . . . . I shall argue that Dworkin's theory thus interpreted fails to describe adequately participant understanding of common social practices."). Dworkin leaves us in no doubt when it comes to the pervasive nature of interpretation in law. For Dworkin, there is no *in principle* distinction between easy and hard cases:

> We have been attending mainly to hard cases, when lawyers disagree whether some crucial proposition of law is true or false. But questions of law are sometimes very easy for lawyers and even for nonlawyers. It "goes without saying" that the speed limit in Connecticut is 55 miles an hour and that people in Britain have a legal duty to pay for food they order in a restaurant. At least this goes without saying except in very unusual circumstances. A critic might therefore be tempted to say that the complex account we have developed of judicial reasoning under law as integrity is a method for hard cases only. He might add that it would be absurd to apply the method to easy cases—no judge needs to consider questions of fit and political morality to decide whether someone must pay his telephone bill—and then declare that in addition to his theory of hard cases, Hercules needs a theory about when cases are hard, so he can know when his complex method for hard cases is appropriate and when not. The critic will then announce a serious problem: it can be a hard question whether the case at hand is a hard case or an easy case, and Hercules cannot decide by using his technique for hard cases without begging the question.
>
> This is a pseudoproblem. Hercules does not need one method for hard cases and another for easy ones. His method is equally at work in easy cases, but since the answers to the questions it puts are then obvious, or at least seem to be so, we are not aware that any theory is at work at all. We think the question whether someone may legally drive faster than the stipulated speed limit is an easy one because we assume at once that no account of the legal record that denied that paradigm would be competent. But someone whose convictions about justice and fairness were very different from ours might not find that question so easy; even if he ended by agreeing with our answer, he would insist that we were wrong to be so confident. This explains why questions considered easy during one period become hard before they again become easy questions—with the opposite answers.

DWORKIN, *supra*, at 353–54. The problem with Dworkin is simple: he confuses the fact that it is always possible that someone will need an interpretation (i.e., an explanation that is usually given) with the false claim that we always interpret in order to understand. *Cf.* Nicos Stavropoulos, *Interpretivist Theories of Law*, THE STANFORD ENCYCLOPEDIA OF PHILOSOPHY (Edward N. Zalta ed., 2003), *at* http://plato.stanford.edu/ archives/ win2003/entries/law-interpretivist (last visited Feb. 28, 2005) (explaining that interpretivism is not fully determined by practice or values served by it).

interpretation is certainly an important element of legal practice, it is an activity that depends upon existing and widespread agreement among legal practitioners with respect to most features of legal practice. In short, interpretation is not the firmament of law.

I do not wish to deny that interpretation is an important aspect of the practice of law. Rather, my aim is to clarify the role of interpretation in law. But before we can begin to understand more clearly the nature of interpretation in law, we must first clarify the nature of understanding, for it is to understanding that interpretation owes its parasitic status.[2]

The need for interpretation arises from the firmament of *praxis*. That is, interpretation in law arises from established forms of action that all participants recognize and employ whenever they make, appraise, and adjudicate claims about the state of the law. Interpretation is grounded in a distinct form of discursive action that we recognize as legal in nature. Thus, before we can truly understand the role of interpretation in law, we must first explicate the particular form of understanding we identify as legal.

Only with a clear view of the nature of understanding in law can we then properly explicate the nature and scope of interpretation in law. When we look at how participants in law engage in interpretation, the activity can best be described by a few general principles. These principles capture what it is that lawyers do when they, of necessity, interpret the law.

This Article is divided into three principal parts. In Part II, I reprise an argument that myself and others have made about the "logical" status of interpretation. I add to the discussion of the role of interpretation in understanding by making the claim that interpretation is a parasitic activity, the efficacy of which is dependent upon understanding already being in place.

2. All interpretation presupposes understanding. No one could interpret the following: Nog drik legi xfom. The term first has to be translated (and, contra Quine, translation is not interpretation) or deciphered before interpretation takes place. W.V. QUINE, ONTOLOGICAL RELATIVITY AND OTHER ESSAYS 51–55 (1969). We interpret an utterance when we choose between different ways of understanding it. Legal interpretation is the activity of deciding which of several ways of understanding a given provision is the correct or preferable way of understanding. This is precisely the sort of activity Wittgenstein has in mind when he writes: "we ought to restrict the term 'interpretation' to the substitution of one expression of the rule for another." LUDWIG WITTGENSTEIN, PHILOSOPHICAL INVESTIGATIONS § 201 (G. E. M. Anscombe trans., 3d ed. 1958).

In Part III, I explicate what it means to *understand* the law. Again drawing on my earlier work,[3] I explain that understanding law is a matter of being the master of a technique, specifically, a technique of argument. I describe the forms of legal argument in detail and make the case that the use of these argumentative forms is the nerve of law.

The forms of argument are central to any understanding of law and legal practice. But the forms of argument conflict, and when they do, the need for interpretation arises. Part IV contains a discussion of three cases that illustrate both the use of the forms of argument and the way in which their conflict requires interpretation. I conclude that interpretation in law is best explained by three principles. These are: minimal mutilation, coherence and generality. When the forms of argument conflict, we must choose between competing resolutions of their conflict. In my discussion of cases where the forms of argument conflict, I will show how the principles of interpretation that I identify provide a perspicuous account of what lawyers do when they interpret the law.

II. UNDERSTANDING IS NOT INTERPRETATION

It has now become quite popular to explicate understanding in terms of interpretation. Interpretivists believe that interpretation is the most perspicuous way to explicate or explain the phenomenon of human understanding. Interpretation knows no disciplinary boundaries. From philosophy to psychology to anthropology and the natural sciences, interpretation plays a central role in the explanation of human action.

So, how do interpretivists account for the phenomenon of human understanding? Interested as we are in law, consider the views of a leading proponent of interpretivism, Stanley Fish. Fish developed the theory of Reader-Response Criticism—the idea that in the act of reading, the reader creates the meaning of the text.[4] This view is a function or corollary of Fish's general philosophical views about the nature of meaning, which he expresses thus:

> All shapes are interpretively produced, and since the conditions of interpretation are themselves unstable—the possibility of seeing something in a "new light," and therefore of seeing a *new* something, is ever and unpredictably present—the shapes that seem perspicuous to us now may not seem so or may seem differently so tomorrow. This applies not only to the shape of statutes, poems, and signs in airplane lavatories, but to the disciplines and forms of life within which statutes, poems, and signs become available to us.[5]

3. *See* PATTERSON, *supra* note 1, at 86–88 (explaining that understanding is the act of properly responding to a request).

4. *See* STANLEY FISH, IS THERE A TEXT IN THIS CLASS? 21–67 (1980) (developing the theory of affective stylistics).

5. STANLEY FISH, DOING WHAT COMES NATURALLY: CHANGE, RHETORIC, AND

In accounting for our understanding of statutes, poems, and airplane lavatory signs, Fish posits an act of interpretation interposed between the object of our understanding and our grasp of its meaning. The interpretive act mediates between the thing we seek to understand and our grasp of its meaning. Interpretation makes understanding possible. Of course, there is often disagreement over the meaning of texts, especially legal texts. Fish thinks that interpretation can account for this phenomenon. In accounting for the divergent perspectives of the majority and dissenting opinions in *Riggs v. Palmer*,[6] Fish writes:

> [I]f it is assumed that the purpose of probate is to ensure the orderly devolution of property at all costs, then the statute in this case will have the plain meaning urged by the defendant; but if it is assumed that no law ever operates in favor of someone who would profit by his crime, then the "same" statute will have a meaning that is different, but no less plain. *In either case the statute will have* been literally construed, and what the court will have done is prefer one literal construction to another by invoking one purpose (assumed background) rather than another.[7]

For Fish, interpretive assumptions are the bridge between a statutory text and our grasp of its meaning. Interpretive assumptions mediate or make possible our grasp of the meaning of the New York Statute of Wills. Without these interpretive assumptions, the requirements of the statute would elude us. But, according to Fish, the interpretive assumptions of the majority and the dissent were different. It is due to these differences in interpretive assumptions that the court divided on the question of the meaning of the rules articulated by the statute. Thus, *per* Fish, interpretation not only accounts for human understanding, it accounts for disagreement in understanding as well.

There is nothing in Fish's account of either understanding or disagreement that can withstand scrutiny. Fish's signature move is the slide from the fact of interpretive dispute to the (false) conclusion that interpretive disputes are best explained by the "fact" that the disputants lack a common ground of understanding. Explicating the common ground of understanding puts us on the road to a better understanding of interpretation.

THE PRACTICE OF THEORY IN LITERARY AND LEGAL STUDIES 302 (1989).

6. Riggs v. Palmer, 22 N.E. 188 (N.Y. 1889) (holding that a man could not receive his grandfather's estate because the principle that no one should be permitted to profit from his own wrong supersedes the applicable statutes).

7. FISH, *supra* note 4, at 280.

With this in mind, consider Wittgenstein:

> A rule stands there like a sign-post.—Does the sign post leave no doubt open about the way I have to go? Does it shew which direction I am to take when I have passed it; whether along the road or the footpath or cross-country? But where is it said which way I am to follow it; whether in the direction of its finger or (e.g.) in the opposite one?—And if there were, not a single sign-post, but a chain of adjacent ones or of chalk marks on the ground— is there only *one* way of interpreting them?—So I can say, the sign-post does after all leave no room for doubt. Or rather: it sometimes leaves room for doubt and sometimes not. And now this is no longer a philosophical proposition, but an empirical one.[8]

Without a practice of following it—a way of acting—the signpost, by itself, leaves considerable room for doubt. There are as many potential ways of following the signpost as there are possible conventions for determining how it is to be used and what counts as following it. But once a convention for following signposts is adopted, a background of understanding evolves. It is against this background that the need for interpretation arises.

In explicating understanding, interpretation is a nonstarter. Even if we were to grant the interpretivist his premise that all understanding involves interpretation, the interpretivist position collapses on its own terms. If all understanding is interpretation, then all interpretation is itself in need of interpretation. That is, if understanding a rule, symbol, or sign is a matter of an act of interpretation standing between the interpreter and the thing interpreted, there is no reason why this same logic should not apply to the interpretation itself. Wittgenstein's point is not to deny understanding. Rather, his argument is that interpretation cannot explicate the very idea of understanding because it gives rise to an infinite regress of interpretations (the Regress Argument).[9] In the end, interpretation obscures rather than illuminates the phenomenon of human understanding.

In addition to the infinite Regress Argument, Wittgenstein advances a second argument, what Meredith Williams calls the "Paradox of Interpretation."[10] First, Wittgenstein:

> This was our paradox: no course of action could be determined by a rule, because every course of action can be made out to accord with the rule. The answer was: if everything can be made out to accord with the rule, then it can also be made out to conflict with it. And so there would be neither accord nor conflict here.[11]

8. WITTGENSTEIN, *supra* note 2, at § 85.
9. *Id.* at §§ 141, 198 (introducing the Regress Argument in two places).
10. MEREDITH WILLIAMS, WITTGENSTEIN, MIND AND MEANING 160 (1999).
11. WITTGENSTEIN, *supra* note 2, at § 201.

The Regress Argument undercuts our ability to prefer one interpretation over another. By contrast, the Paradox of Interpretation argument shows that no matter what action we deem "correct," we can interpret the rule in question in such a way that the action can be made either to accord with the rule or not. Williams sums up the situation thus:

> The Regress Argument shows that the view of objectified meaning as embodied in decision, formula, or any other candidate for the role cannot account for the *necessity of rules*, for the fact that rules constrain the behavior of the agent. The Paradox shows that the view cannot account for the *normativity of rules*, for the fact that there is a substantive distinction between correct and incorrect. There is nothing in the mind of the agent or in the behavior of the agent that shows what rule he is following, so long as we think of rules as embodying objectified meaning. In sum, there is no explanatory role (via the Paradox) nor epistemic role (via the Regress) for objectified meaning to play.[12]

If interpretation is a dead end, how do we explain the fact that we do understand signposts and that we do grasp the requirements of all sorts of norms (that is, follow rules)? Wittgenstein rejects the idea of interpretation as a necessary mediating device between a rule and our grasp of its requirements. His point is not only that interpretation is a logically incoherent explanation of understanding. He goes further, arguing against the very picture of understanding embraced by interpretivists. For Wittgenstein, *nothing* stands between a rule and what counts as following a rule (that is, correct action). And yet, we still do not have a clear picture of the nature of understanding. Precisely what, we may still ask, does understanding consist of?

Wittgenstein's answer is twofold: technique[13] and practice.[14] We show our understanding of a concept when we use the concept correctly. The "giving of a correct explanation is a criterion of understanding."[15]

---

12. WILLIAMS, *supra* note 10, at 161.

13. WITTGENSTEIN, *supra* note 2, at § 199 ("To understand a language means to be [the] master of a technique.").

14. G.P. BAKER & P.M.S. HACKER, 2 WITTGENSTEIN: RULES, GRAMMAR AND NECESSITY 136 (1985).

15. G.P. BAKER & P.M.S. HACKER, WITTGENSTEIN: UNDERSTANDING AND MEANING 667 (1980).

> [G]iving a correct explanation is a criterion of understanding, while the explanation given is a standard for the correct use of the expression explained. Correspondingly, using an expression in accordance with correct explanations of it is a criterion of understanding, while understanding an expression presupposes the ability to explain it.

Id. Thus, when a lawyer is asked why two persons are required to witness a will, the connection between attestation and validity will be explicated, thereby demonstrating the lawyer's understanding of the concepts.

Correct understanding is not a function of something that goes on in our head (for example, a private act of interpretation or translation). Concept possession is the demonstrated ability to participate in the manifold activities in which the concept is employed (for example, rule following).[16]

Interpretation is a nonstarter because interpretation draws our attention away from the techniques that make understanding possible. Correct and incorrect forms of action are immanent in practices. Thus, correct forms of action cannot be imposed on a practice, by interpretation or otherwise. It is only when we master the techniques employed by participants in a practice that we can grasp the distinction between correct and incorrect action.[17]

But where does this leave interpretation? If understanding—knowing how to engage in a practice—is exhibited in action, what role is there for interpretation? Again, Wittgenstein is instructive here. When it comes to interpretation, we can see that interpretation depends upon understanding—unreflective action—already being in place.[18] We should, as Wittgenstein argues, "restrict the term 'interpretation' to the substitution of one expression of the rule for another."[19] Interpretation is an activity—one that not only depends upon understanding already being in place, but an activity that is actuated by a breakdown or failure in understanding. In short, interpretation is a therapeutic, not foundational, activity.

III. Understanding Law: The Grammar of Legal Argument

I have argued that interpretation is an activity that depends upon understanding. I have said that understanding—be it of law or any other human practice—is a matter of being the master of a technique. But what is the technique grasped by a competent practitioner of law, and in what does mastery of such technique consist?

---

16. *See* WILLIAMS, *supra* note 10, at 176.

> The rule as formula, the standard as chart, or the paradigm as an instance have no normative or representational status in their own right. They have this status only in virtue of the way the formula or the chart or the instance is used. It is the use that creates the structured context within which sign-posts point, series can be continued, orders obeyed and paradigms be exemplary. Only then can we see a particular action as embodying or instancing a grammatical structure. In short, the mandatory stage setting is social practice.

Id.

17. *See* ROBERT B. BRANDOM, MAKING IT EXPLICIT 13 (1994) ("[T]he meaning of a linguistic expression must determine how it would be *correct* to use it in various contexts. To understand or grasp such a meaning is to be able to distinguish correct from incorrect uses.").

18. WITTGENSTEIN, *supra* note 2, at § 219 ("When I obey a rule, I do not chose. I obey the rule *blindly*.").

19. *Id.* at § 201.

The nerve of law is argument. Facility in legal argument is the measure of the degree to which one has mastered the grammar of justification that is central to the practice of law. The grammar of legal argument is immanent in the practice of law. By immanent, I mean to say that law is an intersubjective practice wherein participants coordinate their behavior through the employment of a grammar of appraisal that is a constitutive feature of the practice itself.[20]

The fundamental form of expression in law is assertion. Argument in law begins with an assertion that something is the case—true—as a matter of law. Everything from a claim that a statute is unconstitutional to averment that a contract is unenforceable are all examples of legal assertions, claims that the purported proposition is true *as a matter of law*.

Lawyers appraise the truth and falsity of legal assertions through forms of legal argument. The forms of argument are themselves neither true nor false. Rather, the forms of legal argument are the means by which lawyers show the truth and falsity of legal propositions.[21] The forms of argument are the grammar of legal argument. They are immanent in the sense that they make possible the assertion of claims for the truth of legal propositions which are then disputed, evaluated, and judged by all who are competent in their use (technique).[22]

There are six forms of legal argument in the American system of law. While some are more familiar than others in different departments of law,[23] these six forms comprise a complete list of the argumentative tools of American law. The forms of argument in law are:

> Textual: taking the words of an authoritative legal text (e.g., a constitution, statute, contract or trust) at face value, i.e., in accordance with their ordinary meaning;

20. In short, I agree with Jules Coleman that law is a conventional practice "sustained by the behavior of participants." JULES COLEMAN, THE PRACTICE OF PRINCIPLE 99 (2001). I believe an account of the forms of argument, and the way the forms of argument are used to show the truth of legal propositions, is the best explanation of the practice of law.

21. "[P]ropositions of law are typically statements not of what 'law' is but of what *the law* is, i.e. what the law of some system permits or requires or empowers people to do." H.L.A. HART, THE CONCEPT OF LAW 247 (2d ed. 1994).

22. Robert Brandom describes well the project of joining the assertoric and the normative. *See* BRANDOM, *supra* note 17, at 167 ("What is it we are *doing* when we assert, claim, or declare something?").

23. The phrase "departments of Law" is Dwokin's. *See* DWORKIN, *supra* note 1, at 250–54.

Doctrinal: applying rules generated from previously decided cases (precedents);

Historical/Intentional: relying on the intentions of the Framers (constitution), legislature (statute), or parties to an agreement (contract);

Prudential: weighing or assessing the consequences (in terms of "costs") of a particular rule;

Structural: inferring rules from relationships created by the structures created by the Constitution or statute; and

Ethical: deriving rules from the moral ethos established by the Constitution or by statute.[24]

I have said that the forms of legal argument in the American practice of law are employed to show the truth and falsity of legal propositions. While this is certainly true, I need to say more about the argumentative framework within which the forms of legal argument are immanent. Once this structure is articulated, I can then explicate the nature of understanding in law as a prelude to my discussion of the role of interpretation in law.

As mentioned, legal argument begins in assertion. An assertion in law is a claim that a given proposition is true as a matter of law. Consider this proposition: p = "The contract between Smith and Jones is unenforceable." I will call this proposition a Claim because it is asserted as a correct or true proposition. Before we can assess the truth or falsity of the Claim, we need to know what it is about the contract between Smith and Jones that might lead one to assert that the contract is unenforceable.

What we seek is a Ground, a reason (for example, a fact) that connects the Claim of unenforceability with some aspect or feature of the contract by virtue of which the contract is allegedly unenforceable. Suppose Smith is fourteen years of age. This fact is the Ground for the Claim that the contract is unenforceable. But what is it that makes this so? In other words, in virtue of what are the Claim and Ground joined such that the Ground supports the Claim (that is, makes it true)?

The answer to this last question is a Warrant. The Warrant makes the Ground significant vis-à-vis the Claim. The Warrant is the means by

24. The six forms of argument in American law, paraphrased in modern terms here, were first explicated by Philip Bobbitt. *See* PHILIP BOBBITT, CONSTITUTIONAL INTERPRETATION (1991) [hereinafter CONSTITUTIONAL INTERPRETATION]; PHILIP BOBBITT, CONSTITUTIONAL FATE (1982). Structural argument in the constitutional context was first articulated by Charles Black. *See* CHARLES L. BLACK, JR., STRUCTURE AND RELATIONSHIP IN CONSTITUTIONAL LAW (1969).

which we can say with certainty that the Ground is a legally relevant reason for concluding that the Claim is true as a matter of law. But Warrants are not self executing. For Warrrants to be meaningful, there must be ways of construing Warrants that make Warrants meaningful. I shall refer to these as Backings.

The forms of legal argument are the Backings for Warrants, the grammar of legal justification with which we show the truth and falsity of Claims from the legal point of view. The following schema depicts these relationships explained in the preceding paragraphs:[25]

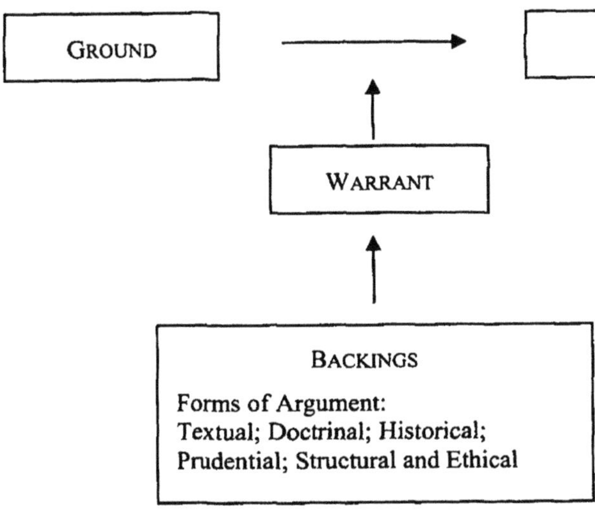

With this schema in view, let us work through the question whether *p* is a true proposition of law. Obviously, Smith's status as a minor is the Ground for the Claim that *p* is true. If the Claim arose in a jurisdiction where the Restatement (Second) of Contracts is deemed to be the controlling law on this question, a textual argument that references the

25. The framework that follows (Claim, Ground, Warrant, Backings) is taken from STEPHEN E. TOULMIN ET AL., AN INTRODUCTION TO REASONING 23–67 (1979). The approach was originally advanced in STEPHEN EDELSTON TOULMIN, THE USES OF ARGUMENT (1958).

operative provision[26] would be sufficient to show the truth of *p*. In addition to the relevant Restatement text, there would no doubt be precedent construing the rule in question (doctrinal argument), noting exceptions, and describing qualifications. Taken together, the textual and doctrinal arguments show the truth of *p*. It is through the use of these forms of argument that we are able to say that *p* is true.

The normativity of law—the distinction between correct and incorrect assertions—is a matter of the proper use of the forms of legal argument. The forms of argument are the (immanent) grammar of legal justification. Understanding in law is best explained as a disposition on the part of individuals to employ the forms of argument in appropriate ways as context requires.[27] The normativity of law assures objectivity in legal judgment.[28] Meaning—the basis of objectivity—is made possible by the harmony in action and judgment of participants in legal practice over time. Most importantly, it is in virtue of what participants in legal practice have *in common*[29] that normativity and objectivity are possible.

IV. INTERPRETATION IN LAW

Interpretation is a constitutive feature of legal practice. Notwithstanding its importance within legal practice, interpretation is an activity that is dependent on understanding already being in place. The need for interpretation arises when our conventional ways of understanding break down. This occurs, in law, when our use of the forms of legal argument "is in some way rendered problematic and thrown in doubt."[30] How does understanding in law break down, and how does interpretation serve to repair the fabric of understanding?

Lawyers use the forms of argument to appraise claims about what is true as a matter of law. In many cases (we may call them easy cases), the relevant forms of argument all point to a single conclusion. But the forms of argument do conflict, and, when they do, the tension must be

26. *See* RESTATEMENT (SECOND) OF CONTRACTS § 12 (1981) (describing capacity to contract).

27. *Cf.* WILLIAMS, *supra* note 10, at 177 (describing a disposition as the ability to act appropriately under the circumstances).

28. *See* Dennis Patterson, *Normativity and Objectivity in Law*, 43 WM. & MARY L. REV. 325, 356 (2001) (showing how normativity arises from a practice of argument with criteria for appraising assertions).

29. Of course, this is directly contrary to the argument made by Ronald Dworkin. *See* DWORKIN, *supra* note 1, at 250–54 (showing the compartmentalization of the departments of law); Postema, *supra* note 1, at 283, 288–89 (making the case for the intersubjective nature of understanding).

30. James Tully, *Wittgenstein and Political Philosophy: Understanding Practices of Critical Reflection*, *in* THE GRAMMAR OF POLITICS: WITTGENSTEIN AND POLITICAL PHILOSOPHY 17, 39 (Cressida J. Heyes ed., 2003).

resolved. Resolving this tension is the activity of legal interpretation.[31] It is in the act of interpretation that the fabric of law is repaired, thereby enabling practitioners to go on with the practice. I shall now discuss three cases to illustrate these points.

A. Statutory Interpretation

Let us start with a case familiar to all students of legal theory, *Riggs v. Palmer*.[32] Having executed a valid will, Francis Palmer intended to leave the bulk of his estate to his grandson, Elmer.[33] Upon the remarriage of his widower grandfather, Elmer feared he would lose his inheritance.[34] To prevent this turn of events, Elmer killed his grandfather by poison.[35]

There was no dispute about the requisite statute at the center of issue in the case. The New York Statute of Wills articulated what all probate statutes required: where there is a valid will, a dead testator, and a named beneficiary, the latter is given the testator's property according to the dictates of the will.[36] The proposition of law to which the parties gave their attention is simple: Elmer is entitled to his grandfather's property in accordance with the dictates of his grandfather's will. Elmer's argument was grounded in the language of the New York Statute of Wills.[37] Before we consider the arguments for and against the asserted proposition of law, a few preliminary remarks are in order. They concern the concept of understanding and its relationship to the forms of argument discussed earlier. As argued above, understanding is exhibited by participants in legal practice in the unreflective employment of forms of argument to show the truth of legal propositions. To see this, consider a case where murder is not an element of the facts—the normal probate context. Once validated by the probate court, the will of the testator dictates the devolution of property of the testator. This requirement is gleaned from a straightforward reading of the Statute of Wills. In short, textual argument is sufficient to show the truth of the proposition that the beneficiary of a valid will is to be given property in

31. Conflict among the forms of argument is a significant but not exhaustive aspect of interpretation in law.
32. Riggs v. Palmer, 22 N.E. 188 (N.Y. 1889).
33. *Id.*
34. *Id.* at 189.
35. *Id.*
36. *Id.*
37. *Id.*

accordance with the dictates of the will. What turns a case of understanding into one where the need for interpretation arises?

The need for interpretation is actuated by facts. In *Riggs*, the actuating fact was the murder of the testator by his grandson. But why is *this* fact an actuating event? Not only does the majority opinion show why the murder actuates the need for interpretation, the opinion shows how the state of the law explains the legal (that is, interpretive) significance of the murder. In other words, we need to explain how understanding (that is, the unreflective act of probating the will in the normal course of things) broke down as the court tried to come to terms with the significance of the murder as the event that precipitated the breakdown in understanding.

The majority opinion in *Riggs* is a sophisticated doctrinal argument. As Professor Dworkin has taught us, the opinion makes good use of the common law maxim: *no man shall profit from his own wrong.*[38] But there is more to the opinion than mere recitation of an equitable maxim. When we look at the ways in which Judge Earl showed the true state of the law, we see why the facts themselves make it clear that a straightforward reading of the requisite statute was all but impossible.

The majority opinion begins in classic fashion with the distinction between law and equity. The distinction is embraced in full measure by the common law systems of both the United States and England and can be traced back to Aristotle. The sheer breadth and diversity of classic writers on the role of equity[39] within all departments of law should cause an educated legal mind to experience a sense of unease when confronted with the facts in *Riggs*.

Having shown how the *no man shall profit from his own wrong* principle is a constitutive feature of law in the most general way (that is, the law and equity distinction), Judge Earl then demonstrated the reach of the principle throughout varied departments of law. Citing cases from the law of wills and insurance, Earl made a strong case for the proposition that precedents both directly on point (that is, the law of wills), as well as those from related departments of law, support an exception to the ordinary meaning of the words of the statute. That is, Earl made a doctrinal argument to the effect that the words of a valid legislative enactment (here, the Statute of Wills) are to be given their normal force and effect unless there is some exception demonstrated by the facts. In short, Judge Earl did not *change* the law; he *clarified* it (by

38. *See* RONALD DWORKIN, TAKING RIGHTS SERIOUSLY 14–45 (1977); DWORKIN, *supra* note 1, at 15–20.

39. In its opinion, the majority cites Puffendorf, Bacon, and Blackstone, among other legal thinkers. *Riggs*, 22 N.E. at 189.

pointing to an underlying and well-established legal principle).[40]

By contrast, Judge Gray, in dissent, argued for a straightforward reading of the words of the statute. Claiming that the court was "bound by the rigid rules of law,"[41] Gray argued that Elmer is being twice punished for his offense.[42] In a clever rebuttal to Judge Gray, the majority pointed out that he begged the question of whether Elmer was entitled to receive his victim's property under the will. The point was that the very question before the court was *whether* the property rightfully belonged to Elmer or not. Judge Gray did not seem to notice his error.

What does *Riggs* teach us about interpretation in law? First, in terms of the forms of argument, it is clear that without the complicating factor of the murder of the testator, the textual argument is decisive. Without the murder of the testator, it is true as a matter of law that Elmer was entitled to receive his grandfather's property according to the dictates of the Statute of Wills. It is only when the complication of the murder is added to the facts that lawyers dispute the true state of the law.

How did Judge Earl persuade enough of his colleagues to see the law as he did? Three factors suggest themselves. First, the majority opinion did no damage to the existing state of the law. I will call this the interpretive principle of *minimal mutilation*.[43] In other words, deciding against Elmer did not put in question the efficacy of any other element of the New York Statute of Wills. Second, through its decision, the majority demonstrated that its conclusion was consistent with everything else it knew to be true about the law of wills. I shall refer to this as *coherence*.[44] Finally, the opinion shows how a decision against Elmer comports with similar decisions in other departments of law. I shall

40. *See* FISH, *supra* note 4, at 327 ("Interpretation is not the art of construing but the art of constructing.").

41. *Riggs*, 22 N.E. at 191 (Gray, J., dissenting).

42. *Id.* at 193 ("[T]o concede appellants' views would involve the imposition of an additional punishment or penalty upon [Elmer].") (Gray, J., dissenting).

43. *See* W.V. QUINE & J.S. ULLIAN, THE WEB OF BELIEF 66–67 (2d ed. 1978) (discussing the virtue of conservatism). *See also* GILBERT HARMAN & JUDITH JARVIS THOMSON, MORAL RELATIVISM AND MORAL OBJECTIVITY 12 (1996) ("It is rational to make the least change in one's view that is necessary in order to obtain greater coherence in what one believes.") (citations omitted). *Cf.* HENRY M. HART, JR. & ALBERT M. SACKS, THE LEGAL PROCESS 147 (1994) (discussing reasoned elaboration).

44. The idea of coherence is apt. *See* CONAL CONDREN, THE STATUS AND APPRAISAL OF CLASSIC TEXTS 148 (1985) ("[A]t its most general level, coherence refers to the ways in which parts are interconnected to form a whole; and at a similar level of generality, the appraisive category of coherence is an abridgment of the range of questions one asks of a text in terms of its parts and the closeness of their interrelationships.").

refer to this aspect as *generality*.[45] Taken together, minimal mutilation, coherence, and generality are the three aspects of the majority's opinion that support the notion that its interpretation of the law is more persuasive than that offered by the dissenting opinion.

More important than the particulars of the majority and dissenting opinions is the fact that neither advanced any *theory* of legal interpretation. Of course, it is always possible to elevate a form of argument into a theory if that means relentless adherence to a single form of argument.[46] However, the move to theory hides the tension felt by practitioners of law as they struggle to persuade one another that their choice of how to go on with the practice is correct. To see such a struggle as a competition of theories obscures this important aspect of the practice.

B. Contract Law

The discernment of legal meaning is a fundamental feature of law. Contracts, trusts, wills, and constitutions all come to us in the form of written instruments. How lawyers construe texts to decide their meaning is a complex and sophisticated undertaking. Interestingly, the forms of argument—previously explained as the means by which lawyers show the truth of legal propositions—are the same whether the document is a contract or a constitution. In fact, it was the existence of the forms of argument at common law that made the American innovation of a *written* constitution workable.[47]

Contracts usually take the form of a writing because the parties wish to hold one another to their bargain. But sometimes the writing—no matter how clear it may be—fails to settle the question of the parties' agreement. *C & J Fertilizer, Inc. v. Allied Mutual Insurance Co.* is illustrative.[48] A building owned by an Iowa corporation whose president was a farmer was burglarized. The thieves made off with chemicals, office equipment, and shop equipment valued at approximately $10,000.[49] The stolen chemicals, which constituted the bulk of the value of the lost items, had been stored in a locked interior room in the warehouse.[50]

45. QUINE & ULLIAN, *supra* note 43, at 73 ("The wider the range of application of a hypothesis, the more general it is.").

46. For an exquisite example *see* MARK TUSHNET, RED, WHITE AND BLUE 179–87 (1988) (reducing all the forms of constitutional argument to prudential argument). For discussion of this point, see Philip Bobbitt, *Is Law Politics?*, 41 STAN. L. REV. 1233 (1989) (reviewing TUSHNET, *supra*).

47. *See* CONSTITUTIONAL INTERPRETATION, *supra* note 24, at 5 ("Since the Constitution was a written law, it had to be *construed*, and this was to be done according to the prevailing methods of legal construction.").

48. C & J Fertilizer, Inc. v. Allied Mut. Ins. Co., 227 N.W.2d 169 (Iowa 1975).

49. *Id.* at 171.

50. *Id.*

Interestingly, there were no visible marks on the exterior of the building, nor was there any sign of tampering upon the Plexiglas door to the warehouse. The court described the facts as follows:

> There were truck tire tread marks visible in the mud in the driveway leading to and from the plexiglas door entrance to the warehouse. It was demonstrated this door could be forced open without leaving visible marks or physical damage.
>
> There were no visible marks on the exterior of the building made by tools, explosives, electricity or chemicals, and there was no physical damage to the exterior of the building to evidence felonious entry into the building by force and violence.[51]

The insurance policy defined burglary as:

> [T]he felonious abstraction of insured property (1) from within the premises by a person making felonious entry therein by actual force and violence, of which force and violence there are *visible marks* made by tools, explosives, electricity or chemicals upon, or physical damage to, the exterior of the premises at the place of such entry.[52]

Following the text of the insurance policy, this loss was not covered, as the burglar left no visible marks on the exterior door. And yet, the Iowa Supreme Court held to the contrary. Its reason for doing so is a lesson in the art of interpretation in law.

The dissent makes the obvious textual argument: "We may not—at least we *should* not—by any accepted standard of construction meddle with contracts which clearly and plainly state their meaning simply because we dislike that meaning, even in the case of insurance policies."[53] In contract law, due to the emphasis on writing, textual argument often enjoys supremacy among the forms of argument. And yet, there are many examples where the plain meaning of the text yields to other considerations.

The majority opinion evinces no lack of appreciation for the power of textual argument.[54] But the majority uses an historical argument to make the case—ultimately persuasive—that the specific language of the contract cannot control the ultimate decision of what rights the parties have under their agreement. In constitutional law, and in the interpretation of statutes, appeal is made to the announced intentions of ratifiers or legislators in interpreting the present meaning of constitutional or

51. *Id.*
52. *Id.* (quoting trial court) (emphasis added).
53. *Id.* at 183 (LeGrand, J., dissenting).
54. *Id.* at 173–75.

legislative provisions. Where circumstances change, the outcome of decisions may well be different from those originally contemplated.

In characterizing the nature of the contractual process, the majority writes: "[m]any of our principles for resolving conflicts relating to written contracts were formulated at an early time when parties of equal strength negotiated in the historical sequence of offer, acceptance, and reduction to writing. The concept that both parties assented to the resulting document had solid footing in fact."[55] But the course of history moved away from the era of parties of equal strength bargaining freely. It is this historical change that, in the view of the majority, merits an outcome not contemplated by a mere reading of the contractual text.[56]

The great change that underlies the majority's historical argument is the rise of standard form contracts.[57] Presented on a *take it or leave it* basis, insurance contracts present the buyer in need of coverage with no options and no ability to negotiate terms (for example, the definition of burglary) or any other material element of the contract. The contract is, in effect, composed of boilerplate terms to which there is no real assent at all.

Owing to the fact that terms cannot be negotiated, purchasers of policies rarely read the terms of the document with care. Of course, any purchaser of insurance will have *reasonable expectations* about the scope and limits of coverage. These expectations, the majority argued, require a different approach to the question whether the purchaser *assented* to the terms offered in the insurance policy. The majority concluded, because of the fact "that modern insurance companies have turned to mass advertising to sell 'protection'"[58] that the law required that the "reasonable expectations" with respect to coverage be of greater importance than the ordinary meaning of contract terms.[59]

How did the majority resolve the conflict between the textual and historical arguments? First, the court showed how the doctrine of reasonable expectations is an established feature of insurance law,[60] thereby demonstrating coherence within the immediate department of law. Minimal mutilation and coherence are both at work, building a persuasive interpretation. But the real strength in the majority's interpretive argument is generality. The majority opinion convinces by showing

55. *Id.* at 173.
56. *Id.*
57. *Id.*
58. *Id.* at 178.
59. *Id.* at 176. However, the majority did make the point that the record demonstrated no actual knowledge of the restrictive definition of burglary in the policies. *See id.* at 176–77. Had such knowledge been shown, the result might well have been different.
60. *Id.* at 176–77.

how the strategy of argument that it employs in the instant case is consistent with what courts are doing in other departments of law. From common law sales contracts[61] to common law leases[62] to transactions governed by the Uniform Commercial Code,[63] the majority used decisions[64] from various departments of law to make the case that the present decision fit within a wide fabric of decisions. It is the feature of generality that enables the majority opinion to favor the historical argument over its textual counterpart.

C. Constitutional Law

In the American legal system, no department of law is more contested than constitutional law. Theories of constitutional law are numerous and wide ranging. Notwithstanding the plethora of theoretical approaches to constitutional law, there is general consensus that the forms of argument outlined above are the grammar for advancement and assessment of constitutional claims.[65]

I will discuss a single opinion of the United States Supreme Court to illustrate the claims made earlier regarding the forms of argument and the role of interpretation in law. While questions in constitutional law are often unique, there is nothing special about the forms of argument in constitutional law. As mentioned earlier, the forms of argument at common law were the very thing that enabled the early Supreme Court to interpret the written Constitution. Thus, everything we learn about interpretation in constitutional law is, *ceteris paribus*, equally applicable to other departments of law.

The late nineteen twenties through the nineteen thirties were a time of great economic turbulence in the United States. Over the course of a decade, state legislatures were repeatedly called upon to stave off the harsh effects of economic depression and widespread fiscal misery. Particularly hard hit by financial crises were American citizens in the middle class, who saw their very ability to shelter their families put at

61. *Id.* at 178.
62. *Id.* at 179.
63. *Id.* at 179–80 (citing Henningsen v. Bloomfield Motors, Inc., 161 A.2d 69, 93 (N.J. 1960)).
64. The majority cited both Iowa precedents and persuasive precedents from other jurisdictions. *Id.* at 178–79.
65. *See* THOMAS E. BAKER & JERRE S. WILLIAMS, CONSTITUTIONAL ANALYSIS 307–36 (2d ed. 2003); PAUL BREST, SANFORD LEVINSON, J.M. BALKIN & AKHIL REED AMAR, PROCESSES OF CONSTITUTIONAL DECISIONMAKING 33 (4th ed. 2000).

risk. In 1933, the Minnesota Legislature passed the Mortgage Moratorium Law. In an effort to mitigate the harsh effects of numerous mortgage foreclosures, the Mortgage Moratorium Law extended the period of time for redemption of property for up to two years, to May 1, 1935.[66]

66. The pertinent section of the statute reads:

Sec. 4. *Period of Redemption May be Extended.*—Where any mortgage upon real property has been foreclosed and the period of redemption has not yet expired, or where a sale is hereafter had, in the case of real estate mortgage foreclosure proceedings, now pending, or which may hereafter be instituted prior to the expiration of two years from and after the passage of this Act, or upon the sale of any real property under any judgment or execution where the period of redemption has not yet expired, or where such sale is made hereafter within two years from and after the passage of this Act, the period of redemption may be extended for such additional time as the court may deem just and equitable but in no event beyond May 1st, 1935; provided that the mortgagor, or the owner in possession of said property, in the case of mortgage foreclosure proceedings, or the judgment debtor, in case of sale under judgment, or execution, shall prior to the expiration of the period of redemption, apply to the district court having jurisdiction of the matter, on not less than 10 days' written notice to the mortgagee or judgment creditor, or the attorney of either, as the case may be, for an order determining the reasonable value of the income on said property, or, if the property has no income, then the reasonable rental value of the property involved in such sale, and directing and requiring such mortgagor or judgment debtor, to pay all or a reasonable part of such income or rental value, in or toward the payment of taxes, insurance, interest, mortgage or judgment indebtedness at such times and in such manner as shall be fixed and determined and ordered by the court; and the court shall thereupon hear said application and after such hearing shall make and file its order directing the payment by such mortgagor, or judgment debtor, of such an amount at such times and in such manner as to the court shall, under all the circumstances, appear just and equitable. Provided that upon the service of the notice or demand aforesaid that the running of the period of redemption shall be tolled until the court shall make its order upon such application. Provided, further, however, that if such mortgagor or judgment debtor, or personal representative, shall default in the payments, or any of them, in such order required, on his part to be done, or commits waste, his right to redeem from said sale shall terminate 30 days after such default and holders of subsequent liens may redeem in the order and manner now provided by law beginning 30 days after the filing of notice of such default with the clerk of such District Court, and his right to possession shall cease and the party acquiring title to any such real estate shall then be entitled to the immediate possession of said premises. If default is claimed by allowance of waste, such 30 day period shall not begin to run until the filing of an order of the court finding such waste. Provided, further, that the time of redemption from any real estate mortgage foreclosure or judgment or execution sale heretofore made, which otherwise would expire less than 30 days after the passage and approval of this Act, shall be and the same hereby is extended to a date 30 days after the passage and approval of this Act, and in such case, the mortgagor, or judgment debtor, or the assigns or personal representative of either, as the case may be, or the owner in the possession of the property, may, prior to said date, apply to said court for and the court may thereupon grant the relief as hereinbefore and in this section provided. Provided, further, that prior to May 1, 1935, no action shall be maintained in this state for a deficiency judgment until the period of redemption as allowed by existing law or as extended under the provisions of

In *Home Building & Loan Association v. Blaisdell*, the United States Supreme Court considered a challenge to the constitutionality of the Minnesota Mortgage Moratorium Law.[67] Pursuant to the statute, the Blaisdells applied for an extension of the redemption period on the foreclosure of a mortgage they had given on land they owned in Minneapolis.[68] The mortgage had been properly foreclosed: the appellant and mortgagee was the purchaser of the mortgage at the foreclosure sale.[69] The Blaisdells applied for relief under the statute prior to the running of the period of equitable redemption, the time during which they were legally permitted to retain ownership of land by paying the mortgagee/purchaser the sum of $3,700.98.[70] The reasonable value of the property, the Court stated, "greatly exceeded the amount due on the mortgage including all liens, costs and expenses."[71]

The Minnesota Supreme Court upheld the constitutionality of the Minnesota statute, finding the statute to be a constitutionally permissible exercise of Minnesota's police power.[72] The question of the statute's constitutionality hinged on the question of whether or not the statute violated the Contract Clause of the U.S. Constitution.[73] In the end, a divided U.S. Supreme Court decided that the Minnesota statute was constitutional. There is much in the opinion to be learned about constitutional interpretation and the role of the forms of argument in showing the truth of propositions of law.

The Court put the question as one of "the relation of emergency to constitutional power"[74] and began with the observation that "[w]hile emergency does not create power, emergency may furnish the occasion

this Act, has expired.

Home Bldg. & Loan Ass'n v. Blaisdell, 290 U.S. 398, 417 n.1 (1934) (quoting Minnesota Mortgage Moratorium Law, ch. 339 § 4, 1933 Minn. Laws 514).

67. *Id.* at 415–16.

68. *Id. at* 418–19.

69. *Id.* at 419.

70. *Id.*

71. *Id.*

72. *Id.* at 420.

73. Article 1, Section 10, Clause 1 reads:

> No state shall enter into any Treaty, Alliance, or Confederation; grant Letters of Marque and Reprisal; coin Money; emit Bills of Credit; make any Thing but gold and silver Coin a Tender in Payment of Debts; pass any Bill of Attainder, ex post facto Law, or Law impairing the Obligation of Contracts, or grant any Title of Nobility.

U.S. CONST. art. I, § 10, cl. 1.

74. *Blaisdell*, 290 U.S. at 425.

for the exercise of power."[75] In deciding the scope and limits of power, the Court must discern the proper relationship between the power sought to be exercised and constitutional limits on that exercise of power. For this, the Court needed to construct the meaning of the Contract Clause. To do this, the Court turned to the forms of legal argument.

The majority began with an historical narrative. History tells us why the ratifiers or framers propounded a constitutional clause and what purpose that clause was meant to serve. The majority maintained that notwithstanding the failure of a clear answer to emerge from the debates in the Constitutional Convention, there could be no doubt as to the reasons which led to adoption of the clause. The Court explained:

> The widespread distress following the revolutionary period, and the plight of debtors, had called forth in the States an ignoble array of legislative schemes for the defeat of creditors and the invasion of contractual obligations. Legislative interferences had been so numerous and extreme that the confidence essential to prosperous trade had been undermined and the utter destruction of credit was threatened. . . . The occasion and general purpose of the contract clause are summed up in the terse statement of Chief Justice Marshall in Ogden v. Saunders, 12 Wheat. pp. 213, 354, 355: "The power of changing the relative situation of debtor and creditor, of interfering with contracts, a power which comes home to every man, touches the interest of all, and controls the conduct of every individual in those things which he supposes to be proper for his own exclusive management, had been used to such an excess by the state legislatures, as to break in upon the ordinary intercourse of society, and destroy all confidence between man and man. This mischief had become so great, so alarming, as not only to impair commercial intercourse, and threaten the existence of credit, but to sap the morals of the people, and destroy the sanctity of private faith. To guard against the continuance of the evil was an object of deep interest with all the truly wise, as well as the virtuous, of this great community, and was one of the important benefits expected from a reform of the government."[76]

This history runs directly counter to the decision the Court ultimately reached. In this regard, the dissenting opinion—written by Justice Sutherland—is particularly instructive. Sutherland was adamant that the historical form of argument was decisive in answering the question of the constitutionality of the Minnesota statute. In constructing the meaning of the Constitution, Justice Sutherland argued: "[t]he whole aim of construction, as applied to a provision of the Constitution, is to discover the meaning, to ascertain and give effect to the intent, of its framers and the people who adopted it."[77] Constitutional interpretation is a matter of "plac[ing] ourselves in the condition of those who framed and adopted it."[78] Doing so, Sutherland maintained, "will demonstrate conclusively

75. *Id.* at 426.

76. *Id.* at 427–28.

77. *Id.* at 453 (Sutherland, J., dissenting) (citing Lake County v. Rollins, 130 U.S. 662, 670 (1889)).

78. *Id.* (Sutherland, J., dissenting) (citing *Ex parte* Bain, 121 U.S. 1, 12 (1887).

that [the Contract Clause] was framed and adopted with the specific and studied purpose of preventing legislation designed to relieve debtors *especially* in time of financial distress."[79]

The weight of history, so thoroughly recited by Justice Sutherland in dissent, meant that the majority opinion had to persuade on some basis other than history. For this, Chief Justice Hughes employed a variety of forms of argument to show why the Minnesota statute survived constitutional challenge. His primary arguments were two: doctrinal and prudential. First, ample precedent exists for the proposition that "the protective power of the State, its police power, may be exercised—without violating the true intent of the provision of the Federal Constitution—in directly preventing the immediate and literal enforcement of contractual obligations, by a temporary and conditional restraint, where vital public interests would otherwise suffer."[80] The example Hughes provided was a series of New York cases where the state extended the periods for residential leases during a housing crisis as long as current residents paid "a reasonable rent or price for their use and occupation."[81] These cases set the stage for the majority's most important argument: the prudential argument.

Finding an emergency existing in Minnesota, the Court granted that the end sought by the State is worthy of protection. But the key question was the means. Could the Court have found that the end of "protection of a basic interest of society"[82] could be accomplished without compromising the Court's obligation to state the law and not remake it according to its own lights? Having recited a variety of considerations—historical, doctrinal, and prudential—Chief Justice Hughes drew the opinion to a conclusive end.

Taking judicial notice of the emergency condition in Minnesota, the majority concluded that the statute was addressed to a legitimate end (that is, it was within the police power). Now Hughes needed to persuade that the end sought is legitimate, and that the means employed to achieve that end was constitutionally permissible. His argument is an entirely prudential one. First, he noted that the period of time for extension of the period of redemption was not unreasonable. Second, the integrity of

79. *Id.* (Sutherland, J., dissenting). Further bolstering his point, Sutherland recited a number of nineteenth and twentieth century Supreme Court precedents where the Court found debtor relief statutes unconstitutional. *Id.* at 465–66 (Sutherland, J., dissenting).

80. *Id.* at 440. This situation, according to the Court, involved debtor relief and leases in the context of scarce housing. *See id.* at 440–43.

81. *Id.* at 440–41.

82. *Id.* at 445.

the mortgage interest was in no way impaired. Third, the mortgagor was required to pay the rental value of the land, which amount was added to the indebtedness. Finally, the legislation was temporary, limited to the period of the exigency.

Chief Justice Hughes' opinion is a model of the interpretive principle of minimal mutilation. Once it had concluded that the police power was legitimate, the majority had to decide whether the exercise of that power could be accomplished in a way that recognized the power of both the textual and historical arguments that were at the center of the dissent. The success of the majority's interpretive argument turned on its ability to cabin the ill effects of trampling the clear language of the Contracts Clause. The majority's appreciation of this was evident in its attempt to emphasize the existence of a unique emergency situation and the very limited scope of the remedy that the decision afforded the respondents.

V. CONCLUSION

Law is a practice of argument. In the day to day practice of law, legal questions often admit of one right answer. Philosophy clarifies the practice of law when it engenders a clear view of the grammar of legal argument—the techniques employed by lawyers to settle disputed questions within a shared, conventional practice.[83]

The forms of argument are a central feature of the practice of law. But the forms of legal argument do not answer the question of what is to be done when they conflict, thereby engendering the need for interpretation. For this, we need to illuminate how it is that lawyers interpret the law when the forms of argument pull in opposing directions.

The forms of argument are immanent in the practice of law. As we have seen, the same is true of interpretation. The principles of minimal mutilation, coherence and generality are the hermeneutic tools of legal interpretation. In bringing these interpretive principles to light, it has not been my purpose to argue for a particular theory of interpretation. Rather, my aim has been to clarify what we already know and obtain a clearer view of what we do when, perforce, we interpret the law.

Clarity with respect to interpretation in law engenders a deeper understanding of the role of argument in law. Interpretation in law has purpose only because the possibility exists that we can persuade others

83. Or, as Jules Coleman puts it: "playing the game 'law'." COLEMAN, *supra* note 20, at 143. *See also* CONSTITUTIONAL INTERPRETATION, *supra* note 24, at 34 ("[I]f you believe the holdings of a court, insofar as they are constructions of the Constitution, are not statements about the world, but are moves within a serious game, movements as practised [sic] as any classical ballet and yet no less contingent, then reductionism is out of the question.").

to embrace our interpretations and that we are, ourselves, likewise capable of being persuaded. Interpretation, while not foundational, is certainly essential; without it, we could not preserve the common fabric of beliefs and dispositions that make law possible.

[6]
Fashionable Nonsense
(Review Essay)

ANTHONY G. AMSTERDAM & JEROME BRUNER,[†] MINDING THE LAW, Harvard University Press (2000), $35.

STEVEN L. WINTER,[‡] A CLEARING IN THE FOREST: LAW, LIFE, AND MIND, University of Chicago Press (2001), $38.

VINCENT DESCOMBES,[‡a] THE MIND'S PROVISIONS: A CRITIQUE OF COGNITIVISM, Princeton University Press (Stephen A. Schwartz trans., 2001), $35.

I. Introduction

There may be no better place to gauge current intellectual fashions than the magazine racks of the local bookstore. Recently *Scientific American* devoted a special issue to "The Hidden Mind." In introducing the articles, the Editor-in-Chief wrote:

> Weighing just three pounds and encompassing some 100 billion neurons, the brain is the most complex organ in the human body. It

---

[*] Distinguished Professor of Law, Rutgers University School of Law (Camden); Visiting Fellow, Department of Politics (Madison Program), Princeton University; Fellow, Center for the Critical Study of Contemporary Culture, Rutgers University (New Brunswick). For comments on drafts of this Essay, I wish to thank Francis Beckwith, Guyora Binder, Brian Bix, Mike Carrier, Mike Dorff, Angelique Haugerud, Richard Hyland, Dick Markovits, Tom Morawetz, Patrick S. O'Donnell, Ralf Poscher, Wes Sharrock, Jeff White, and Meredith Williams. Special thanks to Kim Ferzan and Mary Eckhardt for reading many drafts of this Essay and making very helpful suggestions for its improvement.

[†] Anthony G. Amsterdam is the Judge Edward Weinfeld Professor of Law at New York University School of Law. Jerome Bruner is a Research Professor of Psychology at New York University and a Senior Research Fellow at New York University School of Law. This book is hereinafter cited by page number as AMSTERDAM & BRUNER.

[‡] Steven L. Winter is the Walter S. Gibbs Professor of Constitutional Law and the Director of the Center for Legal Studies at Wayne State University School of Law. This book is hereinafter cited by page number as WINTER.

[‡a] Vincent Descombes is Director, Centre de Recherches Politiques Raymond-Aron. This book is hereinafter cited by page number as DESCOMBES.

> and the spinal cord supervise all physical operations. And yet it has proved to be a most elusive organ, hiding the inner workings of the mind, which defines and creates our unique personalities, intellect and consciousness.[1]

Notwithstanding the "popular" nature of the publication, this characterization of mind is most tendentious.[2] Even if one is inclined to dismiss these remarks as editorial hyperbole, the picture of mind articulated is by no means a careless rendering of sophisticated matters for mass consumption. In fact—and as the works discussed herein illustrate—the quoted passage expresses quite well a view of mind that now seems ascendant. But there are reasons to believe that this picture of mind is problematic, or worse.

At issue in the current fascination with mind is the appropriate characterization of mental life.[3] This task is philosophical in nature. Notwithstanding important advances in our comprehension of the brain's physiology, none of these empirical insights yields—nor could they yield—answers to the philosophical question of how to understand and characterize mental phenomena.[4] It is this question that frames discussion of the works under review.

But what does the relationship of mind to brain have to do with law? In the opinion of the authors of two of the works discussed in this Essay, law is a product of mind.[5] Thus, a better understanding of mind will yield insights

---

1. John Rennie, Letter from the Editor, *On Our Minds*, SCI. AM., Aug. 31, 2002, *at* http://www.sciam.com/special/toc.cfm?issueid=3.

2. At a minimum, what is tendentious is the notion that an incorporeal substance—"mind"—is somehow "contained" within a material organ, the brain.

3. *See* DESCOMBES p. 1 ("[T]he question of mind is the epitome of a contested philosophical problem.").

4. Descombes describes mental life from the cognitivist point of view:

> Like the philosopher of the subject, the mentalist also believes that books—and signs in general—have a subordinate mental status: the book would contain neither language nor meaning if these things did not exist in someone's head. The attribute of mentality belongs first and foremost to what happens inside someone and only secondarily to what happens outside: words, gestures, and written signs. For such a philosopher, "mental" is a synonym for "intrinsically meaningful," precisely because this word refers to whatever it is inside us that allows a meaning to be attached to external things which are otherwise devoid of meaning, like the sounds of a voice or the traces of a pen on paper. In order to be intrinsically mental or meaningful, the phenomena of mind must be internal and not external. They must be sought inside people and not in the world.

DESCOMBES pp. 3–4.

5. Throughout this Essay I often use the term "mind/brain" rather than separately reference each term. I do this because many cognitivists are of the view that the mind and the brain are either reducible one to the other or are simply "the same entity." Professors Amsterdam and Bruner virtually ignore the distinction (*e.g.*, there are no Index references to either "mind" or "brain"). Professor Winter uses the terms "mind" and "brain" interchangeably. Professor Descombes, in his capacity as a critic of cognitivism, is always careful to distinguish the two terms.

into law.[6] Is cognitivism—explaining human action by reference to hidden internal cognitive processes[7]—a "better theory of mind," and does it provide us otherwise unattainable insights into law? These two questions are the focus of this Essay.

This Essay is composed of three parts. In each of the first two parts, I describe and evaluate the arguments of the works devoted to the application of cognitive theory to law. In the course of articulating each author's arguments, I suggest reasons why the arguments fail to sustain the author's claims on behalf of a cognitivist approach to mind and law. One way to evaluate works that apply cognitivism to law is to attack the arguments of cognitivism directly, bypassing altogether the applied dimension of the position. I forsake this approach because I believe the arguments of Amsterdam/Bruner and Winter are weak, quite apart from any questions one might raise about cognitivism.

This does not mean that I think cognivitism is a useful picture of mind. I do not. I raise questions about the plausibility of the cognitivist picture of mind in the third and final part of the Essay.[8] In that discussion I use Vincent Descombes's book as a resource for framing and advancing arguments for the proposition that cognitivism is an implausible approach to the nature of mind. One of the virtues of Descombes's book is that he shows that, while *au courant* in appearance, the research agendas of contemporary cognitivists suffer from some of the same problems that beset the position when it was first staked out in the seventeenth century by René Descartes.

In a recent essay, Judge Richard Posner suggests that the survival of interdisciplinary legal scholarship may depend on its relevance to practitioners and judges and not just legal scholars.[9] He cites cognitive psychology as one discipline of increasing relevance beyond the borders of legal theory.[10]

---

6. *See* WINTER pp. xi–xii ("The project rests on the straightforward premise that a better theory of the mind should facilitate a better understanding of the products of the mind. Law is one of those products and, so, should be amenable to an analysis informed by the tools of cognitive theory.").

7. "[C]ognitivism is the view that the organization of behavior is best explained by an inner mental structure." MEREDITH WILLIAMS, WITTGENSTEIN, MIND AND MEANING 240 (1999). *Cf.* JOHN HAUGELAND, HAVING THOUGHT: ESSAYS IN THE METAPHYSICS OF MIND 9 (1998) ("Cognitivism in psychology and philosophy is roughly the position that intelligent behavior can be explained (only) by appeal to internal 'cognitive processes'—that is, rational thought in a broad sense.").

8. In the works on cognitivism and law discussed in this Essay, virtually none of the arguments against cognitivism is mentioned, let alone discussed. This is regrettable, if for no other reason than that the viability of cognitivism as a point of view on questions of law and legal theory depends on its success in addressing fundamental philosophical questions.

9. Richard A. Posner, *Legal Scholarship Today*, 115 HARV. L. REV. 1314, 1317 (2002).

10. *Id.* at 1326 ("My conclusion is that interdisciplinary legal scholarship is problematic unless subjected to the test of relevance, of practical impact. I hope I will not be accused of self-serving parochialism in suggesting that economic analysis of law passes this test; it has led to significant changes in legal doctrines and institutions, in the way law is practiced in certain fields, and in the

If this claim is true, it raises at least two questions. First, is there good work being done which shows the relevance of cognitivism to law? Second, and more fundamentally, is cognitivism a viable approach to the nature of mind such that we should welcome it into what Perry Dane calls "the legal conversation"?[11] This Essay offers an answer to both of these important questions.

II. Minding The Law—Categorization and Beyond

Minding the Law is the work of Anthony Amsterdam and Jerome Bruner. Bruner is an influential and well-respected psychologist, whose work has concentrated on curricular development at the primary school level, cultural psychology, and cognitive studies.[12] Bruner's co-author, Anthony Amsterdam, is a legal academic with a celebrated record of litigation successes in civil rights cases.[13]

---

teaching of those fields in law school. The same is increasingly true of cognitive psychology.") (footnote omitted).

11. *See* Perry Dane, *Spirited Debate: A Comment on Edward B. Foley's* Jurisprudence and Theology, 66 FORDHAM L. REV. 1213, 1221 (1998) ("[T]o whatever extent religion and religious (or anti-religious) views are inserted, explicitly or implicitly, into the legal conversation, the law will understand them, just as it understands Rawlsianism and Pareto economics and all the other ingredients of our larger normative field, through its own categories and practices.") (footnote omitted).

12. *See, e.g.*, JEROME BRUNER, ACTS OF MEANING (1990); JEROME BRUNER, ACTUAL MINDS, POSSIBLE WORLDS (1986); JEROME BRUNER, THE CULTURE OF EDUCATION (1996); JEROME BRUNER, MAKING STORIES: LAW, LITERATURE, LIFE (2002); JEROME S. BRUNER, ON KNOWING: ESSAYS FOR THE LEFT HAND (1979); JEROME S. BRUNER, TOWARD A THEORY OF INSTRUCTION (1966); JEROME S. BRUNER, THE PROCESS OF EDUCATION (1960); JEROME S. BRUNER ET AL., A STUDY OF THINKING (1956). Howard Gardner both summarizes Bruner's approach to mind and clearly distinguishes it from "scientific" cognitivists like Chomsky:

> I see Bruner today as deeply influenced by literary studies of narrative on the one hand and by anthropology on the other. Drawing on the work of such critics as Paul Ricoeur, Bruner proposes the existence of two primary modes of knowing: a logical or scientific mode, usually explored (and epitomized) by scientists; and a narrative mode, of interest not only to artists and writers but to all of us who try to make sense of our daily experiences. From anthropological writings, particularly those of Clifford Geertz, Bruner has been stimulated to investigate the particular cultural milieus in which people . . . have been formed, the conceptions they have of themselves, and the ways in which they think, imagine, and make decisions. Bruner's writings appeal to readers like me who have long despaired of psychology as a unitary pursuit and who view it instead as a computer-centered cognitive science at one extreme and as a study of different cultural idioms at the other. But it must be noted that Bruner's vision is as remote from Chomsky's syntactic structures as the study of the genetic code is from the taxonomy of animal species.

Howard Gardner, *Green Ideas Sleeping Furiously*, N.Y. REV. BOOKS, Mar. 23, 1995, at 32, 38 (reviewing STEVEN PINKER, THE LANGUAGE INSTINCT: HOW THE MIND CREATES LANGUAGE (1994); ANNETTE KARMILOFF-SMITH, BEYOND MODULARITY: A DEVELOPMENTAL PERSPECTIVE ON COGNITIVE SCIENCE (1995); JEROME BRUNER, ACTS OF MEANING (1992)).

13. *See* New York University School of Law Faculty Biography, *at* http://www.law.nyu.edu/faculty/profiles/bios/amsterdama_bio.html (last visited Jan. 6, 2003). Among the cases Amsterdam has argued before the United States Supreme Court are *Lockett v. Ohio*, 438 U.S. 586 (1978);

Of the three books under review, *Minding the Law*[14] is the most accessible to lawyers. This is, in part, because the argument will sound familiar chords with the legal reader. Amsterdam and Bruner write very much in the tradition of American Legal Realism. The gravamen of their position is that legal analysis and justification are the work of rationalization for decisions reached on other grounds. *Minding the Law* is a book-length effort to sustain this claim. For a variety of reasons, their argument fails. After explicating their point of view on cognitivism, I consider in detail the application of their arguments to a single Supreme Court case. Even on their own terms, they fail to make their case. The authors claim that their version of cognitivism provides insights into law that enable lawyers to see things they would otherwise miss. This claim, which is the central thesis of their book, is not sustained. Thus, even if everything they say about cognitivism is true, the authors fail to show how any of these insights matter at the level of lawyering, the very place they claim it makes all the difference.

A. Cognitive Lite

Amsterdam and Bruner pursue their goal of making "the already familiar strange again,"[15] with a distinctly "lite" form of cognitivism. Their stated aim "is to explore the ways in which human beings, including judges and lawyers, must inevitably rely upon culturally shaped processes of categorizing, storytelling, and persuasion in going about their business."[16]

Roberts v. Louisiana, 428 U.S. 325 (1976); *Lewis v. Martin*, 397 U.S. 552 (1970); and *Bachellar v. Maryland*, 397 U.S. 564 (1970).

14. *Minding the Law* is organized with chapters alternating between "theory" topics ("Categories," "Narrative," "Rhetorics," and "the Dialectic of Culture") and application of the theoretical material to legal issues, specifically Supreme Court decisions, largely ones devoted to matters of race. The first of the theory chapters—"On Categories"—is the most ambitious chapter in the book. In it, Amsterdam and Bruner lay out their perspective on mind and culture, preparing the way for later exploration of cases. AMSTERDAM & BRUNER pp. 19–53.

15. *Id.* at 1. In a lengthy review of *Minding the Law*, Professor Winter chides the authors for failing to transcend "garden variety legal realism." "At this stage of the game," Winter writes, "a book on cognitive theory and law should take up the big questions." Steven L. Winter, *Making the Familiar Conventional Again*, 99 MICH. L. REV. 1607, 1610 (2001) (reviewing ANTHONY G. AMSTERDAM & JEROME BRUNER, MINDING THE LAW (2000)).

16. AMSTERDAM & BRUNER p. 7. The law, they tell us, is about making choices. *Id.* at 247. There is a tension between two claims Amsterdam and Bruner consistently make. First, they claim that law is about "making choices." Second, many of these choices are made "unconsciously," as the work of judges reflects or embodies larger cultural narratives. *Id.* at 110–13. It is an open question whether the concept of "unconscious choice" makes any sense. An implication of a view like Amsterdam and Bruner's is that in writing opinions judges make no "choices" at all. They are merely conduits for larger cultural narratives and are, as Stanley Fish would say, "doing what comes naturally." *See* STANLEY FISH, DOING WHAT COMES NATURALLY: CHANGE, RHETORIC, AND THE PRACTICE OF THEORY IN LITERARY AND LEGAL STUDIES ix (1989) ("I intend it to refer to the unreflective actions that follow from being embedded in a context of practice. This kind of action—and in my argument there is no other—is anything but natural in the sense of proceeding independently of historical and social formations; but once those formations are in place (and they always are), what you think to do will not be calculated in relation to a higher law or an overarching

These categories, which are "*made in the mind*" and not found in the world,[17] are the mental element in their cognitivism. As we shall see, Amsterdam and Bruner locate the mental internally (i.e., in the mind). However, the "mental" is not a product of an internal code or physical process, as it is for many obviously "cognitive" theorists. Theirs is a softer, more culturally grounded form of "cognitivism."[18]

---

theory but will issue from you as naturally as breathing."). These choices are constantly being made by judges who use cognitive devices "to conceal their choices and avoid responsibility for their decisions . . . ." AMSTERDAM & BRUNER p. 247. It is in bringing these choices to light—and showing how choice is hidden—that Amsterdam and Bruner claim that cognitivism is important. *Id.*

17. AMSTERDAM & BRUNER p. 9. Amsterdam and Bruner elaborate:

> For the most part, our categories do not derive from the shape of the world but create it. We inherit an important few from our phylogenetic past: survival categories that predispose even newborn infants to divide up the world in characteristically human ways. (Thus, human infants sort out "faces" and differentiate them from all other shapes: they will smile at schematized circles containing two dark spots *as if* they were "faces.") But most of our category systems are inherited not from our genetic makeup but from our culture . . . .

Id. at 27 (citation omitted).

18. *Minding the Law* is a critique of legal argument from the perspective of cultural anthropology. Above all, the authors' interest lies in the relationship of mind to culture.

> As Clifford Geertz has made a point of reminding us through his long and distinguished career (with many other anthropologists assenting), there is no mind without culture. If culture is anything, it is a network of models of the world, of ways of getting on in it, of tools for thinking and imagining that range from systems of mathematics to genres of storytelling.

Id. at 39 (citing CLIFFORD GEERTZ, THE INTERPRETATION OF CULTURES (1973); BRADD SHORE, CULTURE IN MIND (1997)).

Geertz is legendary for bringing the hermeneutic perspective to anthropology. A basic tenet of hermeneutics is the idea that human understanding is the product of interpretation. Key texts are HANS-GEORG GADAMER, TRUTH AND METHOD (Joel Weinsheimer & Donald G. Marshall trans., 2d rev. ed. 1999) and MARTIN HEIDEGGER, BEING AND TIME (John Macquarrie & Edward Robinson trans., 1962). For an excellent discussion of hermeneutic theory and law, see GUYORA BINDER & ROBERT WEISBERG, LITERARY CRITICISMS OF LAW 112–200 (2000).

Geertz legitimated the non-empirical study of culture. Geertz did this by, among other things, highlighting the "thick" aspects of culture that are missed by the natural scientific approach to social science. Academic culture was ready for an argument like Geertz's. The work of Thomas Kuhn prepared the path. *See* THOMAS S. KUHN, THE STRUCTURE OF SCIENTIFIC REVOLUTIONS (2d ed. 1970). The following passage is representative:

> As in political revolutions, so in paradigm choice—there is no standard higher than the assent of the relevant community. To discover how scientific revolutions are effected, we shall therefore have to examine not only the impact of nature and of logic, but also the techniques of persuasive argumentation effective within the quite special groups that constitute the community of scientists.

Id. at 94.

Peter Novick expresses well both the reaction to Kuhn's argument and Kuhn's immediate reaction to its reception: "[T]o those for whom science was meaningful only insofar as it was teleological, approaching closer and closer to 'the objective truth,' Kuhn's picture was unacceptably 'relativist,' a characterization he neither accepted nor unequivocally repudiated." PETER NOVICK, THAT NOBLE DREAM: THE "OBJECTIVITY QUESTION" AND THE AMERICAN HISTORICAL PROFESSION 532 (1988).

They begin by distinguishing their view from what they describe as "an older, more rationalistic way of looking at categorization . . . ."[19] According to "the rationalist," categories and categorical systems were the result of "combinatorial mental operations"[20] of contrast and overlapping.[21] The problem with this approach, so the authors explain, is its failure to distinguish so-called "natural seeming" categories (e.g., "apple" and "bird") from artificial categories (e.g., "attractive nuisance" or "intellectual property").[22] Citing the work of Eleanor Rosch and George Lakoff,[23] Amsterdam and Bruner note that natural-seeming categories are best explained as originating from a "prototype experience."[24]

They believe this approach leaves unanswered certain key questions that are essential to our understanding of how legal categories are developed and employed. They want to know "*what kind of salience* makes something into a prototype."[25] This is important because it impacts the "*similarity question*": that is, "how similar to the prototype must a newly encountered event be to qualify for inclusion in a category?"[26] Rounding out their endorsement of the

---

Kuhn regularly returned to the topic of relativism. *See* Thomas S. Kuhn, *Postscript*, *in* THE STRUCTURE OF SCIENTIFIC REVOLUTIONS 174–210 (2d ed. 1970); Thomas S. Kuhn, *The Road Since Structure*, *reprinted in* THE ROAD SINCE STRUCTURE 90 (James Conant & John Haugeland eds., 2000). *The Road Since Structure* was Kuhn's Presidential Address to the biennial meetings of the Philosophy of Science Association in October 1990.

For an insightful and corrective assessment of Kuhn's work and the variety of misunderstandings that have attended it, see WES SHARROCK & RUPERT READ, KUHN (2002). For an informative short introduction to the role of Kuhn's thought in the cultural dispute over the meaning of "science," see ZIAUDDIN SARDAR, THOMAS KUHN AND THE SCIENCE WARS (2000). For a reading of Kuhn that sees him as the Chauncey Gardner of academia, see STEVE FULLER, THOMAS KUHN: A PHILOSOPHICAL HISTORY FOR OUR TIMES (2000).

Amsterdam and Bruner embrace the mildly anti-scientific and soft-relativist dimensions of Geertz's hermeneutic holism when they put mathematics and story-telling on the same level. They reinforce this soft relativism in their discussion of categorization. Their approach to categorization is, not surprisingly, the central theoretical aspect of *Minding the Law*. Categorization is central for Amsterdam and Bruner because it is through this process that we make meaning, organize experience, and classify persons. *See* AMSTERDAM & BRUNER pp. 28–29.

19. AMSTERDAM & BRUNER p. 40. The view described by Amsterdam and Bruner is discussed in detail in GEORGE LAKOFF, WOMEN, FIRE, AND DANGEROUS THINGS: WHAT CATEGORIES REVEAL ABOUT THE MIND (1987).

20. AMSTERDAM & BRUNER p. 40.

21. Amsterdam and Bruner give the following examples: "[C]ontrast (as with the category 'citizen' presuming the category 'non-citizens'), overlapping (as in Venn diagrams when two categories, say 'women' and 'U.S. Presidents,' are combined to yield 'female U.S. Presidents') and the like." *Id.*

22. *Id.* at 40–41.

23. *Id.* at 41, 315 n.50 (citing Eleanor Rosch, *Principles of Categorization*, *in* COGNITION AND CATEGORIZATION 27–48 (Eleanor Rosch and B.B. Lloyd eds., 1978); LAKOFF, *supra* note 19).

24. For example, "[a] sparrow . . . may be the prototype of the category of 'BIRD'; penguins are, as it were, outliers in this category. *The closer* something is to the prototype, the more confident we are that it is *in* the category." *Id.* at 41.

25. *Id.*

26. *Id.* at 42.

soft-relativist stance, Amsterdam and Bruner caution that "neither categories nor their prototypes are fixed and once-for-all. Categories form in response to what you are up to, talking about, thinking about."[27]

But how do we come to have the categories we do?[28] Under the "older, more rationalistic notion of category formation"[29] a strategy of necessary and sufficient conditions was employed. Such a model, they emphasize, does not describe every category, but it does work well in formal category systems.[30] But formal category systems have their limitations, the principal one being their artificiality. It is this aspect of formal category systems "that makes them serviceable sorting instruments.... They can hold our operating programs but not our dreams or values or anything we care enough about to contest."[31] As they see the matter, there is a normative hierarchy of different types or forms of concepts.[32] Clearly the ones we care about in the law are more important than formal concepts having necessary and sufficient conditions. What sorts of concepts are these and how do they function?

To answer this question, Amsterdam and Bruner introduce the concept of "implicit praxic knowledge."[33] Two key concepts lie at the heart of praxic understanding. These are scripts and narratives.[34] Scripts are learned responses to low-level recurrent situations that we assimilate from our surroundings.[35] A child, for example, describes a waiter as "somebody who waits on you in a restaurant."[36] The point of view for this description is not the waiter's but the customer's. This script, as with all others, "centers on what *we* expect from the activity related in the script."[37]

---

27. *Id.*

28. The topic of categorization is quite large, and there are any number of methodologies to employ in understanding them. One particularly fruitful approach is that of ethnomethodology. In the right hands the approach combines sociology, philosophy of language, and pragmatics. A stellar exemplar is LENA JAYYUSI, CATEGORIZATION AND THE MORAL ORDER (1984) (analyzing methods of membership categorization).

29. AMSTERDAM & BRUNER p. 43.

30. *Id.* Examples include passports, driver's licenses, and similar formal legal documents. *Id.*

31. AMSTERDAM & BRUNER p. 44.

32. *Id.*

33. *Id.* They characterize this form of understanding with the term "folk psychology" and describe this form of understanding as follows:

> This is the kind of understanding about how the world operates that typically takes the form, 'the right way to do that is so-and-so'—some prescriptive account of *what you do* to avoid snakes, to counteract spells of witchcraft, to show guests a good time, to survive New York City street life, to win lawsuits, or whatever. Virtually everything we do in daily life is kept on course by such praxic understandings; and if you ask people to explain why they are following a particular line of action, they will typically tell you what-you-are-supposed-to-do and then recite some beliefs about how the business at hand 'works.'

Id. at 44–45.

34. *Id.* at 45.

35. *Id.*

36. *Id.* at 46.

37. *Id.*

Narratives can incorporate scripts but they are much larger stories.[38] Like scripts, narratives have a foothold in everyday life but have a more universal quality; embedded in them are categories such as treachery, revenge, honor, reward, defeat, and overcoming.[39] It is through the use of these categories in narratives "that we come to see people as heroes, villains, tricksters, stooges (and so forth), and that we come to see situations as victories, humiliations, career opportunities, tests of character, menaces to dignity (and so forth)."[40]

Amsterdam and Bruner's thesis is that the practice of judicial decisionmaking is accomplished within and against the background of scripts and narratives. The task of lawyering, they maintain, is to present a legal narrative that employs cultural characterizations in a way that persuades the listener to adopt the lawyer's view of the world expressed through the rhetorical categories she chooses.[41] Lawyering is characterization and characterization is rhetoric. While there may be natural-kind categories for concepts like "dog," most of the concepts we find in law are not of this type. In addition, as Stanley Fish might argue,[42] our scripts and narratives are so deeply embedded we are hardly conscious of them.[43] Thus, the point of the argument, and the basic premise of Amsterdam and Bruner's book, is that we will come to understand law better when we bring to the surface the scripts and narratives of which we are only vaguely aware. Does cognitivism afford us such insights? Let us turn to a case that Amsterdam and Bruner believe does just this.

B. The Case Of Michael H.–Cognitive Myths

The fundamental premise of *Minding the Law* is that the law is all about categorization, and the central claim is that cognitive theory will do two things. First, it will "introduce us to the complex ways of categorization in the law."[44] Second, it will serve "to intensify awareness of the decisions and choices constantly being made by the people who make the law—and of the cognitive devices that those people are forever using to conceal their choices and avoid responsibility for their decisions."[45]

38. *Id.* Amsterdam and Bruner mention Northrop Frye's four subspecies of narratives: tragedy, comedy, romance, and irony. *See* NORTHROP FRYE, ANATOMY OF CRITICISM: FOUR ESSAYS 158–239 (1957) (discussing the four generic plots of literature).

39. AMSTERDAM & BRUNER p. 46.

40. *Id.*

41. *Id.* at 48.

42. *See* Stanley Fish, *Still Wrong After All These Years*, 6 L. & PHIL. 401, 403 (1987) ("A meaning that seems to leap off the page, propelled by its own self-sufficiency, is a meaning that flows from interpretive assumptions so deeply embedded that they have become invisible.").

43. AMSTERDAM & BRUNER p. 51.

44. *Id.* at 54.

45. *Id.* at 247.

Among the cases the authors use to illustrate their thesis is *Michael H.*[46] The biological father (Michael H.) of a child (Victoria D.) born to a woman (Carole D.) who was at the time of her daughter's birth married to another man (Gerald D.) challenged the constitutionality of a California statute that precluded him (and Victoria) from visitation.[47] The case presented the United States Supreme Court with a well-defined question: Did the California statute deprive Michael, Victoria, or both, of their due process rights under the Fourteenth Amendment to the United States Constitution?[48] Justice Scalia wrote the plurality opinion for the Court, finding no constitutional protection for the relationship between Michael and Victoria.[49] Amsterdam and Bruner focus on how Justice Scalia came to this conclusion, and the manner in which he articulated his reasons.

Justice Scalia begins his opinion with the observation that "the subject of this litigation is . . . more than a century old."[50] Then, in a sentence that Amsterdam and Bruner make much of,[51] Scalia observes that "California law, like nature itself, makes no provision for dual fatherhood."[52] Michael sought visitation rights with Victoria from the California courts. The problem he faced was that the only way he could get visitation was by establishing paternity of Victoria. As Justice Scalia observes: "All parental

46. Michael H. v. Gerald D., 491 U.S. 110 (1989).

47. In May 1981, Victoria D. was born to Carole D. who, at the time, was married to, and resided with, Gerald D. Victoria's birth certificate listed Gerald D. as her father, but blood tests demonstrated to a 98.07% probability that Michael H., with whom Carole had had an adulterous affair, was in fact Victoria's father. During the first year of Victoria's life, she and her mother lived alternately with Michael H. and Gerald D. In November 1982, Michael began a legal action in California's Superior Court to establish both his paternity and his right to visitation with Victoria. For her part, Victoria—through her court-appointed guardian ad litem—filed a cross-complaint seeking maintenance of filial relationships with both Michael and Gerald. The California Superior Court granted Gerald's motion for summary judgment under CAL. EVID. CODE § 621, which provides that where a child is born to a married woman who, at the time, is living with her husband, and the husband is neither impotent nor sterile, such child is presumed to be a child of the marriage. CAL. EVID. CODE § 621 (1965) (current version at CAL. FAM. CODE § 7540 (1995)). Further, this presumption may be rebutted only by the husband or wife and, in that instance, only in limited circumstances. CAL. EVID. CODE § 621 (1965) (current version at CAL. FAM. CODE § 7541 (1995)). In addition to granting Gerald's summary judgment motion, the court denied the motions of Michael and Victoria seeking visitation pending appeal under CAL. CIV. CODE § 4601 (current version at CAL. FAM. CODE § 3100 (1995)). On appeal, the California Court of Appeal affirmed the Superior Court rulings, rejecting Michael's procedural and substantive due process challenges to § 621, as well as Victoria's due process and equal protection claims. Finally, the California Court of Appeal rejected Victoria's claim to continued visitation with Michael under § 4601, holding that California law denies visitation against the wishes of the mother to a putative father who is precluded from establishing his paternity under § 621. *Id.* at 113–16.

48. That amendment forbids any state to "deprive any person of life, liberty, or property, without due process of law." U.S. CONST. amend. XIV, § 1.

49. *Michael H.*, 491 U.S. at 129–30.

50. *Id.* at 117.

51. AMSTERDAM & BRUNER pp. 81–82.

52. *Michael H.*, 491 U.S. at 118.

rights, including visitation, were automatically denied by denying Michael status as the father."[53]

Michael sought validation and protection of his liberty interest in his relationship to Victoria. Unfortunately for Michael, Justice Scalia prefers his liberty "negative." That is, while the meaning of the term "liberty" in the Due Process Clause goes beyond mere freedom from physical restraint, that "core textual meaning" limits the power of the court to expand the scope of constitutionally protected rights.[54] Further, an asserted liberty interest must "be rooted in history and tradition . . . ."[55] Justice Scalia cites *Pierce v. Society of Sisters*[56] and *Meyer v. University of Nebraska*[57] for the proposition that liberty extends beyond mere freedom from physical constraint to support his consideration of the "liberty interest . . . created by biological fatherhood plus an established parental relationship."[58] How do these principles and precedents come together for Justice Scalia?

Citing Blackstone, Kent, and other eminent authorities, Justice Scalia argues that protection of the family unit was the driving force behind the presumption of legitimacy at common law.[59] Neither the common law cases nor learned commentaries addressed "specifically the power of the natural father to assert the parental rights over a child born into a woman's existing marriage with another man."[60] Again, the presumption of legitimacy was for the protection of the child, and that presumption could only be rebutted by proof that a husband was incapable of procreation or was otherwise unavailable.[61]

---

53. *Id.* at 119. Justice Scalia remarks:

> While Cal. Civ. Code Ann. § 4601 places it within the discretionary power of a court to award visitation rights to a nonparent, the Superior Court here, affirmed by the Court of Appeal, held that California law denies visitation, against the wishes of the mother, to a putative father who has been prevented by § 621 from establishing his paternity.

Id.

54. Michael framed his constitutional challenge to the statute in terms of *procedural* due process. Justice Scalia characterized this approach as proceeding from "a fundamental misconception of the nature of the California statute," because, Scalia asserts, the claim is substantive and not procedural. *Id.*

55. *Id.* at 123.

56. 268 U.S. 510 (1925).

57. 262 U.S. 390 (1923).

58. Michael H. v. Gerald D., 491 U.S. 110, 123 (1989).

59. *Id.* at 125.

60. *Id.*

61. Justice Scalia asserts that this was the rule at common law, and he quotes Blackstone for authority: "'if the husband be out of the kingdom of England (or, as the law somewhat loosely phrases it, *extra quatuor maira* [beyond the four seas] for above nine months . . . .' 1 BLACKSTONE'S COMMENTARIES 456 (J. Chitty ed. 1826)." *Id.* at 124. Because Victoria was born to a mother who was, at the time of Victoria's birth, in a marriage, and who remained in that marriage, Justice Scalia is able to narrow the facts of the case and exclude Michael's claims. The following quote is representative: "What counts is whether the States in fact award substantive parental rights to the natural father of a child conceived within, and born into, an extant marital

But the details of Scalia's legal argument are not what interest Amsterdam and Bruner. According to them, Scalia's opinion is crafted around a core "construct," that of "adultery as combat myth."[62] In their view, clear evidence for this "construction" is Scalia's pronouncement that "'California law, like nature itself, makes no provision for dual fatherhood.'"[63] With the three words "like nature itself" deftly placed within three lines of the beginning of his legal analysis, "Justice Scalia has installed the conceptual and narrative engine that will power everything to come—the necessary and sufficient machinery to demolish all of Michael's and Victoria's constitutional claims."[64]

Let us turn to the authors' cognitive analysis of Scalia's opinion. First, dual fatherhood is a "natural" impossibility.[65] Second, the rule prohibiting dual fatherhood allows Scalia to set up Gerald and Michael as rivals fighting over Victoria.[66] Third, the rule against dual fatherhood subserves the need to protect "the unitary family."[67] To do otherwise is to countenance "*not* that Victoria should have two acknowledged fathers, but rather that Victoria's mother should have two acknowledged lovers. It is this licentious model which cannot be squared with Justice Scalia's cuckold-phobic vision of the 'unitary family.'" [68] There are strong reasons, it seems, for Justice Scalia to extol his vision of "the family" by keeping the concept narrowly defined. With this approach, Justice Scalia "perpetuates a basic symbol of established hegemonies—political and religious, as well as social and sexual—by consecrating a patriarchal notion of the family that simultaneously excludes outsiders and rank-orders insiders in proper-top-down fashion."[69]

In addition to the myths of Western culture, Amsterdam and Bruner see important narrative structures covertly expressed in Justice Scalia's opinion. As if his embrace of the combat myth were not damning enough, Justice Scalia's prose evinces the work of narrative structures "of the apocalyptic combat myth, on the one hand, and the villainous form of the adultery story,

---

union that wishes to embrace the child. We are not aware of a single case, old or new, that has done so. This is not the stuff of which fundamental rights qualifying as liberty interests are made." *Id.* at 127.

62. AMSTERDAM & BRUNER p. 81.

63. *Id.* (quoting *Michael H.*, 491 U.S. at 118).

64. *Id.* at 81. Of course, the "machinery" at work in Justice Scalia's opinion is that of the rationalistic "necessary and sufficient conditions" variety.

65. *Id.*

66. *Id.* at 82.

67. *Id.*

68. *Id.*

69. *Id.* at 82–83.

on the other."[70] It seems that from the Near East to the West one may find stories of battle between the "High Hero" and the "Abysmal Adversary."[71]

Amsterdam and Bruner are irked by what they perceive as Justice Scalia's rigidity. They argue that for him "no accommodation is possible between the combatants"[72] and that this struggle can only have one victor. The authors tell us that if they had written the opinion, it would have opened with the following paragraph:

> We take Michael's claims first. California law makes parental rights indivisible, requiring that either Michael get them all or Gerald get them all. Nature requires the same all-and-nothing [sic] distribution. Because of these requirements, we must deem Michael's claims to be that he is entitled to enjoy all parental rights with respect to Victoria and that Gerald is entitled to enjoy none. Michael's filiation action requested a declaration of paternity for (so far as we can tell) the purpose of obtaining visitation rights. But California law and nature deny him the option of making so modest a claim, and we are bound to treat him as seeking everything that California law and nature make inseparable from what he sued for.[73]

While they may concede an all-or-nothing quality to some aspects of nature, Amsterdam and Bruner reject it completely in the case of parental rights. They ask: "why is *Michael* to be treated as the maker and the seeker of the consequent all-or-nothing combat? He had no opportunity to limit the scope of conflict."[74] But Scalia, they allege, does not wish to take up this or any other question. In his narrative, there could only be one villain, and that is Michael.[75]

---

70. *Id.* at 84.

71. *Id.* The narrative structure proceeds, so Amsterdam and Bruner tell us, in twelve movements. These are: lack/villainy; hero emerges/prepares to act; donor/consultation; journey; battle; defeat; enemy ascendant; hero recovers/new hero; battle rejoined; victory; enemy punished; triumph. *Id.* at 85 (citing NEIL FORSYTH, THE OLD ENEMY: SATAN AND THE COMBAT MYTH 448–51 (1987)). Amsterdam and Bruner compare this sequence with Arthurian exemplars of cuckoldry "because of the central preoccupation of much Arthurian material with the problem of King Arthur and Queen Guinevere." *Id.* We are told—interestingly—that the Arthur and Guinevere stories were the outgrowth of a traditional Celtic abduction or elopement narrative. For those with a taste for detail, three Arthurian exemplars are charted over the course of six pages. *Id.* at 92–93. How does the narrative become law? Amsterdam and Bruner begin their answer by presenting a chart that sets out every active verb in Justice Scalia's opinion. *Id.* We are told that "Michael is portrayed as substantially more active than Gerald throughout the opinion" and that "not a single verb depicts Michael going about the ordinary, productive, work a day business of life: his entire activity consists of *distraining, disputing, and despoiling.*" *Id.* at 93. This is, of course, the familiar figure of the traditional Satan opposed by the "Adversary's Other," that is Gerald, "whose activities are *providing* and preserving—and whose preserve must *naturally* be protected against poaching." *Id.*

72. *Id.* at 95.

73. *Id.* at 96.

74. *Id.* at 97.

75. Justice Scalia, the authors inform us, "uses three well-known rhetorical techniques" to "preserve his orderly and hard-edged rules against the messy little facts that might disorder them." *Id.* at 105. First, he devalues the concrete: Justice Scalia uses classificatory labels instead of taking

Clearly, Amsterdam and Bruner disdain the categories Justice Scalia employs[76] to conclude that Michael has not been deprived of a constitutionally protected liberty interest.[77] However, agreement or disagreement with Justice Scalia's conclusion is not our concern. We want to know whether any of this is useful to lawyers. Not surprisingly, Amsterdam and Bruner believe it is, stating that "[i]n unpacking opinions like *Michael H.*, the perspectives and techniques of literary and linguistic study and rhetorical criticism can therefore be useful *supplements* to more traditional modes of legal analysis."[78] Does cognitive theory, as articulated by Amsterdam and Bruner, bring to the surface hidden dimensions of Justice Scalia's thought processes which, without the benefit of cognitive theory, we might fail to notice?

Before we evaluate the author's claim that their cognitive techniques provide insights otherwise unavailable, we should examine the case in terms of an alternative approach to the legal issues involved. For this, we may consider the dispute between Scalia and Brennan, author of the dissenting opinion. Contrary to his typical affinity for textual and historical argument,[79]

---

the time to describe the facts with some particularity. *Id.* at 105–06. Second, he devalues the individual: throughout the opinion, we are told that "quantitative values trump qualitative values: the general is privileged over the unique." *Id.* at 106–07. Third, he devalues the uncertain: for Justice Scalia, "nothing is important that cannot be known with certainty." Anything that Justice Scalia disagrees with is simply rejected as "unintelligible." *Id.* at 106–09.

76. Amsterdam and Bruner tell us that categories and their use are an essential aspect of daily life. While we take categories for granted, their chosen subheadings remind us that: "Categories Are Made, Not Found," *id.* at 27; "Categorizing Is an Act of Meaning Making," *id.* at 28; "Categories Imply a World That Contains Them," *id.* at 29; "Categories Serve Particular Functions," *id.* at 32; "Categories Become Entrenched in Practice," *id.* at 36; "Categories Are Never Final," *id.* at 37.

77. As mentioned earlier, one of the problems with categories is that they can sometimes appear "natural" when they are not. Justice Scalia, it seems, is a master of this sleight of hand. He makes value choices look like natural events and he does it with alarming ease. Amsterdam and Bruner concede that the very act of categorization "involves matching *some awareness of the situation one is in* with *some standard for what a situation of this sort should be like.*" *Id.* at 109. Judges who deny this are simply engaged in self-deception, merely giving voice to "their predilections when they pretend to themselves or others that their job involves no interpretative work but consists simply of sorting the *objective* facts of cases into the *objective* categories of *objective* rules." *Id.* at 108.

78. *Id.* at 108 (emphasis added). The phrase "useful supplements" puts Amsterdam and Bruner at odds with their claim (discussed earlier) that cognitivism reveals how judges make choices and then hide those choices behind a veil of legal justification. *See supra* note 16. The authors repeatedly make a stronger causal claim, *viz.*, that the real causes of judicial decisions are unconscious choices that are "masked" by the language of legal justification. In other words, legal argument is just a façade. Unfortunately, no proof in support of this strong claim is offered. For discussion of a similar claim, see RICHARD A. POSNER, THE PROBLEMATICS OF MORAL AND LEGAL THEORY 266–70 (1999) (discussing Duncan Kennedy's claim that reasoning from authoritative legal materials never constrains judges).

79. *See* Roger Colinvaux, *What is Law? A Search for Legal Meaning and Good Judging Under a Textualist Lens*, 72 IND. L.J. 1133, 1134 (1997) (labeling Scalia a textualist); Benjamin C. Zipursky, *The Pedigrees of Rights and Powers in Scalia's Cruzan Concurrence*, 56 U. PITT. L. REV. 283, 287 (1994) (noting criticism of Scalia's historical approach to rights analysis); David M.

Justice Scalia makes a relatively straightforward doctrinal argument in *Michael H.* His task is to develop a principled account of the concept of "liberty," one derived from prior decisions of the Court. Justice Scalia approaches precedent from a certain perspective of tradition, one which both his dissenting colleagues and Amsterdam and Bruner reject.

Justice Scalia states the doctrinal question this way: "What counts is whether the States in fact award substantive parental rights to the natural father of a child conceived within, and born into, an extant marital union that wishes to embrace the child. We are not aware of a single case, old or new, that has done so."[80] Justice Brennan, in turn, cites four cases in which the Supreme Court considered the question whether an unwed father has a constitutionally protected interest in his relationship with his child.[81] He argues that while a biological link alone is not sufficient to guarantee a constitutionally protected status in the natural father's relationship with the child, "such a link combined with a substantial parent-child relationship will do so."[82]

Justice Scalia identifies the most important relationship as that of the family. Justice Brennan points out that the plurality identify "family" with "marriage." But—and this is the point of the argument—Supreme Court precedents demonstrate that "marriage is not decisive in answering the question whether the Constitution protects the parental relationship under consideration. [The decided cases] are, after all, important precisely because they involve the rights of *unwed* fathers."[83] In drawing attention to this aspect of previously decided cases, Justice Brennan identifies the precise point of disagreement. In short, Scalia and Brennan are not disputing different things; they are disputing the same thing: Supreme Court precedents. What they dispute is which aspect of precedent is more important.

What is Amsterdam and Bruner's lesson for Justice Brennan? Might they claim the battle over precedent is all smoke and mirrors? "Why not," they might urge, "simply come out and criticize Scalia on the merits for giving voice to the combat myth through the guise of parsing cases?" Is this not their point: that it is simply evading the "real issues" to argue these matters in the language of law and that by engaging Scalia in doctrinal argument, Brennan not only fails to undermine Scalia's efforts, he actually underwrites future exercises in obfuscation?

Zlotnick, *Justice Scalia and his Critics: An Exploration of Scalia's Fidelity to his Constitutional Methodology*, 48 EMORY L.J. 1377, 1382 (1999) (explaining Scalia's methodology as a text-based inquiry).

80. Michael H. v. Gerald D., 491 U.S. 110, 127 (1989).

81. *Id.* at 142 (Brennan, J., dissenting). Those four cases are *Stanley v. Illinois*, 405 U.S. 645 (1972); *Quilloin v. Walcott*, 434 U.S. 246 (1978); *Caban v. Mohammed*, 441 U.S. 380 (1979); *Lehr v. Robertson*, 436 U.S. 248 (1983).

82. *Michael H.*, 491 U.S. at 142–43 (Brennan, J., dissenting).

83. *Id.* at 144 (Brennan, J., dissenting).

But is their claim this strong? Are they actually contending that no substance lies beneath the rhetoric of the combat myth? If so, what are we to make of Amsterdam and Bruner's own argument? Are they themselves not telling a mythic combat story, where Scalia is the villain and they are the heroes? Despite their rhetorical gloss, they expect us to take their account as accurate, or true. But they have already told us that there are only "choices." If there are no standards for choice (just rationalizations), then how can a choice ever be criticized?[84]

Clearly, two very different models of legal analysis are at work. In the first model (the "cognitive" model), Amsterdam and Bruner use their cognitive techniques to explicate judicial reasoning in terms of myths and covert cultural beliefs. The second model (conventional legal analysis) uses basic legal categories to analyze and differentiate the majority and minority judicial reasoning. Both discussions explicate legal choices made, but differ radically in their account of how those choices are made.

There are two objections to their cognitivist model of analysis. The first takes exception to the claim that the "normative" content expressed in the judicial opinion can be characterized as essentially a cultural "construction"—one that mimics those widely disseminated in narrative forms. If the "normative" content of law reduces to "cultural constructs," then there is little defense to subjectivism. (Admittedly, cognitive theorists do not have an interest in defending against subjectivism.) More importantly, reduction of normative content to cultural "constructs" leaves us with no way to account for legal authority.

The second objection involves the weaker claim that the model of cognitive analysis merely "supplements" more traditional legal analysis, and in no way eliminates or displaces it. The problem here, of course, is that the notion of "supplementation" requires us to find some connection between the two models, whereas, in fact, there is an obvious disconnect between the two frameworks. Explicating the Scalia opinion as a "construction" of "adultery as combat myth" has little chance in "supplementing" conventional legal analysis. As a technique, cognitive analysis superimposes narrative structure onto the legal discourse of judicial opinion. While it is novel to transform the legal case into a literary narrative with mythic proportions, it fails the test of joining the "legal conversation."[85]

One last claim of *Minding the Law* deserves attention. Throughout their intricate description of categories and their function in social life, Amsterdam and Bruner repeatedly claim that their observations matter at the level of legal practice.[86] In other words, they contend that their insights into the

84. My thanks to Kim Ferzan for this point.

85. *See supra* note 11 and accompanying text.

86. Here is how Amsterdam and Bruner describe lawyering from their point of view:

cognitive dimensions of law pay dividends for lawyers. One obvious benefit for those studied in the ways of cognitivism would be improvement of their rhetorical skills as advocates. Sadly, as Amsterdam and Bruner's discussion of Justice Scalia's opinion in *Michael H.* demonstrates, the authors do not attempt to assist an advocate in countering the force of the cultural mythology that seemingly pervades Justice Scalia's opinion. Yes, Amsterdam and Bruner tell us what Justice Scalia might have written.[87] But if one's concern is really with making lawyers more effective, some attention has to be given to a rhetorical counter to Justice Scalia's approach to the issues. Amsterdam and Bruner offer nothing other than their own account of what they would have written had they been in Justice Scalia's position.[88] None of the insights to be gained through retroactive analysis of the opinion is of much value unless it has demonstrable, forward-looking rhetorical countereffect.

Amsterdam and Bruner conclude their analysis of Justice Scalia's opinion with this comment: "His entire opinion is a demonstration of the limitless license that judges acquire to reify or deify their predilections when they pretend to themselves or others that their job involves no interpretive work but consists simply of sorting the *objective* facts of cases into the *objective* categories of *objective* rules."[89] This characterization borders on hyperbole. If Justice Scalia's opinion was so obviously radical, what explains the fact that three other justices (including the less than "right wing" Justices O'Connor and Kennedy) joined his opinion in large part, and Justice Stevens concurred in the judgment? Ultimately, Amsterdam and Bruner's greatest objection to Justice Scalia's opinion is to the result in the case: they would have decided the case differently. One does not need cognitivism to reach this conclusion.

> So, what does our lawyer do? In effect, the lawyer designs a *rhetorical strategy*. To be sure, the lawyer's (and the client's) categorization problem will eventually require a decision, but it will not be solely the lawyer's decision. It will involve an arbiter (real or imagined) who must decide which of two (or more) *contending categorizations* is the fitter one. The lawyer is called upon to present (or imagine) the best possible case for the contract being either valid or invalid, and must do so in full knowledge that a lawyer for the other party may, presumably with equal assiduity, present a contrary brief. Immediately or potentially, categorizing under law is an adversary process (though, to be sure, much of legal practice consists of advising clients how to avoid entanglement in formal adversarial procedures). In the end it is guilty as charged or not, liable or not, contract performed or not.

AMSTERDAM & BRUNER p. 48.

87. *See supra* text accompanying note 73.

88. Of course, one must question what categories Amsterdam and Bruner will themselves employ—for, as they make perfectly clear, we are all the product of our own personal narratives and frames.

89. AMSTERDAM & BRUNER p. 108. This remark sounds like classic Legal Realism. There is nothing here that can be identified or characterized as "cognitive."

Even if one finds merit in the analysis of mind and law Amsterdam and Bruner present, the important test of their analysis is whether it enables us to engage frameworks other than our own, thereby improving lawyering skills. Some Supreme Court advocates are consistently successful over time.[90] Obviously, their "frames of mind" are different from the Justices' and, more importantly, the Justices are each themselves different from one another. What is it that successful advocates are doing that unsuccessful ones are not? If Amsterdam and Bruner's cognitivism illuminated this aspect of law, they would have made an interesting contribution to our knowledge of the legal process. They have not done so.

III. A Clearing in the Forest: Cognitivism and Jurisprudence

Professor Steven Winter's book "pulls together . . . ideas worked out in a series of articles written over the ten-year period beginning in 1986."[91] In the first five of his twelve chapters, he articulates an elaborate cognitive perspective,[92] which is directed at a variety of legal and theoretical issues in

---

90. Solicitor General Theodore Olson and Professor Laurence Tribe come to mind as examples. *See* Tony Mauro, *Supreme Advocates: Four Top Litigators*, LEGAL TIMES, Oct. 30, 2000, at 18 (listing Olson's lifetime Supreme Court record as of 2000 as 8-4 and Tribe's as 19-9-1).

91. WINTER p. xix.

92. Winter concentrates on the work of George Lakoff, Mark Johnson, and to a lesser extent, Gerald Edelman. Works by Lakoff and Johnson include: GEORGE LAKOFF & MARK JOHNSON, METAPHORS WE LIVE BY (1980); GEORGE LAKOFF & MARK JOHNSON, PHILOSOPHY IN THE FLESH: THE EMBODIED MIND AND ITS CHALLENGE TO WESTERN THOUGHT (1999); GEORGE LAKOFF & RAFAEL F. NÚÑEZ, WHERE MATHEMATICS COMES FROM: HOW THE EMBODIED MIND BRINGS MATHEMATICS INTO BEING (2000); LAKOFF, *supra* note 19; MARK JOHNSON, THE BODY IN THE MIND: THE BODILY BASIS OF MEANING, IMAGINATION, AND REASON (1987). Edelman's books include: GERALD M. EDELMAN & GIULIO TONONI, A UNIVERSE OF CONSCIOUSNESS: HOW MATTER BECOMES IMAGINATION (2000); GERALD M. EDELMAN, BRIGHT AIR, BRILLIANT FIRE: ON THE MATTER OF MIND (1992); GERALD M. EDELMAN, NEURAL DARWINISM: THE THEORY OF NEURONAL GROUP SELECTION (1988); GERALD M. EDELMAN, THE REMEMBERED PRESENT: A BIOLOGICAL THEORY OF CONSCIOUSNESS (1989).

Winter identifies three themes central to his perspective:

> *Human thought is irreducibly imaginative* . . . . A growing body of empirical and theoretical work demonstrates that human brain processes are *imagistic* and *cross-modal*. They are imagistic in that they involve highly schematic images that are not dependent on any particular sensory modalities such as the visual, the kinesthetic, or the spatiotemporal[;]
>
> *Imagination is embodied, interactive, and grounded.* Imagination is embodied in the sense that it emerges from the neural structure of the brain . . . . There is nothing magical or mysterious about this; it is, rather, a consequence of the cross-modal character of neural processes. Imagination, therefore, is dependent on the kinds of bodies that we have and on the ways in which those bodies interact with our environment. It is grounded in the sense that it is contingent on these experiences[; and]
>
> *Imagination operates in a regular, orderly, and systematic fashion.* Indeed, it is now possible to describe the structures of imagination. These mechanisms . . . include mental operations such as basic-level categorization, conceptual metaphor, metonymy, image-schemas, idealized cognitive models, and radial categories.

WINTER pp. 5–6.

subsequent chapters. While Winter does discuss the application of his cognitivist viewpoint to matters of legal doctrine, the bulk of his effort is directed toward demonstrating the superiority of cognitivism in addressing problems in legal theory.[93] It is to these jurisprudential dimensions of Winter's position that I will devote considerable focus.[94]

I evaluate Winter's claim for the jurisprudential superiority of cognitivism through consideration of his treatment of one of the fundamental debates in contemporary legal theory, that between Ronald Dworkin and legal positivism. As I will show, not only does Winter fail to illuminate this debate, he fundamentally misunderstands the nature of the debate itself. Before considering the particulars of Winter's comments on the Hart/Dworkin debate, I explain what the debate is about and what is at stake in the debate. I then turn to the internal coherence of Winter's arguments in favor of cognitivism, and find them wanting. At the heart of Winter's account of cognitivism is a contradiction, one that law makes all too clear. If persons are endowed with the same cognitive mappings, how does cognitivism account for and explain the fact of disagreement? Either persons have different cognitive mappings or some other factor is at work. Winter seems to be of two minds on this question; it is not clear that the contradiction is, or can be, eliminated.

A. The Embodied Mind

Winter asserts the implications of cognitive theory for law are "momentous."[95] We simply cannot comprehend "meaning, rationality, intellectual change, law, or any other human phenomenon without an understanding of imagination and its central, constitutive role in the interaction between the human organism and the environment. Quite simply, no field remains untouched by what we are finding out about the mind."[96]

Winter believes that a better understanding of mind will lead to a better understanding of law, for law is a product of mind.[97] Meaning, it seems, is "an embodied process,"[98] one that arises from imaginative interactions between mind and world. Philosophers—especially contemporary ones like Richard Rorty and Hilary Putnam—have it all wrong when they maintain that an understanding of "how our cognitive processes work cannot be useful

93. At least one commentator thinks he succeeds in doing so. *See* Jeremy Paul, *Changing the Subject: Cognitive Theory and the Teaching of Law*, 67 BROOK. L. REV. 987, 987 (2002) (asserting that *A Clearing in the Forest*, "offers a path . . . out of our oldest and least fruitful debates.").

94. In subpart IV(B), I discuss the implausibility of several central cognitivist theses, using Professor Winter's account of cognitivism as a representative example.

95. WINTER p. xi.

96. *Id.* at 6.

97. *Id.* at xi–xii.

98. *Id.* at xii.

in criticizing and reconstructing what we think we 'know.'"[99] But philosophers of language are not alone in their naïveté, for all manner of legal theorists, from positivists like H.L.A. Hart to Ronald Dworkin to Critical Legal Studies folks like Duncan Kennedy, all fail to appreciate how cognitive theory "radically transforms . . . many . . . traditional jurisprudence debates."[100]

Let us start with a fundamental topic, that of legal reasoning. On what Winter characterizes as "the standard view,"[101] legal reasoning "consists in abstracting from a judicial opinion or other authoritative legal text the principles that express the necessary and sufficient conditions, properties, or criteria that characterize it."[102] Once those essentials have been extracted, "one decides the next case by determining whether it corresponds with this abstracted form of which the original is only a manifestation (as in a judicial decision) or expression (as in a rule)."[103] Without satisfaction of these two criteria, so the conventional view holds, "objectivity is impossible."[104]

The perspectivalist counters by rejecting the conventionalist assumption that "there is a single, privileged view of reality."[105] Perspectivalism then leads to relativism and the indeterminacy critique,[106] the claim that "reasoning and characterization are not natural or given but are relative to particular languages, cultures, histories, or conceptual schemes."[107] Thus, legal decisions may appear objective, but that "objectivity" masks the unbridled power of the judge, in whose hands "legal doctrines are often masks for power because they purport to derive from the neutral application of objective reason by a disinterested judiciary when, all the while, they are merely expressions of the needs or values of the culture's elites."[108]

Winter argues that the very terms of the conventional debate are false, for both sides "assume the same ideal of reason as top-down, linear, definitional, and characterized by closure (as in the law of the excluded middle)."[109] Reason, he argues, is not propositional, analytic, and reductive. Reason is imaginative. We must eschew "meta" debates and look to "cognitive and cultural *infra*structures, if we are going to make any sense of

99. *Id.*

100. *Id.* at 4.

101. *Id.* at 7. This is the view discussed *supra* text accompanying notes 28–32.

102. *Id.* at 7–8.

103. *Id.* at 8.

104. *Id.*

105. *Id.*

106. *See* Joseph William Singer, *The Player and the Cards*, 94 YALE L.J. 1, 11 (1984) (defining the indeterminacy critique as the claim that legal doctrine allows choice rather than constraining or compelling it).

107. WINTER p. 8.

108. *Id.*

109. *Id.*

the phenomenon of law."[110] We should resort to the tools of cognitive theory to "make much of this tacit knowledge explicit."[111] The key to the enterprise is metaphor. Thus, we move from legal reasoning to the embodied mind.

According to cognitive theory, metaphor is a "matter of thought and not mere language."[112] A metaphor is a "set of conceptual mappings."[113] But a metaphor is not to be confused with "metaphorical expressions that are its linguistic manifestations."[114] Comprehension and reasoning are accomplished by means of conceptual mappings and not, as philosophers such as Donald Davidson suppose, "by means of language and propositions."[115]

Our metaphorical understanding of the world is embodied because, as humans, we possess a body. "[W]e achieve upright posture and balance in the world."[116] Each of our basic interactions with the world is generalizable—that is, it can be "generalized across a series of other domains."[117] This occurs by way of a "'recurring structure' or 'repeatable pattern' by which we are able to understand the world as a 'unified place that we can make sense of.'"[118]

Brain, body, and the extension of the two are structural features of Winter's cognitivism. The body-brain interactions of early life engender basic level characterizations. Thought is not propositional, as philosophers of language maintain. There is "thought without language," for thought "originates in our sense of spatial and kinesthetic origination in the world. In

110. *Id.* at 11.

111. *Id.* at 12.

112. *Id.* at 13. Metaphor is a broad and philosophically rich topic. Works of interest include the following: MAX BLACK, MODELS AND METAPHORS: STUDIES IN LANGUAGE AND PHILOSOPHY (1962); DAVID E. COOPER, METAPHOR (1986); EVA FEDER KITTAY, METAPHOR: ITS COGNITIVE FORCE AND LINGUISTIC STRUCTURE (1987); EARL R. MACCORMACK, A COGNITIVE THEORY OF METAPHOR (1985); Donald Davidson, *What Metaphors Mean*, 5 CRITICAL INQUIRY 31 (1978).

113. WINTER p. 13.

114. *Id.*

115. *Id.* Metaphorical mappings define semantic content. It is important to bear in mind that seemingly related metaphorical mappings may in fact be premised on "different metaphorical mappings." Here is an example: "The 'breaking' in the phrase 'to break the law' is not the destruction or elimination of the law, but a breach or transgression (from the Latin *trans gredi*, 'to step across' or 'to step beyond') of its limits." *Id.* at 14.

116. *Id.* at 15.

117. *Id.* Lest we underestimate the importance of the body, we need only consider the important connection between body and brain:

> The very capacity of the brain to recognize patterns and form concepts depends on the structures of bodily experience. These basic structures or *image-schemas*—such as BALANCE, PART-WHOLE, OBJECT, SOURCE-PATH-GOAL, FORCE-BARRIER, and CONTAINER—provide structure to human thought and a measure of apparent unity and determinacy in our interaction with the world. Image-schemas are neither representations nor literal "pictures" but . . . schematics that emerge from cross-modal linkages in neural processes that transcend any specific sensory modality.

Id.

118. *Id.*

both these ways—and many others—human cognition is a fundamentally *embodied* activity."[119]

We learn basic level characterizations best because we learn these categories first and because the names of these categories are short and readily identified.[120] What determines basic level categories is, in the opinion of George Lakoff, "a matter of correlations."[121] The basic level is "the point at which gestalt perception, motor interaction, mental image formation, and general knowledge correlate."[122]

Brains, neurons, and mappings are the next level of development in the picture of the "embodied mind." Information is "in the brain"[123] but it is not stored in discrete locations as one might expect of a computer chip. Neurons—organized into networks or "neural nets"[124]—are the basis for memory and, ultimately, our experience of the world.[125] Metaphor extends neural mappings by taking topographic mappings in the source domain and moving them to a target domain. Throughout, "the structure of the source domain is preserved in the target domain because the neurons of the former map to (i.e., stimulate) the latter through reentrant signaling (or its

---

119. *Id.* at 23.

120. *Id.* at 25. So "chair" is a basic level category but "furniture" is a superordinate category. Basic level categories are the most useful for satisfaction of practical purposes. When one wants to sit in Professor Winter's classroom, for example, one asks not whether there is "furniture in the room" because all he might encounter is tables and desks. Similarly, "the person who delivers our mail will be more interested in knowing that we do not have a dog than in finding out either that we have an animal (a gerbil) or that we do not have a cocker spaniel." *Id.*

121. *Id.* at 26 (citing LAKOFF, *supra* note 19, at 50).

122. *Id.* at 26.

123. *Id.* at 28.

> "Information" in the brain is not stored in discrete locations like pigeonholes nor coded on individual brain cells as on the chips of a computer. To the extent there is anything like a "record" of a memory or event it lies in the multitudinous connections or synapses between very large numbers of neurons. Each neuron has an axon that makes contact across a synapse with the body (soma) or dendrite of another. Electrical activity down the axon causes the release of a chemical neurotransmitter that in turn induces or inhibits the electrical activity of the next neuron. Each time the firing one neuron stimulates (or inhibits) the firing of the next, the chemical connections between those neurons (that is, the ability to reproduce the same chemical activity) is strengthened.

Id. (citing Roger A. Nicoll & Robert C. Malenka, *Contrasting Properties of Two Forms of Long-term Potentiation in the Hippocampus*, 377 NATURE 115, 115–18 (1995)).

124. *Id.* at 28. Neural processes are organized through a process Gerald Edelman terms "reentrant cortical integration (RCI)." *Id.* at 29. In this process, neuronal groups organized into "mappings" coordinate with each other through "reentrant" and "topographic" connections. *Id.* at 29–30. These mappings produce images "that we experience in consciousness." *Id.* at 31.

125. Winter uses the example of a person drinking coffee: "Her visual cortices will respond to the colors of the cup and of its contents as well as to its shape and position. The somatosensory cortices will register the shape the hand assumes as it holds the cup, the movement of the hand and the arm as they bring the cup to the lips, the warmth of the coffee, and the body change some people call pleasure when they drink the stuff." *Id.* at 28 (quoting Antonio R. Damasio & Hanna Damasio, *Brain and Language*, SCI. AM., Sept. 1992, at 89, 91).

equivalent)."[126] How are such connections forged?[127] Consider the pervasive yet simple example MORE IS UP.[128] There is an abstract domain—quantity or value—that correlates "with relative changes along the vertical axis in the spatial domain."[129] How do these correlations occur? Each of these domains is characterized by a neural network which is "co-activated in everyday experience as when we pile more books on [a] desk and their height goes up or add water to a container."[130]

From this discussion of the neural basis for cognition, Winter draws the following three conclusions:

1. Cognition is experientially grounded. Cognition is a function of our embodied interactions with the world.[131]
2. The brain is "a self-organizing system."[132] True, the brain is to some degree "hard wired."[133] But it is clear that "some post-genetic organization is taking place."[134]
3. Brain processes, "by their very nature, are synthetic and constitutive rather than propositional and analytic."[135]

When it comes to the connection between mind and world, Winter concludes "the brain *constructs* rather than *mirrors* the reality with which it interacts."[136] It is through this process of construction that "we *have* a world."[137]

For cognitive science, "[e]xperience, categorization, meaning . . . are among the central issues."[138] According to Winter, we will achieve a better understanding of these issues only when we eschew the agenda of philosophy of language (specifically the claim that thought occurs in language) and

---

126. *Id.* at 31.

127. *Id.*

128. *Id.*

129. The following expressions are representative:

- my stocks *plummeted*
- her fame *skyrocketed*
- nationwide, crime is *down*
- productivity is way *up*

Id. at 31. Because all of these activities are unconscious, one wonders how the brain "knows" that any of these activities has been done correctly. This issue was raised earlier in the discussion of the Amsterdam and Bruner book. *See supra* notes 1–4 and accompanying text. The issue will also reappear in the final part of this Essay. *See infra* notes 270–79, 282–89 and accompanying text.

130. *Id.* at 31 (quoting LAKOFF & JOHNSON, PHILOSOPHY IN THE FLESH, *supra* note 92, at 54–58).

131. *Id.* at 32.

132. *Id.*

133. *Id.*

134. *Id.* at 32–33.

135. *Id.* at 33.

136. *Id.*

137. *Id.*

138. *Id.* at 42.

embrace the cognitivist agenda. Wittgenstein was wrong when he wrote "[*t*]*he limits of my language* mean the limits of my world,"[139] for Wittgenstein did not have the benefit of the empirical research that is so important to Winter.[140] Thought is "imagistic" and metaphorical. These research results, he argues, "show conclusively that the capacity both to individuate objects and reason about them is prior to and independent of language."[141]

---

139. LUDWIG WITTGENSTEIN, TRACTATUS LOGICO-PHILOSOPHICUS 5.6, at 115 (David F. Pears & Brian F. McGuinness trans., 2d ed. 1971).

140. For example, Winter writes:

> I will be drawing (both directly and indirectly) on extensive empirical work in psychology, anthropology, neuroscience, and linguistics that has taken place over the last thirty years .... [L]anguage is an empirical phenomenon no less than any other form of human behavior. Economists study market transactions (and all sorts of other conduct); sociologists study social behavior; and linguists study language—all in an effort to discern regularities and induce rules. Philosophers of language—and here we may include literary theorists—take language as an a priori capable of being theorized without regard to the actual patterns of current (synchronic) usage or historical (diachronic) development. But the evidence, as we shall see, is remarkably inconsistent with their theories. Indeed, as I hope to persuade you, the data support a radically new and different view.

WINTER pp. xv–xvi.

Ironically, one of Winter's own empirical assertions has been proven false. *See* SAM GLUCKSBERG, UNDERSTANDING FIGURATIVE LANGUAGE 96–97 (2001):

> Winter claims that the meaning of "under color of law" is motivated by two conventional conceptual metaphors. The first is HAVING CONTROL IS UP, with its corollary BEING SUBJECT TO CONTROL IS DOWN. The second is UNDERSTANDING IS SEEING. The "under" rests on the first metaphor, the "color" on the second. Armed with this analysis, Winter concludes that "the phrase *under color of law* is an unlikely, even counterintuitive way in which to express the position advocated by Frankfurter. Rather a cognitive analysis of the metaphor demonstrates that it connotes something like 'under a deceptive appearance of authority' and that this meaning is *overdetermined*."
>
> We tested this hypothesis by asking twelve people to interpret the assertion "The property was foreclosed under color of law." If the "appearance of law" meaning is indeed overdetermined by the two conceptual metaphors cited by Winter, then at least a majority of our informants should have given that interpretation. We found just the opposite. Eleven people said that it meant under the authority of the law; one person also said that it meant under the authority of law but added that it involved taking advantage of a loophole in the law. And, of course, none of our respondents recalled having encountered the color-of-law phrase before. Clearly, the meaning of "under the color of law" is not overdetermined in the direction claimed and justified by Winter. The post hoc rationalization in terms of conceptual metaphors is just that: a rationalization and not a viable linguistic or cognitive analysis.

Id. (citation omitted). Chapter 7 of *A Clearing in the Forest*, entitled "What Is the 'Color of Law'?," contains Winter's argument.

141. WINTER p. 40. Not only is metaphorical thinking brain-based and imagistic, it is *unconscious*. The synaptic process of metaphor is the best explanation of the fact that

> a fully acculturated person can go straight to the conventional meaning—*i.e.*, automatically, without the need consciously to retrace the inferential steps—does not indicate that a metaphor is 'dead,' only that it need not be conscious. These processes of metaphorical inference are performed unconsciously all the time; indeed, they are indispensable to meaning.

We come, then, to the final element in Winter's cognitivism, that of categorization. As we saw in the earlier discussion of Amsterdam and Bruner, categorization is a broad and complicated topic.[142] With his cognitivism, Winter promises to "transform our notion of categorization almost beyond recognition and, with it, everything that depends on categories."[143]

Philosophical approaches to categorization are variations on two major themes. First is the essentialist approach. Essentialism posits that every instance of a general category shares one or more essential traits that make the thing in question what it is. This approach works well with natural kind terms like "mammal" or "gold" but is less successful when it comes to artificial concepts like "games." Wittgenstein introduced the term "family resemblance"[144] to describe concepts like "game." These things, Wittgenstein maintained, did not share essential traits. Rather, family resemblance concepts exhibit a crisscross of similarities. It was through this network of similarities that we bring together otherwise dissimilar things under the same rubric.

George Lakoff extends Wittgenstein's family resemblance metaphor with the concept of "radial category."[145] Despite Lakoff's extension of Wittgenstein with the concept of radial category, Winter believes Wittgenstein's family resemblance approach "makes categorization seem as

---

Id. at 50–51.

142. *See* discussion *supra* Part II.

143. *Id.* at 69.

144. *See* LUDWIG WITTGENSTEIN, PHILOSOPHICAL INVESTIGATIONS § 67 (G.E.M. Anscombe trans., 3d ed. 1972):

> I can think of no better expression to characterize these similarities than "family resemblances"; for the various resemblances between members of a family: build, features, colour of eyes, gait, temperament, etc. etc. overlap and criss-cross in the same way.-And I shall say: 'games' form a family.
>
> And for instance the kinds of number form a family in the same way. Why do we call something a "number"? Well, perhaps because it has a-direct-relationship with several things that have hitherto been called number; and this can be said to give it an indirect relationship to other things we call the same name. And we extend our concept of number as in spinning a thread we twist fibre on fibre. And the strength of the thread does not reside in the fact that some one fibre runs through its whole length, but in the overlapping of many fibres.
>
> But if someone wished to say: "There is something common to all these constructions-namely the disjunction of all their common properties" —I should reply: Now you are only playing with words. One might as well say: "Something runs through the whole thread—namely the continuous overlapping of those fibres".

Id.

145. Following Lakoff, Winter describes a radial category thus:

> A radial category consists of a central model or case with various extensions that, though related to the central case in some fashion, nevertheless cannot be generated by rule. Because they may derive from the central case in different ways, the extensions may have little or nothing in common with each other beyond their shared connection to the central case.

WINTER p. 71 (citing LAKOFF, *supra* note 19, at 79–114).

arbitrary and unpredictable as a fictive category from a story by Borges . . . ."[146] This "misimpression," we are told, "is merely an artifact of the rationalist insistence on the logic of P or not-P."[147] It is this rationalist model that "obscures the systematic connections that link these different uses in a single categorical structure."[148]

To provide a more general approach to the idea of category structure, Winter introduces another term of art employed by George Lakoff, that of an *Idealized Cognitive Model* (ICM).[149] An ICM is "a 'folk' theory or cultural understanding that organizes knowledge of events, people, objects, and their characteristic relationships in a single gestalt structure that is experientially meaningful as a whole."[150] The concept of an ICM improves upon concepts such as frame, script, or schema in two important respects: "First, it provides a more general, overarching abstraction capable of accommodating the many different forms of categorical and conceptual structures identified in the literature. Second, it provides a more supple theoretical tool that better explains the complexities of radial categories."[151]

What does all this mean for legal theory? Winter makes sweeping claims for the cognitive approach to law: he believes cognitivism will change

---

146. *Id.* at 72.

147. *Id.* Consider the radial category "mouth." The mouth of a living thing (e.g., a human) is the "central case." We extend the central case "by means of an image-mapping to other apertures through which things flow." Standard extensions such as the "mouth" of a bottle or river are "fixed by convention." Unusual extensions "such as Homer's description of mouths as wounds—or a phrase like 'the yawning gates of hell'—are related metaphorical expressions that have nevertheless remained unconventionalized." *Id.*

148. *Id.* Radial categories produce "prototype effects" in that the meanings we attach to such terms are structured by their use in standard contexts. Thus, when in a restaurant we encounter a person with a pad and pencil, we "know" this person is here to take our order. We "know" this because "we have automatically and unreflectively assumed a 'restaurant scenario' that organizes our understanding of the events around us." *Id.* at 87–88.

149. *Id.* at 88 (citing LAKOFF, *supra* note 19, at 45, 56–57).

150. *Id.*

151. *Id.* at 89. Winter illustrates the complexity of ICMs with a discussion of the concept of "mother." There are many conventional uses of the term "mother." These include: "*working* mothers, *unwed* mothers, *biological* mothers, *birth* mothers, *genetic* mothers, *surrogate* mothers, *single* mothers, *adoptive* mothers, *foster* mothers, and good-old-fashioned *step*mothers." *Id.* Winter considers one of these types of mother, that of "surrogate mother." The term is usually used to refer to the biological/birth mother and not to the woman who, after the birth of the child, adopts and cares for it. Winter asks: "Why is it the birth mother and not the adoptive mother who is understood as the substitute?" It seems the category "mother" has a "complex internal structure." The concept "mother" is described as "a cluster model characterized by the convergence of several cognitive models, including a birth model, a nurturance model, and a marital model." "Surrogate mother," it seems, is "defined relative to the marital and nurturance models." Like the concept "unwed mother," the surrogate mother submodel is "characterized by a negative social stereotype." The surrogate mother, it seems, is like the unwed mother in that she "is prepared to give up her offspring to someone else. The woman who undertakes to nurture the child is the one who is socially esteemed as the 'real' mother. Conversely, the birth mother is denigrated as the 'substitute' because she does not care for the child she bore." Not surprisingly, the concept "mother" is characterized as a "complex radial category characterized by a cluster of converging models." *Id.* at 90–91.

the nature of debates in legal theory. Much of *A Clearing in the Forest* is taken up with an evaluation of, and arguments against, virtually every major position in legal theory from the last half century. In the next section, I contend that Winter's analysis of these positions rests on a fundamental misunderstanding of the nature of these debates.

B. Dworkin, Positivism, and the Nature of Law

1. The Debate.—Armed with the tools he has forged from reading Lakoff, Johnson, and Edelman, Winter sets off to make good on his claim that once the virtues of cognitivism are fully appreciated, we will free ourselves from the "suffocating conventional wisdom,"[152] and come to see the landscape of legal theory in an entirely new light.

A long-standing debate in jurisprudence is that between legal positivism and its most persistent critic, Ronald Dworkin. In an article that would set the terms of debate in analytic jurisprudence for the next twenty-five years, Dworkin asserted in a 1967 article that H.L.A. Hart's theory of law was fatally defective.[153] In *The Concept of Law*,[154] Hart displaced the then-reigning positivist theory—John Austin's command theory[155]—and replaced it with a picture of law as a system of rules.[156] In *The Model of Rules*, Dworkin argued that Hart's account of law was defective because it was incomplete.[157] Dworkin's claim was simple: there is more to law than simply rules. Rules, Dworkin argued, were part of law but law was also—and more importantly—a matter of principle.[158] Defenders of Hart took up a variety of defenses, but, over time, many acknowledged the force of Dworkin's critique.[159]

---

152. *Id.* at xiii.

153. Ronald Dworkin, *The Model of Rules*, 35 U. CHI. L. REV. 14, 22 (1967).

154. H.L.A. HART, THE CONCEPT OF LAW (2d ed. 1994).

155. *See* JOHN AUSTIN, THE PROVINCE OF JURISPRUDENCE DETERMINED (1832). For a discussion of Austin and his place in analytic jurisprudence, especially legal positivism, see Brian Bix, *John Austin*, *in* STANFORD ENCYCLOPEDIA OF PHILOSOPHY, http://plato.stanford.edu/entries/austin-john/ (last modified Feb. 23, 2001).

156. The first six chapters of *The Concept of Law* do two things. First, Hart explicates and then decisively criticizes the Austinian Command Theory of law. The second thing Hart does is articulate his account of a legal system as composed of primary and secondary rules. In addition to explicating his account of a modern legal system as a system of rules, Hart introduces important notions like "the internal point of view." HART, *supra* note 154, at 88–90. In Chapter Seven of *The Concept of Law*, Hart turns his attention to the activity of judges: adjudication. If Hart has a theory of adjudication (some think he does not), it is found here. The key ideas are core/penumbral meaning, discretion, and rule-skepticism. For an introduction to Hart's thought, see NEIL MACCORMICK, H.L.A. HART (1981).

157. Dworkin, *supra* note 153, at 22–23.

158. Dworkin defined a principle as "a standard that is to be observed, not because it will advance or secure an economic, political, or social situation deemed desirable, but because it is a requirement of justice or fairness or some other dimension of morality." *Id.* at 22.

159. Even Hart admitted that he should have said more about the role of principles in legal reasoning. *See* HART, *supra* note 154, at 259 (stating in the *Postscript*: "I certainly wish to confess

After *The Model of Rules*, Dworkin went on to write a series of influential papers in which he developed the idea that the concept of "law" was closely connected with concepts of justice, rights, and fairness.[160] In a later article,[161] Dworkin argued that a complete theory of law was not possible without due attention to the connections between law and political theory. Most controversially, Dworkin argued that in virtually every legal dispute there is a "right answer."[162]

In 1986, Dworkin published *Law's Empire*. *Law's Empire* was a capacious and wide-ranging account of the nature of law. The book took up the question of what it means to say that a proposition of law is "true."[163] This question, Dworkin opined, was a matter of finding the "true grounds of law."[164] Consider the claim "the speed limit in California is 55 m.p.h."[165] To discern the truth of this proposition of law, lawyers must consult the California statutes in search of a text that decides the matter. Of course, lawyers might disagree over the existence of such a provision. But this disagreement is factual, a form of disagreement Dworkin labels "empirical disagreement."[166]

Suppose lawyers acknowledge the fact of the text regarding the 55 m.p.h. speed limit but disagree with one another over whether the existence of the statute sufficiently answers the question of the truth of the asserted proposition of law. Dworkin labels this sort of disagreement "theoretical disagreement."[167] The disagreement is "theoretical" because it is a disagreement not about a fact (e.g., whether or not there is a statutory provision on point) but a disagreement over how that fact is to be interpreted (the "true grounds of law").[168]

---

now that I said far too little in my book about the topic of adjudication and legal reasoning and, in particular, about arguments from what my critics call legal principles. I now agree that it is a defect of this book that principles are touched upon only in passing."). For discussion, see ANTHONY J. SEBOK, LEGAL POSITIVISM IN AMERICAN JURISPRUDENCE 287–93 (1998) (discussing incorporationism). *See generally* HART'S POSTSCRIPT: ESSAYS ON THE POSTSCRIPT TO THE CONCEPT OF LAW (Jules Coleman ed., 2001).

160. *See, e.g.*, Ronald M. Dworkin, *Social Rules and Legal Theory*, 81 YALE L.J. 855, 855 (defending the claim that "in complicated legal systems . . . no ultimate distinction can be made between legal and moral standards, as positivism insists").

161. Ronald Dworkin, *Hard Cases*, 88 HARV. L. REV. 1057 (1975). Both *The Model of Rules* and *Hard Cases* are reprinted in RONALD DWORKIN, TAKING RIGHTS SERIOUSLY (1997).

162. Dworkin, *supra* note 161, at 1057–60.

163. RONALD DWORKIN, LAW'S EMPIRE 4–15 (1986); *see also* Ronald Dworkin, *On Gaps in the Law*, *in* CONTROVERSIES ABOUT LAW'S ONTOLOGY 84–90 (Paul Amselek & Neil MacCormick eds., 1991) (exploring "gaps in the law," a theory that claims that "there are some, perhaps many, concrete propositions of law . . . which are neither true nor false").

164. DWORKIN, *supra* note 163, at 6.

165. *Id.* at 4–5.

166. *Id.* at 5.

167. *Id.*

168. *Id.* at 5–6. For the best discussion of the philosophical aspects of *Law's Empire*, see Gerald J. Postema, *"Protestant" Interpretation and Social Practices*, 6 LAW & PHIL. 283 (1987).

Law's Empire is Dworkin's answer to the question of the true grounds of law. In giving his answer, Dworkin reprises and extends his criticism of Hart's legal positivism. Dworkin thinks that theoretical disagreement is a very real aspect of law.[169] Hart, Dworkin maintains, makes no place for theoretical disagreement in his account of the nature of law. Thus, Dworkin argues, positivism is a defective theory of law because it fails to account for the role of theoretical disagreement in law.[170]

2. *Winter on Dworkin.*—Now we come to Winter's cognitive evaluation of Dworkin's critique of positivism and Dworkin's alternative account of the nature of law. He begins by describing Dworkin's metaphor for the judicial construction of precedent (i.e., constructive interpretation), that of the "chain novel."[171] As each appellate judge comes to the task of making sense of precedents, she must decide the present case in a way that makes the law (including past decisions) "the best it can be."[172] Winter finds that, while Dworkin's interpretive account of law might "have intuitive appeal," it is nevertheless "unpersuasive."[173] It seems there are several reasons for Winter's conclusion. What is less than clear is how these reasons are related.

First, Winter brings in Dworkin's arch-nemesis, Stanley Fish.[174] Having earlier criticized Fish as one who "maintain[s] the entire superstructure of the objectivist model of rationality,"[175] Winter now cites Fish for the proposition that when it comes to writing the individual chapters of the chain novel, "the authors of the subsequent chapters remain free to reinterpret the plot, the characters, or the genre in ways that drastically change the enterprise."[176]

169. To illustrate his point in a general way, Dworkin asks us to consider how an imaginary community might debate the meaning of the concept of "courtesy." In an effort to decide what courtesy "really requires," the participants will no doubt point to a variety of things, including context, behavior, gender, and the like. Their discussion will include debate over what should count as relevant to a decision about the true meaning of courtesy. This type of debate is "theoretical" (each participant engages in "constructive interpretation") in that the participants disagree not only about facts (e.g., that certain behaviors are or have been thought to be true examples of "courtesy") but about what should count in deciding the meaning of "courtesy." DWORKIN, *supra* note 163, at 46–49.

170. *Id.* at 37–44.

171. WINTER p. 130 (citing DWORKIN, *supra* note 163, at 225–38).

172. *Id.* at 129–30 (quoting at length from DWORKIN, *supra* note 163, at 52).

173. *Id.* at 130.

174. Professors Dworkin and Fish have traded potshots. *See* Fish, *supra* note 42, at 417–18 (arguing that Dworkin's account of "law as integrity" suffers from the same weaknesses as external skepticism, and characterizing this problem as "the mistake that *is* the book"); Ronald Dworkin, *Pragmatism, Right Answers, and True Banality*, *in* PRAGMATISM IN LAW AND SOCIETY 359, 377 (Michael Brint & William Weaver eds., 1991) ("Professor Fish has been on my case . . . for almost a decade.").

175. WINTER p. 10. Early on in *A Clearing in the Forest*, Winter identifies Fish and Richard Rorty as anti-foundationalists who "nevertheless maintain the entire superstructure of the objectivist model of rationality." *Id.*

176. *Id.* at 130 (citing FISH, *supra* note 16, at 87–119, 356–71).

Winter acknowledges Dworkin's point that judges will construct their chapter of the chain novel "relative to interpretive strategies and commitments."[177] In contrast, Fish claims that judges are free to "drastically change the enterprise."[178] Does Winter favor Fish's "radical" account or the more "sober" Dworkinian analysis? It cannot be Fish because, in Winter's view, Fish's arguments all exhibit an "all-or-nothing structure."[179] Fish is part of the "rationalists' dilemma,"[180] it seems. But if Fish's approach to interpretation is not a useful alternative to Dworkin's constructive interpretation,[181] then what is Fish's analysis doing in Winter's critique of Dworkin?

According to Winter, Dworkin, in response to what Winter characterizes as Fish's "objectivist assumptions,"[182] maintains that as each chapter of the chain novel is written, "the very accretion of detail progressively constrains subsequent authors because they must account for the data within their own interpretive conceptions of what a coherent story can be."[183] In short, while there is freedom in the judicial extrapolation of precedent, details such as doctrine, rule, and precedent limit the absolute power of judges to make law.[184] Regrettably, says Winter, "this claim will not wash either."[185] Why not?

---

177. *Id.* (citing DWORKIN, *supra* note 163, at 52–53, 234–35).

178. *Id.* at 130 (citing FISH, *supra* note 16, at 87–119, 356–71).

179. *Id.* at 353.

180. *Id.* (quoting MAURICE MERLEAU-PONTY, THE PHENOMENOLOGY OF PERCEPTION 442 (Colin Smith trans., 1962)).

181. I agree with Winter to the extent he believes Fish's approach to meaning is flawed, although my criticism of Fish would apply equally well to Winter. The idea that all understanding is interpretation is a non-starter. For discussion, see Dennis Patterson, *The Poverty of Interpretive Universalism: Toward the Reconstruction of Legal Theory*, 72 TEXAS L. REV. 1 (1993). Fish replies in Stanley Fish, *How Come You Do Me Like You Do: A Response to Dennis Patterson*, 72 TEXAS L. REV. 57 (1993). My rebuttal to Fish is Dennis Patterson, *You Made Me Do It: My Reply to Stanley Fish*, 72 TEXAS L. REV. 67 (1993).

182. WINTER p. 130 (citing Ronald Dworkin, *My Reply to Stanley Fish (and Walter Bevin Michaels): Please Don't Talk About Objectivity Anymore*, *in* THE POLITICS OF INTERPRETATION 287 (W.J.T. Mitchell ed., 1980)).

183. *Id.*

184. Two criteria—fit and justification—are the standards by which any interpretation is judged. *See* DWORKIN, *supra* note 163, at 230–31.

> The first is what we have been calling the dimension of fit. He cannot adopt any interpretation, however complex, if he believes that no single author who set out to write a novel with the various readings of character, plot, theme, and point that interpretation describes could have written substantially the text he has been given. That does not mean his interpretation must fit every bit of the text. It is not disqualified simply because he claims that some lines or tropes are accidental, or even that some events of plot are mistakes because they work against the literary ambitions the interpretation states. But the interpretation he takes up must nevertheless flow throughout the text; it must have general explanatory power, and it is flawed if it leaves unexplained some major structural aspect of the text, a subplot treated as having great dramatic importance or a dominant and repeated metaphor . . . . He may find, not that no single interpretation fits the bulk of the text, but that more than one does. The

Winter gives this reason: "[T]he accretion of detail does not foreclose alternative interpretations even within a single interpretative conception like the ICM of narrative. Because the ICM is sufficiently generalized to allow many instantiations and many different elaborations, the details of a given story can be reordered in terms of many other points of view."[186] But, as mentioned, Dworkin acknowledges that more than one story can be written with the same materials. It must be that Dworkin is too narrow. But if Fish is too wild, and Dworkin too tame, what are we to do?

Why, Winter asks, does Dworkin's conception of constructive interpretation "work?"[187] It is *not* because it is "analytically sound,"[188] but because his account of law is "the beneficiar[y] of our suspension of disbelief."[189] It seems that "something is 'best' only relative to our set of idealized assumptions or model of what we think it should be—a point that, as we have seen, Dworkin concedes."[190] Winter wants to say Dworkin's theory of constructive interpretation "is logically indistinguishable from and necessarily collapses back into the cultural values that unconsciously animate the practice or object under consideration."[191] Our unconscious "unreflective level of thought is structured by means of culturally shared ICMs . . . ."[192] Finally, we come to the point of all this:

> Thus, interpreting a practice to make it 'the best it can be' is not a constraint; it is a tautology. Constructive interpretation is what we do every time we speak, read, or write. It is the ordinary cognitive process by which one configures new input in a manner that makes sense—in a manner, that is, that makes the input a coherent whole or a 'best example' of an existing idealized cognitive model or reigning paradigm. Constructive interpretation is, in other words, nothing more than the phenomenon of prototype effects presented in fancy philosophical dress. If Dworkin succeeds in leading us to think that he has said more, it is only because he has exploited the fabric of our

---

> second dimension of interpretation then requires him to judge which of these eligible readings makes the work in progress best, all things considered. At this point his more substantive aesthetic judgments, about the importance or insight or realism or beauty of different ideas the novel might be taken to express, come into play. But the formal and structural considerations that dominate on the first dimension figure on the second as well, for even when neither of two interpretations is disqualified out of hand as explaining too little, one may show the text in a better light because it fits more of the text or provides a more interesting integration of style and content.

Id.

185. WINTER p. 130.

186. *Id.* This point is reprised at *infra* text accompanying notes 220–28.

187. *Id.*

188. *Id.*

189. *Id.* at 131.

190. *Id.*

191. *Id.* (citing FISH, *supra* note 16, at 364–65).

192. *Id.*

> expectations and engaged us in the act of contrivances of plot and character necessary to make his story work.[193]

Winter finds fault with Dworkin's account of constructive interpretation because it says too little.[194] Winter seems to think that each time we speak, read, or write, we do so through a process of interpretation. There are reasons to think this account of the nature of understanding and expression is fundamentally flawed.[195] Even if Winter is right about the nature of understanding (i.e., that to understand is to interpret) that would still not settle whether Dworkin is right in his criticism of Hart on the nature of law.

First, Dworkin's point about constructive interpretation is that constructive interpretation is the best way to account for an essential feature of legal practice (i.e., theoretical disagreement) that, Dworkin maintains, positivism ignores. Critics can respond either by arguing that Dworkin has misdescribed the claims positivists make about the nature of law[196] or that Dworkin has overstated the role of theoretical disagreement in law. If Winter had shown that the question of the nature of law were somehow tied to the nature of understanding, he might have moved the debate along. Instead, Winter does not comment on any of these issues and, thus, says nothing informative about this long-standing debate over the nature of law.

For this reason, it is difficult to take seriously his earlier claim that cognitivism will transform our view of debates in legal theory.[197] This is regrettable if for no other reason than the significance of Dworkin's challenge to positivism. If Dworkin is right, and law and morality are indeed conceptually connected, then Dworkin may indeed be correct that law and morality are not two different enterprises but, in some sense, the same. Nothing in Winter's discussion of Dworkin helps decide this question.

3. Winter on Hart.—The Concept of Law is a central text in legal theory. Among other things, Hart provides an account of the meaning of concepts in law.[198] Central to Hart's account is his distinction between core and penumbral meanings.[199] Winter focuses on this discussion and its role in Hart's positivist theory of law. He believes that cognitivism provides a far

193. *Id.*

194. I have my own doubts about Dworkin's approach to the question of the nature of law, specifically his account of the role of interpretation in law. For discussion, see DENNIS PATTERSON, LAW AND TRUTH 71–98 (1996) (characterizing Dworkin as an interpretive universalist and criticizing his view by arguing that "[t]he notion that every act of textual and verbal comprehension is a matter of some act or theory of interpretation is a deeply misconceived idea").

195. For my discussion of the fallacy of the proposition that all understanding requires interpretation, see discussion *infra* subpart IV(B)(2).

196. Hart himself disputes Dworkin's account of Hart's positivism. *See* HART, *supra* note 154, at 238–54 (describing, in the *Postscript*, a variety of misunderstandings on Dworkin's part).

197. WINTER p. 4.

198. *See generally* HART, *supra* note 154.

199. *Id.* at 79–99.

more perspicuous account of the nature of meaning.[200] He seeks to make this point through a critique of Hart, specifically Hart's Separability Thesis.

Winter's analysis of Hart's approach to rules and rule-following begins with this quote from Hart:

> A legal rule forbids you to take a vehicle into the public park. Plainly this forbids an automobile, but what about bicycles, roller skates, toy automobiles? What about airplanes? Are these, as we say, to be called 'vehicles' for the purpose of the rule or not? If we are to communicate with each other at all, . . . then the general words we use . . . must have some standard instance in which no doubts are felt about its application. There must be a core of settled meaning, but there will be, as well, a penumbra of debatable cases in which words are neither obviously applicable nor obviously ruled out. These cases will each have some features in common with the standard case; they will lack others or be accompanied by features not present in the standard case.[201]

Hart's notion of a core of settled meaning is, in Winter's view, now recognizable as "the phenomenon of prototype effects."[202] He describes prototype effects as follows: "Some category members—that is, those that

---

200. Winter's critique of Hart occurs in a chapter entitled "How Do Rules Work?" As Winter acknowledges, "one's view of rules is intimately related to one's understanding of language and categorization." *Id.* at 188. Rules, rule-following, and meaning are, of course, important topics in the philosophy of language. Winter claims throughout *A Clearing in the Forest* that philosophers of language are among the folks who fail to understand the nature of language, the very thing cognitivism will illuminate. Given his sweeping claims of the failure of philosophers to appreciate the merits of cognitivism, one can only be puzzled by the fact that in the entirety of Winter's book, no mention is made of the most notable discussion of rule-following and meaning, that of Saul Kripke. *See* SAUL KRIPKE, WITTGENSTEIN ON RULES AND PRIVATE LANGUAGE (1990). In this book, Kripke advanced a reading of Wittgenstein's *Philosophical Investigations* that concluded with the startling proposition that there was no good argument against the skeptical conclusion that when I use a word, there is nothing to justify my current claim to "know" the meaning of the word in question. *Id.* at 11–12. If this were true—and Kripke argues that Wittgenstein thought it true—then rule-following would be impossible because we could never know what the terms of any rule "meant." *Id.* Alas, neither Kripke nor Wittgenstein is anywhere to be found in Winter's discussion. One must wonder how Winter intends to transform the jurisprudential landscape by ignoring the most-discussed treatment of rule-following in the literature. For an accessible account of Kripke's argument and its importance for questions of meaning and mind, see COLIN MCGINN, THE MAKING OF A PHILOSOPHER 145–55 (2002) (offering a concise explanation of the differences between McGinn's and Kripke's readings of Wittgenstein). For a website that literally "has it all," see *Wittgenstein on Rules and Private Language Ultimate HomePage*, *at* http://krypton.mankato.msus.edu/~witt/ (last visited Oct. 19, 2002). Kripke's reading of Wittgenstein has also been a frequent topic of discussion in legal academic journals. *See, e.g.*, Russell Pannier, *D'Amato, Kripke, and Legal Indeterminacy*, 27 WM. MITCHELL L. REV. 881 (2000); Ahilan T. Arulanatham, *Breaking the Rules?: Wittgenstein and Legal Realism*, 107 YALE L.J. 1853 (1998); Christian Zapf & Eben Moglen, *Linguistic Indeterminacy and the Rule of Law: On the Perils of Misunderstanding Wittgenstein*, 84 GEO. L.J. 485 (1996); Mark V. Tushnet, *Following the Rules Laid Down*, 96 HARV. L. REV. 781 (1983).

201. WINTER p. 197 (quoting H.L.A. Hart, *Positivism and the Separation of Law and Morals*, 71 HARV. L. REV. 593, 607 (1958)).

202. *Id.* at 198.

most fully embody the characteristic features of the model—would readily be perceived as paradigmatic examples of the category and could be expected to serve as cognitive reference points in reasoning about the category."[203]

In addition, it seems that "Hart's claim that words have a 'core' meaning and 'penumbral' cases describes a radial category."[204] Taken together, Winter is persuaded that "Hart's discussion foreshadowed the approach to legal rules . . . [and] . . . recognized that word-categories form radial categories; that they produce prototype effects; and, consequently that rules operate as guidelines rather than rigid directives."[205]

Nevertheless, Hart's analysis is found to be "marred" by an "inadequate account of meaning."[206] And why is this? It seems Hart's description of the core relies on intuition rather than purpose.

> The metaphor of "open texture" captures some of the fluidity of language. But it also suggests the image of a tapestry that, though unfinished at the margins, is tightly woven at its center. In fact, Hart treated prototype effects in just this way: For him the plain case or standard instance represented a *hard* core of *settled* meaning, rather than the contingent product of a motivated, adaptive process of categorization. Thus [Hart takes] the existence of prototype effects as evidence of meaning sufficiently stable to make the conventional model of rules work. [Hart fails to appreciate] the degree to which prototype effects are themselves the product of the tacit knowledge of context and purpose that is integral to categorization.[207]

Owing to his philosophical errors, Hart "cannot admit a semantic role for purpose without undermining the positivist view of law . . . ."[208] The "positivist view of law" to which Winter adverts is the so-called Separability Thesis.[209] The Separability Thesis states that there is no necessary conceptual connection between law and morality.[210] As we saw earlier, this is precisely the claim that Dworkin disputes and makes the basis of his attack on the positivist theory of law. According to Winter, the Separability Thesis

203. *Id.* at 144.

204. *Id.* at 198.

205. *Id.*

206. *Id.*

207. *Id.*

208. *Id.* at 198–99.

209. *See* HART, *supra* note 154, at 185–86 (describing the Separability Thesis as the "simple contention that it is in no sense a necessary truth that laws reproduce or satisfy certain demands of morality, though in fact they have often done so").

210. *See, e.g.*, FREDERICK F. SCHAUER, PLAYING BY THE RULES: A PHILOSOPHICAL EXAMINATION OF RULE-BASED DECISION-MAKING IN LAW AND LIFE 197–99 (1991) (explaining that positivists deny any necessary connection between law and morality); Jules Coleman, *Negative and Positive Positivism*, 11 J. LEGAL STUD. 139, 143–44, 148–49 (1982) (identifying the positivist view that law and morality are not necessarily connected). Winter misdescribes the Separability Thesis (which he explicitly identifies by name) as "the notion that the legal is conceptually distinguishable from the larger universe of the non-legal." WINTER p. 199.

"suffers from a relatively obvious kind of category mistake."[211] This, he says, is the mistake:

> The fallacy of the separability thesis is that it mistakes social distinctiveness for conceptual autonomy: There can be no purely positivist system of legal norms when categorization and comprehension already implicate the legal decisionmaker in the process of making classifications and distinctions relative to the practical commitments and normative assumptions of her culture.[212]

If I understand Winter's point, he says nothing with which Hart would disagree. As one who himself embraced the "linguistic turn" in analytic philosophy,[213] Hart would in no way dispute the general point that conceptual classifications and distinctions are made relative to the practical and normative assumptions of one's culture. In fact, Hart said as much.[214] As in his earlier discussion of Dworkin, Winter's arrow misses its intended target. The reason is quite simple: the Separability Thesis is not a linguistic thesis. Everything Winter says about prototype effects, social distinctiveness, and conceptual autonomy could be true, and none of it would touch Hart's claim.

The Separability Thesis is a *negative* thesis. The claim is simple: there is no necessary conceptual connection between law and morality. As everyone on both sides of this issue knows, one sure way to defeat this claim is to show that such a connection exists. Dworkin believes he has demonstrated that the Separability Thesis is false.[215] Positivists deny the success Dworkin claims for his argument.[216] But Winter mentions none of this literature. The reason for this is simple: he misunderstands the debate over the Separability Thesis. As in his discussion of Dworkin, Winter makes no progress because he fails to understand the debate.

---

211. *Id.*

212. *Id.*

213. For a discussion of the linguistic turn in philosophy, see THE LINGUISTIC TURN: RECENT ESSAYS IN PHILOSOPHICAL METHOD (Richard Rorty ed., 1967).

214. *See* HART, *supra* note 154, at 127–36. For a discussion of Hart's embrace of linguistic philosophy, with specific reference to Wittgenstein, see Anthony J. Sebok, *Finding Wittgenstein at the Core of the Rule of Recognition*, 52 SMU L. REV. 75, 105–06 (1999).

215. Dworkin believes this because he believes he has shown that morality—however conceptually or linguistically understood—is a constitutive feature of legal argument. *See* Dworkin, *supra* note 154, at 17–45 (arguing that the legal positivist assumption of a fundamental separation between law and morality fails because decisionmaking in hard cases often requires reference to principles, which rely on "justice or fairness or some other dimension of morality").

216. *See, e.g.*, JULES L. COLEMAN, THE PRACTICE OF PRINCIPLE: IN DEFENCE OF A PRAGMATIST APPROACH TO LEGAL THEORY 105 (2001) ("[N]o one nowadays considers this argument convincing . . . ."). For a spirited rebuttal, see Ronald Dworkin, *30 Years On*, 115 HARV. L. REV. 1655, 1682 (2002) (book review) ("[Coleman] attributes important views to me that I have never, so far as I can recall, either held or expressed.").

C. *What Difference Does Any of This Make?*

Winter claims that a better understanding of mind will lead to a better understanding of law, for law is a product of mind.[217] Because Winter asks that his book be taken seriously as a contribution to legal theory, I have evaluated it from that point of view. Because Winter misunderstands the central debates in contemporary jurisprudence, his book makes no contribution to those debates. If the book fails to illuminate debates in legal theory, does it nevertheless enhance our understanding of law and legal practice? Sadly, it does not. In fact, taken on its own terms, Winter's argument leaves unaddressed—and, thus, unanswered—key questions about the practice of law and the exercise of legal judgment.

A central tenet of Winter's cognitivism is that we are each endowed with a basic cognitive infrastructure. In making this claim, Winter's cognitivism aligns with similar claims made by linguists, neuroscientists, and other proto-rationalist theorists. The unique dimension of Professor Winter's cognitivism is the "embodied" dimension. Lakoff and Johnson—Winter's favorite cognitivists—champion the idea that a theory of mind can be generated by theorizing interactions between the mind/brain and its environment.

As persons, we come to the world with a mind/brain composed of neural networks, image-schemas, ICMs, and cognitive sedimentations. Armed with this cognitive infrastructure, we make sense of our world through prototype effects and radial categories. But, we are told, there are constraints. In fact, "[t]here are always constraints, and they are as difficult to escape precisely because they are embodied in and constantly reinforced by the sedimented social field of public interactions, cultural objects, and common experiences—'the meaning saturated milieu' in which we are always implicated as participants."[218] Getting beyond these sedimentations is difficult because we are "prisoners of the social field—the very clearing in the forest—that we ourselves have made."[219] It is astonishing that having begun his book with the claim that a better understanding of the nature of mind will lead to a better understanding of law, Winter ends by saying that we are trapped within our own cultural web of belief.

One problem with this perspective is that if everyone is endowed with the same cognitive structures, then what explains the fact that lawyers and judges often disagree over legal questions?[220] If *everyone* is driven by

---

217. WINTER p. xii.

218. *Id.* at 357 (citing KERRAH WHITESIDE, MERLEAU-PONTY AND THE FOUNDATION OF AN EXISTENTIAL POLITICS 75 (1988)).

219. *Id.* at 357.

220. Another reviewer of *A Clearing in the Forest* makes the point this way:

> Winter repeatedly claims that the same basic cognitive structure shapes ALL normal human cognitive outputs. But if that is true, then Sunstein, Schauer, and Dworkin must

imagistic cognitive mappings, then why is it that some folks have different thoughts and perspectives than others?[221] Either they have different cognitive mappings or some other factor is at work.[222] Either way, Winter's account of thinking—legal or otherwise—fails to account for this obvious fact.[223]

And suppose people disagreed because their embodied neural mappings were different from one another? This would explain *why* people come to different conclusions in their respective analysis of legal questions, but it would leave unanswered the questions of who, with respect to any given question, was "right."[224] In fact, in a (theoretical) universe where normative questions are reduced to internal neural firings, it is not at all clear that concepts like "right," "wrong," "correct," or "incorrect" even have a place.

It might be objected that Winter answers the normative question because he not only acknowledges the fact that judges and lawyers disagree, he also explains how disagreements are resolved. His claim is that disagreements are resolved through a process of persuasion. He writes:

> It is precisely here that cognitive theory makes its most powerful contribution. From a cognitive perspective, it does not matter that legal decisionmaking is a product of tacit knowledge rather than doctrinal logic. The process is one of persuasion. To ask about the characterizations that people are likely to find convincing is to inquire into what will make the most sense to them under the circumstances. It is to inquire into the nature of their categories and concepts—for it is our categories and concepts that define our expectations and, in so

---

> not be wrong. Rather, they must be using some image-driven cognitive mapping that differs from Winter's. Their thought is embodied and motivated, too.

Lief Carter, *A Clearing in the Forest: Law, Life, and the Mind*, 12 LAW & POL. BOOK REV. 278, 281 (2002), *at* http://www.bsos.umd.edu/gvpt/lpbr/subpages/reviews/winterclear.html (book review).

221. I want to emphasize that I do not dispute that there may be answers to these questions. My point is simply that Winter never addresses what, given his point of view, are obvious questions.

222. Winter might seek to avoid the effect of this criticism with his acknowledgement that despite the effect of hard-wiring, "some postgenetic organization is taking place." WINTER pp. 32–33. But this move is of no help. Suppose two judges disagree over how best to decide a case. This disagreement is the result of differing "postgenetic organization." With opposing cognitive frameworks, we cannot favor either one without begging the question of which judge has the "correct" framework. The fact that the two evolved "postgenetically" and not through hard-wiring in no way mitigates the need to make a choice.

223. For excellent treatment of this issue, see Thomas Morawetz, *Understanding Disagreement, The Root Issue of Jurisprudence: Applying Wittgenstein to Positivism, Critical Theory, and Judging*, 141 U. PA. L. REV. 371 (1992) (examining legal reasoning to show the jurisprudential importance of the heterogeneity of justification and belief).

224. At many points throughout his book, Winter says that one judgment or another is "right" or "correct." Other than mere assertion, it is unclear how on his own terms he can make such judgments. *See, e.g.*, WINTER p. 142 (analyzing differing views of Supreme Court Justices over the right to counsel and concluding "[c]learly, Blackmun is correct."); *id.* at 246 (stating that a case involving preaching in public parks would be "correctly decided" under the modern public forum doctrine).

doing, powerfully shape what we find believable, what we judge accurate, what we experience as cogent, compelling, and convincing. Persuasion . . . is a function of the cognitive models by which we cognize our world.[225]

This answer simply begs the question at issue. Consider again this sentence from the quote just given: "It is to inquire into the nature of their categories and concepts—for it is our categories and concepts that define our expectations . . . ."[226] Here Winter seems to want to have it both ways.[227] When he speaks of persuading people with "their categories," he seems to be saying that we each have our own individuated set of cognitive mappings. But, in the very next sentence, when he speaks of "our categories," Winter goes back to his universalist stance—*viz*, that we are all wired with the same neural mappings. With such fundamental contradictions in his argument, one wonders how Winter can expect to make much progress.[228]

In reviewing Winter's arguments for a cognitivist perspective on law and legal theory, I have evaluated his arguments with a view to whether they make any contribution to ongoing debates about the nature of law and the simple vantage point of internal coherence of the arguments. Regrettably, Professor Winter's arguments fail on all counts.[229]

225. WINTER pp. 152–53.

226. *Id.*

227. This tendency is evident in Winter's review of the Amsterdam and Bruner book:

> Categorization and adjudication are both social processes. Judges must communicate; more than that, they must persuade. They must persuade us that what they decide is worthy of our obedience, worthy of designation as Law. To do that, *their* categories must connect with *ours* in a profound way. That is why judges, even Supreme Court Justices, write like advocates. And that is one of the reasons that culture necessarily works its way into law . . . . But once we understand that function and purpose are built-in, constitutive dimensions of *our* categories, we cannot escape the conclusion that categorization (like narrative) is profoundly normative. With that realization must come the recognition that adjudication is not only intensely political, but also in some sense inherently conservative. For the judge cannot approach the case—any case—without bringing with her the entire repertoire of cultural categories with their normatively loaded understandings. And if the judge is to be persuasive, *her* categories will have to reflect the most mainstream values and understandings. Which means that adjudication (if not, indeed, law more generally) is typically conservative in the sense that it enforces—and reinforces—the dominant normative views of the culture.

Winter, *supra* note 15, at 1635–36 (emphasis added).

228. Winter himself seems to doubt (or does he?) the universality of his cognitive thesis. *See* WINTER p. 157. ("[T]he fact that cognition is grounded means that even the judges' 'own' categories are already constrained by the socially constructed contexts in which they find themselves.").

229. Nevertheless, some are persuaded of the merits of this approach. *See* Paul, *supra* note 93, at 987 ("For those of us teaching legal theory to American law students at the beginning of the twenty-first century, Steven Winter's book . . . has arrived just in time. It offers a path . . . out of our oldest and least fruitful debates.").

IV. Fashionable Nonsense

In *The Mind's Provisions*, Vincent Descombes takes his readers on a wide-ranging tour of cognitivism. Descombes's book is remarkable for a number of reasons, not the least of which is that he shows first-class philosophical work is possible, even from France, where post-structuralism and deconstruction have been the most celebrated recent exports. Descombes begins with a clear statement of what is at stake in the debate over the nature of mind. The central question is not whether there are mental phenomena "but rather where they are to be located."[230] Cognitivists find mental life to be "inside" the person, specifically in the mind/brain.[231] By thus locating the source of mental activity, the cognitivist sets the stage for a series of related claims: thinking is internal; reading takes place in the head; a science of thinking is both possible and recommended; and introspection will yield insight into the nature of thought and consciousness.[232]

Descombes's most intense disagreement with cognitivism is the move to interiority.[233] As they have done since Descartes, cognitivists look to internal processes—however understood—as the ground of philosophical speculation. Descombes challenges the very starting point of cognitivism with his claim that mental phenomena manifest themselves not directly but in human action.[234] Descombes's project is to understand thought in historical context where, he maintains, agents' self-understanding of their actions and their reasons for actions are best explicated.[235]

I began this Essay with the observation that the cognitivist view of the relationship between mind and world was not only far from obviously true but also a tendentious thesis. In the previous two parts of this Essay, I described and evaluated the arguments from two works, the authors of which laud the insights engendered by a cognitivist approach to law. For a variety of reasons, I argued that none of the arguments support the claims to enhanced understanding of law. I shall now turn my attention from arguments in favor of a cognitive approach to law to more general considerations. The focus will now be on the philosophical presuppositions of cognitivism. There are serious reasons to question the plausibility of cognitivism as a view of mind.

230. DESCOMBES p. 1.
231. *Id.* at 2.
232. *Id.* at 2–9.
233. *Id.* at 2.
234. *Id.* at 12–13.
235. *Id.* at 13, 19–29.

A. A View of the Terrain

Notwithstanding the wealth of attention given to cognitivism, both in scholarly journals and elsewhere,[236] disputes over the explanatory adequacy of cognitivism have a long history. In fact, many of the contemporary debates reprise the terms of argumentation and context first articulated in the seventeenth century when Descartes broached the possibility of "mind" as an object of scientific inquiry.[237]

If it means anything, "Cartesianism" identifies a certain approach to the question of how we can be sure any of our beliefs are true. Descartes answered the question of belief by developing the epistemic viewpoint known as "foundationalism."[238] According to Descartes, we can never be sure of the truth of our beliefs unless those beliefs ultimately rest on an indubitable foundation.[239]

But how can we be certain that what we take to be our knowledge of the external world is in fact the product of correct ideas? Descartes—the rationalist[240]—argues that as humans, we are "hard-wired" by God with

236. Steven Pinker was recently featured in the Science section of the *New York Times* in a very flattering story. *See* Nicholas Wade, *Scientist at Work/Steven Pinker: In Nature vs. Nurture, a Voice for Nature*, N.Y. TIMES, Sept. 17, 2002, at F1 (discussing Pinker's ideas about innate behavior differences and the controversy such ideas have caused). Pinker's works include: THE BLANK SLATE (2002); WORDS AND RULES: THE INGREDIENTS OF LANGUAGE (1999); HOW THE MIND WORKS (1997); THE LANGUAGE INSTINCT: HOW THE MIND CREATES LANGUAGE (1994); LEARNABILITY AND COGNITION: THE ACQUISITION OF ARGUMENT STRUCTURE (1989); LANGUAGE LEARNABILITY AND LANGUAGE DEVELOPMENT (1984).

237. Another area of Cartesian focus is philosophy of mind and the problem of consciousness. Of course, it was Descartes who bequeathed to modernity the framework of the "mind-body problem," specifically the presupposition that the mind and the brain are separate entities. Given this presupposition, the question is how to connect consciousness with the brain. Reductionists argue that the mind is "in" the brain (or, that "consciousness" is just a physical process). This view is called "eliminativism." *See* Samuel Guttenplan, *An Essay on Mind*, *in* BLACKWELL COMPANION TO THE PHILOSOPHY OF MIND 6, 21 (Samuel Guttenplan ed., 1994). By contrast, a functional explanation of consciousness acknowledges the existence of consciousness but demurs to the notion that consciousness presents a mystery to be explained. Sure, we may not know how consciousness and the brain are connected, but there is nothing to be gained by the inquiry. Lastly, there is "mysterianism." On this view, consciousness is deemed to be a natural phenomenon but one whose mysteries we will never discern. Consciousness, on this view, is best left alone. *See* COLIN MCGINN, MYSTERIOUS FLAME: CONSCIOUS MINDS IN A MATERIAL WORLD 68–69 (1999). McGinn discusses mysterianism and other approaches to philosophy of mind in his recent memoir, *The Making of a Philosopher*. *See* MCGINN, *supra* note 200.

238. For a discussion of foundationalism, with attention to its importance for jurisprudence, see PATTERSON, *supra* note 194, at 152–57.

239. RENE DESCARTES, DISCOURSE ON THE METHOD OF RIGHTLY CONDUCTING ONE'S REASON AND SEEKING THE TRUTH IN THE SCIENCES (1637), *reprinted in* 1 THE PHILOSOPHICAL WRITINGS OF DESCARTES 1 (John Cottingham et al. trans., 1984).

240. Rationalism is "the view that knowledge about the world is the development of what, in some sense, we already know in the form of clear, distinct, and mutually consistent ideas present to our consciousness." ROBERT ACKERMANN, DATA, INSTRUMENTS, AND THEORY 7 (1985).

innate resources.[241] Owing to the innate resources of the human mind, persons need not worry about the question of whether there are laws of nature that can account for the way the world is. God has guaranteed their presence. The only challenge is epistemic: identifying these laws. The method of doubt[242]—the hallmark of Cartesian epistemology—is the philosopher's contribution to this endeavor.

Empiricists like Locke and Hume attacked Descartes's rationalism, specifically the theory of innate ideas.[243] For empiricists, all understanding and knowledge of the world is best explained by reference to experience. Empiricists place the senses at the foundation of knowledge. Understanding is the product of sensory evidence combined with empirical method.[244]

While empiricism ultimately triumphed in analytic philosophy, many debates in the philosophy of mind remain firmly within the Cartesian paradigm. The central problem remains the separate realms of mind and brain and their connection. The pervasive character of the Cartesian paradigm can best be appreciated by a look at the variety of contemporary research programs that embrace this picture of mind. I shall discuss three: Noam Chomsky's generative grammar; Jerry Fodor's computational model; and Alan Turing and his "Turing test."

Chomsky's program in linguistics (the theory of generative grammar[245]) is the most far-reaching application of the Cartesian paradigm since Descartes first gave us this picture of mind. Chomsky's rise to fame began with a work in criticism,[246] specifically a critique of the then-dominant school of psychology, behaviorism. In *Verbal Behavior*,[247] B. F. Skinner explained language facility in terms of the behaviorist model of stimulus and response. Chomsky's criticism of Skinner's argument was as simple as it was devastating: if behaviorists were right about language, how could they

241. Here is how Descartes connects the idea of indubitable foundations with innate ideas: "I have noticed certain laws which God has so established in nature, and of which he has implanted such notions in our minds, that after adequate reflection we cannot doubt that they are exactly observed in everything which exists or occurs in the world." DESCARTES, *supra* note 239, at 111–31.

242. *See id.* at 117, 127 (discussing the "method of doubt").

243. For an interesting discussion of the debate between rationalists and empiricists over matters of mind, and the implications of the debate for cognitivism, see Francis F. Steen, *Empiricism vs. Rationalism: The Debate Continues* (Dec. 22, 1996), *at* http://cogweb.ucla.edu/CogSci/Empiricism.html.

244. The clearest example of this approach to knowledge is induction. Induction eschews appeal to *a priori* truths and, instead, relies on inference to general laws from repeated sensory impressions (experience).

245. The central element in the idea of "generative grammar" is the notion that persons are born with an innate knowledge of language. For an entertaining and informative website that treats the topic of generative grammar, see RAY C. DOUGHERTY, NATURAL LANGUAGE COMPUTING fig.7.1 (1994), http://www.nyu.edu/pages/linguistics/f0701w5.html.

246. *See* Noam Chomsky, *A Review of B.F. Skinner's* Verbal Behavior, 35 LANGUAGE 26 (1959).

247. B.F. SKINNER, VERBAL BEHAVIOR (1957).

account for the fact that speakers often utter sentences they have never heard?[248] Given that behaviorists relied upon the reinforcement of behavior as the ground of conduct, they could not explain the presence of novel verbal behavior.

With the explanatory apparatus of behaviorism now in shambles, Chomsky stepped in with a new theory of language facility, that of generative grammar. Chomsky not only adopted Descartes's explanatory framework, he championed it. In addition, Chomsky wrapped his work in the mantle of science, calling his new theory a science of mind.[249] The nub of his theory was that we understand a sentence by interpreting it through "a computational process of unconscious inference."[250] Like Descartes's innate cognitive resources, Chomskian persons are endowed with a faculty for the instantaneous translation of verbal input into meaningful utterances.[251] To understand is to interpret, and to interpret is to engage in a computational process, all of which occurs within the mind/brain.[252]

Another vigorous defender of the Cartesian picture of mind is the philosopher Jerry Fodor. Fodor is an excellent example of a pure cognitivist. Fodor is interested not in the scientific facts about the mind and mental life as much as he is concerned with the proper model of cognitive processes.[253] Here is Fodor's account of the parameters of the field: "Contemporary cognitive psychology is, in effect, a revival of the representational theory of mind. . . .T[he] mind is conceived of as an organ whose function is the man-

---

248. Chomsky, *supra* note 246, at 41–42.

249. NOAM CHOMSKY, LANGUAGE AND PROBLEMS OF KNOWLEDGE 2 (1988).

250. *Id.* at 55. I discuss the plausibility of the notion of "unconscious computation" at *infra* text accompanying notes 268–69. For a thorough rout of this and other assertions by Chomsky, see P.M.S. Hacker, *Chomsky's Problems*, 10 LANGUAGE & COMM. 127 (1990).

251. Additionally,

> [t]he computations involved may be fairly intricate . . . . But since they rely on principles of universal grammar that are part of the fixed structure of the mind/brain, it is fair to suppose that they take place virtually instantaneously and of course with no conscious awareness and beyond the level of possible introspection. In these respects these computations are similar to the complex calculations of the mind/brain that inform me that I am seeing a group of people sitting in a lecture hall, though the actual visual information that my eye receives is limited and chaotic.

CHOMSKY, *supra* note 249, at 90–91.

252. John Searle makes the case that the revolution engineered by Chomsky is over. *See* John Searle, *End of the Revolution*, N.Y. REV. OF BOOKS, Feb. 28, 2002, at 33, 36 (reviewing NOAM CHOMSKY, NEW HORIZONS IN THE STUDY OF LANGUAGE AND MIND (2000)) ("Chomsky has now given up on the idea that Universal Grammar is a matter of unconscious rule-following. But he also dismisses the idea that real human languages are governed by rules. That, I believe, cannot be right.").

253. Fodor has recently expressed doubts about cognitivism's ability to reveal the nature of mind. *See* JERRY FODOR, THE MIND DOESN'T WORK THAT WAY: THE SCOPE AND LIMITS OF COMPUTATIONAL PSYCHOLOGY 100 (2000) ("So far, what our cognitive science has found out about the mind is mostly that we don't know how it works."). For further expression of Fodor's doubts, see Jerry Fodor, *Making the Connection*, TIMES LITERARY SUPPLEMENT, May 17, 2002, at 3 (reviewing JOSEPH LEDOUX, SYNAPTIC SELF: HOW OUR BRAINS BECOME WHO WE ARE (2002)).

ipulation of representations and these, in turn, provided the domain of mental processes and the (immediate) objects of mental states. That's what it is to see the mind as something like a computer."[254]

A final model for the mind (as a computational device) is the computer. If cognitivism is truly a science of mind, then it is only natural to turn to the computer as a model for our own processes of "thinking." As Descombes notes:

> The computer offers, as is often said, a model. The fact that computers are machines—physical systems—provides what would seem to be this model's principal virtue. For the cognitivist hypothesis does not require that the specific operations of human psychology be exactly the same as those of the computer. What matters above all is the assurance that at no point has one taken leave of the physical world.[255]

The most well-known use of a computer in the world of cognitivism is the "Turing test,"[256] invented by the famous mathematician and code-breaker Alan Turing.[257] In 1950, Turing devised a test wherein participants were asked to discriminate between samples produced by a person and those produced by a computer.[258] When participants failed to distinguish between responses by the computer and those of persons, some concluded[259] that the age of the "thinking machine" was upon us.[260]

---

254. JERRY A. FODOR, PSYCHOSEMANTICS: THE PROBLEM OF MEANING IN THE PHILOSOPHY OF MIND 203 (1987). Fodor's model of mind is captured by his phrase "a language of thought." *See* JERRY A. FODOR, THE LANGUAGE OF THOUGHT (1975).

255. DESCOMBES p. 67.

256. For an interesting website devoted to the Turing Test, see The Turing Test Page, *at* http://cogsci.ucsd.edu/~asaygin/tt/ttest.html (last modified Apr. 8, 2002). *See also* B. Jack Copeland, *Church-Turing Thesis*, *in* STANFORD ENCYCLOPEDIA OF PHILOSOPHY, http://plato.stanford.edu/entries/church-turing (last modified Aug. 19, 2002).

257. For a short and elegant discussion of Turing's life, the Turing test, and Turing's code-breaking work, see ANDREW HODGES, TURING (1999). For a superb website on Turing, the man and his accomplishments, see The Alan Turing Home Page, *at* http://www.turing.org.uk/turing/ (last modified Oct. 13, 2002).

258. The point of the test was simple:

> [t]o determine with what frequency people are unable to discriminate between sample output from human beings and sample output from computing machines. If the test results show that the frequency with which the test's subjects can discriminate between the human output and the machine output is statistically insignificant, then the fact that they *cannot* discriminate between these outputs would (it is asserted) mean that *it is right to say that* there is no (essential) difference between a 'thinking' human being and such a sophisticated piece of robotics, and also, therefore, that *it is right to say that* the latter is as much capable of 'thinking' as the former (insofar as the outputs are of the sort which, when produced by human beings would *be said* to involve 'thinking').

GRAHAM BUTTON ET AL., COMPUTERS, MINDS AND CONDUCT 13 (1995).

259. An excellent summary and discussion of the claims for Turing machines is found in John Preston, *Introduction* to VIEWS INTO THE CHINESE ROOM: NEW ESSAYS ON SEARLE AND ARTIFICIAL INTELLIGENCE 1–50 (John Preston & Mark Bishop eds., 2002).

260. Descombes believes the Turing test has a special place in cognitivism because the test bridges the gap between the mental and the material in ways that underwrite and serve the

The Turing Machine, and the success claimed in its name, raise a central philosophical point about just what the Turing Test actually proves.[261] To say that the Turing Test "proves" that machines can think begs the question, "What is thinking?" The Turing Test produced a definite empirical result: participants could not distinguish machine responses. Does this result license the conclusion that because participants could not discriminate between machine and human responses, the Turing Machine "thinks?" The question whether the performance of calculations by a machine shows that "machines think" raises the question of what "thinking" consists of and whether a machine that performs as programmed is really "thinking" at all.[262]

---

reductionist impulses of cognitivism. The impulse for reductionism is the desire to bring human behavior under the explanatory apparatus of natural science (*i.e.*, explanation by resort to natural laws). In short, by reducing the mental to the material, cognitivism makes thinking an (explanatory) object of science. Because the Turing machine is a mechanical device, if the machine shows itself to be capable of "intelligence," then it is possible in theory to reduce "thinking" not so much to a mechanical process but a law-like process that can be replicated on a machine. In short, rationality and thus humanity, become less mysterious and more transparent. Descombes seems disturbed by this:

> The problem is that we have great difficulty in distinguishing rationality and humanity. It is not that we lack imagination: we have never had any difficulty imagining intelligent creatures not of the human species (be they angels or Martians). But when we ask ourselves what makes such creatures seem intelligent to us, we can come up with nothing other than the fact that they speak to us and that we are able to converse with them. It is here, in this manifestation of mind, that intelligence plain and simple tends to be confused with a human form of life.

DESCOMBES p. 115.

261. Fodor, for example, contests the conclusion that a Turing machine can engage in intelligent behavior at all.

> Turing's test, strictly interpreted, does not provide a sufficient condition for successful simulation of human cognitive behavior [since] it could be passed by machines that are incapable of indefinitely many performances that lie well within the capacities of normal humans; performances that may well be argued to constitute types of intelligent behavior. Thus, the ability of a machine to pass Turing's test would not, by any means, entail that it could also obey such simple commands as "Mind the baby while I go shopping." This is in part because the ability of a machine to win at Turing's game would not ensure that the machine is able to integrate the results of its putative mentations with its ongoing behavior in anything like the normal human fashion.

JERRY A. FODOR, PSYCHOLOGICAL EXPLANATION 125 (1968).

262. For clear discussion of this point, see PETER M.S. HACKER, WITTGENSTEIN: MEANING AND MIND 160–70 (1990). The following passage is representative of Hacker's argument:

> One can programme a machine to execute an algorithm. If its parts do not malfunction, its causal connections will ensure the correct output. But what makes the output *correct* is not the causal inevitability with which it is produced. In what seems to be a direct reply to Turing, Wittgenstein wrote:
>
> > Does a calculating machine *calculate*?
> >
> > Imagine that a calculating machine had come into existence by accident; now someone accidentally presses its knobs (or an animal walks over it) and it calculates the product of 25 X 20.
> >
> > I want to say: it is essential to mathematics that its signs are also employed in *mufti*.

B. Critiquing Cognitivism

Strong arguments support the view that cognitivism proceeds from false premises. I think it uncontroversial to observe that above all else, cognitivists of every stripe are committed to the proposition that the best explanations of human action are those that proceed from within the mind/brain. Thus, simple behaviors such as recognizing a friend across a train platform are best explained as a series of neural firings in the brain. It is to the brain that the cognitivist gives credit for "recognition," for it is the brain that is the focus of mental (neural) activity that is taken to constitute "recognition."

Cognitivists err when they construe behaviors such as recognizing, thinking, and understanding (i.e., psychological predicates) in terms of internal processes. It is not my position that when persons engage in human activities, nothing occurs within the brain.[263] My point is conceptual in nature, and it is this: no matter what is going on in one's head, it is fallacious to think that we are right (i.e., free from logical error) to explain human action in terms of these internal operations.[264]

I shall make three arguments. The first of these concerns what is known as the "Homunculus Fallacy." Simply stated, the Homunculus Fallacy is committed when the properties or abilities of a person are attributed to a bodily organ.[265] Second, I shall attack the notion that understanding is the result of the unconscious interpretation of external input. My argument here is not empirical, but it is conceptual: that is, that these claims simply make no

---

> But, one could add, our calculating machines are always in uniform, never in *mufti.* We use these machines (computers) to save us the tedious labour of calculating; but it does not follow, and is indeed nonsense to assert, that the machine infers or draws conclusions.

Id. at 166 (quoting LUDWIG WITTGENSTEIN, REMARKS ON THE FOUNDATIONS OF MATHEMATICS 257 (G.H. von Wright et al. eds., rev. ed. 1978)).

263. *See* WITTGENSTEIN, *supra* note 144, at § 427 (stating that "one is not thinking of brain-processes, but of thought-processes.").

264. *See* M.R. Bennett & P.M.S. Hacker, *Perception and Memory in Neuroscience: A Conceptual Analysis*, 65 PROGRESS IN NEUROBIOLOGY 499, 512–13 (2001):

> Our point, then, is a conceptual one. It makes no sense to ascribe psychological predicates (or their negations) to the brain, save metaphorically or metonymically. The resultant combination of words does not say something that is false, rather, it says nothing at all, for it lacks sense. Psychological predicates are predicates that apply essentially to the whole living animal, not to its parts. It is not the eye (let alone the brain) that sees, but *we* see *with* our eyes (and we do not see *with* our brains, although without a brain functioning normally in respect of the visual system, we would not, of course, see). So too, it is not the ear that hears, but the animal whose ear it is. The organs of an animal are parts of the animal, and psychological predicates are ascribable to the whole animal, not to its constituent parts.

Id.

265. *See* ANTHONY KENNY, THE METAPHYSICS OF MIND 106 (1989) (describing the Homunculus Fallacy as "the attempt to explain human experience and behavior by postulating a little man within an ordinary man").

sense. Finally, and most fundamentally, I will argue that concepts such as recognition, thinking, and understanding (i.e., psychological predicates) can be understood only as "achievement words." In other words, it simply makes no sense to talk about these concepts in terms of inner mental processes. It is only in the context of intersubjective human practices that these terms can be properly understood.[266]

1. The Homunculus Fallacy.—It is an empirical fact that our sense organs are the means by which we gain data about the world. The five senses provide us with a multitude of data which enable us to perform acts as mundane as judging air temperature, as well as more complex activities like calculating the speed of objects in space. But these organs of sense do not perform higher order functions such as seeing, thinking, or ratiocination. To think they do is to commit the Homunculus Fallacy.[267]

When we attribute to an organ capacities only a person can have we commit the Homunculus Fallacy.[268] Descartes provides a perfect example of

---

266. *See* DESCOMBES p. 121.

> The mental processes that interest us . . . can take place inside a head or on a piece of paper. In the sense of the word "mental" that interests the philosophy of mind, so-called mental calculation or calculating in one's head is no more "mental" than are calculations carried out on a chalkboard or on paper. . . . [T]he criteria that allow one to say whether someone has calculated in his head the result of an operation are exactly the same as those one would apply to a calculation done on a sheet of paper. The same could be said about silent reading, about reasoning, about memorization: in each of these cases, one looks at whether the person has calculated correctly (i.e., whether he has found, through his "mental calculation" the result he was supposed to), whether he has read correctly (i.e., whether he has understood what the text says), whether he has come to the correct conclusion or whether he has remembered rightly.

Id.

267. *See* KENNY, *supra* note 265, at 107:

> What is wrong with the homunculus fallacy? In itself, there is nothing misguided in speaking of images in the brain, if one means patterns in the brain which can be mapped on to features of the sensory environment. There is nothing philosophically objectionable in the suggestion that these schematic images may be observable to the neurophysiologist investigating the brain. What is misleading is to say that these images are visible to the soul, and that seeing consists in the soul's perception of these images.
>
> The misleading aspect is that such an account pretends to explain seeing, but the explanation reproduces exactly the puzzling features which it was supposed to explain. For it is only if we think of the relation between a soul and an image in the pineal gland as being just like the relation between a human being and pictures seen in the environment that we will think that talk of an encounter between the soul and the image has any illuminating power at all. As a metaphor, manikin talk may be no more than a harmless necessary fancy; but as an element in a theory a manikin bedevils understanding. For whatever needs explaining in the behaviour of the man turns up, grinning and unexplained, in the shape of the manikin.

Id.

268. Ironically, Winter mentions "an homunculus" but seems unaware of the Homunculus Fallacy. *See* WINTER p. 30 ("Note that, as Edelman points out, topographic connections enable maps to correlate neural responses without any higher-order supervisor. (In philosophical terms,

the fallacy when he makes the pineal gland a mysterious mediator between the world and the human soul.[269] The mind/brain is the modern cognitive analogue to Descartes's pineal gland. Just as the soul encounters images in the pineal gland, the mind/brain performs acts of recognition, understanding, and computation. But is this "personification of bodily organs" anything more than just metaphoric talk, or is something more pernicious afoot?

The mistake the fallacy highlights is the loss of intelligibility. As Descombes asks, if I ask my secretary to write a letter, it is he who "puts his talent and his pen to work for me: he replaces me."[270] But if I write the letter myself, would it make sense to say that my hand is writing the letter for me? Something is awry. Descombes identifies the source of our disquiet:

> When we turn to the brain, the application of the verbs "to write" and "to have someone write" becomes unintelligible. Do we mean to say that I charge my brain with composing and formulating a letter in my stead (i.e., that my brain is a suppositum serving as my auxiliary)? What, then, is the difference between this and the role played by my brain in cases where *I am not* replaced in my writing activity?[271]

In a way, the Homunculus Fallacy is the fallacy of begging the question (*petitio principii*) writ large. Cognitivists want to say that "the brain knows" or "the brain thinks."[272] But this cannot be right. Suppose the details of the flight schedule from Munich to Berlin were "recorded" in the brain.[273] We might say that the brain contained "information." But would it make sense to

---

there is no need to postulate an homunculus or 'little man' inside the brain who directs the action.)").

269. *See* RENE DESCARTES, THE PASSIONS OF THE SOUL (1649), *reprinted in* 1 THE PHILOSOPHICAL WRITINGS OF DESCARTES 325 (John Cottingham et al. trans., 1984).

Descartes provides us a perfect example of the fallacy:

> [I]f we see some animal approaching us, the light reflected from its body forms two images, one in each of our eyes; and these images form two others, by means of the optic nerves, on the internal surface of the brain facing its cavities. Then, by means of the spirits that fill these cavities, the images radiate towards the little gland which the spirits surround; the movement forming each point of one of the images tends towards the same point on the gland as the movement forming the corresponding point of the other image, which represents the same part of the animal. In this way, the two images in the brain form only one image on the gland, which acts directly upon the soul and makes it see the shape of the animal.

Id. at 341–42.

270. DESCOMBES p. 187.

271. *Id.*

272. Consider these remarks by Professor Winter: "The very capacity of the brain to recognize patterns and form concepts depends on these structures. . . ." *Id.* at 15. "The brain is . . . a dynamic associative mechanism whose active correlations shape what we perceive and how we think." *Id.* at 27. "[T]he brain is a self-organizing system . . . ." *Id.* at 32. "[T]he brain *constructs* rather than *mirrors* the reality with which it interacts." *Id.* at 33 (emphasis added). "[T]he brain thinks in terms of its situation, forms its categories in contact with experience, and modifies that situation and that experience by the meaning it thus constitutes." *Id.* at 36.

273. This is a variation on an example in ANTHONY KENNY, THE LEGACY OF WITTGENSTEIN 129 (1984).

say that the brain "knows" the schedule for flights between Munich and Berlin? Could we ask the brain when the next plane for Berlin leaves the Munich airport? We could not. Could the brain be "right" or "wrong" about when the next flight leaves Munich for Berlin? No, it could not. And why not?

The answer is that there is a categorical difference between information and knowledge. As Anthony Kenny reminds us, "[t]o contain information is to be in a certain state, while to know something is to possess a certain capacity."[274] Even if one has a certain capacity, one may act rightly or wrongly, correctly or incorrectly.[275] In addition, there is no single way in which one may express one's knowledge of information.[276] This is why we may conclude that it is only of persons[277] that we may say they see, know, and think.[278]

2. *Always Interpreting?*—Because they attribute capacities to the brain, cognitivists need to explain how the brain performs functions that are only rightly attributed to persons. When cognitivists explain that the brain "recognizes," "knows," or "computes," a process is necessarily postulated. This process, it seems, is unconscious and denominated "interpretation."[279]

---

274. *Id.* at 129. This is not merely a debate about a "form of words" or *façon de parler*. *See* Bennett & Hacker, *supra* note 264, at 516 ("To say that our ordinary talk of the mind is a mere *façon de parler* is *not* to say that there are no minds. On the contrary, it is to insist that there are, but they are not kinds of things. The mind, one might say, adapting a phrase which Wittgenstein used in a different context, is not a *nothing*, but it is not a *something* either.").

275. For example, with knowledge of the flight schedule, one may answer correctly the question "When is the next plane for Berlin?"

276. In addition to answering another's questions about planes and their times of departure, we might use the information to compile a survey of frequency of service between the cities on weekdays versus weekends.

277. *See* WITTGENSTEIN, *supra* note 144, § 281 ("[O]nly of a living human being and what resembles (behaves like) a living human being can one say: it has sensations; it sees; is blind; hears; is deaf; is conscious or unconscious.").

278. *See* KENNY, *supra* note 273, at 130 ("[T]o know is to have the ability to modify one's behaviour in indefinite ways relevant to the pursuit of one's goals. It is because the airline schedule does not have any behaviour to be modified by what is written on it that it does not know what the flight times are.").

279. Once again, Winter's words are representative: "The promise of cognitive theory lies precisely in its ability to make explicit the unconscious criteria and cognitive operations that structure and constitute our judgment." WINTER p. xiii. "These processes of metaphorical inference are performed unconsciously all the time; indeed, they are indispensable to meaning." *Id.* at 51. "Once one recognizes such unconscious processes of metaphorical reasoning, the questions change radically." *Id.* "Constructive interpretation is what we do every time we speak, read, or write. It is the ordinary cognitive process by which one configures new input in a manner that makes sense. . . ." *Id.* at 131. "[W]e unconsciously replicate and maintain our socially constructed contexts." *Id.* at 114.

What is most surprising about Winter's failure to evince any knowledge of the Homunculus Fallacy is the fact that many people in legal theory have made this point for at least the last ten years. *See, e.g.*, BRIAN BIX, LAW, LANGUAGE, AND LEGAL DETERMINACY 196 (1993) (proposing that law can be characterized as both interpretive and descriptive); Martin Stone, *Focusing the Law:*

Again, the ship of cognitivism runs aground on the shoals of sense. It is simply nonsensical to say that the brain performs unconscious acts of cognition through a process of interpretation. Interpretation is an activity we engage in when there is a failure of understanding.[280] Again, a simple example makes the point. If I ask my wife "What time is the next flight to Berlin?"[281] and she replies, "Two flights just took off," I may have to ask what she means to say. But if she replies, "The next flight is at 3 p.m.," no interpretation—unconscious or otherwise—is required.

The cognitivist is committed to the absurd proposition that all understanding requires interpretation. The problem with this assertion is logical in nature.[282] Peter Hacker sums up the dilemma in admirably clear fashion:

What Legal Interpretation is Not, *in* LAW AND INTERPRETATION 31, 80 (Andrei Marmor ed., 1995) (showing that legal judgment does not always require interpretation); Timothy Endicott, *Putting Interpretation in its Place*, 13 LAW & PHIL. 451 (1994) (supporting Marmor's work on interpretation); Dennis Patterson, *The Poverty of Interpretive Universalism: Toward the Reconstruction of Legal Theory*, 72 TEXAS L. REV. 1, 55–56 (1993) (critiquing Dworkin's theory that we make sense of the world through interpretation and arguing that we make sense of the world through activities); ANDREI MARMOR, INTERPRETATION AND LEGAL THEORY 34, 60 (1992) (arguing against the importance of interpretation and supporting legal positivism).

280. Wittgenstein made the point this way:

> "But how can a rule shew me what I have to do at *this* point? Whatever I do is, on some interpretation, in accord with the rule."—That is not what we ought to say, but rather: any interpretation still hangs in the air along with what it interprets, and cannot give it any support. Interpretations by themselves do not determine meaning.

WITTGENSTEIN, *supra* note 144, § 198. *See also* ROBERT B. BRANDOM, MAKING IT EXPLICIT 508–09 (1994) ("Linguistic understanding depends on interpretation . . . only in extraordinary situations—where different languages are involved, or where ordinary communication has broken down."); Jeff Coulter, *Is Contextualising Necessarily Interpretive?*, 21 J. PRAGMATICS 689, 692 (1994) ("Understanding is not an activity: it is akin to an ability. To understand is to have achieved *knowledge* of some kind, whilst interpreting is an activity which is akin to *hypothesis formation* or, in a different sense, to the assignment of significance (explanatory or otherwise) broader than the determination of intelligibility.").

281. Of course, nothing in the cognitivist view precludes cognitivists from believing (indeed, they are committed to believing) that we have to interpret our *own* utterances before we can understand what we ourselves have said!

282. There is a great deal more at stake in the debate over the relationship between understanding and interpretation than correction of a dubious philosophical thesis. As Descombes explains in the following passage, Foucault's central thesis of the ubiquity of power in discourse springs from a hermeneutic sleight of hand:

> If we take away the decorations around the way it is formulated, it boils down to a decision to homogenize the question of sense or meaning. It comes down to saying that there is one and only one passage from *signs* to *meaning*: interpretation. A crucial distinction is thereby lost: that between directly accessible meaning and meaning accessible only by inference. It is the difference between *understanding* and *interpreting*. The hermeneuticist whose philosophy is expressed by Foucault recognizes no difference between the *act* of interpreting, which is an intellectual operation by an active mind, and the fact of understanding, which is neither an act nor a performance but the possession of a *capacity*. This hermeneuticist takes a capacity to be an act and, like the fact of taking the Pireus to be a man, it is an error of category, therefore a metaphysical error. Or, as Wittgenstein would say, a grammatical misunderstanding. We may also note that the distinction in question is also overlooked

> [I]t is a grievous error to think that in understanding an utterance one always or even usually engages in interpretation. To interpret an utterance is to explain it, typically to paraphrase it in the same language or to translate it into a different language. . . . Obscurities, ambiguities or complexities may call out for an interpretation, but it would be wholly incoherent to think that all understanding is interpreting. For then the interpretation given, i.e., the paraphrase, would itself stand in need of an interpretation in order to be understood; and a vicious regress would be generated. This misconception has manifold roots. One is the bizarre idea that what we hear or utter are mere sounds which have to be correlated with or mapped on to meanings in order to be understood. But we no more hear or utter *mere* sounds than we see or paint *mere* patches of colour. We hear and utter meaningful words and sentences. . . .[283]

It seems the cognitivist picture of the nature of human action has backed into a vicious regress. This regress cannot be eliminated or avoided so long as the explanatory realm of human action is limited to the interiority of persons. In other words, to avoid the deleterious consequences of the Homunculus Fallacy and the problem of infinite regress, we must look elsewhere for a proper explanatory vantage point. Let us now turn to this more perspicuous vantage point.

3. *Explaining Human Action.*—We make substantial progress toward a proper view of the nature of human action when we recognize that words like "recognition," "understanding," and "knowing" are best understood not as states of mind but as achievement words.[284] We "know" a fact, or how to do something, when we manifest our ability in action.[285] We free ourselves

---

> by those hermeneuticists inspired not directly by Nietzsche but by Heidegger. For them, too, to understand is already to interpret.

Vincent Descombes, *Nietzsche's French Moment*, *in* WHY WE ARE NOT NIETZSCHEANS 71, 80 (Luc Ferry & Alain Renaut eds., Robert de Loaiza trans., 1997). The distinction in question will on the contrary be familiar to a reader of Wittgenstein. He will also see in this blindness to the difference between an act and a capacity of the mind the effect of an as-yet-unquestioned adherence to the Cartesian philosophy of *cogitatio*. For it is quite precisely in Cartesian philosophy of mind that the differences between acts, states, and capacities are erased in favor of only *conscientia*. *Id.*

283. P.M.S. Hacker, *Language, Rules and Pseudo-Rules*, 8 LANGUAGE & COMM. 159, 168 (1988).

284. This point was made over fifty years ago in GILBERT RYLE, THE CONCEPT OF MIND 149–53 (1949) (arguing that "mind" is a set of capacities manifested in action).

285. Importantly, this is in no way to recommend behaviorism as an explanatory account of the nature of mind. *See* HACKER, *supra* note 262, at 310. Hacker notes:

> It may seem that [Wittgenstein] is a behaviourist in disguise. For is he not denying that anything goes on in the mind and insisting that thinking *is*, or is *reducible* to, just saying or doing? This is wrong. He is denying nothing but the misleading picture of an 'inner (incorporeal) process' that goes with the concept of thinking (cf. PI § 305). 'Thinking' is not the name of an introspectible inner process; but to insist on that is not to deny that people think, nor is it to *equate* thinking with saying or doing. Wittgenstein does not deny that when one is thinking, a variety of things may cross

from the cognitivist picture when we appreciate to the fullest this very simple but powerful insight. It is through what Descombes, explicating Wittgenstein, calls "the exteriorization of the mental"[286] that we will come to see that everything we want to say about mental life can be said without reference to machinations in the mind/brain.[287]

Consider a simple case of mental calculation from the opening sections of Wittgenstein's *Philosophical Investigations*. A man running errands stops in a shop and hands the shopkeeper a slip of paper marked "5 red apples." Descombes asks "what does the shopkeeper do if he proves himself able to understand what is being asked of him? In what does his understanding consist?"[288] The answer is simple, perhaps deceptively so: his understanding consists in handing over 5 red apples. But, the cognitivist will ask, "[H]ow does the shopkeeper get from the three words written on the slip of paper to handing over the apples?"[289] In *Philosophical Investigations*, Wittgenstein gives this answer:

> [T]he shopkeeper . . . opens the drawer marked "apples"; then he looks up the word "red" in a table and finds a colour sample opposite it; then he says the series of cardinal numbers—I assume that he knows them by heart—up to the word "five" and for each number he takes an apple of the same colour as the sample out of the drawer.[290]

Does an "understanding" of the message on the slip of paper require that each of the words on the slip of paper "call to mind a mental object (an image of an apple, an image of a color, an image of the number five)"?[291] Wittgenstein disputes the notion that in order to account for the shopkeeper's understanding, we need to give an account of his internal mental operations.[292]

> one's mind—words, phrases, mental images, and the rest. But a description of *this* 'stream of consciousness' would *not* be a report of what one was thinking or of the *reasoning* underlying the conclusion reached.

Id.

286. DESCOMBES p. 121.

287. For a critique of this view in the context of learning words such as "pain," see GALEN STRAWSON, MENTAL REALITY 215–50 (1994).

288. *Id.* at 121.

289. DESCOMBES pp. 121–22.

290. WITTGENSTEIN, *supra* note 144, § 1.

291. DESCOMBES p. 122.

292. Descombes summarizes the point in the following:

> The shopkeeper demonstrates that he understands the message by carrying out the appropriate operations: he makes use of the words. His linguistic ability is above all a syntactic ability that is given full expression in the order of his actions: he begins by opening the apple drawer, then he seeks out those that meet the condition imposed by the red color sample, then he counts out five of them. In other words, linguistic comprehension is primarily the ability to apprehend the message as a syntactic unit whose elements have functions that are both heterogeneous and complementary. . . . Wittgenstein's analysis is meant to highlight what it is that deserves to be called understanding a message: grasping an order in the application of the different concepts.

But the cognitivist will respond that we cannot really say that the shopkeeper has understood the message on the slip of paper until we have given an account of the mental activities that lie behind his actions. The Wittgensteinian critic—Descombes—will retort that, at some point, such questions become pointless.[293] In short, the meaning of "5" is how the word is used. There is nothing left to explain.

We can, perhaps, see this point more clearly in the context of law. Suppose a judge decides that a baby stroller is not a "vehicle" for purposes of the rule "No vehicles are permitted in the park." The skeptic challenges the judge by asking, "How do you know that a baby stroller does not fall under the concept of 'vehicle' in the rule?" The cognitivist judge replies, "Because I know that 'vehicle' is a radial category and, owing to what I know about prototype effects, ICMs, and tacit knowledge, I know I am right."

Perhaps the most obvious problem with the answers our imaginary judge provides is that the answers beg the question. The question is normative,[294] not empirical.[295] Even if the cognitivist is right about the brain and neural firings, that would explain only *how* we learned the meaning of words. It would never—because it logically could never—answer the question whether we were using our words correctly.[296] No amount of fact—scientific or otherwise—will preclude the need for legal argument.

> In what does the application of a concept consist? The above explanation is the *entire* psychological description of the operation: the words are used according to their meaning, i.e., according to the rules of their application (in the correct order). Understanding that the customer wants apples does not amount to reading the word and thinking about apples, nor does it amount to entering into a relation with the idea of apples: to understand is to open the apple drawer. This gesture is not an external effect indicating that the correct mental association has taken place in the shopkeeper's mind. Rather, it is a manifestation of the shopkeeper's ability to use the word "apple" correctly.

Id. at 122–23.

293. The cognitivist starts from the premise that we cannot explain "understanding" without exploring the inner workings of the mind. Thus, the cognitivist does not even regard it as a *question* whether the very idea of "understanding" could be explicated without resort to the realm of the mental. This is why I began this Essay with the claim that a description of the brain as the focal point of mental activity is not a description but a tendentious thesis.

294. I discuss the normative dimensions of legal argument in Dennis Patterson, *Normativity and Objectivity in Law*, 43 WM. & MARY L. REV. 325 (2001) and in Dennis Patterson, *From Postmodernism To Truth In Law*, 26 HARV. J.L. & PUB. POL. (forthcoming Jan. 2003).

295. Professor Winter insists again and again that "language is an empirical phenomenon" and that empirical evidence can falsify philosophical theories. This is simply incorrect. In fact, every scientist recognizes that before any empirical inquiry (e.g., an experiment) can begin, terms must be defined. *See* FRED N. KERLINGER, FOUNDATIONS OF BEHAVIORAL RESEARCH 26–41 (3d ed. 1986) (discussing constructs, variables, and definitions). This is precisely where philosophical dispute arises. It simply begs the question to insist otherwise.

296. The basic problem is that normativity is not reducible to a neural state. Two examples will prove my point. Consider the following: 2 + 3 = 5. The question "How much does 2 plus 3 equal?" is posed to a child. Additionally, the sums are entered in a computer and in a calculator. The answer that each provides is "5." What makes each answer correct? According to Professor Winter, the correct answer lies within the process that generated the answer. But this is obviously

V. Conclusion

Cognitivism promises a new dawn in our understanding of the mind. Lawyers enamored of cognitivism believe it will provide insights into the nature of law which have previously been unavailable or obscured. None of the claims made on behalf of cognitivism by the works discussed in this Essay withstands scrutiny. In their brief for cognitivism, Amsterdam and Bruner do little more than reprise Legal Realist homilies that have, for good reason, been abandoned. Their promise that cognitivism will improve lawyering skills is empty, even on its own terms. Even if one is persuaded of the truth of their claims about frames and narratives, Amsterdam and Bruner never show how these insights—if they are insights—ever make a difference at the level of lawyering.

Winter's argument for cognitivism is detailed and enthusiastic. While he has managed to assimilate the details from one corner of the cognitivist universe, he fails to show how any of these claims alters current debates in legal theory. The fault for this may not lie with cognitivism for, as we saw, Winter simply does not understand the terms of current debates. But even if he did, fundamental problems remain. Among these problems is the fact that cognitivism fails to illuminate the nature of disagreement in law. No matter how detailed the explication, disagreement about legal outcomes cannot be reduced to cognitive activity. A better understanding of mind may lead to a better understanding of law. Winter has given us neither.

Cognitivists believe the mind is located in the head. The brief against cognitivism is not that the mind is located somewhere other than the head. The argument is more radical: mind is not "located" anywhere.[297]

---

wrong. "5" is the answer because that is the meaning of "plus." But "plus" means the same thing whether the calculation is done in one's head, in a computer, or in a calculator. Again, the question is never how one arrives at the answer; rather, the question is what we mean when we say that an answer is "correct" or "true."

Consider a second example. Joe and Jane are playing chess. Joe and Jane have roughly the same chess ability, but Jane is extraordinary for a simple reason: she is blind. How does Jane play chess? Whatever else we say about her ability, it is certainly the case that Jane plays chess in a manner that is fundamentally different from Joe. Joe can see every piece on the board in front of him, but Jane can see nothing. She must play the game by extraordinary use of the process of memory. This is a task Joe need not undertake. It is no doubt the case that Jane has had to undergo tremendous training to enable her to get to the point where she can play the game of chess as well as Joe. Whatever that training is, and whatever her memory capacity might be, have nothing to do with the answer to the question whether Jane is playing the game of chess well or not. Again, the answer does not lie within (e.g., the mind/brain) but somewhere else.

297. *Cf.* LUDWIG WITTGENSTEIN, THE BLUE AND BROWN BOOKS 7 (1958):

> We say, "surely the thought is *something*; it is not nothing"; and all one can answer to this is, that the word "thought" has its *use*, which is of a totally different kind from the use of the word "sentence".
>
> Now does this mean that it is nonsensical to talk of a locality where thought takes place? Certainly not. This phrase has sense if we give it sense. Now if we say "thought takes place in our heads", what is the sense of this phrase soberly understood? I suppose it is that certain physiological processes correspond to our thoughts in such a

Cognitivism cannot explicate the nature of mental life until its advocates recognize that what we refer to as thinking, believing, and understanding are best explained as human activities, not hidden, internal, cognitive functions.

One of the important contexts for mind is that of law. Law is a matter of argument.[298] Cognitivism purports to explain legal reasoning by reference to hidden processes that lie within the mind/brain. It may be true that a better understanding of mind will give us a better understanding of law. There is no reason to believe that cognitivism will give us a better understanding of either.

> way that if we know the correspondence we can, by observing these processes, find the thoughts. But in what sense can the physiological processes be said to correspond to thoughts, and in what sense can we be said to get the thoughts from the observation of the brain?

Id.

298. For discussion, see PATTERSON, *supra* note 194, at 169–79 (outlining the structure of legal argument); PHILIP BOBBITT, CONSTITUTIONAL INTERPRETATION 11–22 (1991) (identifying six modalities of constitutional argument).

[7]
Normativity and Objectivity in Law

TABLE OF CONTENTS

The agreement of people in calculation is not an agreement in opinions or convictions.
-Ludwig Wittgenstein[1]

* Distinguished Professor of Law, Rutgers University, School of Law (Camden).

For comments on drafts of this Article, I thank Brian Bix, Michael Carrier, Kim Ferzan, Beth Hillman, Tom Morawetz, Jefferson White, and Meredith Williams.

1. LUDWIG WITTGENSTEIN, REMARKS ON THE FOUNDATIONS OF MATHEMATICS VI-30 (G.H. von Wright Rush et al. eds., rev. ed. 1978) [hereinafter WITTGENSTEIN, FOUNDATIONS].

INTRODUCTION

The protagonists battle on. Trumpeting right answers,[2] foundations,[3] and truth,[4] objectivists lash out against the unrelenting tide of nihilism, postmodernism, and deconstruction.[5] Armed with the tools of literary theory, antifoundationalism, and Kuhnian[6] "relativism," subjectivists[7] dismiss the dreams of objectivism as philosophical illusions. But the "conflict" between these two camps is vastly overstated. In fact, the entire debate depends upon a shared premise, one that is both false and unnecessary. The objectivism/subjectivism debate assumes a picture of mind and law that should be extirpated rather than explicated.[8] In this Article, I argue in favor of objectivity but do so

---

2. RONALD DWORKIN, TAKING RIGHTS SERIOUSLY (1977) [hereinafter DWORKIN, SERIOUSLY] (arguing that even in so-called "hard cases" there is a right answer to every legal question).

3. For a discussion of the work of Michael Moore, see *infra* notes 23-25 and accompanying text.

4. Dworkin must be given credit here, for he was the first to notice the connection between questions of "truth" in the philosophy of language and issues in jurisprudence. Ronald Dworkin, *Introduction*, *in* THE PHILOSOPHY OF LAW 1 (Ronald Dworkin ed., 1977) ("Even the debate about the nature of law, which has dominated legal philosophy for some decades, is, at bottom, a debate within the philosophy of language and metaphysics.").

5. Although certainly not an objectivist, Ronald Dworkin does give voice to the impatience felt by some in the objectivist camp. Ronald Dworkin, *Objectivity and Truth: You'd Better Believe It*, 25 PHIL. PUB. AFF. 87, 87 (1996):

> Is there any objective truth? Or must we finally accept that at bottom, in the end, philosophically speaking, there is no "real" or "objective" or "absolute" or "foundational" or "fact of the matter" or "right answer" truth about anything, that even our most confident convictions about what happened in the past or what the universe is made of or who we are or what is beautiful or who is wicked are just our convictions, just conventions, just ideology, just badges of power, just the rules of the language games we choose to play, just the product of our irrepressible disposition to deceive ourselves that we have discovered out there some external, objective, timeless, mind-independent world what we have actually invented ourselves, out of instinct, imagination and culture?

6. THOMAS S. KUHN, THE STRUCTURE OF SCIENTIFIC REVOLUTIONS (2d ed. 1970) (arguing that scientific knowledge is a function of a "paradigm" of scientific inquiry).

7. For more on the particulars of subjectivism, see *infra* notes 33-52 and accompanying text.

8. Objectivism and subjectivism (relativism) need each other: without its opposite, neither position would get off the ground. *See* BRIAN FAY, CONTEMPORARY PHILOSOPHY OF SOCIAL SCIENCE 220 (1996):

> [O]bjectivism and relativism are not true opposites; indeed, they exist on the same spectrum albeit at opposite ends. Both assume that objectivity requires

from a more perspicuous framework. I seek to change the terms of the debate from one of mind to one of action. After this change is effected, the current debate will simply fade away, and a new, more revealing focus shall take its place.

Objectivity is often theorized as a relationship between an assertion and some state of affairs in virtue of which the assertion is "objectively true."[9] The nub of the argument is that assertions or beliefs are true in virtue of the way things are (i.e., facts).[10] Facts make assertions and beliefs true, and objectively so, for facts are not mere matters of mind: they are a function of the way things are.[11] By conceptualizing objectivity in terms of a connection

> unmediated access to the world, the only difference between them being that objectivists believe this access attainable at least in theory, while relativists deny this access attainable even in theory. Objectivism and relativism are simply opposite sides of the very same coin.

9. This is "the venerable notion that truth is the property of *corresponding with reality*." PAUL HORWICH, TRUTH 8 (2d ed. 1998). For a succinct discussion of the correspondence theory of truth in a wider context of theories, see Paul Horwich, *Theories of Truth*, *in* BLACKWELL COMPANION TO METAPHYSICS 491-96 (Jaegwon Kim & Ernest Sosa eds., 1995).

10. Objectivity and truth are often seen as metaphysically related. Andrei Marmor, *Three Concepts of Objectivity*, *in* LAW AND INTERPRETATION 177, 181 (Andrei Marmor ed., 1995) ("Objectivity in the metaphysical sense ... implies that there is a truth of the matter consisting in the fact that there is an object with properties corresponding to its description by the statement in question."); NICOS STAVROPOULOS, OBJECTIVITY IN LAW (1996) (discussing the links between law and metaphysics).

11. John Searle is one staunch defender of a strong conception of objectivity. JOHN R. SEARLE, THE SOCIAL CONSTRUCTION OF REALITY (1995). He argues:

> [T]wo senses are crucial, an *epistemic* sense of the objective-subjective distinction and an *ontological* sense. Epistemically speaking, "objective" and "subjective" are primarily predicates of judgments. We often speak of judgments as being "subjective" when we mean that their truth or falsity cannot be settled "objectively," because the truth or falsity is not a simple matter of fact but depends on certain attitudes, feelings, and points of view of the makers and the hearers of the judgment. An example of such a judgment might be, "Rembrandt is a better artist than Rubens." In this sense of "subjective," we contrast such subjective judgments with objective judgments, such as the judgment "Rembrandt lived in Amsterdam during the year 1632." For such objective judgments, the facts in the world that make them true or false are independent of anybody's attitudes or feelings about them. In this epistemic sense we can speak not only of objective judgments but of *objective facts*. Corresponding to objectively true judgments there are objective facts. It should be obvious from these examples that the contrast between epistemic objectivity and epistemic subjectivity is a matter of degree.
>
> In addition to the *epistemic* sense of the objective-subjective distinction, there is also a related ontological sense. In the ontological sense, "objective" and "subjective" are predicates of entities and types of entities, and they ascribe

between a belief or assertion and a mind-independent state of affairs, proponents of objectivity all but guarantee creation of objectivism's opposite, subjectivism. Subjectivists deny the efficacy of the objectivist account of the relation between mind and world, locating the seat of truth and belief in the individual subject. The debate is intractable.

I argue that the choice between objectivism and subjectivism is false. Just because we are free to describe a situation in a variety of ways (rejecting objectivism)[12] does not dictate the conclusion that, within each vocabulary, there are no standards for correct and incorrect assertion (rejecting subjectivism).[13] I propose to approach objectivity from the point of view of normativity. By "normativity" I mean to identify the ways in which speakers of a language appraise assertoric utterances in terms of "correct" and "incorrect" or "true" and "false." I want to replace the conventional understanding of objectivity with an account of the notion that grows out of the actual practice of law. My claim is that the normativity and objectivity of legal judgment is a function not of the way the world is, but is forged in community agreement over time. Action, not mind, is the basis of this alternative approach to normativity and objectivity.

Law exhibits an argumentative framework employed by participants in legal practice to show the truth of legal propositions.[14] Identifying this framework, and describing how it is

> modes of existence. In the ontological sense, pains are subjective entities, because their mode of existence depends on being felt by subjects. But mountains, for example, in contrast to pains, are ontologically objective because their mode of existence is independent of any perceiver or any mental state.

Id. at 8.

12. I argue against the idea that any given discourse or vocabulary is "primary." This second-order or "meta" perspective is the philosophical pretension I wish to deny. For an excellent recent discussion of this issue in the context of ongoing struggles between practitioners of analytic and continental philosophy, see Richard Rorty, *Being That Can Be Understood is Language*, LONDON REVIEW OF BOOKS, Mar. 16, 2000, at 23-25 (book review) (arguing against the view that any language or discourse—e.g., the language of science—enjoys ontological privilege).

13. In other words, "propositions, true or false, are *indexed* to some conceptual scheme or schemes." MICHAEL P. LYNCH, TRUTH IN CONTEXT: AN ESSAY ON PLURALISM AND OBJECTIVITY 21 (1998).

14. For discussion of propositions of law and claims to truth, see RONALD DWORKIN, LAW'S EMPIRE 4 (1986) [hereinafter DWORKIN, EMPIRE] ("Let us call 'propositions of law' all the

used to appraise propositions of law, is a central feature of my argument. Objectivity is a product of the recursive use of this argumentative framework. I shall describe the framework in detail, explain how action, not mind, is the central feature of normativity, and then explain both the presence and limits of objectivity in law.

This Article has five parts. I begin by describing the current state of the objectivity debate in legal theory.[15] The two leading positions, objectivism and subjectivism, are discussed in the context of exemplary examples of each position. The conclusion of this part of the Article is that the debate between objectivism and subjectivism rests on a false premise. Having identified that premise, I explain in Part II why normativity can best be thought of in social rather than cognitive terms. Here I discuss the oft-trodden topic of rule-following[16] to set the stage for Part III, where I argue for the social basis of normativity. In Part IV, we reach the practice of law. Here I detail why a social approach to normativity provides a more perspicuous account of the nature of objectivity in legal practice. Finally, in Part V, I consider possible objections to my account of normativity and objectivity. Specifically, I explain why law seems less objective than practices such as science and arithmetic.[17]

---

various statements and claims people make about what the law allows or prohibits or entitles them to have.").

15. The discussion of the current state of the debate is broader than that found in analytic jurisprudence, although I believe analytic jurisprudence is the place where one finds the most well-developed positions. That said, analytic philosophy does not comprise the entire field of legal theory. The discussion of objectivity, as well as related topics such as interpretation, indeterminacy, and linguistic meaning, is much wider than what is captured in the discourse of analytic philosophers. I think it important to consider this wider perspective in any discussion of objectivity. A recent and quite successful example of such an approach is GUYORA BINDER & ROBERT WEISBERG, LITERARY CRITICISMS OF LAW (2000) (presenting a sophisticated and wide-ranging discussion of literary and philosophical approaches to the reading of texts).

16. The discussion in Part II centers around two logically distinct forms of explanation: causal and normative. My argument is that normative explanation is logically distinct from, and not reducible to, the language of causal explanation. For a discussion of the variety of forms of explanation, see DANIEL LITTLE, VARIETIES OF SOCIAL EXPLANATION (1991).

17. For an argument that law is less objective than naturalistic inquires such as the natural sciences, see Brian Leiter, *Objectivity and the Problems of Jurisprudence*, 72 TEX. L. REV. 187 (1993) (reviewing KENT GREENAWALT, LAW AND OBJECTIVITY (1992)). *See also* Jules L. Coleman & Brian Leiter, *Determinacy, Objectivity and Authority*, 142 U. PA. L. REV. 549 (1993) (arguing for an account of law as "modestly objective").

I. OBJECTIVISM AND SUBJECTIVISM

Current discussions of objectivity in the jurisprudential literature come down to the question of grounds for legal judgments.[18] There are two views, in both the philosophical and jurisprudential literature, that dominate the discussion. These views—which I will label "objectivism" and "subjectivism"—name two radically distinct approaches to the question of what it means to follow a normative standard such as a legal rule.[19] Before we can consider a fresh approach to the question of normativity and the possibility of objectivity in law, thorough familiarity with the leading views in the objectivity debate is both necessary and appropriate.

A. Objectivism

When we look at various applications of a rule, it is quite natural to ask "In what sense are these different applications each an application of the same rule?" This question is an aspect of a broader philosophical inquiry, namely how are we able to look at a variety of different objects and say "These are the same." Consider fruit. If the rule in question is "Only fruit will be served for snacks," then we know the following items may be served: oranges, bananas, peaches, and grapes. This all seems quite straightforward. What is the philosophical issue?[20] The philosopher asks "In virtue of what

18. These include questions about what the law permits or requires; whether a given legal standard has been violated; or whether a judge's decision is correct as a matter of law.

19. Everything said herein about rules applies equally well to principles and policies. In some jurisprudential theories, distinctions among types of legal norms makes a difference. *E.g.*, DWORKIN, SERIOUSLY, *supra* note 2, at 22 (arguing that rules and principles are logically distinct). Nothing I say turns on such distinctions.

20. The philosophical debate has traditionally been framed in terms of Realism and Nominalism. For example, Renford Bambrough explains that:

> It is assumed as obvious by both the nominalist and the realist that there can be no objective justification for the application of a general term to its instances unless its instances have something in common over and above their having in common that they *are* its instances. The nominalist rightly holds that there is no such additional common element, and he therefore wrongly concludes that there is no objective justification for the application of any general term. The realist rightly holds that there is an objective justification for the application of general terms, and he therefore wrongly concludes that there must be some additional common element.

are all these items 'fruits'?" Or, put differently, the philosopher might ask "What is it about all these items that makes them properly called 'fruits'?"

The first answer we shall consider comes from the objectivist. It is not enough for the objectivist that all these things are *called* fruits. The objectivist believes that they are all called fruits because they are, in some sense, *really* fruits.[21] What, one might ask, is the difference between something merely being called a fruit and it, in fact, being a fruit? To this question the objectivist has a distinct and well-wrought answer.

When we set out to follow a rule, we never believe that whether we have complied with the rule is a matter of opinion. We may believe that we have complied with the dictates of a rule, but that belief cannot be grounds for our claim that we have in fact complied. This shows that rules exhibit what we might term "epistemic primacy." By this, I mean that the broad application of rules "seems to imply a standard of correctness that is independent of applications."[22] To explain this phenomenon, the objectivist asserts the existence of a standard independent of the rule which enables rule application in a variety of contexts. Let us consider a jurisprudential example.

More than anyone, Michael Moore has championed the objectivist position[23] in modern analytic jurisprudence.[24] Moore explicitly

---

Renford Bambrough, *Universals and Family Resemblances*, *in* WITTGENSTEIN: THE PHILOSOPHICAL INVESTIGATIONS 199 (George Pitcher ed., 1968).

21. Ronald Dworkin makes frequent use of the word "really" in sentences such as the following: "[*Riggs v. Palmer*] was a dispute about what the law was, about what the real statute the legislators enacted really said." DWORKIN, EMPIRE, *supra* note 14, at 20. In putting the matter as he does, Dworkin hints that there may be a difference between what we may *think* the law requires and what the law "really" requires. Does Dworkin thereby intend to suggest a realist jurisprudence? The point is that such phrasing suggests at least the possibility of a gap between the way things are (i.e., what the law "really" requires) and the way things seem to be (i.e., what we think the law requires). My point is that such a distinction is vacuous. Despite his hinting otherwise, Dworkin never attempts to supply the metaphysical scaffolding to support his hints at realism.

22. MEREDITH WILLIAMS, WITTGENSTEIN, MIND AND MEANING 158 (1998).

23. Moore self-identifies his position as "realism." His view is certainly "realist" in the sense that he believes "reality" is mind-independent and has a structure which, in principle, can be grasped by the mind. For a definition of "realism," see MICHAEL DUMMETT, TRUTH AND OTHER ENIGMAS 146 (1978) ("Realism I characterise as the belief that statements of the disputed class possess an objective truth-value, independently of our means of knowing it: they are true or false in virtue of a reality existing independently of us."). I think Moore is

rejects the claim that the meaning of our words turns on anything but a standard of correctness independent of our discourse. Consider his treatment of the concept of "death." He writes:

> A realist theory asserts that the meaning of "death," for example, is not fixed by certain conventions. Rather, a realist theory asserts that "death" refers to a natural kind of event that occurs in the world and that it is not arbitrary that we possess some symbol to name this thing. (It may be arbitrary *what* symbol we assign to name this class of events, but it is not arbitrary that we have *some* symbol to name it). Our intentions when we use the word "death" will be to refer to this natural kind of event, whatever its true nature might turn out to be. We will guide our usage, in other words, not by some set of conventions we have agreed upon as to when someone will be said to be dead; rather, we will seek to apply "dead" only to people who are really dead, which we determine by applying the best scientific theory we can muster about what death really is.
>
> ....
>
> Finally, a realist theory of meaning will not view a change in our conventions about when to apply a word as a change in its meaning. If we supplant "heart stoppage" with "revivability" as our indicator of "death," we will do so because we believe revivability to be a part of a *better* theory of what death is than

---

more an "objectivist" than a "realist." Objectivism presupposes realism, but realism in no way entails or requires it. Objectivists share with realists the view that the world exists beyond our ideas and quite apart from anything we may believe about it. But the objectivist believes not only that the world exists independently of our ideas of it, but that the world has an order or structure that is, in principle, discernible. That said, not all objectivists adhere to the same set of philosophical ideals. The following is a description of "pure objectivism":

> [O]bjectivism is a complex of ideas. It includes a realist ontology; a positivist epistemology; a correspondence theory of truth and scientific progress; and an axiology of disinterest. Within this complex, objectivity is conceived as a property of the results of inquiry, namely the property of these results being true. A theory or a fact is said to be objective if it fits with reality as it is in itself. Secondarily, persons or methods are said to be objective if they eliminate the subjective elements which typically prevent achieving objective truth.

FAY, *supra* note 8, at 204.

24. For a position with objectivist aspirations, see Brian Leiter, *Objectivity, Morality, and Adjudication*, *in* OBJECTIVITY IN LAW AND MORALS 66, 88 (Brian Leiter ed., 2000) ("Objective domains must generally answer to the world at some point: only then can we distinguish between mere hegemonic conventions from practices of argument about genuinely objective domains.").

> heart stoppage. We will not have changed the meaning of "death" when we substitute one theory for another, because by "death" we intended to refer to the naturally occurring kind of thing, whatever the true nature of the event turned out to be. Our linguistic intentions are constant, on the realist theory, even if our scientific theories change considerably.[25]

In *Philosophical Investigations*, Wittgenstein characterizes views like Moore's as advancing a "rules on rails" thesis.[26] The idea is that the applications of a rule extend into the future much as a rail extends the length and direction of a train. The train (rule) is connected to the rail (the essential property or natural kind term) and proceeds in a predetermined direction. The rule operates "as if" it were on a rail in that future applications of the rule (its extension) are already determined by the independent property (e.g., the natural kind term).

Wittgenstein reveals a basic problem with this picture (of a mind grasping an objective standard) of what it means to follow a rule with the argument that even if there were a standard like that imagined by the objectivist, the standard would be of no use to us unless we knew how to use it.[27] And once we entertain the question

25. Michael S. Moore, *A Natural Law Theory of Interpretation*, 58 S. CAL. L. REV. 277, 294 (1985).

26. LUDWIG WITTGENSTEIN, PHILOSOPHICAL INVESTIGATIONS § 218 (G.E.M. Anscombe trans., 2d ed. 1967) [hereinafter WITTGENSTEIN, INVESTIGATIONS] ("And infinitely long rails correspond to the unlimited application of a rule."). John McDowell characterizes the view this way:

> What counts as doing the same thing, within the practice in question, is fixed by its rules. The rules mark out rails along which correct activity within the practice must run. These rails are there anyway, independently of the responses and reactions a propensity to which one acquires when one learns the practice itself; or, to put the idea less metaphorically, it is in principle discernible, from a standpoint independent of the responses that characterize a participant in the practice, that a series of correct moves in the practice is really a case of going on doing the same thing. Acquiring mastery of the practice is pictured as something like engaging mental wheels with these objectively existing rails.

John McDowell, *Non-Cognitivism and Rule-Following*, *in* STEVEN HOLTZMAN & CHRISTOPHER LEICH, WITTGENSTEIN: TO FOLLOW A RULE 145-46 (1981).

27. *See* JOHN MCDOWELL, PROJECTION AND TRUTH IN ETHICS 11 (1987) (arguing that "we have some way of telling what can count as a fact, prior to and independent of asking what forms of words might count as expressing truths, so that a conception of facts could exert some leverage in the investigation of truth").

of how to use the "objective standard," the whole point of the exercise evaporates.[28] Put differently, the problem is that anything that serves as a standard can be variously interpreted.[29] And if a standard is amenable to various interpretations, one interpretation must be chosen. But the standard does not tell us which interpretation is the "correct" one. Thus, the very thing (the objective standard) introduced to solve the problem serves only to recapitulate the dilemma.[30]

Thus, objectivism fails. What to do? One possibility is to embrace objectivism's opposite, that is, subjectivism. There are of course, many meanings to subjectivism, with possible candidates ranging from deconstruction[31] to idealism.[32] In addition to questioning the determinacy of linguistic meaning, subjectivist positions all embrace the view that linguistic meaning is located in the individual subject. Let us now turn to an example of this view.

B. Subjectivism

If objectivity is unattainable, then what? A favorite alternative—subjectivism—is well-represented in contemporary legal theory. The positions are various, to be sure. Yet each seems to make the failure of objectivism the starting point of analysis. An oft-quoted expression of this view is found in the work of Joseph Singer:

---

28. *See* Jeremy Waldron, *The Irrelevance of Moral Objectivity*, *in* NATURAL LAW THEORY 158 (Robert P. George ed., 1992) (arguing against the usefulness of meta-ethics based on metaphysical realism).

29. Hilary Putnam argues that the problem may be even deeper than I suggest:

> [E]ven when we see such a "reality" as a tree, the possibility of that perception is dependent on a whole conceptual scheme in place (one which may or may not legislate an answer to such questions as "Is the tree identical with the space-time region that contains it?" and "Is the tree identical with the mereological sum of the time-slices of elementary particles that make it up?").

HILARY PUTNAM, REPRESENTATION AND REALITY 113 (1988).

30. Wittgenstein discusses the use of drawn figures and the language of calculation in WITTGENSTEIN, FOUNDATIONS, *supra* note 1, at I-38. I discuss this further in Dennis Patterson, *Wittgenstein and Constitutional Theory*, 72 TEX L. REV. 1837, 1848-49 (1994).

31. *See, e.g.*, JACQUES DERRIDA, OF GRAMMATOLOGY (Gayatri Spivak trans., 1976) (criticizing "logocentrism" and "presence" in Western metaphysics).

32. "Idealism" is "the view that mind is the most basic reality and that the physical world exists only only as an appearance to or expression of mind." CONCISE ROUTLEDGE ENCYCLOPEDIA OF PHILOSOPHY 379 (2000).

> We cannot expect the new to emerge phoenix-like from the old. Traditional legal theorists have assumed that theory is, or should be *determinative*—that the goal of theory is to *generate answers*. For this view to make sense, we must believe that it is possible to find out what to do by thinking in the right way....
>
> But in the end, all the sophisticated versions of theory that seek to describe it as a decision procedure based on a sure foundation are supremely unconvincing; they cannot convince precisely because they are so sophisticated. The dilemma comes down to this: For a theory to generate answers, it must be mechanical, yet no mechanical theory can render an adequate account of our experience of legitimate moral choice. We cannot even escape the dilemma by trying to make some of our choices (the "core") mechanical and some (the "periphery") open-ended: *No* mechanical choices appear to be unequivocally valid.[33]

Bereft of a mechanical decision-procedure for making choices, we are left to our own devices. Our only compasses in a world of indeterminate values, and equally indeterminate meaning, are our own predilections, what has come to be known as our "politics."[34]

There is one figure in the subjectivist camp who affirms the basic tenets of the position but has a totally different response to the

---

33. Joseph W. Singer, *The Player and the Cards*, 94 YALE L.J. 1, 61 (1984). For a similar view, see JEROME FRANK, LAW AND THE MODERN MIND 129 (1963) ("The law is not a machine ...."). A superb critique of the skeptical arguments of Critical Legal Studies is found in Christian Zapf & Eben Moglen, *Linguistic Indeterminacy and the Rule of Law: On The Perils of Misunderstanding Wittgenstein*, 84 GEO. L.J. 485 (1996).

34. At least one early champion of the indeterminacy/politics thesis has recently tempered his opinion, stating:

> The radicalization of indeterminacy is ... a mistake; not merely a mistake about law and language but also a mistake about the relation between what the radical indeterminists mean and what they say. Emerging as the all but inexorable outcome of a long progression of ideas, the radicalization of the indeterminacy thesis makes us realize that something has long since gone wrong in the terms of this discussion.
>
> ....
>
> We cannot, just by saying so, turn a political defeat into a word game. We must sacrifice the metaphor to the campaign, and recognize that law can be something, and that it matters what it is. Having rejected the radicalization of indeterminacy as a misstatement of radical intentions, we must then go on to repudiate the central role of the problem of determinacy and discretion in legal theory.

ROBERTO MANGABEIRA UNGER, WHAT SHOULD LEGAL ANALYSIS BECOME? 121-22 (1996).

"problem." I have in mind Stanley Fish. Although it is certainly true that Fish's views have gone through a number of iterations,[35] he has consistently adhered to a basic hermeneutic[36] theme: all understanding is interpretation. The following is representative:

> The point is a simple one: All shapes are interpretively produced, and since the conditions of interpretation are themselves unstable—the possibility of seeing something in a "new light," and therefore of seeing a *new* something, is ever and unpredictably present—the shapes that seem perspicuous to us now may not seem so or may seem differently so tomorrow. This applies not only to the shape of statutes, poems, and signs in airplane lavatories, but to the disciplines and forms of life within which statutes, poems, and signs become available to us.[37]

---

35. The following summary of the evolution of Fish's thought is instructive:

> Stanley Fish ... has long since committed himself to the initial assertions of reader-response criticism and ... continues to do so but, by changing his position a number of times, has struggled with the kinds of unacceptable consequences of those assertions.... But his latest reformulation [STANLEY FISH, IS THERE A TEXT IN THIS CLASS? (1980)], which is offered as if no more than a refinement, amounts in fact to his abandoning its essentials completely. His most recent version, then, involves the postulation of interpretive communities, with assumptions and conventions that guide interpretation; this, in his view, allows communication to take place and so rescues him from the consequences of earlier formulations. Now it is, of course, true that a text means nothing without conventions shared by the speakers of the language concerned, but to acknowledge this *fully* would, as Fish sees, abolish his reader-response position: if readers are guided by the rules of language, they do not have the freedom envisaged by reader-response theory, and so the text together with its relation to the linguistic system can be the place to which disputes are appealed after all, contrary to the statement by Fish that I cited. In order to continue to cling to his reader-response position, then, Fish continues to deny that it is sharing a language and "knowing the meanings of individual words and the rules for combining them" that is involved in communication but, instead, a "way of thinking, a form of life." But this direct denial that the shared rules of language makes communication possible is surely bizarre, and the distinction he makes here is certainly untenable. Oddly enough, Fish's language here recalls Wittgenstein's, but in using it Wittgenstein was pointing out precisely that a language with its rules, conventions, and agreements *is* a way of thinking and form of life!

JOHN ELLIS, AGAINST DECONSTRUCTION 121 n.6 (1989).

36. For discussion of the hermeneutic tradition, see *infra* note 43.

37. STANLEY FISH, DOING WHAT COMES NATURALLY: CHANGE, RHETORIC, AND THE PRACTICE OF THEORY IN LITERARY AND LEGAL STUDIES 302 (1989).

The meaning of everything is "interpretively produced." The conditions of interpretation themselves are unstable. Therefore, linguistic meaning is unstable. Today's "correct" interpretation is tomorrow's "error." All of this is quite controversial and hotly contested.[38] Having already advanced an in-depth critique of Fish's views,[39] I do not wish to rehash those arguments here. There is, however, an aspect of Fish's thought that is quite widely shared,[40] and that is the idea that the world comes to us through acts of interpretation.[41] The idea is most fully developed[42] in the hermeneutic philosophical tradition,[43] but is a commonplace in

---

38. For a particularly harsh critique of Fish's views, see Terry Eagleton, *The Estate Agent*, LONDON REVIEW OF BOOKS, Mar. 2, 2000, at 10-11 (reviewing STANLEY FISH, THE TROUBLE WITH PRINCIPLE (1999)). An intelligent comparison of Fish and Wittgenstein is found in Charles Altieri, *Going On and Going Nowhere: Wittgenstein and the Question of Criteria in Literary Criticism*, *in* CHARLES ALTIERI, CANONS AND CONSEQUENCES 81-107 (1990) (arguing that Fish's relativism is born, among other things, of a failure to appreciate the normative role of grammar in practices).

39. *See* DENNIS PATTERSON, LAW AND TRUTH 99-127 (1996) [hereinafter PATTERSON, TRUTH]. For an exchange with Fish over my reading of his work, see *Colloquy*, 72 TEX. L. REV. 1-77 (1993) (including article by Patterson, reply by Fish, and rebuttal by Patterson).

40. *See, e.g.*, DRUCILLA CORNELL, THE PHILOSOPHY OF THE LIMIT 101 (1992) ("It is interpretation that gives us the rule, not the other way around."); FREDERICK SCHAUER, PLAYING BY THE RULES 207 (1991) ("*[E]very* application of a rule is also an interpretation."). For an excellent critique of Cornell on interpretation, see Martin Stone, *Focusing the Law: What Legal Interpretation Is Not*, *in* LAW AND INTERPRETATION, *supra* note 10, at 31-96 (discussing the limits of interpretation in law).

41. Fish's jurisprudential nemesis, Ronald Dworkin, shares this view. DWORKIN, EMPIRE, *supra* note 14 (advancing the thesis that "law" is an interpretive practice and that the truth of legal propositions is a matter of interpretation).

42. The idea of interpretation as a function of "perspective" comes from Nietzsche:

> "Everything is subjective," you say; but even this is interpretation. The "subject" is not something given, it is something added and invented and projected beyond what there is.—Finally, is it necessary to posit an interpreter behind the interpretation? Even this is invention, hypothesis.
>
> In so far as the word "knowledge" has any meaning, the world is knowable; but it is *interpretable* otherwise, it has no meaning behind it, but countless meanings.—"Perspectivism."
>
> It is our needs that interpret the world; our drives and their For and Against. Every drive is a kind of lust to rule; each one has its perspective that it would like to compel all the other drives to accept as a norm.

FRIEDRICH NIETZSCHE, THE WILL TO POWER 267 (Walter Kaufmann ed., Walter Kaufmann & R.J. Hollingdale trans., 1968).

43. *See* MICHAEL INWOOD, A HEIDEGGER DICTIONARY 106 (1999).

> Our everyday life is pervaded by interpretation, both of ourselves and of other entities. Everyday, 'circumspect' interpretation is prior to the systematic interpretation undertaken by the humane sciences, and prior to the

contemporary, sophisticated academic thought.[44] This notion, I believe, is philosophically flawed.[45]

> explanations of the natural sciences. A scientist has to find the way to the library or laboratory, and interpret its contents as books or other equipment, before doing any science. According to Heidegger, we interpret all the way down. We do not *first* see uninterpreted black marks on a white background or first hear pure sounds, and *then* interpret them as printing or as speech. We perceive them right away as printed or spoken words, even if we cannot understand them: 'What we "first" hear is never noises or complexes of sounds, but the creaking wagon, the motor-cycle. [...] It requires a very artificial and complicated frame of mind to 'hear' a 'pure noise'. [...] Even where the speech is indistinct or the language unknown, we immediately hear *unintelligible* words, not a multiplicity of tone-data.' Heidegger was at this stage influenced less by Nietzsche and far more by Dilthey, who had in his later writings travelled a good way along Heidegger's own path. The ubiquity of interpretation does not, for Heidegger, imply Nietzschean scepticism. The fact that I immediately interpret speech as speech or a tool as a tool does not entail that my interpretation is unreliable or incorrigible or that it creates the meaning of what is interpreted. At most it undermines the view that interpretations are based on, or answerable to, uninterpreted foundations.

Id. (quotations as in original) (alterations in original) (citation omitted). Heidegger represents the high point in the development of the hermeneutic tradition starting from Dilthey. Although there are certain surface similarities between the thought of Heidegger and Wittgenstein, the commentary just reproduced highlights a key difference in approach to the nature of understanding. Because Heidegger comprehends "understanding" as an internal and personal operation of mind, he remains within the philosophical tradition that starts with Descartes in so far as he locates meaning in the individual. For his part, Wittgenstein's later thought represents a break with the philosophical tradition starting with Descartes in that he locates meaning not within persons but outside them, that is, in public practices. One need only consider Dworkin's approach to legal interpretation to realize that philosophy remains within the grip of the Cartesian picture of mind. *See* DWORKIN, *supra* note 4 (building a theory of law out of a theory of interpretation).

44. *See, e.g.*, the classic collection of interdisciplinary essays in THE POLITICS OF INTERPRETATION (W.J. Thomas Mitchell ed., 1982) (including classic essays by Fish and Dworkin).

45. The notion of meaning being "up for grabs" or "indeterminate" is a pervasive feature of contemporary critical theory, in law and elsewhere. Despite its pervasive character in European thought, this view is coming under increasing scrutiny. The following is a superb critique:

> Is this conception of language viable? If we take away the decorations around the way it is formulated, it boils down to a decision to homogenize the question of sense or meaning. It comes down to saying that there is one and only one passages [sic] from *signs* to *meaning*: interpretation. A crucial distinction is thereby lost: that between directly accessible meaning and meaning accessible only by inference. It is the difference between *understanding* and *interpreting*. The hermeneuticist whose philosophy is expressed by Foucault recognizes no difference between the *act* of interpreting, which is an intellectual operation by an active mind, and the fact of understanding, which is neither an act nor a performance but the possession of a *capacity*. This hermeneuticist takes a

The problem with the interpretivist (subjectivist) response to the failure of objectivism is identified by what has come to be known as the "infinite regress argument."[46] Wittgenstein puts it this way:

> "But how can a rule shew me what I have to do at *this* point? Whatever I do is, on some interpretation, in accord with the rule."—That is not what we ought to say, but rather: any interpretation still hangs in the air along with what it interprets, and cannot give it any support. Interpretations by themselves do not determine meaning.[47]

Why does Wittgenstein question the importance of interpretation for meaning?[48] His point is that if the understanding of an utterance or sign were a matter of advancing an interpretation (which is just another utterance or sign) then the interpretation itself would require its own interpretation, and so on, infinitely.[49]

> capacity to be an act and, like the fact of taking the Pireus to be a man, it is an error of category, therefore a metaphysical error. Or, as Wittgenstein would say, a grammatical misunderstanding. We may also note that the distinction in question is also overlooked by those hermeneuticists inspired not directly by Nietzsche but by Heidegger. For them, too, to understand is already to interpret.

Vincent Descombes, *Nietzsche's French Moment*, *in* WHY WE ARE NOT NIETZSCHEANS 80 (Luc Ferry & Alain Renaut eds., Robert de Loaiza trans., 1997).

46. Saul Kripke made this argument the basis of his controversial reading of Wittgenstein. SAUL A. KRIPKE, WITTGENSTEIN ON RULES AND PRIVATE LANGUAGE (1982) (arguing for a skeptical reading of Wittgenstein's remarks on rule-following). For a legal application of the skeptical misreading of Wittgenstein, see Mark Tushnet, *Following the Rules Laid Down: A Critique of Interpretivism and Neutral Principles*, 96 HARV. L. REV. 781, 825 (1983).

47. WITTGENSTEIN, INVESTIGATIONS, *supra* note 26, § 198; *see also* ROBERT BRANDOM, MAKING IT EXPLICIT 508-09 (1994) ("Linguistic understanding depends on interpretation ... only in extraordinary situations—where different languages are involved, or where ordinary communication has broken down.").

48. Consider James Tully, *Wittgenstein and Political Philosophy*, 17 POL. THEORY 172, 196 (1988):

> [Interpretation] is a practice we engage in when our understanding and use of signs is in some way problematic or in doubt. Here we attempt to come to an understanding of the sign in question by offering various interpretations (expressions) as opposed to different ones, adjudicating rival interpretations, in some cases calling the criteria of adjudication into question, and so on.... Interpretation should thus be seen as one important practice of critical reflection among many, resting comfortably in more basic ways of acting with words (self-understandings) that cannot themselves be interpretations.

49. Wittgenstein makes a second argument about interpretation which builds on the

The infinite regress argument is not designed to, and should not, move us to a point of frustration or failure. Rather, Wittgenstein urges us to rethink the notion that before we can understand an utterance we must first interpret it. As he says, "there is a way of grasping a rule which is *not* an *interpretation* ...."[50]

There are few voices in contemporary legal theory speaking on behalf of objectivism.[51] More vocal, and more numerous, are the voices of subjectivism.[52] Subjectivism, I have argued, is a natural response to the failure of objectivism. Its ubiquity notwithstanding, subjectivism is a troubled and troubling philosophical stance. Whatever one's metaphysics, subjectivism eats away at our aspirations for law. We want law to be more than opinion, collective or otherwise. The question whether a legal standard has or has not been violated should turn on more than the caprice of who is asked

---

regress argument. This is the paradox of interpretation.

> This was our paradox: no course of action could be determined by a rule, because every course of action can be made out to accord with the rule. The answer was: if everything can be made out to accord with the rule, then it can also be made out to conflict with it. And so there would be neither accord nor conflict here.

WITTGENSTEIN, INVESTIGATIONS, *supra* note 26, § 201. The paradox is that "[g]iven the fact of multiple interpretations, for any action, that action can be characterized both in a way that accords with a given rule and conflicts with it—even if the interpretation of the rule itself were transparent." WILLIAMS, *supra* note 22, at 160. It is perhaps due to the difficulties presented by the paradox of interpretation that Wittgenstein introduces the idea of a practice. Anthony O'Hear states that:

> It is my contention that Wittgenstein introduces the practice of a community into his analysis of rule-following in order to put a stop to the difficulties that arise from the insight that on some interpretation, anything can be seen as following from a rule, difficulties which would dog my individualistic attempt to follow out the implications of a self-imposed rule, whether or not I was interested in communicating my understanding of the rule to others.

Anthony O'Hear, *Wittgenstein and the Transmission of Traditions*, *in* WITTGENSTEIN CENTENNARY ESSAYS 41, 47 (1991).

50. WITTGENSTEIN, INVESTIGATIONS, *supra* note 26, § 201.

51. Other than Michael Moore, I would note only Ernest Weinrib. ERNEST WEINRIB, THE IDEA OF PRIVATE LAW (1995) (arguing for an inherent moral order to private law).

52. There are many facets of subjectivism, from the rejection of objectivity as a value to the embrace of "identity politics" in legal theory. Movements or schools of thought include Critical Race Theory, strong versions of "narrative" scholarship, and proponents of radical indeterminacy. Exemplars are mentioned in Richard A. Posner, *The Skin Trade*, THE NEW REPUBLIC, Oct. 13, 1997, at 40-43 ("Every intellectual movement has a lunatic fringe. Radical legal egalitarianism is distinguished by having a rational fringe and a lunatic core.") (reviewing DANIEL A. FARBER & SUZANNA SHERRY, BEYOND ALL REASON: THE RADICAL ASSAULT ON TRUTH IN AMERICAN LAW (1997)).

to decide the matter. Providing an alternative to objectivism that avoids the excesses of subjectivism is the task at hand. Let us turn to that endeavor.

II. FORMS OF EXPLANATION: CAUSAL AND NORMATIVE

Objectivism and subjectivism are both attempts to explain the normativity of rule-following. Objectivism searches for the means by which disparate applications of a rule (or concept) can be said to be applications of the "same" standard. Subjectivism despairs of ever finding the Holy Grail of objectivism and resorts to individual and collective subjectivity to explain the phenomenon of rule-following and, hence, normativity. Despite their differences, objectivism and subjectivism share one fundamental: each theory adheres to the thesis that rule-following is an operation of mind. For the objectivist, the mind grasps the external measure of compliance. For the subjectivist, rule-following is the result of individual proclivity or the consensus of similarly-inclined subjects.

The central insight that enables us to break free of the existing debate is this: rule-following is not a mental phenomenon. Consistent with his critique of psychologism, Wittgenstein relocates normativity in action, specifically social action. A complete articulation of normativity as a social phenomenon leads to a surprising result: a new conception of objectivity.[53] As we shall see, objectivity is neither a property, nor a relation: it is a collective achievement. In short, objectivity is produced and not found.

In *Philosophical Investigations*, Wittgenstein overcomes the limits of the objectivism/subjectivism debate by asking a different question. This question enables him to break new ground in our understanding of normativity and, ultimately, objectivity. He writes:

> Let me ask this: what has the expression of a rule—say a sign-post—got to do with my actions? What sort of connexion is there here?—Well, perhaps this one: I have been trained to react to this sign in a particular way, and now I do so react to it.[54]

53. *See infra* notes 110-38 and accompanying text.

54. WITTGENSTEIN, INVESTIGATIONS, *supra* note 26, § 198.

The remark is met with an immediate objection from Wittgenstein's imaginary interlocutor: "But that is only to give a causal connexion; to tell how it has come about that we now go by the sign-post; not what this going-by-the-sign really consists in."[55] But Wittgenstein's point is that the sign-post exists as such by virtue not of training but by virtue of a social practice, a custom.[56] He states: "On the contrary; I have further indicated that a person goes by a sign-post only insofar as there exists a regular use of sign-posts, a custom."[57] What Wittgenstein is pointing to here is the connection between meaning and training. The meaning of the signpost is a "social" meaning: it is in the regular *use* of the signpost that normativity (correct and incorrect use of the signpost) is established. And how do we understand "correct" and "incorrect?" This is where training comes in. Wittgenstein maintains that the key to normativity lies in the ways in which we have been trained to respond to the sign or rule. The philosophical challenge is to extract an account of normativity from the details of training.

Normativity is concerned not with how we make judgments of correctness and incorrectness, but in what those judgments consist.[58] An example will help make the point. Consider a chess

---

55. *Id.* The mistake identified here is often made. The error lies in trying to explain how to do something correctly or incorrectly by appealing to a causal story regarding training. A good example of this is Stanley Fish's use of the idea of "interpretive communities." Fish accounts for different persons being in the same interpretive community by appealing to a story about training. FISH, *supra* note 37, at 141 (In addition to facility in a language, one needs to be in possession of a certain structure of interests, described by Professor Fish as "distinctions, categories of understanding, and stipulations of relevance and irrelevance ...." These are acquired, Professor Fish tells us, "only after one has 'passed through a professional initiation or course of training' whose effect is to homogenize persons who were disparate and heterogeneous before entering—and becoming inhabited by—the community's ways."). The problem is that the narrative about training does not illuminate *what* seeing the world the same way means. It is only an account of the training involved. For a detailed account of this error, see PATTERSON, TRUTH, *supra* note 39, at 99-127.

56. Wittgenstein's conclusion is that "'obeying a rule' is a practice." WITTGENSTEIN, INVESTIGATIONS, *supra* note 26, § 202.

57. *Id.* § 198.

58. For discussion of normative explanation, see GORDON B. BAKER & PETER M.S. HACKER, LANGUAGE, SENSE & NONSENSE (1984), who note that:

> A normative explanation, therefore, explains a normative act, a normative situation, or a normative consequence by reference to some relevant rule or aspect of a rule. The manner in which the rule is invoked in, or involved in, the explanation will vary from case to case according to the nature of the question. Since such explanations are not causal (i.e. do not serve as explanations in

match between Smith and Jones. Jones is a good player, but Smith is said to be better. Each time Smith makes a move, he engages in all the normal mental processes that lead up to his decision of which piece to move and where to move it on the board. In addition, Smith has to remember where every other piece is on the board for, as it turns out, Smith is blind.

How Smith makes a correct move (the causal account) is a logically distinct question from whether he makes a correct move (the normative account). When it comes to normativity, our interest is not in how Smith is able to do what he does. This is not to deny that what Smith is able to do is impressive—but from the point of view of normativity, it is of no interest. The reason it is of no interest is that how someone does something does not tell us to what his "doing" amounts, that is, of what it consists, nor does it tell us whether the act is correct or incorrect.[59] Standards for the correct/incorrect, successful/unsuccessful doing of anything are not a matter of how the doing is accomplished (causal explanation). Nothing in Smith's head can tell us whether he has moved a piece correctly. For this, we must look elsewhere.

A causal account of a practice or activity fails to explain what constitutes correct and incorrect action, e.g., following a rule.[60] By

---

> virtue of subsuming an individual case under a general causal law), we do not seek these explanations by experimental observations and inductions. If we want to know what rules inform certain activities and give them meaning, we typically *ask the participants*. Their specifications of what rules they are following or are trying to follow typically have an authoritative status. An agent's sincere assertion that he was making a promise, kicking a goal, buying a ticket, checking his opponent's king, voting for the amendment to the motion, and so on, or that he was trying to effect these acts, are not *hypotheses*. And such an agent's explanation of what makes his utterance a promise, his kick a goal, his handing over money a purchase, etc. are not theories which he concocts on the basis of past observations. They are rather explanations of the rules which he is following or trying to follow.

Id. at 258.

59. For discussion of the immanent role of rules in training, see PETER M.S. HACKER, WITTGENSTEIN'S PLACE IN TWENTIETH-CENTURY ANALYTIC PHILOSOPHY 209 (1996) ("The relevance of teaching is not causal or genetic, but rather immanent: 'what matters is *what is given in the explanation*'.") (quoting WITTGENSTEIN'S LECTURES, CAMBRIDGE 1930-32: FROM THE NOTES OF JOHN KING AND DESMOND LEE 38 (Desmond Lee ed., 1980)).

60. The meaningful character of action cannot be reduced to physical phenomena such as bodily movement, brain waves, behaviorist responses, or other materialist grounds. For the hermeneutic tradition, this is expressed by the question "Is there a sense in which interpretation is essential to explanation in the sciences of man?" *See, e.g.*, CHARLES TAYLOR,

emphasizing the social character of rules and the role of training in understanding how the correct/incorrect distinction is inculcated, Wittgenstein moves us to the following two conclusions. First, the normativity of rules is forged in community agreement over time. The second is epistemic—we normally follow rules "unreflectively."[61] Rules of courtesy, driving, and the like are never the product of anything save our instinctive sense of appropriateness. The logic of our actions, and our ability to understand our actions as "rule-governed," presupposes a social context in which the regularities, customs, and patterns of action over time are found.[62] Some elaboration is in order.

Judgments of correctness and incorrectness are an everyday feature of social life. How do we go about making such judgments? And how should we characterize or account for judgments of correctness and incorrectness? Finally, what do we mean when we characterize the statements, behavior, and assertions of others?

In many, but by no means all, situations in which we characterize the action of others as correct or mistaken, we appeal to rules. For example, when a person speeds through a red light at an intersection, we say that by his action the person has violated the motor vehicle laws. Were our judgment to be challenged, we would cite the rule requiring one to stop at a red traffic signal and the fact that the person in question failed to stop. Here we want to say that the statement "*X* violated the Motor Vehicle Code" is true. The truth of the statement is not a matter of opinion. "Objectivity" names the difference between one's thinking a rule has been violated and its in fact having been violated.

I have said that it is through the use of rules that we distinguish between correct and incorrect action. How is it that rules enable us to make such judgments? In other words, what is it about rules that we may successfully employ them in appraisive activities such as judging the actions of others? What is required is an account of the

---

Interpretation and the Sciences of Man, *in* 2 PHILOSOPHICAL PAPERS (PHILOSOPHY AND THE HUMAN SCIENCES) 28 (1985) (analyzing practices such as negotiation and voting to make the point that meaningful human action is not reducible to physical phenomena: interpretation is essential to meaning).

61. For discussion of this point in the context of law, see Philip Bobbitt, *What It Means to Follow a Rule of Law*, *in* RULES & REASONING: ESSAYS IN HONOUR OF FRED SCHAUER 55-60 (Linda Meyer ed., 1999).

62. WILLIAMS, *supra* note 22, at 169.

normativity of rules, one that explains and justifies claims for a social basis of normativity.

III. THE SOCIAL BASIS OF NORMATIVITY

If normativity is not reducible to causality, does that mean that no connection exists between the two? For Wittgenstein, the *fact* that we are trained in certain ways does not answer the question whether, in a given circumstance, we are acting in accord with the appropriate norm. Yet Wittgenstein maintains that an element of the causal story—training—holds the key to normativity.[63] Unpacking the connection between training and normativity reveals an important connection between the normativity of rules and community agreement (properly understood). As we will see, action replaces both metaphysical foundations (objectivism) and community consensus (subjectivism) in the explanation of normativity and, ultimately, objectivity itself.

Before we turn to the role of training (specifically in the legal context), one preliminary matter needs to be addressed. The question can be put simply: Is it an essential aspect of normativity that rule-following requires an *actual* practice?[64] When Wittgenstein says "there is a way of grasping a rule which is *not* an *interpretation*,"[65] the question we need to ask is whether the act of grasping a rule can take place independent of an actual practice. Consider the practice of law. If normativity exists only in actual practices, and we accept law as a practice, then the task of jurisprudence becomes importantly descriptive,[66] for we cannot

63. Wittgenstein, Investigations, *supra* note 26, § 190 (indicating the criterion for how to apply a formula lies in "the way we are taught to use it").

64. For an argument that an "internal relation" does the normative work of connecting a rule and its applications, see G.P. BAKER & P.M.S. HACKER, WITTGENSTEIN: RULES, GRAMMAR AND NECESSITY 102-03 (1985) [hereinafter BAKER & HACKER, GRAMMAR] (containing commentary on Wittgenstein's PHILOSOPHICAL INVESTIGATIONS, Volume 2).

65. WITTGENSTEIN, INVESTIGATIONS, *supra* note 26, § 201.

66. H.L.A. Hart had a similar insight. This may be why he described his work in THE CONCEPT OF LAW as "descriptive sociology." H.L.A. HART, THE CONCEPT OF LAW v (2d ed. 1994) ("Notwithstanding its concern with analysis the book [THE CONCEPT OF LAW] may also be regarded as an essay in descriptive sociology ...."). The task of philosophy is noncognitive. Hacker, *supra* note 59, at 110 ("The *Investigations* delineates a purified non-cognitive conception of philosophy.").

know what rules "mean" apart from an actual practice of law.[67] This is what I mean when I say the focus should shift from mind to action. In short, apart from an actual community of legal rule-followers, it is impossible for an individual to discern whether he or she is following a rule, interpreting a rule, or correcting error.[68]

It is clear that Wittgenstein believed that, to be meaningful, rules must be used repeatedly, and over time. He wrote: "Is what we call 'obeying a rule' something that it would be possible for only *one* man to do, and to do only *once* in his life?... It is not possible that there should have been only one occasion on which someone obeyed a rule."[69]

Could a radically-isolated individual—say, Robinson Crusoe—follow rules in much the same way as one does in normal social contexts? The literature on the question is vast,[70] but the explanatory options are well-defined. According to two leading philosophical commentators, solitary rule-followers require "*regularities* of action of sufficient *complexity* to yield normativity."[71] Where do we find such complexity? In other words, must rule-following be *both* public and social?

Consider the following pattern: _ _ . . . _ _ . . .[72] Imagine Robinson Crusoe using this pattern to decorate the walls of his house. As he applies the pattern on and around his walls, he applies the pattern uniformly, keeps the lines level, and corrects any errors in application which require reapplication or other emendation of his work. We can evaluate what Crusoe is doing just as if he were here among us. Likewise, he can apply the pattern just as we might. It is as though he were one of us.

---

67. Williams, *supra* note 22, at 183 ("What is correct is shown in what we do."); PHILIP BOBBITT, CONSTITUTIONAL INTERPRETATION 24 (1991) [hereinafter BOBBITT, INTERPRETATION] ("Law is something we do, not something we have as a consequence of something we do.").

68. *See* WITTGENSTEIN, FOUNDATIONS, *supra* note 1, Part VI § 41 ("The word 'agreement' and the word 'rule' are *related*, they are cousins. The phenomena of agreement and of acting according to a rule hang together.").

69. WITTGENSTEIN, INVESTIGATIONS, *supra note* 26, § 199.

70. A representative sample of the various points of view is found in HOLTZMAN & LEICH, *supra* note 26. The most controversial work on Wittgenstein and rule-following is KRIPKE, *supra* note 46. A thorough critique of Kripke's reading of Wittgenstein is G.P. BAKER & P.M.S. HACKER, SCEPTICISM, RULES & LANGUAGE 1-55 (1984) [hereinafter BAKER & HACKER, SCEPTICISM].

71. BAKER & HACKER, SCEPTICSIM, *supra* note 70, at 42.

72. This is borrowed from WITTGENSTEIN, FOUNDATIONS, *supra* note 1, Part VI § 41.

But think about this from the point of view of "corrective behavior." How does Crusoe decide whether or not he has made a "mistake"? And how does he decide what constitutes "correction" of "error"? Is it not the case that the evaluation of Crusoe's behavior as correct or incorrect issues not from some neutral standpoint but from assimilation of his behavior into our practices?[73] Imagine if we were able to view Crusoe's work, and saw that after every use of a dot he used six dashes? If we were to claim that he had erred in his use of the pattern, we would appeal to nothing beyond *our* way of using the pattern. "Correct" use of the pattern begs the normative question. Without appeal to some way of *using* the formula, the meaning of "correct" and "incorrect" does not seem to take hold.[74]

Wittgenstein tells us as much when he rejects characterization of Crusoe's conduct as "rule-following": "There might be a cave-man who produced *regular* sequences of marks for himself. He amused himself, e.g., by drawing on the wall of the cave: _ . _ _ . _ _ . _ _ or _ . _ . . _ . . . _ . . . . _ But he is not following the general expression of a rule."[75]

Why are we precluded from characterizing Crusoe's conduct as following a rule, i.e. engaging in normative behavior? Apart from a practice of use, Crusoe has only "the master pattern." He could interpret it as he sees fit but, as we saw earlier, interpretation

---

73. Without a public practice of application, Crusoe cannot distinguish between applying the pattern and merely *thinking* he is applying the pattern. The argument about the need for a public language extends even to the language of sensation. *See* ROGER TRIGG, UNDERSTANDING SOCIAL SCIENCE: A PHILOSOPHICAL INTRODUCTION TO THE SOCIAL SCIENCES 26 (2d ed. 2001).

> How do we learn the word 'pain.' We can all communicate with each other about pain and teach the word, but it apparently refers to a private sensation. Wittgenstein was concerned to show how the meaning of such a word can only be rooted in a public language, with public checks that it is being used correctly. He was looking for a 'criterion of correctness,' and argued that one cannot have a private rule for using a word. In that case there would be no distinction between my having a rule which I kept, and my having a rule which I thought I was keeping even when I was not. The rules of the private language could not be *impressions* of rules.

Id. (footnotes omitted). Wittgenstein's argument against a private language is found in WITTGENSTEIN, INVESTIGATIONS, *supra* note 26, §§ 243-81.

74. *See* BARRY STROUD, MEANING, UNDERSTANDING, AND PRACTICE 83 (2000) ("For there to be ... correctness and incorrectness of performance there must be some practice or pattern of behaviour which an individual's actions either do or do not conform to.").

75. WITTGENSTEIN, FOUNDATIONS, *supra* note 1, Part VI § 41.

cannot provide grounds for meaning.[76] The only other alternative, one we have also rejected,[77] is the idea that the master pattern is "self-interpreting;" that its meaning can be discerned, as it were, in the abstract.[78] This leaves us with the conclusion that the meaning of the pattern, like the meaning of the signpost, and legal standards, is a function of use; of our practices. Wittgenstein says as much when, at the end of his analysis of rule-following, he states "'obeying a rule' is a practice."[79]

The normativity of rule-following—the ground of correctness and incorrectness—is not to be found in the agreement of others *as such*.[80] Agreement is a necessary feature of the normativity of our practices, but the "agreement" must be regularity in reaction to use.[81] In short, when we say there must be "agreement in actions" what we are really saying is that there must be harmony in application, over time. This harmony in reaction and application is constitutive of legal practice and, thus, is the basis of our legal judgments.[82]

---

76. *See supra* notes 33-52 and accompanying text.

77. *See supra* notes 20-32 and accompanying text.

78. *See* WILLIAMS, *supra* note 22, at 175 ("Wittgenstein's point is that a rule or master-pattern is such only from within a practice that is itself a kind of complex regularity, namely, community regularity as expressed in agreement in action and judgment.").

79. WITTGENSTEIN, INVESTIGATIONS, *supra* note 26, § 202.

80. For discussion of the relationship between normativity and "consensus," see DAVID BLOOR, WITTGENSTEIN: RULES AND INSTITUTIONS (1997). He notes that:

> [I]n following a rule we move automatically from case to case, guided by our instinctive (but socially educated) sense of 'sameness.' Such a sense does not itself suffice to create a standard of right and wrong. It is necessary to introduce a sociological element into the account to explain normativity. Normative standards come from the consensus generated by a number of interacting rule followers, and it is maintained by collectively monitoring, controlling and sanctioning their individual tendencies. Consensus makes norms objective, that is, a source of external and impersonal constraint on the individual. It gives substance to the distinction between rule followers thinking they have got it right, and their having really got it right.

Id. at 17.

81. This is precisely the point at which a theory like Stanley Fish's Reader-Response theory founders. Fish is right to reject practice-transcendent accounts of meaning but wrong in thinking that the collective presuppositions of members of an interpretive community are the key to meaning. For discussion of this point, see PATTERSON, TRUTH, *supra* note 39, at 99-127.

82. WILLIAMS, *supra* note 22, at 176.

> It is in this sense that community agreement is constitutive of practices, and that agreement must be displayed in action. There are two important features

Harmony in action is a function of an intersubjective grammar of appraisal, one that is used consistently and over time. Grammar is immanent in our practices.[83] It is agreement in reaction among participants to occasions for the use of this grammar that enables us to follow rules, appraise action, and engage in the multiple normative practices of rule-following. But from where does this grammar—specifically legal grammar—come? And how is its use inculcated in participants? For answers, we must return to training but this time in the context of law.

IV. THE NORMATIVITY OF LAW

Consider the most basic of learning tasks. Even something as simple as basic arithmetic requires instruction, which itself includes correction of error. Training takes a novice and inculcates a skill. In many activities, skills are imparted by one fully competent in the practice and capable of transmitting those skills to an initiate. When asked to describe why the student carries out the mathematical series as she does, she is likely to answer "That

---

> about this account that need to be highlighted. First, it is the *social* practice that provides the structure within which individual understanding can obtain or individual judgment be made. Central to Wittgenstein's thought is the claim, repeatedly argued for, that no isolated event or behavior can correctly be described as naming or obeying or understanding. The rule as formula, the standard as chart, or the paradigm as an instance have no normative or representational status in their own right. They have this status only in virtue of the way the formula or the chart or the instance is used. It is the use that creates the structured context within which sign-posts point, series can be continued, orders obeyed and paradigms be exemplary. Only then can we see a particular action as embodying or instancing a grammatical structure. In short, the mandatory stage setting is social practice.
>
> Second, community agreement does not constitute a justification for particular judgments. What is indispensable for correct, or appropriate, judgment and action is that there *is* concord, *not* that each individual justifies his (or anyone else's) judgment and action by appeal to its harmony with the judgment of others.

Id. (footnote omitted).

83. The understanding of language from an immanent perspective is a hallmark of the later work of Wittgenstein. ROBERT JOHN ACKERMANN, WITTGENSTEIN'S CITY 8 (1988) ("Wittgenstein always operated with an immanent understanding of language, according to which, when we have a puzzle that seems to call for philosophical treatment, some localized language use is recognized as perfectly clear, and other language use as obscure.").

is how I was taught to do it."[84] We might say that "how we are trained, how we learn, is constitutive of what we mean."[85] Understanding the normativity of our practices requires attention to the ways in which we are trained to employ the rules of the game. In this way, we can explicate the connection between rules and action, thereby grounding normativity in the latter. As I will show, the philosophical task is ultimately descriptive: we seek nothing less than a perspicuous view of legal practice.[86]

A look at training in the legal context brings us to the normative dimension of law. While complicated and richly varied, legal training provides novice lawyers with a unique set of argumentative skills.[87] The practical dimension of lawyering is a matter of producing persuasive arguments to the effect that one's assertions about what the law permits, requires, or prohibits are correct.[88] How do lawyers do this? How do lawyers show the truth of legal propositions?

As Ronald Dworkin has noted, legal argument is a matter of assertion.[89] But how, in the law, do we go from asserting a legal proposition to sustaining a claim of truth? I treat the word "Claim"

84. WITTGENSTEIN, INVESTIGATIONS, *supra* note 26, § 190 ("It may now be said: 'The way the formula is meant determines which steps are to be taken.' What is the criterion for the way the formula is meant? It is, for example, the kind of way we always use it, the way we are taught to use it.").

85. WILLIAMS, *supra* note 22, at 179.

86. This is the proper task of philosophy. *See* PETER M.S. HACKER, WITTGENSTEIN 9 (1997) ("The only kinds of explanation in philosophy are explanations by *description*—description of the use of words.").

87. This is not to deny that other skills are imparted. I would go so far as to say, however, that if the argumentative skills were not imparted, legal education would be incomplete.

88. This means that a practice-based account of law is an extension of a general account of the role of practices in creating meaningful discourses. Stephen Turner notes that:

> Our powers of persuasion and explanation, it seems, stop at the borders of our own localities. It is our *shared practices* that enable us to be persuaded and persuade, to be explainers, or to justify and have the justifications accepted. But the same justifications would not be accepted for a Roman, and thus there is no universal touchstone to which we could both refer either our disputes or failures of mutual understanding. The same holds true for the law. The point of legal training is to inculcate skills, skills that enable a lawyer to understand and formulate legal reasons and distinctions.

STEPHEN TURNER, THE SOCIAL THEORY OF PRACTICES 11 (1994).

89. *See* DWORKIN, EMPIRE, *supra* note 14, at 4 (describing legal propositions as "statements and claims people make about what the law allows or prohibits or entitles them to have").

as a term of art.[90] Consider the claim "Smith's will is invalid." This Claim asserts that, as a matter of law, Smith's will cannot be an instrument for probate transfer of her property. To sustain the claim of invalidity, more is required than mere assertion of the Claim (proposition of law). There has to be a reason supporting the claim of legal invalidity.

Suppose Smith's will is witnessed by only one person. This is the Ground of the Claim that Smith's will is invalid. The Ground supports the Claim. The relation may be represented this way:

To show the truth of the Claim more than the Ground is required. Grounds function as reasons, but reasons of a special sort. In this case, the Ground is a fact (i.e., that Smith's will has only one witness). What is it that makes that fact significant? The answer is a Warrant.

A Warrant connects a Ground with a Claim. The Warrant makes the Ground significant vis-à-vis the Claim. In this case, the Warrant is the Statute of Wills, for in that statute one will find the appropriate Warrant, specifically the provision requiring two witnesses to a will. We may represent the relations between Claim, Ground, and Warrant thus:

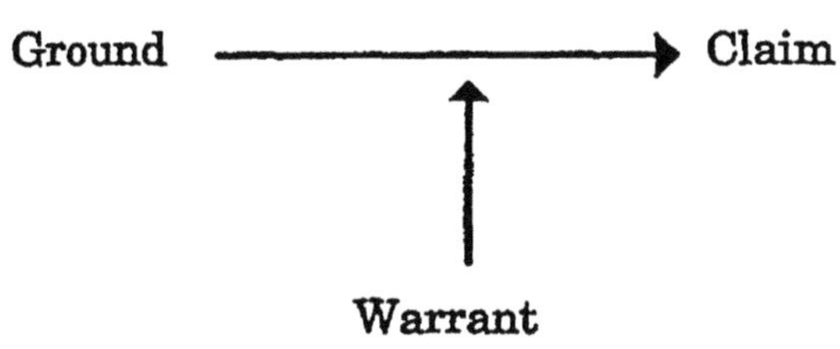

It is a commonplace that statutory texts are not self-executing. All texts, especially legal texts, must be construed. The way we give

90. The framework that follows (Claim, Ground, Warrant, Backings) is taken from STEPHEN TOULMIN ET AL., AN INTRODUCTION TO REASONING 23-67 (1979). The approach was originally advanced by Toulmin in STEPHEN EDELSTON TOULMIN, THE USES OF ARGUMENT (1958). For an exemplary employment of the of the framework in the field of theology, see NANCEY C. MURPHY, REASONING AND RHETORIC IN RELIGION (1994). I discuss this approach to legal argument in PATTERSON, TRUTH, *supra* note 39, at 169-75.

meaning to legal rules is with Backings.[91] This process is one of application; it is the way legal rules come to have meaning. There are four principal Backings (I shall call them "forms of argument") for legal Warrants. These forms of argument are: Textual, Historical, Doctrinal, and Prudential.[92] While certain departments of law may have additional forms of argument,[93] these four—which were present in the English Common Law[94]—are found in every

91. This is a corollary of the point Wittgenstein makes when he says "'obeying a rule' is a practice." WITTGENSTEIN, INVESTIGATIONS, *supra* note 26, § 202. Andrew Lugg elaborates:

> There is no such thing as a rule that fixes how it is to be followed (or a self-interpreting signpost). Far from determining its own application, a rule can always be interpreted in more than one way. Not even a straightforward rule about the use of a word dictates how it is to be obeyed. 'Use the word "game" to apply to competitive activities involving skill, chance and endurance' no more fixes its own application than a signpost to Paris fixes how it is to be followed. The rule does not tell us that 'competitive' is to be understood as involving conflict, not cooperation, any more than the signpost to Paris tells us to go in the direction of the finger, not in the opposite direction .... (It is no argument against this observation that signs that exert forces making us go where they point fix their applications. Following such a sign is a natural phenomenon on a par with the Moon's tracking the Earth as it goes around the Sun. It is not a phenomenon involving interpretation, never mind one that can be sensibly praised or blamed.)

ANDREW LUGG, WITTGENSTEIN'S INVESTIGATIONS 1-133, 146 (2000).

92. The idea of forms of argument or "modalities" was developed in the American context by Philip Bobbitt. *See* PHILIP BOBBITT, CONSTITUTIONAL FATE (1982); BOBBITT, INTERPRETATION, *supra* note 67. Bobbitt identifies six forms of argument (he refers to them as "modalities") in constitutional law. Two not mentioned above, structural and ethical arguments, are, in my view, unique to constitutional law. For discussion of interpretation in the context of German law, see KARL LARENZ, METHODENLEHRE DER RECHTSWISSENSCHAFT 312-65 (6th ed. 1991).

93. I have in mind the structural and ethical forms of argument in constitutional law. BOBBITT, INTERPRETATION, *supra* note 67, at 73-75, 80-81.

94. *See* BOBBITT, INTERPRETATION, *supra* note 67, at 5 ("The ways in which Americans interpret the Constitution could have been different.... For Americans, however, these ways have taken the forms of common law argument, those forms prevailing at the time of the drafting and ratification of the US Constitution."); NORMAN F. CANTOR, IMAGINING THE LAW 373 (1997) ("The common law today is what it has been since since it crystallized in the fourteenth century."); H. Jefferson Powell, *Constitutional Investigations*, 72 TEX. L. REV. 1731, 1737 (1994) ("There is nothing sacred or philosophically fundamental about these modes; they derive historically from the professional discourse of early-modern English common lawyers, and over time they may change.") (citation omitted) (footnote omitted).

department of law.[95] The argumentative structure of legal argument—the grammatical skeleton—may be represented thus:

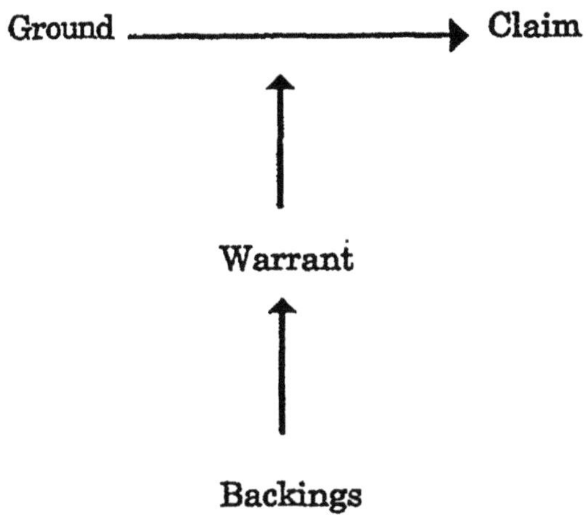

Consider the most common form of argument, textual argument.[96] Textual argument is not about plain meaning or the like. Rather, it is simply taking the meaning of words at face value (ordinary meaning).[97] For example, when parties to a contract reduce their agreement to writing, the writing is the first place to go for an answer to the question "What is the parties' agreement?" The same is true of trust instruments. The settlor of the trust expresses her intentions in words, which are given their ordinary meaning.[98] Finally, even in constitutional law—as complicated as it can sometimes be—textual argument plays a prominent role. Few

95. *E.g.*, Mark P. Gergen, *The Jury's Role in Deciding Normative Issues in the American Common Law*, 68 FORDHAM L. REV. 407 (1999); Craig Allen Nard, *Legitimacy and the Useful Arts*, 10 HARV. J.L. & TECH. 515 (1997); Carlos Manuel Vázquez, *Laughing at Treaties*, 99 COLUM. L. REV. 2154 (1999).

96. Richard H. Fallon, Jr., *A Constructivist Coherence Theory of Constitutional Interpretation*, 100 HARV. L. REV. 1189, 1195 (1987) ("Arguments from text play a universally accepted role in constitutional debate.").

97. *See* LAWRENCE H. TRIBE & MICHAEL C. DORF, ON READING THE CONSTITUTION 11 (1991) ("Constitutional commentators sometimes seem to forget that history serves to illuminate the text, but that only the text itself is law.").

98. Bobbitt compares the reading of trust instruments and written constitutions in BOBBITT, INTERPRETATION, *supra* note 67, at 4 ("[A] written constitution is like a trust agreement. It specifies what powers the trustees are to have and it endows those agents with certain authority delegated by the settlor who created the trust.").

constitutional issues are resolved without perusal of the Constitution's text. Of course, this analysis is not likely to end the discussion, but in many instances, textual argument plays a necessary role.

Historical argument is the form of argument one often encounters in the context of constitutional law. In construing a particular clause or provision of the Constitution, the reader seeks the meaning the terms in question had for those who authored the provision.[99] In the context of statutory interpretation, historical analysis focuses on the aspirations of the legislative body that promulgated the text in question.[100] Doctrinal argument represents a record of past efforts to discern the meaning of texts (statutes, etc.) as well as divining principles that can be said to "inform" prior decisions. The variety of ways of coming to terms with past decisions (e.g., analogy) is the province of doctrinal argument.[101] Of course, an important dimension of doctrinal argument is discerning when mistakes have been made.[102]

Finally, there is prudential argument. Prudential arguments focus on the effects or consequences of deciding a case one way rather than another.[103] Prudential arguments are, in effect, arguments of policy: the pursuit of collective goals.[104] The most common form of appeal is to economy—decision one way raises the costs of judicial administration without a correlative benefit.[105]

99. For a superb treatment of historical argument in the context of claims for Originalism in constitutional interpretation, see H. Jefferson Powell, *The Original Understanding of Original Intent*, 98 HARV. L. REV. 885 (1985).

100. A sophisticated account of the vicissitudes of historical argument is found in William N. Eskridge, Jr., *Dynamic Statutory Interpretation*, 135 U. PA. L. REV. 1479 (1987).

101. Arguments from "precedent" are not limited to those originating in case law. BOBBITT, INTERPRETATION, *supra* note 67, at 18 ("[T]here are also precedents of other institutions, e.g., the practices of earlier Presidents as well as the various corollaries incident to fashioning rules on the basis of precedent").

102. *See* DWORKIN, SERIOUSLY, *supra* note 2, at 118-23.

103. The most sophisticated example of an emphasis on this form of argument in constitutional scholarhship is MARK TUSHNET, RED, WHITE AND BLUE: A CRITICAL ANALYSIS OF CONSTITUTIONAL LAW (1988) (evaluating forms of argument as "ideologies" from the point of view of prudential argument).

104. In the course of his commentary on Bobbitt's approach to constitutional law, Richard Markovits makes a compelling axiological case for the limits of prudential argument in law. RICHARD MARKOVITS, MATTERS OF PRINCIPLE: LEGITIMATE LEGAL ARGUMENT AND CONSTITUTIONAL ADJUDICATION 60-74 (1998).

105. For discussion of this point in the context of the common law process, see MELVIN

The importance of the forms of argument is quite simple: without them rule-following and, thus, law is impossible.[106] How can this be? Rules are not self-executing. Like Wittgenstein's signpost, we have to know how to *act* with rules. The forms of argument are the ways in which we make meaning with rules (or do meaningful things with rules). The forms of argument make it possible for us to engage in the myriad activities we call "law" (e.g., arguing, asserting, deciding). The forms are the very thing that give law its normativity, for they enable us to show how assertions are correct and incorrect, true and false. The forms are the grammar of law.[107]

I began this part by connecting normativity with training. When we look at training in law, a distinct grammar of argument emerges. That grammar—the forms of legal argument—is the shared, intersubjective basis of legal judgment. The normativity of law depends upon an identifiable grammar of justification and consistent recognition (agreement) among participants in the practice that these are the forms of legal appraisal.[108] In addition to agreement on the forms themselves, it is crucial that participants in our legal practice agree in their reactions to the use of the forms.[109] As we shall see directly, agreement in judgment is an essential component of objectivity, and not always easy to come by.

ARON EISENBERG, THE NATURE OF THE COMMON LAW 144 (1988) (discussing competing interests of doctrinal consistency and pragmatism).

106. The forms of argument are themselves neither true nor false. They are the means for making true and false assertions (similarly, consider arithmetic functions).

107. One commentator states that:

> Anyone who failed to acknowledge the relevance of the various argument forms to the enterprise of justifying claims based on a legal text would, quite frankly, lack a rational capacity, in the same way as would a person who did not admit the relevance of visual observation to justifying claims about the natural world.

Brian Winters, *Logic and Legitimacy: The Uses of Constitutional Argument*, 48 CASE W. RES. L. REV. 263, 306 (1998).

108. For important discussion of this point in the context of internal and external approaches to law as a practice, see Thomas Morawetz, *Understanding Disagreement, The Root Issue of Jurisprudence: Applying Wittgenstein to Positivism, Critical Theory, and Judging*, 141 U. PA. L. REV. 371, 378-79 (1992) ("I refer to individuals within the practice as having a commitment to a particular interpretive strategy for applying rules and norms in the light of a conception of the purposes they serve.").

109. I am not suggesting that there is always agreement over every use of the forms of argument. Disagreement is a pervasive feature of legal practice. But if there were no agreement in the use of the forms of argument, disagreement would be impossible.

V. NORMATIVITY AND OBJECTIVITY

We come, then, to objectivity. If the forms of argument are the normative grammar of law, how do they engender objectivity? One might think this question has already been answered. If we understand "objectivity" as an account of the difference between one's *thinking* one is following a legal norm and one's *in fact* following the norm then, indeed, the question has been answered. By linking normativity to public forms of argument, we identify the means by which actors in a practice such as law conduct their discourse in constitutive, intersubjective terms.[110] Legal norms are objective to the degree the forms of argument continue to be recognized as legitimate forms of legal justification. The forms of argument are a culturally endorsed form of legal appraisal. They "exist" only to the extent they continue to be employed by the "caste of lawyers."[111]

But perhaps this answer fails to satisfy. True, law seems more "objective" than literary criticism but less objective than science or arithmetic. What accounts for this sense, and how can it be explained? It might be objected that while some practices admit of objective judgment (e.g., arithmetic), law does not. Let us consider an illustration of this point from the realm of commercial law.

Under the Uniform Commercial Code (UCC) Statute of Frauds provision, a contract for the sale of goods in an amount greater than $500 must be in writing, otherwise the contract is unenforceable.[112] If Smith sues Jones for breach of contract, and the value at stake in the contract is over $500, Jones may assert the Statute of Frauds as a defense and move for summary judgment. Jones's claim is that the contract is unenforceable (Claim). His basis (Ground) for the claim is the fact that the contract is for an amount in excess of $500. The Statute of Frauds (Warrant) permits such a defense to preclude enforcement of the contract against the party to be charged (Jones). Smith's argument will be the most basic argument

110. *See* BAKER & HACKER, GRAMMAR, *supra* note 64, at 170 ("[T]he fundamental issue is to clarify how a practice yields objective standards for determining what is correct.").

111. Brian Simpson, *The Common Law and Legal Theory*, *in* LEGAL THEORY AND COMMON LAW 8, 20 (William Twining ed., 1986).

112. U.C.C. § 2-201 (1995).

of all: the ordinary meaning of the words (Backing-Textual Argument) of Section 2-201 of the UCC.

From the point of view of objectivity, there seems to be little room for disagreement over Jones's assertion of the defense of the Statute of Frauds. The textual argument is dispositive. There are exceptions, of course, to the formal requirement of a writing. One of these is found in UCC Section 2-201(3)(b). It states that notwithstanding the lack of a writing signed by the party to be charged, a contract is enforceable if the party to be charged "admits in his pleading, testimony or otherwise in court that a contract for sale was made."[113] How do we use the forms of argument to handle a more difficult case?

In *DF Activities Corp. v. Brown,*[114] DF sought to purchase a Frank Lloyd Wright chair owned by Brown. DF contended, and Brown denied, that Brown agreed by phone to sell the chair for $60,000, to be paid in two equal installments. DF followed up with a confirmation letter and a check for $30,000. Two weeks later Brown returned both with a note indicating that the chair was no longer available. Brown then sold the chair for $198,000. DF sued and Brown moved to dismiss, attaching an affidavit stating that she had never agreed to sell the chair to DF.

The issue was whether, under the Statute of Frauds, a sworn denial of the existence of a contract ends the case or whether the plaintiff may press forward and insist on discovery, intending to use the judicial-admission exception[115] to the statute. Judge Posner held that once the defendant denies under oath that a contract had been formed, discovery may not proceed. Posner's argument is pure prudentialism. He writes: "[T]he chance that at a deposition the defendant might be badgered into withdrawing his denial is too remote to justify prolonging an effort to enforce an oral contract in the teeth of the statute of frauds."[116]

113. U.C.C. § 2-201(3)(b).

114. 851 F.2d 920 (7th Cir. 1988).

115. U.C.C. § 2-201(3)(b) (indicating a contract that does not satisfy the requirements of the Statute of Frauds is enforceable if the party against whom enforcement is sought admits in a pleading, testimony or otherwise in court that a contract for sale was made).

116. *DF Activities Corp.*, 851 F.2d at 923-24.

Is there an argument from the other side? In dissent, Judge Flaum argued against what he described as a "blanket rule"[117] against further discovery where the party against whom enforcement is sought denies the existence of a contract. His basis for this was the simple, yet powerful observation that the rule announced by the majority renders the testimonial admissions provision "virtually meaningless."[118] Sympathetic to the view expressed by his colleague (Judge Posner) but mindful of the pull of the text, Judge Flaum stated his preference for reposing discretion in the hands of the trial court, eschewing a general, blanket prohibition on discovery after the critical affidavit is filed.

This example illustrates two things about the normative character of the forms of legal argument. Judges Posner and Flaum agree on what text is relevant to the dispute (UCC Section 2-201). Their disagreement is over how that text is to be construed.[119] The four forms of argument are always available to show how the text is to be construed, but the forms do not themselves indicate their appropriateness to a given case, nor do they tell us what to do when different forms pull in opposite directions.[120] It is the breakdown of consensus at this level that fuels claims for lack of objectivity in law.

As proof of this thesis, one might point to the fact that in matters arithmetic, consensus is far easier to come by than in law. Why is it that disagreement—which seems pervasive in law—is comparatively absent in arithmetic? Are we not permitted to say

117. *Id.* at 925 (Flaum, J., dissenting) ("A blanket rule prohibiting any further discovery once the defendant denies under oath that a contract was formed is therefore too inflexible.").

118. *Id.*

119. Judges Posner and Flaum both employed prudential arguments. The relevant text posed the issue but contributed nothing to the resolution of the question raised by the ingenious lawyering of the defendant. The facts of the case actuated neither doctrinal nor historical arguments.

120. Conflict among the forms of argument is an occasion for interpretation. Bobbitt resolves the problem of conflict by resort to "conscience." BOBBITT, INTERPRETATION, *supra* note 67, at 184 ("The recursion to conscience is the crucial activity on which the constitutional system of interpretation that I have described depends."). I criticize this aspect of Bobbitt's position in Dennis Patterson, *Conscience and the Constitution*, 93 COLUM. L. REV. 270, 301-07 (1993) (reviewing BOBBITT, INTERPRETATION, *supra* note 67). Richard Fallon proposes to solve the problem of conflict among the forms of argument by resort to a theory of coherence. Fallon, *supra* note 96, at 1237-51. I have argued that Fallon's solution—lexical ordering of the forms of argument—"states, rather than resolves, the problems under consideration." Patterson, *supra* at 305 n.111.

that arithmetic, or for that matter, science, is simply "more objective" than law?

Could it be that the appearance of objectivity in arithmetic and its comparable absence in law, is due not to the subject matter but to desiderata?[121] In doing sums, there is universal agreement about what counts as a correct answer. It is not the agreement *as such* which "produces" objectivity,[122] rather, universal agreement is the corollary of a prior consensus on criteria of correctness.[123] In looking at practices like science and arithmetic, we are tempted to think the "hardness" of these practices is a function of the objects of investigation. We are tempted to believe that rocks and theorems enjoy an ontological and epistemological status that is simply of a higher order than propositions of law or literary criticism.

---

121. Richard Rorty, *Texts and Lumps*, *in* 1 PHILOSOPHICAL PAPERS (OBJECTIVISM, RELATIVISM, AND TRUTH) 90 (1991) ("I think of objectivity as a matter of ability to achieve agreement on whether a particular set of desiderata has or has not been satisfied. So I think that we can have objective knowledge at any level without necessarily having it at any other."). Rorty's account of the constitutive role of the interaction between the interplay of causal and intentional elements is instructive:

> [An] object can, given a prior agreement on a language game, cause us to hold beliefs, but it cannot suggest beliefs for us to hold. It can only do things which our practices will react to with preprogrammed changes in belief. So when he is asked to interpret the felt difference between hard and soft objects, the pragmatist says that the difference is between the rules of one institution (chemistry) and those of another (literary criticism).

Id. at 83-84.

122. This is the subjectivist view of someone like Stanley Fish.

123. *See* WITTGENSTEIN, INVESTIGATIONS, *supra* note 26, § 241 ("'So you are saying that human agreement decides what is true and what is false?'—It is what human beings say that is true and false; and they agree in the language they use. That is not agreement in opinions but in form of life."); *see also* RICHARD RORTY, *Thomas Kuhn, Rocks and the Law of Physics*, *in* PHILOSOPHY AND SOCIAL HOPE 175, 179-80 (1999).

> The main reason admirers of physics distrust literary critics is that no consensus ever seems to form about the right interpretation of a text: there is little convergence of opinion. At the opposite extreme, mathematicians are usually unanimous about whether or not a theorem has been proved. Physicists are closer to the mathematics end of the spectrum, and politicians and social scientists closer to the literary criticism end. Analytic philosophers claimed (not very plausibly, as things turned out) that analytic philosophers were more capable of consensus than non-analytic philosophers, and in that sense were more scientific.
>
> The trouble is that intersubjective agreement about who has succeeded and who has failed is easy to get if you can lay down criteria of success in advance.

Id.

When the litmus paper turns blue we are inclined to say that the results of the test are "objective."[124] The use of the word seems fine enough—but it begs the question: What is doing the "normative heavy lifting," the world or the fact that everyone already agrees on what it means when the paper turns blue?[125] This is where the objectivist wants to give science the advantage and declare that "the world" has told us what is the case.[126] The "facts" are now known.

Here, again, the causal and the normative are confused. One cannot, and need not, deny that causal processes are at work, both in the case of the litmus test and the reading of texts. But I want to agree with Richard Rorty when he suggests that there is

---

124. Quine himself provides a wonderful example of how what we "see" is dependent upon a network of associations already in place:

> [S]omeone mixes the contents of two test tubes, observes a green tint, and says 'There was copper in it.' Here the sentence is elicited by a non-verbal stimulus, but the stimulus depends for its efficacy upon an earlier network of associations of words with words; viz., one's learning of chemical theory .... [T]he verbal network of an articulate theory has intervened to link the stimulus with the response.
>
> The intervening theory is composed of sentences associated with one another in multifarious ways not easily reconstructed even in conjecture.

WILLARD VAN ORMAN QUINE, WORD AND OBJECT 10-11 (1960).

For further discussion of Quine's thought and its implications for jurisprudence, see PATTERSON, TRUTH, *supra* note 39, at 158-59. *See also* Dennis Patterson, *Law and Truth: Replies to Critics*, 50 SMU L. REV. 1563, 1589-98 (1997) (responding to Brian Leiter, *Why Quine Is Not a Postmodernist*, 50 SMU L. REV. 1739 (1997)).

125. For an interesting and informative discussion of the cognitive status of science against the background of recent work in science studies, see JOHN ZIMAN, REAL SCIENCE (1999) (containing an exhaustive analysis of the cultural and cognitive dimensions of science practice). The following characterization of objectivity is relevant to the present discussion:

> [T]he notion of "objective knowledge" is linked with the academic norms of communalism, universalism, and disinterestedness. The culture built around these norms in the natural sciences has produced a solid core of *established* knowledge. There is no *absolute* basis for our belief in the cognitive objectivity of scientific entities such as gravitating planets, atomic nuclei, tectonic plates or the genetic code. Nevertheless, this is a well-founded belief, as natural as our attitude to the rest of the shared furniture of all human lives. What is more, these are entities that exist independently of our individual thoughts about them, and operate even-handedly for everyone. This consensus is so overwhelming that nobody can seriously deny that they are simultaneously 'socially' and 'cognitively' objective in full measure.

Id. at 179 (citations omitted).

126. *See* Leiter, *supra* note 124. I reply to Professor Leiter in Patterson, *supra* note 124, at 1589-98.

> no way to transfer nonlinguistic brutality to *facts*, to the truth of sentences. The way in which a blank takes on the form of the die which stamps it has no analogy to the relation between the truth of a sentence and the event which the sentence is about. When the die hits the blank something causal happens, but as many *facts* are brought into the world as there are languages for describing that causal transaction.[127]

There is a well-known anecdote about Wittgenstein wherein he explained how he first came to his ideas about the relationship of language to the world.[128] It seems Wittgenstein read a magazine account of a trial in a French court on the question of liability for an auto accident.[129] By way of explaining how the accident occurred, one of the lawyers assembled some wooden block figures, each representing the automobiles involved in the accident as well as the details of the accident scene. Upon seeing this arrangement, an idea came to Wittgenstein: perhaps our words relate to the world in the same way the figures stand for the participants in the accident. Words "stand for" things in the world: words are proxies for things.

I want to use the accident scene for a purpose different than that of Wittgenstein. I want to say that when it comes to the question "what happened?," there is no single "best" vocabulary or language of description. The simple accident scene can be described in at least three different vocabularies, each an expression of what Hilary Putnam would call "a point of view."[130] No one of these points of view is "correct."[131] Each is useful for different purposes. Finally,

---

127. RORTY, *supra* note 121, at 81.

128. These ideas were published as LUDWIG WITTGENSTEIN, TRACTATUS LOGICO-PHILOSOPHICUS (David Pears & Brian McGuinness trans., 1961).

129. The story is recounted in RAY MONK, LUDWIG WITTGENSTEIN: THE DUTY OF GENIUS 118 (1990). My thanks to Dr. Peter M.S. Hacker for assistance with this reference.

130. *See* HILARY PUTNAM, REPRESENTATION AND REALITY 114 (1988):

> We can and should insist that some facts are there to be discovered and not legislated by us. But this is something to be said when one has adopted a way of speaking, a language, a "conceptual scheme." To talk of "facts" without specifying the language to be used is to talk of nothing; the word "fact" no more has its use fixed by the world itself than does the word "exist" or the word "object."

131. However, I would argue that within each point of view it is possible to make correct and incorrect assertions or statements.

none is reducible one to the other,[132] nor to the individual predilections of anyone employing a vocabulary.[133]

Consider the familiar concept of "duty." Did one of the drivers proceed in such a way as to create risk for others? If the question receives a positive answer, it is likely that that party will be found liable for injuries caused thereby. The discussion will proceed in the juridical language of duty, risk, and causation. With this language, the trier of fact will devolve to a conclusion on the question of liability and a judgment will issue.

An entirely different description of the event is also possible. Imagine a physicist is asked "what happened?" She will answer that objects proceeding through space and time met at a certain point in mereological space and repelled one another. No mention of duty, risk, or causation will be made. Why? Because these are not concepts of physics. Physics and law are independent languages (discourses) of description, each with their own distinct vocabulary.[134] It is these vocabularies that allow for distinctly different answers to the question "what happened?"

A third answer is also possible. We could ask an economist "what happened?" She might say "the cheapest cost avoider failed to take suitable precautions." Other economic descriptions are possible, but the point is that the language of economic description will be in a vocabulary that is in no way coextensive with the discourses of law or physics. And that is the point: in answer to the question "what happened?," three plausible and logically distinct responses are possible. None of the three modes of description is "the" correct one. The very idea of "the" correct one simply makes no sense.[135]

---

132. A well-known approach to reductionism is Steven Weinberg's work. *E.g.*, STEVEN WEINBERG, DREAMS OF A FINAL THEORY 55 (1992) ("The reason we give the impression that we think that elementary particle physics is more fundamental than other branches of physics is because it is.").

133. This is why I maintain that Fish is not a pragmatist: he is a subjectivist. The focus of the relativism is the individual—collective or isolated—not the practice.

134. These vocabularies are the appraisive tools of their disciplines. It is in the use of these vocabularies that true and false assertions or statements are made.

135. This is the nub of the problem. Economists, philosophers, and theorists of all stripes write as if some nonlegal language can "rescue" law from itself. For an argument to the effect that this is an illusory undertaking, see Gunther Teubner, *How the Law Thinks: Toward a Constructivist Epistemology of Law*, 23 LAW & SOC'Y REV. 727 (1989).

What, then, of objectivity? The conclusion we inevitably reach is that objectivity is relative to a domain. Within different fields, practices, or discourses, one finds different forms of argument—different ways of showing the truth of propositions.[136] The truth of assertions within a domain cannot be proven nor disproven with the forms of argument of other disciplines. There is no "form of forms" or metaprinciple which can identify a given set of argumentative forms as "the" correct ones, for the choice of forms is a matter of history and utility.

The forms of argument in law could have been different[137] and may yet become different. The forms of legal argument are an inheritance, not a dictate. As I hope I have shown, this does not make law any less "objective" than any other discipline. Law is more argumentative than physics or arithmetic.[138] If law is less objective than physics, the explanation lies more with us than the world. In thinking about objectivity, it is a mistake to believe that objectivity depends more on "the world" than on those who inhabit the world. This, I have suggested, rests on a view of the relationship of mind to world that no longer seems plausible.

---

136. I would go so far as to say that it is the various forms of argument that demarcate one field or discipline from others. Why would we reject an opinion which, after recitation of the facts of the case, provides three differential equations and the statement "Motion denied?" The answer is that this decision—even if correct on the merits—expresses the judgment of the court in a nonlegal discourse. One is reminded that, in law as in most things, *how* a conclusion is reached is as important as *what* conclusion is reached.

137. BOBBITT, INTERPRETATION, *supra* note 67, at 5 ("The ways in which Americans interpret the Constitution could have been different; indeed the forms of constitutional discourse are very different in other societies.").

138. Dean Wellington spoke eloquently of this phenomenon in the context of the disconnect between legal academics and practitioners. Harry Wellington, *Challenges to Legal Education: The 'Two Cultures' Phenomenon*, 37 J. LEGAL EDUC. 327, 327 (1987):

> On the one hand, [the] methodology [of the academic] is apt to mirror the style of political and moral philosophy, and accordingly, appear to the practitioner as overly general and abstract, insufficiently particularistic and attentive to institutional considerations....
>
> [Another] factor is vocabulary: law teachers talk differently from practicing lawyers. In the Sterling Law Buildings and elsewhere one hears heated conversations about hermeneutics, externalities and deconstruction.

A reaction, extreme in the view of some, to the proliferation of these extra-legal orientations may be found in Judge Posner's recent rejection of the relevance of moral philosophy to law. RICHARD POSNER, THE PROBLEMATICS OF MORAL AND LEGAL THEORY (1999). For a critique of Posner's position, see Jeremy Waldron, *Ego-Bloated Hovel*, 94 NW. U. L. REV. 597 (2000) (book review).

[8]
Explicating the Internal Point of View

THE Concept of Law is the most important book in twentieth-century analytic jurisprudence.[1] Its importance is a function of many things, not the least of which is the fact that Hart's approach to jurisprudence was forged at a time of great intellectual ferment in analytic philosophy.[2] *The Concept of Law* was written during a period when analytic philosophy's commitment to language as the focal point of philosophical reflection had been firmly cemented.[3] At the time he wrote *The Concept of Law*, Hart was in a unique position to take advantage of then-recent work in philosophy of language. Yet, when the book was published, no one could foresee just how sharp the linguistic turn in philosophy would be. I would suspect that even Hart, prescient as he was, could not have predicted the depth and breadth in the expansion of language as the central focus of philosophical activity.

Like any great work, there is much in *The Concept of Law* that demands attention and explication. Before I introduce the topic on which I will focus, I would like to say a few things about how I see the book. First, it is properly located in the tradition of analytic jurisprudence known as positivism. Central to positivism is the idea that the true ground of legal obligation—the source of validity for what is referred to as "law"—is an origin. This notion, central to the thought of Hobbes and John Austin, is contemporarily expressed in Joseph Raz's felicitous phrase, the "sources thesis." For a norm to be law, it must be the case that it originates in an act of some official, that possesses the requisite authority.

John Austin gave expression to this idea in the nineteenth century when he argued that the best way to think of law was as the imperative of a sovereign backed by threat of reprisal for non-compliance. Hart famously demolished this conception by pointing out that on Austin's picture of the nature of law, there is no material difference between "the

* Distinguished Professor of Law, Rutgers University, School of Law (Camden). B.A., J.D., State University of New York at Buffalo. My thanks to Professor Brian Bix for very helpful comments on a draft of this Article.

1. H.L.A. HART, THE CONCEPT OF LAW (2d ed. 1994).

2. An excellent discussion of the intellectual history of the period is found in P.M.S. HACKER, WITTGENSTEIN'S PLACE IN TWENTIETH-CENTURY ANALYTIC PHILOSOPHY (1996).

3. For an account of the rise of analytical philosophy, especially philosophy of language, see MICHAEL DUMMETT, ORIGINS OF ANALYTICAL PHILOSOPHY (1994).

law" and the command of a gunman to turn over one's purse.[4]

Paying attention to Hart's critique of Austin leads me to see *The Concept of Law* as a book in two parts. The first part—the first six chapters—is dedicated to two tasks. The first is the articulation and demolition of the Austinian conception of legal obligation. From the vantage point of the present, there can be little question that Hart's critique of Austin is successful.

The second major theme in *The Concept of Law* is the advancement of Hart's account of the nature of law: the notion that law is a matter of rules. According to Hart, law has a nature that is best thought of in terms of a distinction between two sorts of rules: primary and secondary. Primary rules are rules of obligation. Secondary rules are rules of change. Taken together, these rules comprise the genetic structure of the legal system.

But what is the (validating) source of primary and secondary rules? What makes these rules valid? Hart says that a "master rule"—the Rule of Recognition—is the validating source for all other secondary rules and primary rules. Hart's discussion of the Rule of Recognition completes his analysis of the nature of law.

We turn, then, to the second part of *The Concept of Law*, chapter seven, which contains Hart's much-discussed comments on the discretion, as well as one of the clearest examples of the influence of linguistic philosophy, the distinction between core and penumbral meaning.

Does chapter seven constitute a "theory of adjudication"? I certainly believe it does, but some dispute this.[5] Perhaps it is safe to say that if one is ever to find a theory of adjudication in Hart's ouvre, this is the best place to look.[6] Chapter seven of *The Concept of Law* has been the focal point of discussion in analytic jurisprudence since Ronald Dworkin first called into question Hart's account of the role of discretion in deciding

4. *See* HART, *supra* note 1, at 82.

> A orders B to hand over his money and threatens to shoot him if he does not comply. According to the theory of coercive orders this situation illustrates the notion of obligation or duty in general. Legal obligation is to be found in this situation writ large; A must be the sovereign habitually obeyed and the orders must be general, prescribing courses of conduct not single actions. The plausibility of the claim that the gunman situation displays the meaning of obligation lies in the fact that it is certainly one in which we would say that B, if he obeyed, was 'obliged' to hand over his money.

Id.

5. *See* Ken Kress, *Modern Jurisprudence, Postmodern Jurisprudence, and Truth*, 95 MICH. L. REV. 1871, 1901 (1997) (reviewing DENNIS PATTERSON, LAW AND TRUTH (1996)).

> This aspect of law is often held to show that any elucidation of the concept of law in terms of rules must be misleading. To insist on it in the face of the realities of the situation is often stigmatized as 'conceptualism' or 'formalism,' and it is to the estimation of this charge that we shall now turn.

Id. (citation omitted).

6. In the Postscript to THE CONCEPT OF LAW, Hart said that while he did speak to the topic, he "said far too little . . . about the topic of adjudication and legal reasoning." HART, *supra* note 1, at 259.

cases.[7]

Let us return to the issue of the nature of law. As I mentioned, the first six chapters of *The Concept of Law* are an articulation and critique of Austin's account of the nature of law, followed by the advancement of Hart's alternative account of the nature of law as a system of rules. The intellectual pedigree of this argument is important to a full understanding of Hart's project.

Central to legal positivism is the denial of any necessary conceptual connection between law and morality (the separation thesis). In simple terms, the idea is that there is a logical distinction between statements of what the law is or requires and statements about whether the law is good or just. Put differently, nothing follows from a statement of what the law requires: to state the law is to take no position on whether the law should be obeyed. To state the law is neither to endorse it nor criticize it.

One of the tasks taken up by legal positivists is articulation of the grounds of law. This enterprise is an effort to identify the "normativity" of law.[8] Bentham, Hart informs us, failed in this undertaking because he reduced the normativity of law to social facts, specifically the acts of legislative officials.[9] Bentham's error, Hart maintains, is the reduction of statements of the law to statements about the law.[10]

But what, exactly, is the problem of the normativity of law? For Hart, the problem is explaining the evaluative dimension of legal language while remaining true to the separation thesis.[11] In *The Concept of Law*, Hart explained this in terms of what he referred to as "internal points of view"[12] toward law. In using the language of legal obligation, officials were exhibiting a discernible attitude towards the law, one of endorsement. This attitude, Hart maintains, explains the normativity of law without sacrificing the separation thesis.

Hart's account of the internal point of view as the key to explaining legal normativity was criticized[13] as insufficiently sensitive to the variety of statements one can make when speaking of law. Internal statements

7. *See* RONALD DWORKIN, TAKING RIGHTS SERIOUSLY 31-39 (1977).

8. Hart puts it this way in describing the shortcomings of the Imperative Theory of law:

> The Imperative Theory . . . fails to account for a feature of statements of legal obligation which cannot be characterized by the aid of Bentham's conceptual resources of command and habit of obedience. This feature is what is now called the 'normativity' of such statements and statements *of the law* or the legal position of individuals under the law.

H.L.A. HART, ESSAYS ON BENTHAM: STUDIES IN JURISPRUDENCE AND POLITICAL THEORY 144 (1982).

9. *See id.* at 144-45.

10. *See id.* at 144.

11. *See id.*

12. HART, *supra* note 1, at 89-90.

13. Hart cites the following from Raz: JOSEPH RAZ, PRACTICAL REASON AND NORMS 123-29, 146-48, 162-77 (1990); JOSEPH RAZ, THE AUTHORITY OF LAW: ESSAYS ON LAW AND MORALITY 153-57 (1979); JOSEPH RAZ, THE CONCEPT OF A LEGAL SYSTEM: AN INTRODUCTION TO THE THEORY OF LEGAL SYSTEM 234-38 (2d ed. 1980). Hart's citation appears in HART, *supra* note 8, at 153 n.73.

(statements of law) are normative in that they express the speaker's endorsement of the rules. By contrast, moderate external statements are in the nature of reports about what participants in a legal system believe about their own legal standards. External statements are not comments on the quality or character of internal statements; they are merely descriptions of the beliefs of others.

In response to criticism of the distinction between committed statements and reports, Hart adds a third category or dimension of normativity, the category of "'detached' judgements," which are "statements of law or legal obligation *from the point of view* of one who accepts or regards as valid the laws in question, but without committing the speaker to that point of view."[14] The distinction between Hart's original external point of view and the newer "detached" external point of view is a matter of the difference between description and commitment. The point of the detached external point of view is to be able to say something true from the point of view of law without implying a "commitment . . . to the truth or validity of the claims made by committed speakers."[15] In short, Hart now wants to differentiate use[16] of the (normative) language of a system like law from endorsement of the system of legal rules.

Can one make a statement like "x has an obligation to y" which is true without thereby endorsing the standard under which x's obligation falls? In other words, is it not possible to state correctly what the law is without thereby being committed to the view that the law correctly deals with the issue in question? The entire point of Hart's newly-minted conception of the external perspective is designed to do just that: to make it possible to state the law without either endorsing it (the original internal point of view) or merely describing it (the original external point of view).

As background for Hart's discussion, one must be mindful of the thought of Professor Dworkin, for whom a statement of the law is not possible without endorsing it.[17] Hart wants to preserve the essential positivist point that a statement of the law carries with it no commitment to principles that may underwrite or justify it.

Do Hart's final distinctions render any clearer our picture of the internal point of view? Neil MacCormick, one of our finest commentators on Hart's work suspects not. MacCormick begins with the observation that the law on any given question varies from one jurisdiction to the next.[18]

14. Gerald J. Postema, *The Normativity of Law*, *in* ISSUES IN CONTEMPORARY LEGAL PHILOSOPHY: THE INFLUENCE OF H.L.A. HART 83 (Ruth Gavison ed., 1987).

15. *Id.*

16. In Hart's original formulation of the normativity of law, a speaker had only two choices: employ legal language and, thereby, endorse it (propositions of law), or merely describe or report on the use of legal language by others (propositions about law).

17. *See* RONALD DWORKIN, LAW'S EMPIRE (1986). For a similar reading, see HART, *supra* note 1, at 253 ("[F]or Dworkin the truth of any proposition of law ultimately depends on the truth of a moral judgment as to what best justifies and since for him moral judgments are essentially controversial, so are all propositions of law.").

18. *See* Neil MacCormick, *Comment*, *in* ISSUES IN CONTEMPORARY LEGAL PHILOSOPHY: THE INFLUENCE OF H.L.A. HART 105-13 (Ruth Gavison ed., 1987).

He provides the following example, one taken from comparative law:

> Scottish testators have neither right nor power to disinherit their children at law, and the executors of their estate are duty-bound to secure the legal rights of the children against the estate. English and *a fortiori* North Carolinan testators have such right and power and their executors are subject to no such duty.[19]

Of the variety of legal norms just described, MacCormick asks the following: "[I]s it possible that somebody somewhere has made a mistake about law, legal rights, legal powers, or legal duties?"[20] The answer is "No." One can only agree with MacCormick's observation that "even the most perfervid jusnaturalist, acknowledges the possibility of variance in positive laws."[21] Thus, MacCormick argues, we are compelled to draw the conclusion that legal validity is "a jurisdictionally relative concept."[22] Whether the legal rights of a child in, say, Scotland, are morally preferable to those of a child in North Carolina is a conceptually distinct matter. As MacCormick puts it, "legal rights and obligations can vary or be varied without corresponding variance in moral rights or obligations."[23]

What is the issue here, and why is it important? Why should we be clear about the relationship of legal norms to the attitudes of those who use them to appraise the conduct of others? Part of the problem in discussing this question is getting clear about what is at stake. For Hart, the issue is one of explanation.[24] What does it mean to explain the law? The explanation is an explanation of the normative aspect of legal rules. This is an explanation of the meaning of legal norms. Thus, the question of the normativity of law is, at bottom, a question about the nature of explanation of legal meaning.

Dworkin once said that jurisprudential questions are ultimately questions in the philosophy of language.[25] If we follow Dworkin here, we would have to ask whether the meaning (normativity) of legal language could be illuminated by recourse to the attitudes of speakers (Hart's claim). We might want to ask to what extent the meaning of legal discourse turns on the attitudes of those using the terms.

The gravamen of the idea of the internal point of view is that the meaning of terms is a function of something within the legal system itself. In other words, the question whether someone is making a true or correct statement of law is determined by resort to something within a particular legal system.

19. *Id.* at 105-06.
20. *Id.* at 106.
21. *Id.*
22. *Id.* at 107.
23. *Id.* at 107-08.
24. *See* HART, *supra* note 8, at 147-48.
25. *See* R.M. Dworkin, *Introduction*, *in* THE PHILOSOPHY OF LAW 1 (R.M. Dworkin ed., 1977) ("Even the debate about the nature of law, which has dominated legal philosophy for some decades, is, at bottom, a debate within the philosophy of language and metaphysics.").

The debate over the question of attitude toward legal statements—the question whether a statement of the law is an endorsement of the law—is really a question about the ultimate meaning of the terms involved. The only reason we are interested in the statement—endorsement distinction is because we harbor the view that some statement of the law may appear correct but is, in fact,[26] incorrect. In short, a statement of the law may be incorrect because the meaning of the statement involved is other than what the speaker supposes it to be.

As we have seen, Hart tried to make sense of the distinction between internal and external from the point of view of attitude. As the important work of other analytically-minded legal philosophers shows,[27] Hart was on to something important with the internal-external (inside-outside) distinction. Driving Hart's analysis is the need to answer the question what, if anything, makes legal statements unique? Put differently, the question is what, if anything, makes a proposition "legal" and not a proposition of some other sort (e.g., moral).[28]

I want to join Neil MacCormick in his puzzlement about the merit of Hart's final effort to express his view about the normative character of law. MacCormick's point is that legal rights are jurisdictionally-relative. As such, statements of the law are true only within jurisdictional boundaries. Thus, legal truth, like legal rights, is (jurisdictionally) relative. The reason MacCormick finds Hart's final effort puzzling, I suspect, is that he does not see that Hart's final distinctions illuminate this relativity.

Where is this debate going? MacCormick claims "[c]onventionalism is all that we should need in order to account for the possibility of true detached statements of law for a given jurisdiction at a given time."[29] I think he is right in this, and I would like to explain why.

The core of MacCormick's criticism of Hart's final reformulation of the internal-external distinction is the idea that the truth of a proposition of law is jurisdictionally relative. In the language of detachment, a statement of the law presupposes it to be a statement of the law in a particular legal system at some particular time. When one says, "The law permits disinheritance of one's children," the question naturally arises, "Where is that type today"?

MacCormick says that "[t]o be detached in legal matters is precisely to discover what the correct view of the law somewhere is."[30] He also states that to acknowledge the correctness of a statement of the law is "to make

26. This is where the idea of "grounds of law" becomes important. The truth of a legal proposition requires identification of the proper grounds of law.

27. *See, e.g.*, Thomas Morawetz, *Understanding Disagreement, the Root Issue of Jurisprudence: Applying Wittgenstein to Positivism, Critical Theory, and Judging*, 141 U. Pa. L. Rev. 371 (1992).

28. I take Dworkin's work to be both a critique of this view (the separation thesis) as well as an alternative to that view. Dworkin's alternative view is that law and morality are not separate discourses but are, in fact, joined at some deep, conceptual level (the relational thesis).

29. MacCormick, *supra* note 18, at 112.

30. *Id.* at 109.

a cognitive commitment."[31] In other words, there is a fact of the matter about (at least some) legal questions. Two questions (at least) arise: what does it mean to say there is a fact of the matter about law and how does this impact Hart's distinction between internal and external points of view?

In a recent work, I argued that the best way of understanding truth in law was in the use of forms of legal argument.[32] Very roughly, I said that law has its own argumentative grammar, and that it is through the use of this grammar that the truth of legal propositions is shown. An assertion like, "In Scotland, it is legally possible to disinherit your children," can be shown to be true or false by employing the familiar forms of legal argument. It is in the use of forms of argument that the truth of legal propositions is possible. In other words, outside these forms, there is no legal truth.

I think Hart was right to say that acceptance is a large part of the normativity of a legal system. But what is accepted in law is not only a system of rules but forms of argumentative appraisal. When a lawyer points to a statute to make the case that a particular legal assertion is true, that text must already be regarded (accepted) as authoritative for the gesture to be meaningful. If lawyers did not already agree in their modes of appraisal (forms of argument), legal argument simply would not be possible.

What does this have to do with the internal point of view and Hart's efforts to respond to his critics? I think Hart was right when he said that the task of jurisprudence is the description of our legal practices. He made the hermeneutic point[33] that the key to this understanding is explicating how participants in legal systems coordinate their rule-following behavior. In short, when Hart describes his "practice theory of rules,"[34] he is identifying what holds the practice together. He thought it was attitude. I think it is forms of argument.

Despite this difference, I join Hart and others[35] in denying any entailment between legal truth and moral truth.[36] People who want the entailment relationship to hold usually argue the connection from the point of view of legal concepts.[37] They say that the meaning (and, hence, truth) of legal assertions depends upon getting clear about the real content of the concepts implicated by our words. In other words, the key to legal truth

31. *Id.*

32. *See* DENNIS PATTERSON, LAW AND TRUTH 169-79 (1996).

33. First observed by Peter M.S. Hacker. *See* P.M.S. Hacker, *Hart's Philosophy of Law*, *in* LAW, MORALITY, AND SOCIETY: ESSAYS IN HONOUR OF H.L.A. HART 9 (P.M.S. Hacker & J. Raz eds., 1977) (relating the internal point of view to the claim of hermeneutics that to understand human phenomena one must understand the practice or activity from the point of view of participants).

34. HART, *supra* note 1, at 255.

35. *See, e.g.*, Postema, *supra* note 14; MacCormick, *supra* note 18.

36. *See* MacCormick, *supra* note 18, at 110.

37. A recent example is NICOS STAVROPOULOS, OBJECTIVITY IN LAW (1996).

lies in uncovering the objective meaning of our concepts (legal and otherwise).

This way of putting things confirms that attention to the philosophy of language can engender progress in legal theory. As I have said, I think Dworkin is correct in this.[38] That said, where does this leave us with respect to Hart's last effort to express the significance of the internal point of view? It leaves me convinced that Hart was right to look for the uniqueness of law— its normativity—in the intersubjective relations of legal actors. More needs to be done in explicating and developing Hart's important insight.

38. *But see* Anne De Moor, *Nothing Else to Think? On Meaning, Truth, and Objectivity in Law*, 18 OXFORD J. LEGAL STUD. 345 (reviewing STAVROPOULOS, *supra* note 37) (expressing skepticism that legal theory can benefit from advances in philosophy of language).

[9]
Langdell's Legacy

Introduction

Langdell aspired to a "scientific" account of law. Labelled variously as a "formalist" or a purveyor of "mechanical jurisprudence," Langdell survives only as a figure to be pilloried. But what was Langdell's vision of a science of law? And how does Langdell's scientific aspiration relate to his enduring legacy, the case method of legal instruction? These are the questions that shall concern us.

There is, I think, a parallel to be drawn between Langdell's scientific vision of the law and the current pedagogical emphasis on interdisciplinary approaches to law. Today, it is almost no longer possible to pick up a modern casebook or set of teaching materials without seeing a certain pattern firmly in place. In addition to questions relating to the cases, statutes, and other legal materials discussed in the case, the student is often presented with a few paragraphs from the "and" side of "Law and." The student is invited to assess the holding of the case in the light of this disciplinary material. What is the point of such an approach to legal materials? And is there any connection between this current approach to pedagogy and Langdell's scientific vision of the law? I think there is. At least that shall be my argument.

I. Langdell and The Sources of Law

There are two elements to Langdell's theory of law.[1] First is his well-known assertion that law is a science.[2] The second is his enduring

---

* Distinguished Professor of Law, Rutgers University School of Law (Camden). The author thanks Richard Hyland for his helpful comments on initial drafts of this Article.

1 Some commentators believe that it borders on overstatement to suggest that Langdell had a "theory" of law. *See, e.g.*, John Henry Schlegel, American Legal Realism and Empirical Social Science 276 n.11 (1995) ("[Langdell's] total output of legal theory is about a page of print.... Conceivably, all that need be said about legal theory could be said in a page or two. But more likely, all that Langdell could say about legal theory was a page or two."). A number of points are worth mentioning. First, however small Langdell's output, his yield—measured in terms of enduring influence—is unequalled. Additionally, while it may be true that Langdell did not produce a "theory" of law, at least in the sense in which that term is used today, he did provide a compelling picture of how best to understand law. As I shall argue, this picture is the dominant mindset in contemporary academic accounts of the nature of law.

2 Christopher C. Langdell, A Selection of Cases on the Law of Contracts at vi (1871) ("Law, considered as a science, consists of certain principles or doctrines.").

contribution to legal education, the case method. What is the relationship between these two elements? Are they two aspects of a unified account of the nature of private law? Is the case method simply the means by which general principles of law are imparted to students? The key to understanding Langdell's idea of law as a science lies in understanding how these two elements of his thought are related.

Langdell's aspiration was that law be like science. But how? What sort of science did Langdell have in mind? Did he see legal knowledge as the product of experimental method? Or did he believe that the first principles of law could be deduced by reason?

In the Preface to the first edition of his contracts casebook, Langdell, who came to the legal academy with no prior teaching experience,[3] identified a practical problem: the necessity of having to teach "a large class of pupils, meet them regularly from day to day, and give them systematic instruction in such branches of law as had been assigned to me."[4] The solution to Langdell's practical problem was to be found in his scientific approach to law.

Langdell considered law to be a science. He said as much.[5] But what sort of science was law? Here the question arises as to Langdell's conception of science; in short, what he meant by the term. An answer to this question provides a clue as to his conception of the role of cases in the science of law and pedagogy. Each legal doctrine, Langdell said,

> has arrived at its present state by slow degrees; in other words, it is a growth, extending in many cases through centuries. This growth is to be traced in the main through a series of cases; and much the shortest and best, if not the only way of mastering the doctrine effectually is by studying the cases in which it is embodied. But the cases which are useful and necessary for this purpose at the present day bear an exceedingly small

3 *Id.* at v. Details of Langdell's career leading up to his Deanship at Harvard Law School can be found in Marcia Speziale, *Langdell's Concept of Law as Science: The Beginning of Anti-Formalism in American Legal Theory*, 5 VT. L. REV. 1, 7-11 (1980).

4 LANGDELL, *supra* note 2, at vii. To meet the task, Langdell set himself three objectives, which he described as follows:

> [F]irst, that the efforts of the pupils should go hand in hand with mine, that is, that they should study with direct reference to my instruction; secondly, that the study thus required of them should be of the kind from which they might reap the greatest and most lasting benefit; thirdly, that the instruction should be of such a character that the pupils might at least derive a greater advantage from attending it than from devoting the same time to private study.

Id.

5 *See id.* at vi.

> Law, considered as a science, consists of certain principles or doctrines. To have such a mastery of these as to be able to apply them with constant facility and certainty to the ever-tangled skein of human affairs, is what constitutes a true lawyer; and hence to acquire that mastery should be the business of every earnest student of law.

Id.

proportion to all that have been reported. The vast majority are useless, and worse than useless, for any purpose of systematic study. Moreover, the number of fundamental legal doctrines is much less than is commonly supposed; the many different guises in which the same doctrine is constantly making its appearance, and the great extent to which legal treatises are a repetition of each other, being the cause of much misapprehension. If these doctrines could be so classified and arranged that each should be found in its proper place, and nowhere else, they would cease to be formidable from their number.[6]

When Langdell described law as a science, did he think of science as "experimental method"? There is historical evidence to suggest that he did.[7] But the nerve of experiment is the postulation of a hypothesis that provides the best account of the phenomena under consideration.[8] In Langdell's case, the "phenomena" under consideration were the cases. If the cases were to be properly explained, the principles of law identified by Langdell would, of necessity, have to account for all of the "data." It is at this point that the identification of "science" with "scientific method" founders.

Langdell saw no need to account for all the data—the cases. Consider his treatment of what came to be known as "the Mailbox Rule." The question answered by the Mailbox Rule is whether the offeree's acceptance is binding on the offeror when posted by the offeree or received by the offeror? Of course, there is no question in modern law—the acceptance is effective upon mailing.[9] But when Langdell came to the question, there was no agreement as to when acceptance was effective. In his celebrated article on Langdell,[10] Professor Thomas Grey summarizes Langdell's analysis of the question:

> According to Langdell, the issue between the alternatives was not merely a practical one. In his view, fundamental principles dictated that the acceptance must be received before the contract could be formed. This followed from the doctrine that a promise could not be binding unless it was supported by consideration. The consideration for the offer was the offeree's return promise. But a promise by its nature is not complete until it is communicated; a "promise" into the air is no promise at all. Since there was no promise, there was no consideration and could be

6 *Id.* at vi-vii.

7 Charles W. Elliot, who, as President of Harvard University, appointed Langdell Dean of Harvard Law School, was impressed that Langdell wished to bring the tools of scientific method to the study of law. *See* Speziale, *supra* note 3, at 7-8.

8 This is the "hypothetico-deductive method." It may be described as follows: "[A] hypothesis is proposed, and consequences are deduced, which are then tested against experience. If the hypothesis is falsified, then we learn from the attempt, and are in a position to produce a better one. If not, then we can try other tests." SIMON BLACKBURN, THE OXFORD DICTIONARY OF PHILOSOPHY 182 (1994).

9 *See* RESTATEMENT (SECOND) OF CONTRACTS § 30(2) (1981).

10 Thomas C. Grey, *Langdell's Orthodoxy*, 45 U. PITT. L. REV. 1 (1983).

no contract, until the letter of acceptance was received and read. The mailbox rule could not be good law.[11]

Professor Grey's summary of Langdell's approach to the consideration doctrine raises a question about Langdell's view of legal knowledge. There are two possibilities: first, knowledge of relevant law is obtained by generating principles consistent with the vast majority of decided cases. The point of this inductive approach is to explain as much of the data (cases) as possible. This is one way of approaching law from a scientific point of view. Following Professor Grey, we might label the second alternative "The Geometric Model."[12] Under this approach, it is the task of legal theory to identify principles basic to the subject under scrutiny. But here normativity and rationality converge. Principles are identified through the use of scientific method; but once identified, those principles must be internally coherent. Formal derivability—the hallmark of the geometric method—is not possible if there are contradictions among first principles.

Professor Gilmore observed that for Langdell, "[t]he doctrine tests the cases, not the other way round."[13] What did Gilmore mean? He must be read to say that for Langdell, cases are not data to be explained by a confirmatory hypothesis. In other words, cases do not confirm doctrine (principles) in the way that an experiment confirms the truth of a scientific hypothesis. Experimental results tell the scientist that her hypothesis is correct (or true). The data (experiment) "tests" the hypothesis. But in law, the cases do not test the doctrine, for "[t]he doctrine tests the cases."[14]

On Langdell's account, cases do not show that doctrines—the rules—are correct. Rather, the cases are illustrations of deeper principles identified by other means.[15] Doctrines are not "correct" because they account for a great number or wide variety of cases. Langdell told us that such criteria are irrelevant.[16] The cases—few in number—illustrate or reflect true legal principles. In short, Langdell

---

11 *Id.* at 3-4 (citing Christopher C. Langdell, Summary of the Law of Contracts 1-2, 7-15 (Boston, Little, Brown & Co. 1880)).

12 *See* Grey, *supra* note 10, at 16-20.

13 Grant Gilmore, The Ages of American Law 47 (1977).

14 *Id.*

15 An excellent contemporary example of this approach is found in Posner and Shavell's account of tort law. For them, the language of justification in tort law is no more than an epiphenomenal expression of "deeper" (*i.e.*, economic) forces. *See* Richard Posner & Steven Shavell, The Economics Analysis of Tort Law 22-23 (1987) ("We think that economic principles are encoded in the ethical vocabulary that is a staple of judicial language, and that the language of justice and equity that dominates judicial opinions is to a large extent the translation of economic principles into ethical language.").

16 Christopher C. Langdell, Cases on Contracts at viii (2d ed. 1879) ("[T]he number of fundamental legal doctrines is much less than is commonly supposed. . . .").

turned scientific method on its head. Unlike science, where data is truth-telling (*e.g.*, through confirmation of a hypothesis), in law, the "true" is always theoretical. In short, theory—not data—is primary.

This account of Langdell's approach to law as a science explains how consideration came to be such a central feature in his account of contract law. As Professor Gilmore has remarked, Langdell favored English cases, from which he imported the doctrine of consideration.[17] But those cases were imported not because they were exotic, but because they were rightly decided. Again, doctrine tests the cases. Consideration was a necessary element in contract not because the cases said so,[18] but because the correct theory of contract required it.[19]

It turns out, then, that there is very little that is "empirical" in Langdell's approach to law. This is why Langdell, even in his own time, was criticized for his "unscientific" approach to law.[20] In science, validity (*e.g.*, of a hypothesis) is a function of confirmation (by the data). A confirmed hypothesis is one that has survived the experimental tribunal.[21] But for Langdell, validity was a function of verisimilitude—the correspondence of case with principle. As principle (doctrine) enjoyed pre-testing validity, it was the case that was always under scrutiny.[22]

Having identified the unscientific aspects of Langdell's scientific approach to law, what, if anything, was scientific in his conception of law? The answer is methodological in nature. Mastery of doctrine is the product of study. What is studied are "the cases in which [the doctrine] is embodied."[23] Again, the proportion (of illustrative cases) is "exceedingly small."[24] Cases are studied not in their own right, but as doctrinal exemplars. This is why Langdell says that "the cases which are useful and necessary for this purpose at the present day

17 *See* Grant Gilmore, The Death of Contract, 14 (Ronald K.L. Collins ed., 2d ed. 1995) (Langdell's casebook "was to contain—and presumably did contain—all the important contract cases that had ever been decided. 'All the cases' turned out to be mostly English cases. . . .").

18 That is to say, the cases did not show that consideration was basic to contract.

19 The best example of the centrality of the consideration doctrine in Langdell's theory of contract is Christopher C. Langdell, Summary of the Law of Contracts 58-122 (Boston, Little, Brown & Co. 1880).

20 *See* Grey, *supra* note 10, at 20 n.70.

21 *See* Karl R. Popper, The Logic of Scientific Discovery (1968).

22 I disagree with Professor Grey's characterization of Langdell's approach to law as "inductive." Grey, *supra* note 10, at 21 ("[I]n the classical conception of legal science, the rules and principles constituting the common law are themselves inductively derived from the cases."). If this were true, Langdell would never have argued against the Mailbox Rule. As a construction of doctrine, the Mailbox Rule was wrong, not because the cases so held, but because Langdell's theory of contract would not permit it. Conversely, consideration was a necessary element of a contract despite the fact that a vast number of cases held to the contrary.

23 Langdell, *supra* note 2, at vi.

24 *Id.*

bear an exceedingly small proportion to all that have been reported."[25]

Langdell's approach to law as the classification of cases under a few general principles became the structure for the organization of legal knowledge when it was adopted as the framework for the National Reporter System and the American Law Institute's Restatement projects. Leading cases were collected along doctrinal lines and ordered in a fashion such that the holdings became all important, for it is in virtue of their holdings that cases are classified.

Legal holdings are true or false, correct or incorrect, to the extent they can be classified in the doctrinal framework. The "science of law" is the science of classification along doctrinal lines. In short, the essence of law is not logic, and it is not experience; it is structure (doctrine). A holding—a proposition of law—is true or correct only if it can be classified under some doctrinal principle. The true is what can be verified.

Langdellian method invites the assessment of decided cases not on the basis of legal analysis or craft, but by reference to an apparatus or structure that lies behind law. Correct legal principles are discovered not in the plethora of decided cases, but in the realm of (ideal) theory. Cases are illustrative, not instructive. Cases stand in need of explanation. Doctrine—explanatory principles—is the (hidden) true legal order.

II. Langdell's Legacy

Surprisingly, Langdell's legacy is strongest in the "Law and" movements that have in the last two decades enjoyed immense growth and popularity. Contemporary accounts of the law exhibit the continuing hold of the Langdellian paradigm by their adherence to an "explanatory" (in the Langdellian sense) account of the law. Contemporary theoretical accounts of the law are not interested in how law creates a world; rather, the interest lies in explaining why the law is as it is: "Why is the law 'efficient'?" "How does the law marginalize 'oppressed groups'?" "Is the law consistent with the demands of moral philosophy?"

One finds the "Law and" expression most readily in the contemporary casebook. First, there is the text—dutifully edited—of the opinion. After the text comes a series of notes, inviting the reader to consider the holding of the case from various "points of view." In keeping with the topical focus of this Symposium, let us consider an example from the law of contracts.

---

[25] *Id.*

The popular casebook *Problems in Contract Law: Cases and Materials*,[26] introduces the student to the study of contract law with the case of *Monge v. Beebe Rubber Co.*[27] *Monge* raises a number of issues, the principal one being the question of whether a cause of action exists for bad faith termination of an "at will" employment contract. Not only is *Monge* the very first case a student reads in her Contracts course, but the case is set off as an "example" that, in the words of the casebook authors, is to be considered in the light of "the questions that follow the opinion."[28] Those questions are the best evidence for the continuing hold of Langdell's "scientific" approach to law.

There are a dozen "Notes and Questions" following the *Monge* opinion. Some of these are unremarkable—they include references to classic treatises, a reference to the Uniform Commercial Code, and mention of state unemployment compensation statutes. Nothing unusual here.

Together with these issues are others of even greater interest. The student is invited to consider:

1. Whether the common law of contracts is efficient? If not, should it be?;
2. In the context of a quotation from an article by two leading members of the Critical Legal Studies (CLS) movement,[29] the student is asked to ponder this question: "How do you think a CLS scholar would react to a decision like *Monge*?";
3. Finally, there is a long quotation from the feminist perspective.[30]

What is the relationship between these questions and Langdell's vision of a science of law? Like Langdell, each of these perspectives looks at the law (the cases) not as a phenomenon to be understood, but as one to be explained. If understanding the cases were the task, the emphasis would be on the quality and character of the court's legal argument. But these questions are not concerned with legal argument *qua* legal argument. Rather, like Langdell, the holding is the thing to be explained. The explanation is not a legal explanation but is one offered from the point of view of a nonlegal perspective. The holding is "true" or "correct" if it is consistent with the dictates of the preferred theory (*e.g.*, economics, critical theory or feminism). As with Langdell, a "true" legal proposition is one that is consistent with the demands of the theory. The theory's the thing, not the cases.

26 Charles L. Knapp & Nathan M. Crystal, Problems in Contract Law: Cases and Materials (3d ed. 1993).

27 316 A.2d 549 (N.H. 1974).

28 Knapp & Crystal, *supra* note 26, at 16.

29 The quotation is from Peter Gabel & Duncan Kennedy, *Roll Over Beethoven*, 36 Stan. L. Rev. 1, 33 (1984).

30 The quotation is from Deborah L. Rhode, Justice and Gender: Sex Discrimination and the Law 236-37 (1989).

One might object that this comparison of Langdell with contemporary teaching materials fails to recognize that, in addition to the "perspective" questions enumerated above, there are a host of other, more "traditional" questions. This objection misses the point; the questions under consideration are not of the same type. The answer to a question like "How do you think a CLS scholar would react to a decision like *Monge*?" tells us nothing true as a matter of law. Of course, it may very well tell us something true about the law, but it will not illuminate any legal truth.[31]

I hasten to add that my point is not that some questions are "out of bounds" and others "appropriate." It seems perfectly clear that both sorts of questions are entirely appropriate. The point is that they are *different* questions. One reason why Langdell's scientific approach to law lost its appeal was that it no longer made sense of much of legal practice.[32] The reason this was inevitable was that the type of question he pressed led away from the actual practice of law and toward the embrace of theory. When the theory could no longer account for the practice, people stopped paying attention to the theory.

Langdell's legacy is an explanatory approach to the nature of law. To the unsuspecting, the current interdisciplinary emphasis in legal academia marks something new and different. But it is neither. Understanding cases by concentration on their holdings in the light of broad explanatory principles was precisely what Langdell had in mind when he recommended a scientific approach to law. Langdell's vision may have been updated, but it has not been displaced.

31 I discuss the distinction between propositions that are true of law and those true about law in Dennis Patterson, *The Pseudo-Debate Over Default Rules in Contract Law*, 3 S. Cal. Int'l L.J. 235, 239-40 (1993).

32 *See* Gilmore, *supra* note 17, at 65 ("What the realists had principally attacked, savagely and successfully, was the essentially Langdellian idea that cases can be arranged to make sense—indeed scientific sense. Such an idea, the realists demonstrated, was purest moonshine and nonsense.").

[10] Wittgenstein and Constitutional Theory

My type of thinking is not wanted in this present age,
I have to swim so strongly against the tide.
—Ludwig Wittgenstein[1]

I. Introduction

Constitutional Interpretation[2] *is* the best book on constitutional law in years. But it is also the most philosophically sophisticated and stylistically subtle and, as a consequence, easily misunderstood.

In *Constitutional Grammar*,[3] Jack Balkin and Sanford Levinson characterize Bobbitt as a "normative grammarian" concerned with policing the discourse of constitutional law. In *The Constitution of Conscience*,[4] Steven Winter employs tools taken from cognitive science to assess what he takes to be the philosophy of Wittgenstein. Neither of these papers gives a satisfactory account of Bobbitt's views, and Winter's treatment of Wittgenstein borders on the bizarre. In this Comment, I propose to bring the reader back to Bobbitt and his remarkable body of work.

II. Bobbitt's Constitutional Jurisprudence

There are two familiar ways to evaluate the law from a jurisprudential point of view. First, a theorist asks of a given body of law, "In the light of which general principles may this body of law be explained?" In the

---

* Professor of Law, Rutgers University School of Law—Camden. Visiting Professor of Law, Georgetown University Law Center. J.D., Ph.D. (Philosophy) 1980, State University of New York at Buffalo. My thanks to Sherry Colb, Michael Dorf, and Thomas Morawetz for helpful comments on a draft of this article.

1. M.O'C. Drury, *Some Notes on Conversations with Wittgenstein*, *in* LUDWIG WITTGENSTEIN: PERSONAL RECOLLECTIONS 91, 94 (Rush Rhees ed., 1981).

2. PHILIP BOBBITT, CONSTITUTIONAL INTERPRETATION (1991) [hereinafter BOBBITT, INTERPRETATION].

3. J.M. Balkin & Sanford Levinson, *Constitutional Grammar*, 72 TEX. L. REV. 1771 (1994).

4. Steven L. Winter, *The Constitution of Conscience*, 72 TEX. L. REV. 1805 (1994).

search for principles that animate the law, the theorist seeks some account of the law which shows that despite the seeming discontinuity of legal doctrine, there lies below the surface an animating structure, one that provides the best explanation of the law as we find it.[5]

The second approach to law is not to explain the law as we find it, but rather to provide an "ideal" account of the object or enterprise to which the law is directed. An example here is the current debate in contract theory over how courts should set default rules.[6] One suggestion, which is illustrative of the jurisprudential approach now under discussion, is to connect the particular question regarding default rules to "a general theory of contractual obligation."[7] Inevitably, the theorist of this orientation will argue that the law must be reconstructed in the light of the ideal theory, against which substantive law is evaluated.[8]

Both of the two jurisprudential perspectives just mentioned purport to provide an explanation of the nature and structure of law. Put differently, each purports to offer legal understanding (in what understanding the law consists). This is the point at which the jurisprudential nature of Bobbitt's work becomes relevant. His book provides both a critique of contemporary jurisprudence as well as an alternative to these two approaches.[9]

In brief, Bobbitt provides a jurisprudentially original account of the nature of law. Central to this account is the distinction between legitimacy and justification. Legitimacy, for Bobbitt, does not arise from a normative stance toward the law; legitimacy, to advert to a phrase Bobbitt uses in *Constitutional Fate*,[10] is a matter of employing "The Rules of the Game."[11] The modalities—the six forms of argument in constitutional law—are the rules of the game of constitutional argument.[12] When Bobbitt says that "[l]aw is something we do, not something we have as a consequence of something we do,"[13] he points to a certain relationship be-

5. *Cf.* THOMAS JACKSON, THE LOGIC AND LIMITS OF BANKRUPTCY LAW (1986) (identifying the general principles behind bankruptcy law in evaluating the Bankruptcy Code).

6. For a recent collection of papers, see Symposium, *Default Rules and Contractual Consent*, 3 S. CAL. INTERDISCIPLINARY L.J. 1 (1994).

7. Jules L. Coleman et al., *A Bargaining Theory Approach to Default Provisions and Disclosure Rules in Contract Law*, 12 HARV. J.L. & PUB. POL'Y 639, 641 (1989).

8. *See generally* Ernest J. Weinrib, *Legal Formalism: On the Immanent Rationality of Law*, 97 YALE L.J. 949 (1988) (defending the formalist account of the nature and structure of private law).

9. In my review of *Constitutional Interpretation*, I considered both of these points in detail. *See* Dennis Patterson, *Conscience and the Constitution*, 93 COLUM. L. REV. 270, 270-307 (1993) (reviewing BOBBITT, INTERPRETATION, *supra* note 2).

10. PHILIP BOBBITT, CONSTITUTIONAL FATE (1982) [hereinafter BOBBITT, FATE].

11. *Id.* at 243; *cf. id.* at 233-42 (explaining that legitimacy is not an evaluation of the truth of a constitutional decision by some external standard).

12. *See generally* BOBBITT, INTERPRETATION, *supra* note 2 (articulating his account of the modalities of constitutional argument).

13. *Id.* at 24.

tween the grammar (the modalities) of constitutional argument and the Constitution. Legitimacy is not delivered to the law from outside, as virtually all contemporary theorists maintain.[14] Legitimacy is preserved over time by employment of the grammar of constitutional law—the modalities.

If legitimacy is decision by employment of the modalities, what, then, is justification? Justification is the activity according to which a decision—whether it is legitimate or not—is evaluated. This assessment determines the justice of a legal decision, and so it is distinguished from legitimation; on the other hand, justification is also validated in so far as it accords with the practices that comprise justifying.

Balkin and Levinson, however, describe Bobbitt's view this way: "Justification is the assessment of whether a legitimate utterance is in fact justified."[15] I think this characterization of Bobbitt's argument gets his position wrong in a subtle, but important, way. By tying justification to legitimate utterance, Balkin and Levinson obscure Bobbitt's point about the relationship of decision to justification. The modalities of argument legitimate; they are not "legitimate." *What* they legitimate are arguments made according to their terms, decisions explained in their terms, and decisions and arguments understood in their terms. Utterances are neither legitimate nor illegitimate. By employing the modalities, legitimacy is preserved.[16] Justification comes after decision: "[W]e assess the justice of a particular decision by reference to some external standard, a system of evaluation outside the modalities of argument. That is how *justifying* is done; but not, I will argue, *deciding*."[17] In short, while decision according to law amounts to decisionmaking that can be accounted for and understood in terms of the modalities, determining the justice of such a decision is a matter of the evaluation of a decision from a nonlegal point of view.

Bobbitt shows that contemporary approaches to understanding law have the wrong picture of the nature of law. Understanding law means knowing how to engage in the enterprise.[18] Law is an activity and not an

---

14. Bobbitt would argue that the debate over the legitimacy of judicial review confirms the truth of this generalization. *See id.* at 6-10 (arguing that the debate over judicial review is a fruitless attempt to find an outside source to legitimize constitutional interpretation); *see also infra* text accompanying notes 25-29 (discussing the implications of Bobbitt's theory for the debate over judicial review).

15. Balkin & Levinson, *supra* note 3, at 1775. The obscurity in this statement is present in other places in their paper as well: "Bobbitt's theory also poses a fundamental distinction between the legitimacy of the practice of constitutional argument and the justification of decisions about what the Constitution means." *Id.* at 1778; *see also id.* at 1779 ("[O]ne justifies an interpretation of the Constitution . . . .").

16. That is why Bobbitt refers to legitimacy as an accretion. *See* Patrick O. Gudridge, *False Peace and Constitutional Tradition*, 96 HARV. L. REV. 1969, 1971 (1983) (reviewing BOBBITT, FATE, *supra* note 10).

17. BOBBITT, INTERPRETATION, *supra* note 2, at 163 (emphasis in original).

18. I join Akhil Amar in celebrating the pedagogical importance of Professor Bobbitt's project. *See* Akhil R. Amar, *In Praise of Bobbitt*, 72 TEX. L. REV. 1703, 1704 (1994) ("Bobbitt's modalities are key tools for me in the classroom.").

object in need of explanation. Contemporary theorists devote their energies to understanding law in the language of their preferred vocabulary—economics, moral philosophy, feminism, or critical race theory—and thereby shift their descriptions of law into justification. There is nothing wrong with this approach per se so long as no legitimation is inferred or implied in the shift.[19]

III. Change and Normativity

Does Bobbitt's account of constitutional argument account for criticism of or change in the practice of constitutional argument? If so, does he explain criticism and change in our constitutional practice in ways that do not sacrifice his account of legitimacy? Legitimacy, as Bobbitt describes it, is an accretion.[20] Legitimacy is maintained by playing the rules of the game—by employing the forms of argument to show the truth of propositions of law.

Balkin and Levinson see a certain danger in Bobbitt's account of legitimacy—one implicating the issues of criticism and change in our constitutional practice. They make their point this way:

> A . . . problem with Bobbitt's theory is that it has difficulty accounting for the possibility of changes in our constitutional grammar. If our practices of constitutional argumentation are legitimate because they are how we live and how we think, then if our practices change, they do not lose legitimacy, because this is how we now live and now think. However, this will not do for Bobbitt because he thinks that constitutional argument has changed for the worse because of the work of the left and the right from the 1950s onward. These people have misunderstood the nature of constitutional argument and have misled everyone else.[21]

For Balkin and Levinson, Bobbitt's project is both descriptive and normative.[22] They argue that Bobbitt wants to defend the existing practice

---

19. *See* Philip Bobbitt, *Is Law Politics?*, 41 STAN. L. REV. 1233, 1306 (1989) (reviewing MARK TUSHNET, RED, WHITE, AND BLUE: A CRITICAL ANALYSIS OF CONSTITUTIONAL LAW (1988)) ("It is simply a mistake to suppose that we consult these disciplines to tell ourselves how to apply a legal rule.").

20. *See supra* note 16 and accompanying text.

21. Balkin & Levinson, *supra* note 3, at 1791 (footnote omitted).

22. The authors describe Bobbitt's project as follows:

> Thus we see that Bobbitt's goal is not only to explicate, but also to defend the existing practices of constitutional discourse from those who would challenge or alter them . . . .
>
> . . . .
>
> . . . According to Bobbitt's own theory, the only legitimate practices are those that actually exist; the only legitimate language games are those that are currently being played, and their legitimacy in each case is established by the fact that they do exist and are currently being played.

Id. at 1780-81.

of constitutional argument from those who would seek to alter the practice. In short, they think Bobbitt bears a certain burden of production:

> Are Berger's, Bork's, and Tushnet's practices normal or deviant, especially if from their standpoint Bobbitt's own practices might be regarded as deviant? In order to answer these questions, Bobbitt must explain and justify his criteria for identifying what counts as normal or deviant practices of constitutional argument. He must offer an account of what makes his account a better interpretation than proffered alternatives. In particular, he must show why one type of practice is better and another type is worse when both can be found within the spoken language of the native speakers of constitutional law talk. Because a simple description of the actual practices of constitutional argument cannot achieve these goals, his project must become both interpretive and normative.[23]

While he never states so directly, Bobbitt cannot accept the proposition that Berger, Tushnet, and Bork determine the practice of constitutional argument to the same extent and in the same way as the legal opinions of judges and the briefs and oral arguments of counsel. Consider the following observation by Bobbitt in a recent encyclopedia contribution:

> Constitutional Interpretation is both the process by which the American Constitution is construed and the study of that process. The latter is principally an academic activity, while the former art is practiced daily by government officials and private lawyers. . . . Let us first look at how judges and practitioners interpret the Constitution and then survey what academics have said about that practice.[24]

Constitutional argument is what lawyers and judges do. Academics comment on that work. Academics do not interpret the Constitution for the purposes of making legal argument. They remark upon the product of those for whom constitutional interpretation is an everyday occupation. Thus, Bobbitt rightly can adopt a normative position toward the politicized claims of Tushnet and Bork while maintaining a descriptive stance toward constitutional argument generally.

What if one were to accept Bobbitt's constitutional jurisprudence? What would be the implications of such a move? If one were persuaded of the virtues of a "descriptive constitutional jurisprudence," which debates would be over and which would begin?

Actually, Bobbitt's point is that arguments within practices are legitimate or not to the extent those arguments employ the modalities of the enterprise.

23. *Id.* at 1790-91.

24. Philip Bobbitt, *Constitutional Interpretation*, *in* THE OXFORD COMPANION TO THE SUPREME COURT OF THE UNITED STATES 183, 183 (Kermit C. Hall et al. eds., 1992).

First, and most obviously, the debate over the legitimacy of judicial review would end. This is not because Bobbitt has defined the debate out of existence.[25] Instead, he has shown that the terms of the debate render it pointless.[26] Bobbitt's goal is to describe how lawyers make constitutional arguments, for it is in how those arguments are made that one discerns how legal propositions are shown to be true and false. Judicial review names a particular practice of constitutional argument. Bobbitt's point is that there is nothing special about judicial review: It is simply one legal activity among many, no more nor less deserving of our attention.[27] Its legitimacy does not depend upon its justification in political (or other) theory.

Bobbitt's position has broader implications for jurisprudence. Take the contemporary debates over "interpretation" in law.[28] From the left,[29] the center,[30] and the right,[31] the debate is over the proper lens for interpreting the Constitution.[32] If Bobbitt is correct, there is no lens—nothing between the Constitution and our understanding of it. When we understand how the modalities are used to show the truth of propositions of constitutional law, we understand how the Constitution has meaning. We do not grasp the meaning of the Constitution with the modalities; rather, the modalities are the means by which constitutional propositions are shown to be true or false.

IV. Wittgenstein and Constitutional Theory

Although Wittgenstein rarely appears explicitly in Bobbitt's work,[33] it has always been clear to philosophically inclined readers that Bobbitt's

25. My point is that Bobbitt's recasting of the debate over the legitimacy of judicial review is not a mere verbal ploy. Rather, the effort is to show that the debate takes up a pseudoproblem.

26. For a discussion and elaboration of this point, see Patterson, *supra* note 10, at 284-93.

27. *See* BOBBITT, INTERPRETATION, *supra* note 2, at 9-10 ("The use of the six forms of constitutional argument is the way we decide constitutional questions in the American legal culture. The practice of judicial review is compelled by such methods. There is no more to say about the legitimacy of such review.").

28. For criticism of the turn to interpretation, see Dennis Patterson, *The Poverty of Interpretive Universalism: Toward the Reconstruction of Legal Theory*, 72 TEX. L. REV. 1 (1993).

29. *See, e.g.*, Robin West, *The Aspirational Constitution*, 88 NW. U. L. REV. 241 (1993) (endorsing a progressive and aspirational interpretation of the Constitution).

30. *See, e.g.*, RONALD DWORKIN, LAW'S EMPIRE (1986) (arguing that legal reasoning is an exercise in constructive interpretation).

31. *See, e.g.*, ROBERT H. BORK, THE TEMPTING OF AMERICA (1990) (arguing that the Constitution should be interpreted consistently with its original understanding).

32. Of course, the Constitution is just one focus of interpretive attention. The primacy of interpretation is pervasive. *See* Patterson, *supra* note 28, at 2-3 ("[I]nterpretation is a central organizing theme of the late twentieth century.").

33. See the allusions to Wittgenstein in epigraphs to BOBBITT, FATE, *supra* note 10, at vii, and PHILIP BOBBITT, DEMOCRACY AND DETERRENCE vi (1988).

project is in considerable sympathy with Wittgenstein's. It is not a matter of "applying" Wittgenstein (would that it were so easy!) as much as approaching problems having been informed by Wittgenstein's insights and approaches. This method runs a certain risk, however, that philosophically inclined, but largely unsophisticated, readers will mangle Bobbitt in much the same way Wittgenstein was mangled for three decades.

Steven Winter's essay, *The Constitution of Conscience*,[34] attacks Bobbitt's *Constitutional Interpretation* by attacking Wittgenstein. I think it can be shown easily that he has no idea what Bobbitt is doing. How does Winter do with Wittgenstein?[35] We are told that reading Wittgenstein is positively disadvantageous to a proper understanding of law. Winter tells us that the "Wittgensteinian point of view" is fallacious,[36] fetishizing,[37] and reductionist.[38] The indictment does not end there. It seems that exposure to a Wittgensteinian text is so corrupting that it causes one to ignore ordinary human activities such as communication.[39] Even human rationality, which Winter describes as "ineradicably imaginative,"[40] escapes the gaze of the Wittgensteinian reader. In the face of such condemnation, one is moved to ask the following: Even if Winter's indictment results in conviction on just a few of these many counts, why would one ever turn to Wittgenstein for a better understanding of law?

Before we can speak about Wittgenstein and constitutional law, it might be helpful to review a few points about Wittgenstein's own aspirations in philosophy.[41] In his later philosophy,[42] Wittgenstein directed his

---

34. Winter, *supra* note 4.

35. Professor Winter has authored many articles in which he adapts the work of others in the field of cognitive science in order to illuminate the nature of law. My efforts here are not directed to this body of work. Rather, I comment solely upon Professor Winter's paper in this Symposium in which he critiques what he thinks are philosophical shortcomings in the thought of Wittgenstein.

36. *See* Winter, *supra* note 4, at 1813 (arguing that the Wittgensteinian approach engenders a "particularist fallacy").

37. *Id.*

38. *Id.* at 1822.

39. *Id.*

40. *Id.*

41. I discuss Wittgenstein's approach to philosophy more expansively in Dennis M. Patterson, *Wittgenstein and the Code: A Theory of Good Faith Performance and Enforcement Under Article Nine*, 137 U. PA. L. REV. 335 (1988).

42. On the question of the two Wittgensteins, I have noted:

> The question whether there is one Wittgenstein or two is endlessly debated. Compare R. Ackermann, Wittgenstein 7 (1988) (one Wittgenstein) with N. Malcolm, Nothing Is Hidden: Wittgenstein's Criticism of his Early Thought ix (1986) (the earlier thought is "purged" by the later). Perhaps the only agreement among scholars is that in his "first phase," Wittgenstein argued that language mirrored reality. Thus, the study of language could be a way of uncovering the logical structure of the world. In his "second phase," which began when he returned to Cambridge in 1929, Wittgenstein took up a whole new approach to philosophy. In this phase of his thought Wittgenstein concerned

energies toward many varied problems and projects. He produced a work on the nature of certainty and doubt.[43] He also wrote a great deal about problems in the philosophy of mind,[44] the philosophy of mathematics,[45] and philosophical psychology.[46] A consistent theme throughout Wittgenstein's work is that the task of philosophy is the clarification of our uses of language.[47] Wittgenstein condemned academic philosophy as arid and pointless.[48] In brief, Wittgenstein rejected a central presumption of the philosophical tradition—that language has a structure that can be revealed through analysis. Language, Wittgenstein believed, reflected no such structure: It is a motley of related uses. Hence, it is impossible to have a unified "theory" about any given linguistic concept.[49]

To understand human activities, Wittgenstein argues, one must understand how the participants in the activity conduct it; understanding a practice is a matter of catching on to the ways the activity is conducted.

> himself with the question of how language acts as a constitutive medium of understanding.
>
> Put succinctly, in his first phase, Wittgenstein believed that language pictured the world.
>
> In his second phase, Wittgenstein believed that language gave us a world.

Dennis M. Patterson, *Law's Practice*, 90 COLUM. L. REV. 575, 576 n.9 (1990) (reviewing KARL N. LLEWELLYN, THE CASE LAW SYSTEM IN AMERICA (1989)).

43. LUDWIG WITTGENSTEIN, ON CERTAINTY (G.E.M. Anscombe & G.H. von Wright eds., Denis Paul & G.E.M. Anscombe trans., Harper & Row 1972).

44. LUDWIG WITTGENSTEIN, PHILOSOPHICAL INVESTIGATIONS §§ 316-427 (G.E.M. Anscombe trans., 3d ed. 1968) [hereinafter WITTGENSTEIN, INVESTIGATIONS].

45. LUDWIG WITTGENSTEIN, REMARKS ON THE FOUNDATIONS OF MATHEMATICS (G.H. von Wright et al. eds. & G.E.M. Anscombe trans., 1956) [hereinafter WITTGENSTEIN, MATHEMATICS].

46. 1 LUDWIG WITTGENSTEIN, REMARKS ON THE PHILOSOPHY OF PSYCHOLOGY (G.E.M. Anscombe & G.H. von Wright eds., G.E.M. Anscombe trans., 1980); 2 LUDWIG WITTGENSTEIN, REMARKS ON THE PHILOSOPHY OF PSYCHOLOGY (G.H. von Wright & Heikki Nyman eds., C.G. Luckhardt & M.A.E Aue trans., 1980).

47. *See, e.g.*, LUDWIG WITTGENSTEIN, TRACTATUS LOGICO-PHILOSOPHICUS 4.112 (D.F. Pears & B.F. McGuinness trans., 1961) ("Philosophy is not a body of doctrine but an activity. . . . Philosophy does not result in 'philosophical propositions', but rather in the clarification of propositions.").

48. A general account of Wittgenstein's view of academic philosophy can be found in D.A.T. Gasking & A.C. Jackson, *Wittgenstein as Teacher*, *in* LUDWIG WITTGENSTEIN, THE MAN AND HIS PHILOSOPHY 53-54 (K.T. Fann ed., 1967).

49. The late Norman Malcolm summarizes well this aspect of Wittgenstein's thought:

> After his return to philosophical research [in 1929], Wittgenstein came to the realization that "what we call 'proposition' and 'language' is not the formal unity that [he] had imagined but is a family of structures more or less related to one another." The implication of this perception was that there could not be a correct philosophical theory of language. If the concept of language is not a unitary concept, we should expect the same of the other concepts with which philosophy has struggled. If the word "cause", as it is actually used, does not have a uniform employment, but an irregular one, then there cannot be a correct theory of the essence of causation. The same holds for the concepts of truth, representation, knowledge, justice, the good and so on. Wittgenstein's new insight into the actual working of language implies that the enterprise of philosophical analysis, as traditionally conceived, is based on a false assumption.

NORMAN MALCOLM, WITTGENSTEIN: A RELIGIOUS POINT OF VIEW? 43 (1993).

A famous example, which comes from the opening paragraph of *Philosophical Investigations*,[50] concerns the meaning of the word "five":

> I send someone shopping. I give him a slip marked "five red apples." He takes the slip to the shopkeeper, who opens the drawer marked "apples"; then he looks up the word "red" in a table and finds a colour sample opposite it; then he says the series of cardinal numbers—I assume he knows them by heart—up to the word "five" and for each number he takes an apple of the same colour as the sample out of the drawer. It is in this and similar ways that one operates with words. "But how does he know where and how he is to look up the word 'red' and what he is to do with the word 'five'?" Well, I assume that he acts as I have described. Explanations come to an end somewhere. But what is the meaning of the word "five"? No such thing was in question here, only how the word "five" is used.[51]

This wonderfully simple example illustrates a general point about Wittgenstein's approach to philosophy. Instead of articulating "theories" about the meaning of the word "five," Wittgenstein recommends that we attend to the uses of the word—obtain a clear picture of how the word is used. The meaning and, thus, correct uses of "five" are shown in the activities in which the word has a role. Study those activities, learn how to use "five" correctly, and you will learn the meaning of "five."[52]

Theoretical approaches to law all take the position that understanding the activity requires the identification of something that mediates between the participant and the activity itself. The leading candidate today is "interpretation." I have argued elsewhere that Ronald Dworkin and Stanley Fish each believe that understanding law is a matter of interpreting it.[53] For Dworkin, a "correct" understanding of law is a matter of "constructive interpretation."[54] For Fish, a "correct" understanding of law means having an interpretation that everyone in one's "interpretive community" agrees is correct.[55] While each unpacks "correct" differently, Dworkin and Fish both believe that understanding is mediated by interpretation.

---

50. WITTGENSTEIN, INVESTIGATIONS, *supra* note 44.

51. *Id.* § 1, at 3e.

52. Does one need a "theory" of carpentry to be a master builder? Does mastery require theoretical prowess?

53. Patterson, *supra* note 28, at 20, 38.

54. *Id.* at 12. Dworkin argues that a "correct" account of law—the truth of a legal proposition—is a matter of finding a political justification of law that puts the law in its "best light." *See* DWORKIN, *supra* note 30, at 225 ("[P]ropositions of law are true if they figure in or follow from the principles of justice, fairness, and procedural due process that provide the best constructive interpretation of the community's legal practice.").

55. Patterson, *supra* note 28, at 35.

Wittgenstein believed interpretation to be a second-order phenomenon, one that could come into play only against a background of understanding.[56] Thus, we see that Bobbitt's constitutional theory is very much in the tradition of Wittgenstein. Like Wittgenstein, Bobbitt rejects the idea that understanding is a matter of the mediation of experience, or of the Constitutional text, through some lens. The modalities are the ways one understands the Constitution from the legal point of view. The grammar of constitutional argument is the way the Constitution has meaning. We do not interpret the Constitution with the modalities, for to put it that way assumes that the Constitution already has a meaning that is then interpreted. This, in part, is why Bobbitt's contribution does not end with constitutional law, but extends well into jurisprudence and philosophy generally.

A. *Interpretation and the Third Term*

Winter insists that the introduction of a third term—something standing between the Constitution and our understanding of it[57]—is necessary because it is only by virtue of a third term that one is able to explain what it means to participate in a practice—a constitutional argument.[58] Because Bobbitt's theory of the Constitution has no such term, his account of constitutional law is deemed a failure.

The rejection of a third term—a mediating device between subject and

---

56. *See infra* text accompanying notes 78-80 (discussing Wittgenstein's account of understanding and interpretation).

57. One might refer to Professor Winter's view as "structuralist" because he uses that term and its cognates with such frequency. *See, e.g.*, Winter, *supra* note 5, at 1824. But Professor Winter is never as clear in his use of these terms as one would like: He seems yet to have decided whether his position is structuralist or not. Compare the following sentences: "[M]any of the constituent facets of a practice will themselves be comprehensible only by reference to things and experiences outside that practice," *id.*; "[E]ven in the hands of its most subtle proponents, the Wittgensteinian account is necessarily impoverished by its elimination of the middle term of the dialectic. Without a moment of objectification or other cognitive consolidation, it has no alternative except to reduce meaning to a 'primordial' and inexplicable dimension of practice," *id.* at 1821; "Our hypothetical Wittgensteinian counsellor is correct in saying that the maxims do not acquire legitimacy by correspondence with some truth-conferring, mind-independent reality. The proverbs are, after all, social constructions," *id.* at 1821-22. The upshot of these passages seems to be that understanding is objective and socially constructed. The problem with such a view is that these terms—objectivity and social construction—are the endpoints on a long continuum, one that contains virtually every available position on legal understanding. Additionally, Professor Winter often confuses metaphysical objectivity—the way things are—with epistemological objectivity—our knowledge of the way things are. *See generally* Brian Leiter, *Objectivity and the Problems of Jurisprudence*, 72 TEX. L. REV. 187, 195 n.30 (1993) (reviewing KENT GREENAWALT, LAW AND OBJECTIVITY (1993)) (arguing that metaphysical objectivity and epistemological objectivity are often confused in legal literature).

58. Of course, Professor Winter does not speak in terms of propositions of law, nor does he speak of truth and falsity. Because he fails to employ the terms and arguments familiar to those in jurisprudence, it is sometimes difficult to discern exactly what his claims and criticisms are.

practice—is central to Winter's critique of Wittgenstein. He states his position:

> We are now in a position to see exactly why the Wittgensteinian approach is prone to the problems and distortions identified earlier. In effect, it goes straight from externalization—that is, ongoing human activity—to internalization without any mediations whatsoever. Thus, even in the hands of its most subtle proponents, the Wittgensteinian account is necessarily impoverished by its elimination of the middle term of the dialectic. Without a moment of objectification or other cognitive consolidation, it has no alternative except to reduce meaning to a "primordial" and inexplicable dimension of practice. Correlatively, we can also see why, for the Wittgensteinian, reflection necessarily drops out. Simply put, the Wittgensteinian has nothing—that is, no "thing"—for practitioners to reflect upon. There is only the purely performative dance of an ongoing practice and its practitioners' inexpressible tacit knowledge: "What they know is either inside them or (at least on this day) beyond them."[59]

There seem to be two claims in this paragraph: First, the Wittgensteinian account of understanding in a practice is impoverished because it lacks a middle term; and second, there is no place for "reflection" in a Wittgensteinian account of understanding in a practice. Neither of these claims is plausible.

One possible inadequacy in the Wittgensteinian account of understanding is that without a middle term, we cannot account for why different people understand the same legal rule in the same way over time.[60] Winter accounts for objectivity in judgment by following the lead of some cognitivists[61] in positing the existence of "structures" through which input is mediated[62] and turned into ideas.[63] The reason for the structure—the

59. Winter, *supra* note 4, at 1821 (quoting STANLEY FISH, DOING WHAT COMES NATURALLY: CHANGE, RHETORIC, AND THE PRACTICE OF THEORY IN LITERACY AND LEGAL STUDIES 373 (1989)).

60. I discuss this issue in the context of Winter's analysis of knowledge of institutional practices. *See infra* text accompanying notes 73-75.

61. *See, e.g.*, MARK JOHNSON, THE BODY IN THE MIND: THE BODILY BASIS OF MEANING, IMAGINATION, AND REASON xxiv (1987) (describing the objectivist view of rationality, which considers reasoning to be "a series of operations in which connections among symbols and rule-governed combinations of symbols are established and traced out according to various logical canons or principles"); GEORGE LAKOFF, WOMEN, FIRE, AND DANGEROUS THINGS: WHAT CATEGORIES REVEAL ABOUT THE MIND 5 (1987) ("There is nothing more basic than categorization to our thought, perception, action, and speech.").

62. *See* Winter, *supra* note 4, at 1824 ("[M]eaning is mediated by imaginative operations that include objectification, transfiguration, and subsequent reflection.").

63. This picture of understanding was formulated in the seventeenth century by the English philosopher John Locke. *See* JOHN LOCKE, AN ESSAY CONCERNING HUMAN UNDERSTANDING bk. 2, ch. 1, §§ 1-4 (Peter H. Nidditch ed., 1975) (proposing that ideas are formed both by the perception of the senses and by the perception of the operation of the mind).

third term—is that we need some measure of consistency. How do we know that when we use a term in the future that use will be consistent with past usage?[64] The third term is the answer.

But the solution provided by the third term turns out to be a pseudo-explanation of the nature of understanding—legal or otherwise.[65] Let us be clear about the form of explanation under attack. Wittgenstein argued against positing a psychologistic inner process between neural input and understanding.[66] He rejected the idea that understanding or recognition is best explained by resort to something going on inside our heads.[67] Winter claims that without that "something," a Wittgensteinian cannot account for the meaning of our words.

What is Wittgenstein's answer? In one discussion of this issue, Wittgenstein imagined someone saying: "You need only look at the figure

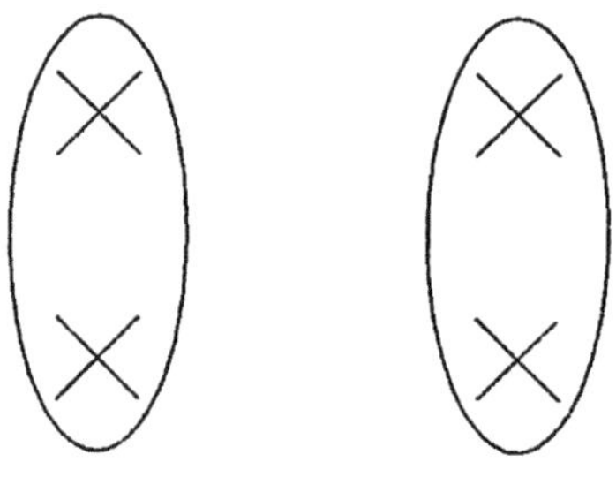

to see that 2+2 are 4."[68] Of course, the set-up here is for the purpose

64. A version of this question is famously taken up in SAUL A. KRIPKE, WITTGENSTEIN: ON RULES AND PRIVATE LANGUAGE 7-54 (1982) (addressing the question: How do I know my present use of a term is consistent with past usage?).

65. Professor Winter consistently confuses two questions. First, one may ask what makes it possible for humans to communicate. This can be an empirical, biological, or linguistic question. A different question—a philosophical question—is what it means to say that an utterance is meaningful. *See* MICHAEL DUMMETT, ORIGINS OF ANALYTICAL PHILOSOPHY app. at 187-88 (1993) ("Philosophy is not concerned with what enables us to speak as we do, but what it is for our utterances to have the meanings that they have, and nothing that happens in the brain can explain that."). Because of his persistent confusion of these two different types of questions, Professor Winter believes scientific progress solves philosophical problems. But this simply cannot be. Consider a blind person playing chess. What enables the person to play the game (a good memory) tells us nothing about whether the person is playing correctly. Likewise in law (or any other discipline), what enables us to participate in the activity tells us nothing about the activity itself (how it is conducted—its rules).

66. *See generally* WITTGENSTEIN, INVESTIGATIONS, *supra* note 44.

67. For a discussion of Wittgenstein and mind, see P.M.S. HACKER, WITTGENSTEIN: MEANING AND MIND (1990). Importantly, Wittgenstein did not reject the notion that we have thoughts or other inner processes; he simply rejected the idea that our thoughts and inner processes explain the meanings of words. *See* WITTGENSTEIN, INVESTIGATIONS, *supra* note 44, §§ 243-315.

68. WITTGENSTEIN, MATHEMATICS, *supra* note 45, at 14e.

of rejecting the realist point that the mathematical significance of the figure may be determined apart from the conventions for manipulation, computation, and synthesizing of information.[69] Wittgenstein demolishes the position with the following rebuttal: "Then I only need look at the figure

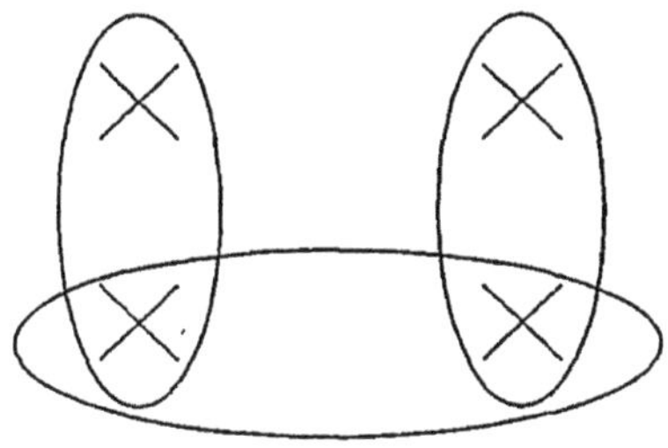

to see that 2+2+2 are 4."[70]

Wittgenstein's point is not that the arithmetical truth has or does not have a relationship to the physical world, but that there is no arithmetical "truth" without the conventions and habits of arithmetic—the "grammar" of arithmetic, the arithmetical equivalent of the modalities. No mathematical truth can be uttered or shown apart from the forms of mathematical expression. These forms make arithmetical truths possible.

Winter has to be read as asserting that the Wittgensteinian account of arithmetical understanding is inadequate because it makes no place for an intermediary between the figures on the page and an individual subject's correct calculation. Unfortunately, Winter's posited third term—a mediating device through which correct answers are discerned—does not account for understanding how to do sums or in what correctly doing sums consists.[71] Winter insists that we must see meaning as "mediated by imaginative operations."[72] Why? He invites us to consider the example of an institution:

> Consider, for example, the development and perpetuation of an insti-

69. This discussion has profited from David Bloor's reading of the passage. *See* DAVID BLOOR, WITTGENSTEIN: A SOCIAL THEORY OF KNOWLEDGE 91, 90-91 (1983) ("The point [of Wittgenstein's example] is that the arithmetical truth has a complex relationship to the physical world, including the physical symbols used to represent it.").

70. WITTGENSTEIN, MATHEMATICS, *supra* note 45, at 14e.

71. Part of the explanation for the failure of Winter's critique is his belief that knowledge is in some measure an empirical concept. But knowledge is not "in the brain." The mind is necessary for a person to have knowledge, but the knowledge is not found in the synapses. Nothing in the brain will tell us what it means "to know the law," for that is dependent upon what participants in the legal system decide counts as knowing the law.

72. Winter, *supra* note 4, at 1824.

tution. If it is to endure, it must be reproduced successfully in the performance of actual actors. To assure such continuity, there must be an educational process through which the relevant recipe knowledge can be transmitted systematically to those whose actions will constitute the institution in the future. Thus, the process of transmission itself creates pressure to reduce this recipe knowledge to canonical, easily memorizable forms—"maxims, morals, proverbial nuggets of wisdom, values and beliefs, myths, and so forth," the familiar "'what everybody knows' about a social world." In this way, "[l]anguage becomes the depository of a large aggregate of collective sedimentations, which can be acquired . . . as cohesive wholes and without reconstructing their original process of formation."[73]

At no point does Winter explain how anything he identifies as a third term accounts for the phenomenon of linguistic meaning. Recall Wittgenstein's discussion of the meaning of "five."[74] Professor Winter is like Wittgenstein's interlocutor who, after having had counting explained to him, asks, "But what is the meaning of 'five'?"

Wittgenstein's philosophical point is that cognition is social in character—that objectivity and rationality are "things that we forge for ourselves [as in the arithmetical example] as we construct a form of collective life."[75] Winter's assertion that this explanation is but a partial picture of the nature of human understanding can convince only when he shows—and not merely asserts—how these "objectified sedimentations" give rise to meaning in the same way as human practices.

B. *Interpretation and Reflection*

Now to the second of Professor Winter's assertions, to wit, that a Wittgensteinian account of law "effaces the role of reflection by situated practitioners in the performance and perpetuation of a practice."[76] Of course, there is a place for reflection in the Wittgensteinian account of understanding in practices.

As we have seen, for Professor Winter, understanding law means explaining the practice through the lens of a mediating device. Winter eschews the language of moral philosophy, economics, history, or sociology and chooses instead his own laws, those of "metaphoric devices." There are, to be sure, several basic philosophical problems with such a

73. *Id.* at 1820 (footnotes omitted) (citing and quoting PETER L. BERGER & THOMAS LUCKMANN, THE SOCIAL CONSTRUCTION OF REALITY: A TREATISE IN THE SOCIOLOGY OF KNOWLEDGE 65 (1966)).

74. *See supra* note 51 and accompanying text.

75. BLOOR, *supra* note 69, at 3.

76. Winter, *supra* note 4, at 1818.

move.[77] Consider just one: the problem of infinite regress of justification. Winter asserts that to interpret the Constitution, one must have a lens—a mediating device—that gives the Constitution meaning. The lens—in Winter's case, metaphor—instructs you how to read the document. Fine, but what tells you how to use the lens? Is the meaning of the lens somehow self-evident? If the lens is a set of rules for applying rules, why are there no rules for the application of the rules, and rules for the application of the rules for the application of the rules? Such basic conceptual problems simply cannot be ignored.

But let us directly answer Winter's charge of lack of reflection. Winter claims that there is no role for reflection in Wittgenstein's account of understanding. But Wittgenstein himself addressed this question directly when he drew the distinction between understanding and interpretation.[78] Interpretation—reflection on how to adjudicate between different formulations of a rule—is a uniquely reflective activity. James Tully describes the reflective role of interpretation in these words:

> [Interpretation] is a practice we engage in when our understanding and use of signs is in some way problematic or in doubt. Here we attempt to come to an understanding of the sign in question by offering various interpretations (expressions) as opposed to different ones, adjudicating rival interpretations, in some cases calling the criteria of adjudication into question, and so on. . . . Interpretation should thus be seen as one important practice of critical reflection among many, resting comfortably in more basic ways of acting with words (self-understandings) that cannot themselves be interpretations.[79]

Interpretation is a reflective activity, one we engage in when conventional meanings—employments of the modalities—are called into question. In the activity of interpretation (reflection), participants advance proposals for

---

77. I canvass these in Patterson, *supra* note 10, at 289-93.

78. Wittgenstein drew this distinction in the course of his famous discussion of rule-following:

> This was our paradox: no course of action could be determined by a rule, because every course of action can be made out to accord with the rule. The answer was: if everything can be made out to accord with the rule, then it can also be made out to conflict with it. And so there would be neither accord nor conflict here.
>
> It can be seen that there is a misunderstanding here from the mere fact that in the course of our argument we give one interpretation after another; as if each contented us at least for a moment, until we thought of yet another standing behind it. What this shews is that there is a way of grasping a rule which is not an interpretation, but which is exhibited in what we call "obeying a rule" and "going against it" in actual cases.
>
> Hence there is an inclination to say: every action according to the rule is an interpretation. But we ought to restrict the term "interpretation" to the substitution of one expression of the rule for another.

WITTGENSTEIN, INVESTIGATIONS, *supra* note 44, § 201, at 81e (emphasis omitted).

79. James Tully, *Wittgenstein and Political Philosophy*, 17 POL. THEORY 172, 196 (1988).

continuing our practice—the practice of constitutional argument—one way rather than another. In addition to the reflective practice of interpretation—adjudicating various proposals in accordance with criteria of interpretation—we may engage in a further, ancillary reflective practice of putting the criteria themselves into question.[80] Throughout each of these practices, the point is to advance interpretations in the hope of reaching agreement about how to go on with our practice of constitutional argument. Far from being fundamental, interpretation (reflection) is dependent upon conventional understandings already in place. Contrary to Winter, we now understand that interpretation is best seen as a therapeutic activity—one for reaching understanding, not explaining it.

Winter's mistake is in believing that all understanding of law is interpretation. The third term—the mediating device—is an interpretive prism. Winter thinks the Wittgensteinian account of understanding comes up short only because Winter embraces this philosophically confused account of the nature of understanding. But Wittgenstein got it right. It simply cannot be the case that everyone is interpreting everything all the time. There must be something that everyone participates in—something shared, something common. In constitutional law, that something is the modalities, the grammar of constitutional argument. Were there not widespread agreement in the application of the modalities, constitutional law simply would not be possible.[81] It is only against a background of widespread agreement that disagreement, interpretation, and reflection are possible.[82]

C. *Interpretation and Indeterminacy*

We come, finally, to Professor Winter's last topic of discussion: indeterminacy. The details of the previous discussion of the role of reflection in Wittgenstein's distinction between understanding and interpretation enable us to quickly see why Professor Winter's remarks about indeterminacy wholly miss their intended target.

Professor Winter begins by affirming what he takes to be Roberto Unger's position that "law can only be the product of a myriad of political and ideological conflicts."[83] He then asks how a Wittgensteinian might

80. This is one way of understanding the jurisprudential project of Ronald Dworkin. *See generally* DWORKIN, *supra* note 30 (challenging positivism with the thesis that law is a thoroughly "interpretive" practice).

81. Wittgenstein argued that while practices required agreement, the fact of agreement explains nothing—it does no normative work. *See* WITTGENSTEIN, INVESTIGATIONS, *supra* note 44, § 241, at 89e.

82. For discussion of this point in the context of early debates over interpretation in law, see Dennis M. Patterson, *Interpretation In Law—Toward a Reconstruction of the Current Debate*, 29 VILL. L. REV. 671, 676-88 (1984) (rejecting debates over interpretation in law that employ terms of subjectivity and objectivity).

83. Winter, *supra* note 4, at 1828.

respond to Unger's claim. Professor Winter reads Bobbitt, the Wittgensteinian under scrutiny, as conceding that law "*is* either ideology or indeterminacy."[84] Bobbitt, so Professor Winter argues, believes himself to have solved the indeterminacy problem "with the resort-to-conscience gambit."[85] This "gambit" is dismissed by Professor Winter for being "like pasting a rhetorical Band-Aid over a very real aporia."[86]

What, in Professor Winter's view, would it take to solve the problem of indeterminacy? To what would a properly informed legal theorist repair to solve the problem of indeterminacy? Professor Winter holds out Charles Taylor as an example of someone who embraces what Professor Winter sees as the correct solution to the problem of indeterminacy—"objectification, institutionalization, and retention of legal meaning."[87] Law, Professor Winter tells us, "cannot be understood apart from the larger social practices—the form of life—in which it participates."[88] We must see that "law is dependent on culture,"[89] for culture "is both anterior and interior to the language and thought of law."[90]

It is truly ironic that Professor Winter chooses Charles Taylor—the most distinguished contemporary exponent of the hermeneutic tradition—to register his objectivist disagreements. Professor Taylor has authored two articles on Wittgenstein's philosophy,[91] both of which run counter to the very position Professor Winter attributes to Taylor. Just a few passages will suffice to make the needed point:

> We can't understand human life merely in terms of individual subjects who frame representations about and respond to others, because a great deal of human action happens only insofar as the agent understands and constitutes him or herself as an integrall part of a "we."[92]

Taylor also notes:

---

84. *Id.* (emphasis in original). Professor Winter employs a familiar false dichotomy with a parenthetical question: "Indeed, without foundations, what other alternatives could there be?" *Id.*

85. *Id.*

86. *Id.*

87. *Id.* at 1829.

88. *Id.*

89. *Id.* at 1830.

90. *Id.* at 1833.

91. *See* Charles Taylor, *To Follow A Rule . . .*, *in* BOURDIEU: CRITICAL PERSPECTIVES 45, 45-60 (Craig Calhoun et al. eds., 1993) [hereinafter Taylor, PERSPECTIVES] (arguing against the idea that understanding requires something to stand between language and the world); Charles Taylor, *To Follow a Rule*, *in* RULES AND CONVENTIONS 167, 177-78 (Mette Hjort ed., 1992) [hereinafter Taylor, RULES] (rejecting causal explanations of rule-following). Additionally, Taylor has endorsed the arguments of his colleague, James Tully, against the primacy of interpretation. *See* Tully, *supra* note 79, at 196 ("Taylor now agrees with this conclusion.").

92. Taylor, PERSPECTIVES, *supra* note 91, at 52.

> What is important about this kind of understanding is its connection to social practice. My embodied understanding exists in me, not only as an individual agent, but as the co-agent of common actions. This, I believe, is how we should understand Wittgenstein's claim that "obeying a rule" is a practice, that is, a social practice. . . .
>
> Standing social usage is what establishes the connection in question here, which cannot, as a result, be understood as a merely causal one.[93]

Taylor's Wittgensteinian point is that whatever our practices turn out to be, it is we who decide their form and content. If law is dependent on culture, it is because we have made it so. Professor Winter's claim is that something else—"sedimentations"—something outside ourselves, regulates what we do in law.[94] Professor Winter's burden of proof is that of the metaphysical realist: to show that the fit "between our thought and the world is determined independently of human cognition."[95] There is little in Professor Winter's critique of Wittgenstein to indicate how this burden of proof could be met.

Professor Winter no doubt would disagree with my characterization of the position he advances in support of his critique of Wittgenstein. The reason for this disagreement is that Professor Winter fails to appreciate fully the philosophical implications of his arguments. Philosophical questions cannot be answered by empirical data; if they could be, philosophy would have been over a long time ago. Thus, nothing we learn about how the brain functions will ever solve a philosophical problem, for philosophy is not an empirical endeavor. It is only because Professor Winter conflates fundamentally different issues and questions that he can believe himself to be advancing a coherent point of view. In this he is mistaken.

As I have previously noted,[96] Much of twentieth-century analytic philosophy is devoted to the proposition that when it comes to our words, "it is we who fix a reference."[97] The legacy of philosophy from the middle of this century to the present has been the systematic replacement of foundationalist epistemology with holism,[98] the substitution of referential

93. Taylor, RULES, *supra* note 91, at 177-78 (citation omitted).

94. Winter, *supra* note 4, at 1820.

95. John Haldane & Crispin Wright, *Introduction* to REALITY, REPRESENTATION AND PROJECTION 3, 3-4 (John Haldane & Crispin Wright eds., 1993). For a discussion of recent jurisprudential work from a realist perspective, see BRIAN BIX, LAW, LANGUAGE, AND LEGAL DETERMINACY 133-77 (1993).

96. Patterson, *supra* note 9, at 304-05.

97. Henry Staten, *The Secret Name of Cats*, *in* REDRAWING THE LINES: ANALYTIC PHILOSOPHY, DECONSTRUCTION, AND LITERARY THEORY 27, 43 (Reed W. Dasenbrook ed., 1989) (emphasis omitted).

98. *See generally* WILLARD V.O. QUINE, *Two Dogmas of Empiricism*, *in* FROM A LOGICAL POINT OF VIEW 20, 20-46 (2d ed. 1961) (arguing against the analytic-synthetic distinction and urging that knowledge is embedded in "the whole of science").

theories of language with an emphasis on speech as action,[99] and a general movement away from the individual as the foundation of empirical, linguistic, and moral judgment. The nineteenth century's emphasis on the individual as the site of judgment has been replaced with various conceptions of "group" knowledge: the language-game,[100] the scientific community,[101] and the web of belief.[102]

Professor Winter seeks a quasi-scientific account of law, one that can bring the objectivity of the scientific enterprise to the human sciences. A singular virtue of Bobbitt's critique of contemporary constitutional theory is in revealing the continuing influence of the scientific approach to legal justification and its attendant shortcomings. Perhaps the time has come to realize that by aping the aspirations of natural scientists, legal theorists manage not only to miss the beauty of law, but worse, they make of it a vulgar illusion.

V. Conclusion

Whatever the merits of Wittgenstein's approach to philosophy might be, Philip Bobbitt's contribution to constitutional theory stands on its own merit. One cannot "apply" Wittgenstein to the law, for there is—literally—nothing to apply. The lesson of Wittgenstein is that philosophizing about a subject is an *ersatz* endeavor. It is better to clarify an enterprise such as law than to theorize about it. Not only has Bobbitt advanced a perspicuous and compelling account of constitutional argument, he has changed the terms of the debate over the nature of law. This is a significant and exciting contribution to jurisprudence.

---

99. *See generally* J.L. AUSTIN, HOW TO DO THINGS WITH WORDS (J.O. Urmson & Marina Sbisà eds., 2d ed. 1975) (exemplifying the analysis of linguistic meaning in terms of use); WITTGENSTEIN, INVESTIGATIONS, *supra* note 44, at 1 (analyzing the use of the word "five").

100. *See* WITTGENSTEIN, INVESTIGATIONS, *supra* note 44, § 7, at 5e ("I shall call the whole, consisting of language and the actions into which it is woven, the 'language-game.'").

101. *See* THOMAS S. KUHN, THE STRUCTURE OF SCIENTIFIC REVOLUTIONS 163-64 (2d ed. 1970) ("[O]nce the reception of a common paradigm has freed the scientific community from the need constantly to re-examine its first principles, the members of that community can concentrate exclusively upon the subtlest and most esoteric of the phenomena that concern it.").

102. *See* QUINE, *supra* note 98, at 42 (concluding that all knowledge is "a man-made fabric," only peripherally attached to experience and so interconnected that reevaluation of one proposition forces reevaluation of others). For discussion of this point, see Peter Galison, *History, Philosophy, and the Central Metaphor*, 2 SCI. IN CONTEXT 197, 203 (1988) ("Quine strongly opposed the total separation of observation from other forms of knowledge; for him, all were up for evaluation."); Nancey Murphy, *Scientific Realism and Postmodern Philosophy*, 41 BRIT. J. PHIL. SCI. 291, 294 (1990) ("Quine not only replaced the foundationalist theory of knowledge with a holist account, but also provided a new picture or metaphor—that of a web or network of beliefs—to replace the 'layer-cake' model.").

[11]

Conscience and the Constitution (reviewing Philip Bobbit, *Constitutional Interpretation*)

> Above all, one should not wish to divest existence of its *rich ambiguity* . . . .
>
> —Nietzsche††

Introduction

This is the best book of constitutional theory in years. Were its argument fully understood and its particulars to become central to academic legal culture, the focus of constitutional theory would change dramatically.[1] The significance of the book, however, extends far beyond the confines of constitutional law: the most exciting aspect of *Constitutional Interpretation* is not what is said about constitutional law but what the argument means for jurisprudence generally. The book represents the further articulation and refinement of an original philosophical approach that provides an alternative to much of contemporary jurisprudence. It is to this aspect of the book that I will draw attention.

The central theme of *Constitutional Interpretation* is that there is nothing more nor less to constitutional law than the practice itself. This is a thoroughly radical view, one that is shared by virtually no one else in constitutional law or theory on the current scene.[2] Bobbitt is

---

* Professor of Law, Rutgers University School of Law (Camden); Visiting Professor of Law, The University of Texas at Austin, School of Law. I have received helpful comments on drafts of this essay from Anne Dalesandro, Richard Hyland, Brian Leiter, and Thomas Morawetz. My thanks to Dean Roger Dennis, Rutgers School of Law (Camden), for productive discussion of a draft of this essay and for financial support of this work. Special thanks to Allan Stein and Jack Balkin.

†† Friedrich Nietzsche, The Gay Science 335 (Walter Kaufmann trans., 1974).

1. For discussion of the concerns of mainstream constitutional theory, see Paul W. Kahn, Community in Contemporary Constitutional Theory, 99 Yale L.J. 1, 2 (1989) (characterizing modern constitutional theory as an effort to find a new synthesis of reason and will). For an assessment that goes beyond modernist sensibilities, see J.M. Balkin, What Is a Postmodern Constitutionalism?, 90 Mich. L. Rev. 1966 (1992).

2. I have myself argued in this spirit in the context of commercial law. See Dennis M. Patterson, Wittgenstein and the Code: A Theory of Good Faith Performance and Enforcement Under Article Nine, 137 U. Pa. L. Rev. 335 425–29 (1988); Dennis M. Patterson, Law's Pragmatism: Law as Practice & Narrative, 76 Va. L. Rev. 937, 991–95 (1990).

critical of the reigning picture of justification in law and is keen to show its faults and replace it with another account. To succeed at such a project, he must do at least three things: accurately describe the conventional picture of legal justification, demonstrate why this picture is inadequate, and provide an alternative account that avoids the shortcomings of the conventional picture without creating new problems in the process.

This essay is structured in a manner consistent with these three tasks. I begin with a description of the conventional approach to the question of the legitimacy of judicial review. A central feature of Bobbitt's argument is his claim that contemporary constitutional theory misconceives the relationship between legitimacy and justification. Because Bobbitt's critique need not be limited to constitutional law, the reach of the argument is extended to the ongoing debate between Ronald Dworkin and Stanley Fish over the nature of interpretation in law. A virtue of this debate over legal interpretation is that it implicates larger themes in the contemporary philosophy of language, which I explore in detail. I then turn to Bobbitt's attempt to use individual conscience as the means for resolving conflicts among the various forms of constitutional argument. My claim is that while the argument does not fully convince, the book remains a profound contribution to contemporary jurisprudence.

I. The Conventional Picture

A. *Legal Justification*

Bobbitt reveals the faults of the reigning picture of legal justification by returning to a debate he first considered in an earlier book, *Constitutional Fate*.[3] In that work, Bobbitt argued that the controversy over the legitimacy of judicial review was a pseudo-debate, driven largely by a false picture of the nature of justification in constitutional law. The essentials of that argument are an important component of Bobbitt's position in *Constitutional Interpretation*.[4]

In brief, Bobbitt argues that the practice of constitutional interpretation is a matter of using six forms of argument (he refers to them as "modalities") to demonstrate the truth of propositions of constitutional law.[5] Justification—the activity of demonstrating the truth of a legal proposition—is a matter of employing the modalities. To be legiti-

3. Philip Bobbitt, Constitutional Fate: Theory of the Constitution (1982).

4. An intermediate step in the present formulation of Bobbitt's position is his extended review of Mark Tushnet's Red, White and Blue: A Critical Analysis of Constitutional Law (1988) in Philip Bobbitt, Is Law Politics?, 41 Stan. L. Rev. 1233 (1989). The book under discussion comprises a portion of Bobbitt's review of Tushnet (pp. 126–40). Because the Tushnet review stands on its own as an example of the power of modal analysis, in the present essay I do not address this aspect of the book under review.

5. The various modalities are discussed in detail infra Part II.A.

mate, a constitutional argument must remain within the modalities. The modalities themselves, either alone or in combination, can never be legitimate, for they are the means by which legitimacy is maintained (through their use in argument). The modalities are the constitutional grammar of justification.

The question of what legitimates judicial review has stimulated a number of important and sophisticated accounts of the nature of the Constitution and its interpretation, not to mention theories of the nature of the judicial process itself.[6] Despite the merits of these many interesting and important works, Bobbitt argues that none has noticed that the debate is a pseudo-debate, driven by a mistaken picture of the nature of justification in constitutional law.

The key to the "problem" of judicial review lies in the relationship between legitimacy and justification. The conventional wisdom is that judicial review cannot be justified unless it is legitimate.[7] To this end, constitutional theorists advance an array of theories of legitimacy.[8] Once the preferred theory is proffered, it is employed as a measure of the legitimacy of specific acts of judicial review. In short, judicial review is justified to the degree it is congruent with the preferred theory of legitimation. Bobbitt's position is that all attempts to find a normative foundation outside the conventions of legal argument confuse legitimacy with justification. Neither the Constitution, the conventions of legal argument, nor judicial review requires legitimation. Legitimacy is obtained when the conventions of legal argument (the modalities) are adhered to. Justification is the use of the modalities to demonstrate that a proposition of constitutional law is true. A constitutional argument in support of the truth of a proposition of constitutional law is legitimate to the extent it employs the modalities. To the degree it does not, it is illegitimate.

The defenders of judicial review advance various arguments in support of the legitimacy of judicial review.[9] Originalists, for example,

---

6. Of course, these questions have occupied generations of scholars. Two leading, recent examples are Jesse H. Choper, Judicial Review and the National Political Process (1980) (arguing that the Court must exercise judicial review to protect human rights), and John H. Ely, Democracy and Distrust: A Theory of Judicial Review (1980) (outlining a theory of representation-reinforcing judicial review).

7. As Alexander Bickel put the objection: "[W]hen the Supreme Court declares unconstitutional a legislative act or the action of an elected executive, it thwarts the will of representatives of the actual people of the here and now; it exercises control, not in behalf of the prevailing majority, but against it." Alexander M. Bickel, The Least Dangerous Branch 16–17 (1962).

8. Each of these theories of legitimacy is a response to the question "What justifies judicial review?" It is to confuse the relationship between legitimacy and justification to argue that judicial review cannot be legitimate unless it is justified by the dictates of a normative or political theory.

9. It turns out that in their effort to legitimate judicial review, each of these theories of legitimacy grabs hold of a form of legal argument and elevates it to the level of a theory of legitimation. For example, the reason arguments of text are appropriate in

contend that judicial review gives voice to the original intent of the framers. These intentions, they argue, must be the overriding normative justification for judicial review, lest judges go about their business without the appropriate degree of restraint on their interpretive activities.

Another "justification" for judicial review, one close in spirit to originalism, is that offered by so-called "textualists." The Supremacy Clause provides: "This Constitution . . . shall be the supreme Law of the Land; and the Judges in every State shall be bound thereby, any Thing in the Constitution or Laws of any State to the Contrary notwithstanding."[10] This, it seems, implies the following:

> (1) all judges, when asked to apply any law, must do so in conformity with "supreme" law; that is the common import of the word "supreme"; and
> (2) that the laws and constitutions of the states, even when construed by state judges, must give way to the provisions of the United States Constitution in case of conflict; "giving way" is . . . the common inference drawn from the use of the term "do as here instructed anything to the contrary notwithstanding"; and
> (3) that insofar as the same Article also carefully provides that only those federal laws "which shall be made in pursuance" of the Constitution are the law of the land, this language indicates that federal laws that conflict with the Constitution cannot be given effect as law (pp. 25–26).

Yet a third "justification" for judicial review lies in the positive effects of the practice, and is advanced by what Bobbitt terms "the prudential advocate" (p. 26). Judicial review, the advocate argues, has the salutary effect of serving "a goal (or goals) with which the advocate associates himself. These goals may be: the protection of minorities; the exercise of vigilance on behalf of civil liberties; the taming of revolution into reform or the fanning of reform into revolt (consciousness raising); and so on" (id.).

Each of these three forms of argument is a response to the question of what legitimates judicial review. Judicial review, it seems, is legitimate because the intentions of the framers, the text of the Constitution, or the effects of judicial review each justify the practice.

Each of these justifications certainly has its detractors. The power of originalism as a normative justification for judicial review is totally dependent upon the ability of present-day interpreters of the Constitution to ascertain correctly the precise content of original intentions. This is no simple task, if only because historical evidence of intention

constitutional practice is that we have a written Constitution. The forms of legal argument are the means by which a proposition of law is shown to be true. A form of argument can no more legitimate legal argument than a ruler can justify or legitimate measuring.

10. U.S. Const. art. VI, cl. 2.

often points in more than one direction, or sometimes in no direction at all.[11] More telling, perhaps, is the question of why the polity of the present should be governed by the dead hand of the past. Originalists have had difficulty formulating an acceptable answer to this objection.[12]

For textualists, the situation appears even more grim. To claim that judicial review is legitimate because the text of the Constitution makes it so is, in effect, to assert that the language of the constitutional text speaks free from the individual perspective of the reader.[13] From Paris,[14] to Durham,[15] to Berkeley,[16] contemporary critics assert that there is no author and that it is the reader who produces the meaning of a text. For the textualist, it seems, there is no escape from the semantic vortex of signs and subjectivity.

Prudentialists—those who argue that judicial review is legitimate because it produces effects worth having—are represented on both the Right[17] and the Left[18]. Each side argues for the legitimacy of judicial review on the basis of the values it promotes. Naturally, there is little agreement over what those values are or should be, but all forms of the prudentialist argument invite a well-known criticism: the problem of the infinite regress of justification. By answering the skeptic's question, "What justifies judicial review?" with a response that identifies one's preferred normative agenda, the prudentialist invites the further question, "What, then, justifies *that* value?" To proffer *yet another* preferred value (for example, the vigilant protection of First Amendment guaran-

---

11. See generally Paul Brest, The Misconceived Quest for the Original Understanding, 60 B.U. L. Rev. 204 (1980) (rejecting strict textualism and strict interpretivism as untenable in constitutional decisionmaking).

12. But see Earl Maltz, Some New Thoughts on an Old Problem—The Role of the Intent of the Framers in Constitutional Theory, 63 B.U. L. Rev. 811, 836–50 (1983) (advancing a noninstrumental, structural justification for interpretive review).

13. That constitutional language is rarely this unambiguous is evidenced by Judge Easterbrook's contention that a sentence containing the number "thirty-five" may not mean what it says:

> When the Constitution says that the President must be thirty-five years old, we cannot be certain whether it means thirty-five as the number of revolutions of the world around the sun, as a percentage of average life expectancy (so that the Constitution now has age fifty as a minimum), or as a minimum number of years after puberty (so the minimum now is thirty or so).

Frank H. Easterbrook, Statutes' Domains, 50 U. Chi. L. Rev. 533, 536 (1983).

14. See generally Michel Foucault, The Archaeology of Knowledge (A.M. Sheridan Smith trans., 1972) (all knowledge is produced within an "episteme" or grid).

15. See generally Stanley Fish, Doing What Comes Naturally (1989) (collection of essays from the perspective of "reader-response" literary theory).

16. See generally Avital Ronnell, The Telephone Book (1989) (deconstruction of the telephone as a technological presence in discourse).

17. See Michael J. Perry, The Constitution, the Courts, and Human Rights 99–119, 225 (1982) (arguing for an active role for the Supreme Court in the "moral evolution" of the polity).

18. See generally Tushnet, supra note 4 (addressing five forms of constitutional argument from a prudentialist perspective).

tees is a good thing *because* the proliferation of viewpoints tends to produce the truth) is not to answer the skeptic, only to put her off. For every answer to the question, "What justifies X?", the skeptic simply takes the answer, fills in the blank, and poses the question anew. More often than not, the infinite regress of justification ends not because some primordial value has been identified,[19] but because no further answer to the skeptic can be given. What this shows, the skeptic argues, is that the prudentialist justification for judicial review is really nothing more than the articulation of a personal, political preference that has been elevated to the status of law.

On the surface, it would appear as if the originalist, the textualist, and the prudentialist disagree deeply over the legitimate ground of constitutional practice. In a sense they do, for each provides a separate and distinct account of its legitimate normative foundations,[20] and their answers partake not at all in a shared or common point of view on the nature of the explanatory or justificatory matrix for constitutional law. These disagreements, however, are only superficial. What is truly important about these various approaches to constitutional argument are not the differences but a striking similarity, one that has even gone unnoticed by the combatants themselves.

The similarity is the one noticed earlier. Proponents of theories of judicial review all start from the premise that in the absence of a theory of legitimation, the act of judicial review is unjustified. Bobbitt's point is that resort to a theory of legitimacy only has the effect of asking a question about law from the point of view of some other enterprise (for example, political theory, history, or moral philosophy). The conclusion that judicial review is legitimate is a claim that can only be justified relative to the argumentative standards of the preferred discipline. This may be interesting, but it is irrelevant; for what interests us are legal propositions. And for these, only legal conventions of argument are appropriate.

B. *Justification and the Ghost of Langdell*

The conventional wisdom treats propositions of constitutional law as if they were propositions about the world. Armed with a theory of legitimacy, the conventional theorist turns her attention to the evaluation of propositions of constitutional law (for example, "the Constitution prohibits busing school children to parochial schools"). If the proposition is consistent with the dictates of the preferred theory of

19. But see John Finnis, Natural Law and Natural Rights 85–97 (1980) (a natural law jurisprudence based on a theory of basic human needs).

20. To this point, I have limited discussion to the question of judicial review. However, Bobbitt's argument is not constrained by any particular topic. He uses the debate over the legitimacy of judicial review to make a larger jurisprudential point about the nature of justification in constitutional law—that is, that the conventional picture misunderstands the relationship between legitimacy and justification.

legitimacy, then the proposition is true; to the degree it is not, it is false. This approach, Bobbitt argues, treats legal propositions as if they were statements "about the world" (p. 34), verifiable in the same ways as empirical propositions. This confusion of legal and scientific modalities lies at the heart of contemporary constitutional jurisprudence. As I will argue later,[21] the same argument can be made about contemporary jurisprudence generally.

To reveal the common ground shared by the divergent camps in contemporary constitutional theory, Bobbitt turns to an unlikely source: Christopher Columbus Langdell, universally regarded as the father of legal formalism[22] and a strong proponent of the use of scientific method in law.[23] In comparing law to science, Langdell believed the task of legal theory to be the discovery of principles that underlie legal doctrine.[24] Langdell's scientific view of law had two methodological presuppositions. First, the number of fundamental principles is small, and second, for that reason, exhaustive knowledge of reported decisions was simply unnecessary.[25] Once the fundamental principles were identified, they were all one needed to "think like a lawyer."

Bobbitt organizes his argument around the question, "What is the nature of a legal proposition?" There are two answers: his own and the "Langdellian" answer, which is a form of "causal" explanation embraced by many approaches to constitutional law and theory. The Langdellian approach attempts to explain constitutional law by identifying "ideological and political commitments [that] are somehow 'behind' or 'beneath' " (p. 23) the surface play of constitutional argument. These approaches

> simply assume an epistemological attitude that is highly controversial, i.e., they undertake to explain events in the world by reference to ideas that allegedly cause such events while maintaining that the explanatory scheme itself is outside the otherwise pervasive causal influence it allegedly describes. No doubt there are many persons who continue to believe that class, or race, or sex or personal history determine "how we see the world"—as though these were spectacles that are put on at a certain age and could be removed, indeed have been removed by the clear-sighted analyst. This is only a modern version of the claim that such influences determine how we behave. But to a growing number this will seem naive. The

21. See infra Part I.C.

22. By "formalism," I mean the view that legal conclusions can be generated solely by rigorous use of law's distinct methodological tools.

23. See Thomas Grey, Langdell's Orthodoxy, 45 U. Pitt. L. Rev. 1, 5 (1983).

24. See Christopher C. Langdell, Address to the Harvard Law School Association (1886), quoted in Grant Gilmore, The Ages of American Law 42 (1977) (comparing law to zoology).

25. See Christopher C. Langdell, Selection of Cases on the Law of Contracts viii–ix (2d ed. 1879).

> world is a human idea, inseparable from our perceptions of it, and thus something we can apprehend only with the spectacles of humanity firmly in place. Nor are our faculties detachable from the perspectives they enable or the world without which they are disabled (id.).

In this paragraph Bobbitt sets off causal from normative explanations.[26] He thinks many theorists make the mistake of advancing causal accounts of law when legal statements are not statements about the world: hence, the "explanations" miss the target and leave the theorist, as they say in New England, "shingling into the fog." Because law is a normative practice, only an account of justification appropriate to law's character as a normative practice will suffice. Bobbitt explains:

> Although most people may to some extent hold the view[] . . . that there *must* be some sublime explanatory mechanism that allows our ideas to interact with the world—there is no reason to think so.
>
> . . . .
>
> Law is something we do, not something we have as a consequence of something we do. Sometimes our activities in law—deciding, proposing, persuading—may link up with specific ideas we have at those moments; but often they do not, and it is never the case that this link must be made for the activities that are law to be law. Therefore the causal accounts of how these inner states come into being, accounts that lose their persuasiveness in contact with the abundance of the world, are really beside the point. If we want to understand the ideological and political commitments in law, we have to study the grammar of law, that system of logical constraints that the practices of legal activities have developed in our particular culture (p. 24).

While resort to principle as an explanatory method is an important element in Langdell's approach to law, there is another aspect of his approach that is of far greater importance. The resort to principle is motivated by a particular conception of what it is to *explain* legal thinking. Langdell's model is driven by the demand to explain legal doctrine by resort to "the unifying theories that underl[ie] the rationales of these cases" (p. 46). Thus, the holdings of cases are not to be explained as the *product* of legal reasoning; rather, they are simply phenomena that *themselves* stand in need of "explanation."[27] From this

26. A causal form of explanation tells you why something happened. For example, one could give an account of the physical processes involved in stopping an automobile at a red light. One could say that the red light sets off a causal reaction in the driver, which itself is the product of training, physical processes, neural firings, etc. A normative explanation tells you what the physical acts amount to (e.g., why stopping at a red light is the "correct" way to drive an automobile).

27. For a survey of recent law and economics scholarship with particular emphasis on the question of explanation of legal doctrine, see Jason S. Johnston, Law, Economics, and Post-Realist Explanation, 24 Law & Soc'y Rev. 1217 (1990).

observation, Bobbitt renders the following diagnosis:

> Every significant casebook and law review reflects this approach, though few of their authors and editors would subscribe to Langdell's description of law as a science. Despite such up-to-date agnosticism, however, these authors and editors usually do in fact share the main consequence of Langdell's description, namely that legal holdings are propositions about the world. As such, they can be verified, if they are *law*, by reference to some feature of the world, some fact outside the control of the verifying judge or scholar. And so the "progressive" casebooks add dubious historical and social science materials, while the "conservative" casebooks confine themselves to reprints of notable cases. But whatever the excerpt, one will always find it followed by a set of leading questions designed to elicit the relevant "fact" and to invite the reader to compare that fact with the holding and rationale of the doctrine. In his lecture, the law professor will, by the use of other cases and hypotheticals, adroitly or fecklessly, demonstrate the competing values and rationales at stake. The more vain the professor, the more it will appear that the court's opinion is a hopeless series of ill-conceived assertions that can be effortlessly shown to contradict the past (precedent) as well as the future (those hypotheticals) (p. 47).

Bobbitt argues that contemporary juridical pedagogy and sophisticated legal theory are still within the grip of the Langdellian picture of legal (i.e., causal) explanation. Sustaining such a claim requires further comment about Bobbitt's assertion that what lies at the root of the Langdellian picture of law is the presupposition that legal propositions are, as Bobbitt explains, "propositions about the world" (p. 47). If the claim is true, then Bobbitt is right about the continuing hold of the Langdellian picture of law. But Bobbitt's argument cuts deeper still. As Bobbitt sees it, legal propositions are not propositions about the world, and illuminating the nature of these propositions is his goal. If he is right about the continuing hold of the Langdellian picture, then virtually the whole of contemporary jurisprudence is locked into a hopeless epistemology, one that fuels such complex but ultimately vacuous debates as the one surrounding the indeterminacy of law, the question of whether law is reducible to politics, and, of course, the ascendancy of the idea that law is an "interpretive" practice.[28]

Is there any debate in contemporary jurisprudence that employs the form of causal explanation Bobbitt describes? There is one debate[29] that fits this description in ways that, at first, may appear quite

28. See generally Ronald Dworkin, Law's Empire (1986) (theory of law as an interpretive concept). See also Fish, supra note 15, at 141–42, 149 (law is a congeries of "interpretive communities").

29. There are others as well, such as the debate over the "indeterminacy" of law and over the question whether race and gender are epistemological prisms.

surprising. I have in mind the feud between Ronald Dworkin and Stanley Fish over the question, among others, of the role of interpretation in law. The details of the Dworkin/Fish debate are worth pursuing, for both Dworkin and Fish represent two of the most widely-discussed views on the nature of interpretation in law. They both seem to think that their views are wildly different; but if Bobbitt is right, the differences are only superficial. Such a startling claim must be supported with an argument equal to the task. Bobbitt does not produce such an argument, but supplying one is surely possible.

C. *The Dworkin/Fish Debate*

Ronald Dworkin and Stanley Fish disagree over what it means to say that some proposition of law is true. At first glance, both provide an answer to the question that appears to be the same: each thinks that interpretations make propositions of law true. Although Dworkin and Fish may mean vastly different things by "interpretation," and we must be careful to point out those differences, they each end up subscribing to the same *form* of answer.

In the latest expression of his position,[30] Dworkin seeks to replace the positivist emphasis on agreement in criteria as the ground of true propositions of law[31] with his notion of "law as integrity": "According to law as integrity, propositions of law are true if they figure in or follow from the principles of justice, fairness, and procedural due process that provide the best constructive interpretation of the community's legal practice."[32] What is important to notice in Dworkin's account of truth in law is his claim that the truth of legal propositions is a function of something that transcends legal discourse, namely principles of justice or fairness. The gravamen of Dworkin's conception of the relationship between the practice of legal argument and political theory is that propositions of law are *made true* because they stand in a certain relationship to political theory. Only the political theory that puts the law "in its best light" can make a proposition of law true.[33]

30. See Dworkin, supra note 28, at 4–6, 31–46, 87, 110–13. For discussion, see Ronald Dworkin, Is There Really No Right Answer in Hard Cases?, *in* A Matter of Principle 119, 134–37, 142–43 (1985) (discussing, inter alia, the notion of a "true proposition of law"). Dworkin's definition of a legal proposition is uncontroversial. See Dworkin, supra note 28, at 4 ("Let us call 'propositions of law' all the various statements and claims people make about what the law allows or prohibits or entitles them to have.").

31. Dworkin criticizes positivism for what he perceives as its anti-realist theory of meaning. See Ronald Dworkin, Introduction to The Philosophy of Law 8 (Ronald Dworkin ed., 1977).

32. Dworkin, supra note 28, at 225.

33. For a recent discussion of the relationship between truth and justification in Dworkin's theory of law, see Andrei Marmor, Interpretation and Legal Theory 39–40 (1992) (law consists "of source-based law as well as all the norms derivable from the soundest political theory justifying the source-based law").

For Stanley Fish, "the text, while always there, is always an interpreted object."[34] The meaning of the legal text is never a property of the text itself, but rather the product of an interpretive community whose members share a reading strategy. As Fish describes the matter: "[M]eanings are the property neither of fixed and stable texts nor of free and independent readers but of interpretive communities that are responsible both for the shape of a reader's activities and for the texts those activities produce."[35] For Fish, it is the reader who produces the meaning of the text by adopting a personal reading strategy, one she applies as do others in her "interpretive community." Thus, "being a member of an interpretive community" means producing meaning from a text by employing (not sharing)[36] the same reading strategy as the rest of the community's members. It is a short step from this construction to the claim that "[a] meaning that seems to leap off the page, propelled by its own self-sufficiency, is a meaning that flows from interpretive assumptions so deeply embedded that they have become invisible."[37] In Bobbitt's view, Fish celebrates "the irreducible nature of every text" (p. 42). This is surely correct. It seems that if the meaning of the text is not a property of the text, then anything is permitted. The only way to achieve stability in meaning is by agreement, and it is agreement in interpretive assumptions which, in Fish's view, makes a proposition of law (or anything else) true.

For both Dworkin and Fish, propositions of law are true because they stand in a certain relationship to something beyond the bounds of "law" as it is conventionally understood. For Dworkin this external element is a political theory: a proposition of law is true because it satisfies the normative demands of law as integrity. Chief among these demands is the requirement that the judge's decision be consistent with what she sees as the best political justification of the practice of law taken as a whole. Fish's counterpart to Dworkin's best political justification are "tacit assumptions" that underlie our legal language. Thus, Fish explains disagreement over the grounds of law as nothing more than a failure in the convergence of interpretive assumptions.[38]

---

34. Fish, supra note 15, at 563 n.31.

35. Stanley Fish, Is There a Text in This Class? 322 (1980).

36. Gerald Postema illustrates the two senses of sharing in the following manner:

> The history of [a] friendship is a common history, and the complex meaning of the relationship is collectively constructed over the course of this history. When friends share a common history, Aristotle points out, it is not like cows sharing a pasture, for the shared life of friends engenders common perception, a common perspective, and common discourse. Friendship is characterized, ultimately, not by sympathy or consensus (*homonoia*), but by common deliberations and thought.

Gerald J. Postema, "Protestant" Interpretation and Social Practices, 6 Law & Phil. 283, 309 (1987).

37. Fish, supra note 15, at 358.

38. For a detailed example of this phenomenon, see Fish's discussion of Riggs v. Palmer, 22 N.E. 188 (N.Y. 1889), in Fish, supra note 35, at 278–81. Fish explains the

But Dworkin and Fish end up with an identical picture of the nature of legal justification. Law is a set of linguistic propositions that are either true or false. The truth or falsity of legal propositions is a function of something beyond the mere surface play of legal justification (for example, appeals to the language or structure of a statute, precedent, or legislative history). Their only disagreement is over what the "something" is that makes legal propositions true or false. For Dworkin it is political theory; for Fish it is interpretive presuppositions.

In the opening pages of *Law's Empire*, Dworkin describes propositions of law as "all the various statements and claims people make about what the law allows or prohibits or entitles them to have."[39] There are two types of disagreements one can have about propositions of law. The first type, which Dworkin identifies as "empirical disagreement,"[40] is exemplified by the type of disagreement that might arise around the claim "the speed limit is 55 miles per hour." Disagreement over the truth of this proposition can be readily settled by resort to the appropriate statute: its existence will determine whether or not the proposition is true.

Of greater interest is the type of disagreement termed "theoretical disagreement," or "disagreement about law's grounds."[41] This type is more problematic, for unlike mere empirical disagreement, theoretical disagreement is disagreement "about what the law *really* is."[42] The question implicates debate over the ultimate or true grounds of law. There is much contestation about this, manifesting itself in debates about whether judges ever "make law." On this question, Dworkin states:

> In a trivial sense judges unquestionably "make new law" every time they decide an important case. They announce a rule or principle or qualification or elaboration—that segregation is unconstitutional or that workmen cannot recover for fellow-servant injuries, for example—that has never been officially

---

disagreement between the majority and the dissent not as a conflict over principle, but as a failure of interpretive assumption:

> If it is assumed that the purpose of probate is to ensure the orderly devolution of property at all costs, then the statute in this case will have plain meaning urged by the defendant; but if it is assumed that no law ever operates in favor of someone who would profit by his own crime, then the "same" statute will have a meaning that is different, but no less plain. In either case the statute will have been literally construed, and what the court will have done is prefer one literal construction to another by invoking one purpose (assumed background) rather than another.

Id. at 280.

39. Dworkin, supra note 28, at 4.

40. Id. at 5. Dworkin argues that, for legal positivists, empirical disagreement is the only form of disagreement in law because, so they argue, "law's grounds" are exhausted by institutional history and criteria (e.g., statutes, precedents, etc.). See id. at 6–11.

41. Id. at 5.

42. Id. (emphasis added)

> declared before. But they generally offer these "new" statements of law as improved reports of what the law, properly understood, already is. They claim, in other words, that the new statement is required by a correct perception of the true grounds of law even though this has not been recognized previously, or has even been denied.[43]

The key to Dworkin's jurisprudence—a realist metaphysics[44]—lies in what he means by the "true [as opposed to apparent] grounds of law" and how he answers the question, "What does the law *really* require?"[45] For Dworkin, the answer to this question lies in his assumption that "it is the 'ground rules' of the legal practice—the principles which establish the 'grounds' of (true propositions of) law."[46] The grounds of true propositions of law transcend the institutional and craft elements of legal practice. Without political theory, identification of the grounds of true legal propositions—that *in virtue of which* propositions of law are true—would be impossible.[47] Legal propositions are true only to the extent that they are consistent with the idea that "the political theory that supplies the best justification for non-controversial propositions of law provides for the rights or duties which the controversial proposition describes."[48]

Not surprisingly, Fish is much more straightforward than Dworkin

43. Id. at 6.

44. I am by no means the first to identify Dworkin's view as realist. See Geoffrey Sayre-McCord, Introduction: The Many Moral Realisms, *in* Essays on Moral Realism 1, 16 (Geoffrey Sayre-McCord ed., 1988). As Sayre-McCord sees it, "a perfectly respectable realist position in philosophy of law is that the truth-conditions for legal assertions make essential reference to the conventions and practices of particular societies and that sometimes those conditions are satisfied." Id. at 16 n.42. He then adds that this is the sort of position defended by Dworkin. See id.

45. Dworkin's continuous appeals to what the law "*really*" requires place him squarely in the realist tradition of thought. See Dworkin, supra note 28, at 20, 64, 66. Compare the following statement of the realist spirit in philosophy of science:

> The basic claim made by scientific realism . . . is that the long-term success of a scientific theory gives reason to believe that something like the entities and structure postulated by the theory actually exists. There are four important qualifications built into this: (1) the theory must be successful over a significant period of time; (2) the explanatory success of the theory gives some reason, though not a conclusive warrant, to believe it; (3) what is believed is that the theoretical structures are *something like* the structure of the real world; (4) no claim is made for a special, more basic, privileged form of existence for the postulated entities.

Ernan McMullin, A Case for Scientific Realism, *in* Scientific Realism 8, 26 (Jarrett Leplin ed., 1984).

46. Postema, supra note 36, at 318.

47. This has been at the heart of Dworkin's efforts to develop a "third" theory of law, that is, an alternative to positivism and naturalism. See John Mackie, The Third Theory of Law, 7 Phil. & Pub. Aff. 3 (1977). For a very interesting and insightful analysis of why Dworkin's project has failed, see Richard H. Fallon, Jr. Reflections on Dworkin and the Two Faces of Law, 67 Notre Dame L. Rev. 553, 555–84 (1992).

48. Dworkin, supra note 31, at 8.

about the extent of his adherence to the conventional, causal picture of justification. For Fish, the world is but a mere projection of individual proclivity[49] or prejudice[50]: "truth" means nothing more than one's own beliefs about the law standing in a certain relation to one's interpretive assumptions. Communication—saying something true—is nothing more than saying things with which your interlocutor already agrees.[51] For example, consider the following:

> All that is necessary for the practice of sexually segregating prisoners to be considered "cruel and unusual" would be a conviction strongly held in a society that sexuality and its exercise were at the very center of man's being; so that if people were asked, "What is the worst, most unbearable, organization of social life you can think of?," one often-given answer would be "sexually segregated." At that point (and it is a point some in *our* society have already reached), the classification of the practice as one enjoined by the Eighth Amendment would be obvious, would "go without saying," and to assert otherwise would amount to being irresponsible.[52]

Fish is the arch-conventionalist; he is unwilling to consider the possibility that meaning could arise other than by tacit or explicit interpre-

---

49. Fish recently reaffirmed this view in a paragraph that reads like a parodic play on itself. See Stanley Fish, Play of Surfaces: Theory and the Law, *in* Legal Hermeneutics 297, 300 (Gregory Leyh ed., 1992).

> Rather than being a stable center of authority and control, the intending self is the continual creation and re-creation of the interpretations it itself performs in relation to its own actions, including the action of intending. We know ourselves no less interpretively (and therefore revisably) than others know us; the fact that it is intentions that we know, or try to know, does not limit the range of interpretation but merely specifies what the object of interpretation will necessarily be.

Id. One quite obvious problem with Fish's claim that all statements and their interpretations are endlessly interpretable is that when his view is turned on itself, it self-destructs. Nothing Fish ever says could be true because for there to be truth, there would first need to be a claim to truth. That claim would be made in the form of an utterance. Because the utterance (like the self who utters it) is endlessly interpretable, it could never state a truth, for the truth is but a function of interpretation. Because no utterance could ever be true, this paragraph is also not "true." For discussion and criticism of this aspect of Fish's views, see Michael S. Moore, The Interpretive Turn in Modern Theory: A Turn for the Worse?, 41 Stan. L. Rev. 871, 912–14 (1989).

50. Fish has applied his view to the interface between culture and geography: "The France you are thinking about will always be the product of the talk about it and will *never* be independently available. What the example of France shows is that all facts are discourse-specific (since no fact is available apart from some dimension of assessment or other)." See Fish, supra note 35, at 199.

51. Fish makes the same basic error as Wittgenstein's interlocutor: he reduces understanding to the anti-realist calculus of agreement. See Ludwig Wittgenstein, Philosophical Investigations § 241 (G.E.M. Anscombe trans., 3d ed. 1968) ("'So you are saying that human agreement decides what is true and what is false?'—It is what human beings *say* that is true and false; and they agree in the *language* they use. That is not agreement in opinions but in form of life.").

52. Fish, supra note 15, at 300.

tive assumption. This is not to deny truth. It is, however, to affirm that it is our interpretive assumptions that make legal propositions true. It is this claim that enables us to say that, at the deepest level of philosophical commitment, Dworkin and Fish are as one. It is not the form of truth about which they disagree, only its content.

D. *Realism and Anti-Realism*

The debate between Dworkin and Fish over the true grounds of law—that which makes propositions of law either true or false—is a local instance of a wider debate in philosophy, that between realists and anti-realists. These perspectives represent the two dominant schools of thought in the contemporary philosophical debate over the question of what determines the truth of a proposition. For realists, a proposition is true by virtue of some feature of the empirical, conceptual, or normative realm that makes it true. For the realist philosopher of science, for example, a claim with respect to some unobservable aspect of nature is made true because of the way the world is.[53] The moral realist similarly asserts that any moral claim is true or false in virtue of certain features of the world, to which we refer when we employ moral concepts.[54]

The anti-realist opposes the realist picture of truth with a variety of alternative pictures. For example, conventionalists assert that there are no features of the world that make propositions true or false. Rather, truth and falsity are a function of agreement among participants in a given practice. For the anti-realist philosopher of science, the only measure of the truth of a scientific proposition is the fact of group assent. On this account, a scientific proposition is "true" if everyone agrees it is true. Likewise, in ethics the anti-realist explains morality as

53. Philosophers of science identifying themselves as realists often disagree with one another over the nature of their realism. See generally Roger Jones, Realism About What? 58 Phil. of Sci. 185 (1991). As Jones frames it,

> While beyond a commitment to a "nature of things itself" advocates of realism are seriously divided, they share the general hope that the scientific enterprise has the capacity to provide accounts of this nature-of-things-itself that are true. In what is more or less the "classical" realist position, this hope is elevated to a belief. Indeed, such classical realists are willing to go out on a limb and claim that theories in the "mature" areas of science should already be judged as "approximately true", and that more recent theories in these areas are closer to the truth than older theories. Classical realists see the more recent theories encompassing the older ones as limiting cases and accounting for such success as they had. These claims are all closely linked to the claim that the language of entities and processes—both "observational" and "theoretical" ones—in terms of which these theories characterize the-nature-of-things-itself genuinely refers. That is, there are entities and processes that are part of the nature-of-things-itself that correspond to the ontologies of these theories.

Id. at 186.

54. See, e.g., Alan Goldman, Moral Knowledge 8–12 (1988) (contrasting coherence theory of law with realism and anti-realism in ethics); Michael Moore, Moral Reality, 1982 Wis. L. Rev. 1061 (1982).

the product of a tacit or hypothetical bargain reached by citizens of a polity. The bargain generates principles of justice that, among other things, provide a basis for the evaluation and criticism of conduct.

Having stated the realist and anti-realist positions with respect to the issue of truth generally, one must examine the specific question central to the Dworkin/Fish debate, that of the meaning of legal propositions. Michael Dummett, who first employed the term "anti-realism," elucidates the connection between the *truth* of propositions and the question of their *meaning*. Let us take a class of propositions, the truth-value of which is in dispute. Dummett says that with respect to that class:

> [T]he realist holds that the meanings of statements of the disputed class are not directly tied to the kind of evidence for them that we can have, but consist in the manner of their determination as true or false by states of affairs whose existence is not dependent on our possession of evidence for them. The anti-realist insists, on the contrary, that the meanings of these statements are tied directly to what we count as evidence for them, in such a way that a statement of the disputed class, if true at all, can be true only in virtue of something of which we could know and which we should count as evidence for its truth. The dispute thus concerns the notion of truth appropriate for statements of the disputed class; and this means that it is a dispute concerning the kind of *meaning* which these statements have.[55]

For both the realist and the anti-realist, knowing the meaning of a sentence means knowing its truth conditions (when, and under what conditions, the sentence would be true). Here, the anti-realist (Dummett) seems to have the upper hand; for the only way to make sense of meaning and understanding is by reference to the procedures for verifying the presence or absence of truth conditions. If all the realist can do is assert *but not adduce* (for example, due to some epistemic failure) the presence of those truth conditions, then the realist has not met her burden of proof.[56] But, the realist will counter, failure to meet the burden of proof on any one occasion does not preclude meeting it on another, nor does it prove that a right answer could not or does not exist.

Some philosophers argue that the realism/anti-realism debate is phony, and believe it can be avoided by looking at questions of knowledge, truth, and meaning from an "antirepresentationalist"[57] point of

55. Michael Dummett, Realism, *in* Truth and Other Enigmas 145, 146 (1978).

56. Dworkin has consistently made this argument in connection with his thesis that there is a right answer to every legal question. See Dworkin, supra note 30, at 119–45; Dworkin, supra note 28, at 264; Ronald Dworkin, Taking Rights Seriously 81–130, 279–90 (1977).

57. Here I follow Richard Rorty's usage. See 1 Richard Rorty, Introduction, *in* Objectivism, Relativism, and Truth (Philosophical Papers) 2–3 (1991).

view.[58] The basic viewpoint against which antirepresentationalism is deployed is that of language set apart from and "over and against" reality. The realist asserts that something in the world is referred to or implicated by a proposition, and it is this that *makes* the proposition true. The anti-realist counters that there is nothing out there beyond our conventional assessments of truth and falsity. Despite their differences, both the realist and the anti-realist claim that the meaning of our propositions *comes from somewhere*; the disagreement is not over the question of how there is meaning, only of its *source*: the world (realism) or conventional criteria (anti-realism).

A philosopher whose recent work points a way out of the realism/anti-realism debate is Hilary Putnam. Putnam has devoted a substantial portion of his career to arguing for the superiority of realism as a form of explanation in science and morals.[59] A few years ago, he radically changed course and recast his view of the relationship between meaning and truth in ways germane to the present discussion. The position, described as "antirepresentationalist,"[60] is directed at the view of language as something set "over and against reality"—against the idea that reality is something that can be captured by language, much as a cookie-cutter captures dough. Putnam argues that the cookie-cutter metaphor is undermined by the fact that

> [w]hat is (by commonsense standards) the same situation can be described in many different ways, depending on how we use the words. The situation does not itself legislate how words like "object," "entity," and "exist" must be used. What is wrong with the notion of objects existing "independently"

> [Anti-realism] is standardly used to mean the claim, about some particular true statements, that there is no matter of fact which they represent. But, more recently, it has been used to mean the claim that *no* linguistic items represent *any* nonlinguistic items. In the former sense it refers to an issue within the community of representationalists—those philosophers who find it fruitful to think of mind or language as containing representations of reality. In the latter sense, it refers to antirepresentationalism—to the attempt to eschew discussion of realism by denying the notion of "representation," or that of "fact of the matter," has any useful role in philosophy. Representationalists typically think that controversies between idealists and realists were, and controversies between skeptics and antiskeptics are, fruitful and interesting. Antirepresentationalists typically think both sets of controversies pointless. They diagnose both as the results of being held captive by a picture, a picture from which we should by now have wriggled free.

Id.

58. This is Bobbitt's strategy. Avoidance of the realism/anti-realism debate is not a direct goal of the book, but that goal is reached in the course of the argument. Nevertheless, Bobbitt does see the relationship of his argument to the realism/anti-realism debate in philosophy. More importantly, he understands well the stakes in the debate (pp. xix–xx).

59. For an entertaining account of Putnam as a realist, see the dialogue between a fictionalized Putnam and "Don Philahue," in Sayre-McCord, supra note 44, at 1.

60. See the discussion of antirepresentationalism supra note 57.

> of conceptual schemes is that there are no standards for the use of even the logical notions apart from conceptual choices. What the cookie-cutter metaphor tries to preserve is the naive idea that at least one Category—the ancient category of Object or Substance—has an absolute interpretation.[61]

What Putnam describes here is the realist position on the relationship between meaning and truth: a statement (proposition) is true if the words used to express the proposition (the cookie cutter) capture some feature of reality (in the dough) that subsists independently of all conceptual schemes. The anti-realist counters with "the view that it's all *just* language."[62] Is there any escape from the anti-realist's claim that "the world" is merely a function of our categories? Putnam answers thus:

> We can and should insist that some facts are there to be discovered and not legislated by us. But this is something to be said when one has adopted a way of speaking, a language, a "conceptual scheme." To talk of "facts" without specifying the language to be used is to talk of nothing; the word "fact" no more has its use fixed by the world itself than does the word "exist" or the word "object."[63]

But if the world does not fix the reference of our words, what does? It is at this point that Putnam makes a very interesting move.

> "Is the tree identical with the space-time region it occupies?" or "Is the chair identical with the mereological sum of the elementary particles that make it up?" . . . "Is a space-time point a concrete individual, or is it a mere limit, and hence an abstract entity of some kind?" [These questions] can all be handled in much the same way. "Identical," "individual," and "abstract" are notions with a variety of different uses. The difference between, say, describing space-time in a language that

61. Hilary Putnam, Representation and Reality 114 (1988). Putnam's way of approaching questions of interpretation and meaning highlights the error in Fish's approach to these questions. Fish agrees with Putnam, Rorty, Sellars, and Davidson that situations can be described, as Putnam puts it, "in many different ways." Id. The problem with Fish is that he does not wish to stay within a given language of description, since, he claims, any description of a situation is always up for grabs. But this claim is false. It is one thing to say that the effects of pollution on riparian owners may be described either in legal terms (e.g., duty, fault, and causation) or in economic terms (e.g., in light of the Coase theorem). However, once one adopts a language of description, one either uses the language correctly or one does not. As I have argued here, the question whether one is using words correctly or not has nothing whatsoever to do with interpreting the intentions of another (Fish) or with the personal interpretation of political theory (Dworkin). This does not preclude the possibility of disagreement, but rather makes disagreement possible. See Paul Feyerabend, Three Dialogues on Knowledge 145 (1991) ("Poems are not without constraints. As a matter of fact, the constraints poets impose on their work are often more severe than the constraints accepted by a botanist, or a birdwatcher.").

62. See Putnam, supra note 61, at 114.

63. Id.

> takes points as individuals and describing space-time in a language that takes points as mere limits is a difference in the choice of a language, and neither language is the "one true description."[64]

But this seems to confirm the anti-realist claim that "the world" is relative to a given conceptual scheme and that there are different worlds to the extent that there exist different languages of description. In short, that truth is simply relative to a conceptual scheme. Putnam responds in this way:

> The suggestion I am making, in short, is that *a statement is true of a situation just in case it would be correct to use the words of which the statement consists in that way in describing the situation*. . . . [W]e can explain what "correct to use the words of which the statement consists in that way" means by saying that it means nothing more nor less than a sufficiently well placed speaker who used the words in that way would be fully warranted in *counting* the statement as true of that situation.[65]

Putnam's point is that whatever it turns out to be, a theory of truth will not provide us with the Archimedean perspective hoped for by the realist and denied by the anti-realist. We will never have an unmediated encounter with that which "makes" our sentences true because it is only through our linguistic practices that there is truth at all. Truth is not a feature of the universe; rather, it is a matter of discerning the meaning of what we have said.[66] The only things that can be true are what we say with our sentences. To chase after truth in the way realists and anti-realists have is to chase ghosts.

I turned to the realism/anti-realism debate in philosophy in the hope that it might shed light on current controversies in jurisprudence over the nature of legal justification. The specific focus has been the Dworkin/Fish debate over the role of justification in law. The problem with the picture of justification embraced by Dworkin and Fish is precisely what Bobbitt notices—it is a causal theory masquerading as a normative explanation.[67] Dworkin and Fish are wedded to a picture of law in which a legal proposition is true or false because something *makes it so*. This picture of the nature of legal justification is, of course, representationalist in nature: a proposition of law is true only when the proposition stands in a certain relation to the preferred external element (political theory (Dworkin) or unarticulated presupposition (Fish)). It is this picture of justification in law that Dworkin and Fish both embrace.

What Putnam's analysis shows is that the way out of the picture of

64. Id. at 114–15.

65. Id. at 115.

66. As we shall see, the modalities are the tools for discerning the meaning of the Constitution.

67. Which is clearly a contradiction in terms.

justification that realists and anti-realists (such as Dworkin and Fish) share is to recast the relationship between meaning and truth. A claim that some proposition of law is true is vindicated if one can show that on any particular occasion one is correctly using the words in question.[68] Of course, this means that jurisprudence will of necessity turn its attention away from an externalist, causal theory of justification (the realist/anti-realist debate) to one that takes as its task the description of law's public, intersubjective practices of justification—the strategies employed by lawyers to demonstrate that some proposition of law is either true or false. This is the direction in which Bobbitt wants to take the debate over the grounds of constitutional law. Before considering the particulars of Bobbitt's alternative, we should consider what exactly are those problems with the conventional view that Bobbitt's perspective must avoid.

There are four basic problems. The first results most directly from the form of the criticism just offered—that is, that "explanations" of law do not get us anywhere. What we are interested in is not an *explanation* of law but an *understanding* of it. Of course, the causal accounts all claim to provide just that: their proponents each assert that one understands law when one gets an explanation of it.

The problem with the causal form of explanation is that the normative means of justification lie only within the practice. By resort to an explanatory mechanism outside the practice, the conventional account misses what is in fact the very thing that makes the practice what it is.[69]

68. This point is illustrated by reminding ourselves that, in contrast to the theories of Dworkin and Fish, we demonstrate knowledge of the meaning of our terms not vertically but horizontally—we demonstrate that meaning is something not "made true" but tied to the manifold uses of a word in contexts. "These horizontal connections are important in displaying and instantiating the language-games which give our sentences their meanings, that is, their various connections with reality." Merrill B. Hintikka & Jaakko Hintikka, Investigating Wittgenstein 216 (1986).

As the following comment confirms, horizontal explanations have only recently begun to displace vertical explanations as the preferred form of justification:

> [L]anguage-games are frequently introduced to contrast *horizontal* with *vertical explanations*, and . . . Wittgenstein invariably prefers the former to the latter. Vertical explanations are characteristic of traditional philosophizing. They get their title from the sorts of the connections with which they render explanations of semantic phenomena. They proceed *from* the level of language or its use *to* another level; say, that of mental episodes or referential ties to language-independent reality. Thus, a typical vertical explanation would be that the meanings of expressions are constituted by their relations to self-interpreting thoughts or mental images, or that the truth of a proposition is constituted by its relation of agreement with a fact, or the justification of a proposition by its vertical relation to certain evidential conditions.

Gerald Vision, Modern Anti-Realism and Manufactured Truth 221 (1988).

69. The best explanation of this point can be found in Thomas D. Eisele, The Activity of Being A Lawyer: The Imaginative Pursuit of Implications and Possibilities, 54 Tenn. L. Rev. 345, 377–85 (1987).

Bobbitt sets the normative apart from the causal (explanatory) in this way:

> The belief that interpretive statements in law (such as: "the Constitution requires that a state cannot be sued in federal court by its own citizen without its consent") are statements about the world, though widely if unacknowledgedly shared, is false. Such statements are descriptions; they are not about things (like the Constitution) but are about interpretations. Thus they are modal descriptions, not empirical ones. Whether they are true or false depends upon a human choice, not a correspondence with facts in the world. It is a measure of the strong grip the false metaphysics has on us that such a distinguished academic [Dworkin] should think that to believe otherwise is to be an "anti-realist" or nominalist. One who expects a further thought to lie behind a decision, and that that thought is determined by a meta-logic, would conclude that in its absence there appears to be no link between the thought and the real world (p. 181).

The second problem with the conventional view is that it builds into its picture of justification the seeds of its own demise. Consider the following statement by Dworkin:

> I think that many positivists rely, more or less consciously, on an anti-realist theory of meaning. They think that no sense can be assigned to a proposition unless those who use that proposition are all agreed about how the proposition could, at least in theory, be proved conclusively. Lawyers are agreed, according to positivism about how the existence of a law or a legal rule could be proved or disproved, and they are therefore agreed about the truth conditions of ordinary propositions of law that assert rights and duties created by rules. But controversial propositions of law, which assert rights that do not purport to depend on rules, are another matter. Since there is no agreement about the conditions which, if true, establish the truth of such propositions, they cannot be assigned any straightforward sense, and must therefore be understood in some special way, if at all.[70]

Of course, the central claim of this paragraph is but one element in Dworkin's overall position on the question of whether there is one "right" answer to all legal questions. Dworkin has never provided an account of what he means by "right,"[71] but has instead rested content

70. Dworkin, supra note 31, at 8.

71. Dworkin has recently indicated that we should all stop asking the questions he has urged upon us for the last 25 years. See Ronald Dworkin, Pragmatism, Right Answers, and True Banality, *in* Pragmatism in Law and Society 359, 360 (Michael Brint & William Weaver eds., 1991).

> We should now set aside, as a waste of important energy and resource, grand debates about whether law is all power or illusion or constraint, or whether texts interpret only other texts, *or whether there are right or best or true or soundest answers or only useful or powerful or popular ones*.

with the assertion that the failure to *demonstrate* what the right answer is in any case does not license denial of the possibility that one right answer might, in some sense, "exist."[72] This lacuna aside, the basic problem with the argument is that it invites the skeptic's assertion that a judge can never know whether or not she has gotten the law right, because she is in a constant state of epistemic failure.[73] Worse still, Dworkin has no telling reply, for he has built into his normative account of law the very gap the skeptic exploits.

The third difficulty I term "the problem of translation." It has been the task of general jurisprudence for at least the last twenty-five years to produce a normative matrix that, when adduced, can serve as an evaluative tool for law. The effort is "to translate legal problems into the informal proof structures of other disciplines" (p. 172). Bobbitt is not against the use of other disciplines in law. However, he wants to limit the use of coordinate disciplines in two ways. First, the coordinate mode of argument must at least complement legal analysis:

> Imagine a judicial opinion with sets of simultaneous equations. It is not the mathematical illiteracy of the judiciary that makes this so implausible; rather it is the idea that law could grapple with human behaviour in such a highly reified way. The standards of mathematics—technique, economy, rigor—have much in common with those of legal argument. But a mathematical argument does not convince unless it is a mathematical question that has been put. It follows from this observation that someone doing law, with the assistance of arguments stolen from other disciplines, is not acting within those other disciplines. Lawyer's history is not just shoddy history; it is the use of historical methods that have been fabricated, re-made for a purpose that is not the historian's purpose (p. 173).

Id. (emphasis added). But if we were to follow Dworkin's advice, what then would we do with ourselves? In the very next sentence of the paragraph just quoted, Dworkin provides this answer: "We could then take up instead how the decisions that in any case will be made should be made, and which of the answers that will in any case be thought right or best or true or soundest *really are*." Id. (emphasis added). One cannot help but notice how in this paragraph Dworkin simultaneously urges giving up the questions he has asked for the last 25 years, only to reaffirm their importance with the claim that there *really are* answers that are right (and not merely *thought* to be so). This is what the realism/anti-realism debate is all about. In the very same article, Dworkin now says that debate is pointless. He states: "[I]t [is] so difficult to state the issue, if any, that divides 'realists' from 'antirealists' in metaphysics, and, more generally, to formulate any philosophically very deep form of skepticism." Id. at 382 n.4.

72. Dworkin has recently affirmed that his view on the right answer thesis has not changed. "Some critics, including Brian Barry and Joseph Raz, suggest that I have changed my mind about the character and importance of the one-right-answer claim. For better or for worse, I have not." Id. at 382 n.1.

73. In other words, no proposition of law can ever be shown in fact to be the principle that provides the "right answer" or, in another *façon de parler*, puts the law "in its best light."

Bobbitt's second point implicates the problem of the loss of law and legal craft. By importing an explanatory model from another discipline,

> we invariably carve away those aspects of the legal situation to which the model is inapplicable. We forget that the model is merely a prototype, and so we resist the reality of the divergence of the actual from our model. In this way we do not enrich legal analysis by resort to coordinate disciplines; we impoverish it. Thus a jurist trying to apply the principles of John Rawls tends to bend the legal analysis to "rights" and inevitably away from the historical claims of the state (id.).

Bobbitt draws the line between "a heuristic object of comparison and . . . a rule of decision" (id.). As others have pointed out,[74] it is not a "critique" of law to replace legal vocabulary with terms and forms of argument from other disciplines. Bobbitt's point, however, is a subtle nuance of this observation. The legitimacy of a decision grounded in Rawls' principles of justice, for instance, "is not itself 'Rawls-governed' and therefore the imported system is never decisive" (p. 174). In short, nothing that cannot be made to fit with the modes of legal justification already in place can ever displace the law. If law is an activity and not a thing, the replacement of legal with economic or philosophical vocabulary is not to change law; rather, it is to do economics or philosophy. As I shall show in the discussion of the modes of justification, because law is something we *do*, the first order of business has to be getting an accurate picture of what it is we in fact do. Doing philosophy or economics will not help us with that task.

The last of the four points has already been mentioned—that of the problem of the infinite regress of justification.[75] As we saw in the discussion of Dworkin and Fish, one of the stock moves in contemporary jurisprudence is to justify some or all of the practice of law by resort to something external to the practice itself. The problem with such a move, however, is that instead of *solving* the problem of justification, the solution manages only to relocate it. Like law, every discipline or discourse to which resort is made to legitimate law will have its own procedures of justification and its own standards of argument. Solving problems of legal justification by resort to, say, philosophy, accomplishes nothing more than a change of vocabulary. But what is it that drives this spirit to find something solid, a spirit shared by many on both the Right and the Left? Bobbitt answers:

> [I]t is their belief that legal statements depend upon some fac-

74. See, e.g., Jules L. Coleman, The Structure of Tort Law, 97 Yale L.J. 1233, 1252 (1988) (reviewing William Landes & Richard A. Posner, The Economic Structure of Tort Law (1987)) ("[B]y reconstructing the key concepts of tort liability in economic terms, economic analysis could hardly be said to be providing an explanation of legal practice as it finds it.").

75. See supra text accompanying note 19.

> tual state of affairs that is their foundation. There *is* a lesson in contemporary philosophy for the legal critic, but it is a cold one. Twentieth century philosophy discredits many of the epistemological assumptions of natural law and positivism, of formalism and realism, but it does not replace those schools (which partly accounts for the curious isolation of political philosophy from the developments in logic and epistemology). The message of such philosophy is: you are on your own; we've done enough to harm you already. Until legal critics absorb this important lesson we will be trapped in problems that have their origins in philosophy's once-proposed solutions; like minotaurs within mazes we await new maps from our captors but are given only new victims (p. 175).

II. The Modalities of Constitutional Argument

A. *The Modalities*

Bobbitt is convinced that contemporary legal theory has the wrong orientation to the question of justification in law. Time and again, a new paradigm for understanding law is announced and, upon examination, turns out to be the same old form of argument merely in a new or more fashionable mode of expression. Bobbitt is eager to avoid both the foundationalism that demands a firm ground for law and the skepticism that ceaselessly exploits the appetite for certainty.

The crux of Bobbitt's argumentative strategy is to separate legitimacy from justification. The key is to see that the practice of judicial review—or, more broadly, constitutional law—requires no justification.[76] The answer to the skeptic's question of what justifies judicial review is: "Why, nothing, of course."[77] But if nothing justifies judicial

76. The problem with virtually all constitutional theory, and much of general jurisprudence, is the continuing need to legitimate law by resort to some external source. For an illuminating discussion of this problem in modern jurisprudence, see Gunther Teubner, How the Law Thinks: Toward a Constructivist Epistemology of Law, 23 Law & Soc'y Rev. 727, 743 (1989). As Teubner describes the problem:

> From a constructivist perspective, there is no way to challenge the epistemic authority of law, neither by social realities themselves, nor by common sense, nor by scientifically controlled observation. A social epistemology on a constructivist basis can explain why law appears to be an "essentially self-validating discourse" which one should expect to be "largely impervious to serious challenge from other knowledge fields." It is simply naive to invoke social "reality" itself against legal conceptualism, against the "heaven of legal concepts" or against the law's "transcendental nonsense." There is no direct cognitive access to reality. There are only competing discourses with different constructions of reality.

Id. (citations omitted).

77. Bobbitt states: "What is the fundamental principle that legitimizes judicial review? There is none. It follows from what I have said thus far that constitutional law needs no 'foundation.' Its legitimacy does not derive from a set of axioms which, in conjunction with rules of construction, will yield correct constitutional propositions." Bobbitt, supra note 3, at 237.

review, then can we ever know that our juridical practices of justification are legitimate? In short, is there no connection between law and justice?

Nothing in Bobbitt's approach precludes the evaluation of a judicial decision from the point of view of one's preferred theory of justice. As he states, "we assess the justice of a particular decision by reference to some external standard, a system of evaluation outside the operation of the modalities of argument." The oft-repeated mistake of contemporary jurisprudence is to treat the conventions of legal argument as if they were just another theory of justice. Law is not a theory; it is a practice, and the modalities are the tools of the trade.

In *Constitutional Fate*, Bobbitt addressed the issue of how lawyers sustain their claims about the truth or falsity of legal propositions. Recognizing that different disciplines each have their own ways of assessing the truth or falsity of substantive claims, Bobbitt described the six forms (modalities) of argument that, taken together, constitute the justificatory matrix of constitutional law:[78]

> [H]istorical (relying on the intentions of the framers and ratifiers of the Constitution);
> [T]extual (looking to the meaning of the words of the Constitution alone, as they would be interpreted by the average contemporary "man on the street");
> [S]tructural (inferring rules from the relationships that the Constitution mandates among the structures it sets up);
> [D]octrinal (applying rules generated by precedent);
> [E]thical (deriving rules from those moral commitments of the American ethos that are reflected in the Constitution); and
> [P]rudential (seeking to balance the costs and benefits of a particular rule) (pp. 12–13).

The most important aspect of the modalities is that it is only through their use that the truth or falsehood of legal claims is determined. Unlike the conventional perspective, which sees the truth of law as a function of something lying outside the law (for example, politics, moral philosophy, etc.) the unique and, if correct, compelling aspect of

78. It is essential to understanding Bobbitt's central contention to realize that there is nothing more to constitutional argument than the six modalities. As he argues repeatedly, there simply is nothing more for "philosophy" to do than describe accurately the *practice* of constitutional argument, for that practice *is* constitutional law. If there is nothing more nor less to constitutional law than the six modes of argument, then there is nothing more to talk about other than how the forms are employed to sustain claims that some proposition of law is either true or false. The question nearly everyone else wants to ask about any and all aspects of constitutional law is, "Is this argument legitimate?" The question makes no sense if it is a question about whether someone is making a valid argument, for the forms of argument answer any question concerning what is being done. The essential point of the argument is that *the very idea* of a "legitimate" form of argument is unintelligible. What would it be like to ask "Is this a legitimate way to play chess?" or "Is this a legitimate way to paint in a neo-impressionist style?" It is not clear that these sorts of questions are amenable to answer.

Bobbitt's account of our constitutional practice is that *nothing is hidden*. There is nothing more to constitutional law (or any other body of doctrine) than the use of the six modalities of argument. For jurisprudence, both constitutional and general, the lesson is clear: the essential task of jurisprudence is the accurate *description* of our legal practices of argument and justification.[79] Theory[80] is banished not because it is wrong, but because it is irrelevant. If law is an argumentative practice composed of the six modalities of argument, then the key to understanding law lies in understanding how these forms are deployed in legal argument.[81]

What, then, justifies a judicial decision? And how is justification related to legitimacy? The judicial decision is justified to the extent that it is rendered according to law. A decision is made "according to law" when one or more of the six modalities is employed to reach the decision (pp. 183–84). The law, it turns out, is an activity—the use of the six modes of constitutional justification. Justification is an argumentative activity by which one reaches a conclusion that some proposition of law is true or false. The modalities are "the way[s] in which a proposition is true; constitutional modalities determine the way in which a constitutional proposition is true" (p. 34).

What then of legitimacy? For Bobbitt, a legal decision is legitimate to the extent that its argumentative character remains within modalities

79. There are connections to be drawn between Bobbitt's description of the modalities and the recent work of scholars in the area of statutory interpretation. In his path-breaking article Dynamic Statutory Interpretation, 135 U. Pa. L. Rev. 1479 (1987), William Eskridge argues that the meaning of statutes changes over time when "the original legislative expectations have been overtaken by subsequent changes in society and law [evolutive considerations]." Id. at 1484. Eskridge's argument is a form of historical argument. What is interesting to notice about Eskridge's argument is what is new in it—it suggests pragmatic reasons why we should look at history differently than in the ways to which we have become accustomed (for example, by examining only legislative intent).

What is important to notice in this connection is that in addition to the use of the modalities as a way of demonstrating the truth of a legal proposition, law is also a practice a part of which is the reflective practice of argument over what constitutes an adequate historical argument. We can agree with Bobbitt that historical argument is one of the modalities used to justify the truth of a proposition of law. What is left out of his account is any notice of the fact that within law, participants contest the adequacy of the forms of argument themselves. For discussion of this point in the context of commercial law, see Dennis M. Patterson, A Fable from the Seventh Circuit: Frank Easterbrook on Good Faith, 76 Iowa L. Rev. 503, 513–29 (1991).

80. By "theory" I mean to follow Bobbitt's usage—that is, a "sublime explanatory mechanism" (p. 24).

81. It is in the use of the forms of argument that legal propositions are shown to be true or false (p. 12). Bobbitt's argument in this connection is consistent with the last writings of Wittgenstein on this point: "But I did not get my picture of the world by satisfying myself of its correctness; nor do I have it because I am satisfied of its correctness. No: it is the inherited background against which I distinguish between true and false." Ludwig Wittgenstein, On Certainty § 94 (G.E.M. Anscombe & G.H. von Wright eds., Denis Paul & G.E.M. Anscombe trans., Harper Torchbook 1972 (1969)).

(p. 151). Legitimacy is not something a system of law can achieve *writ large*. The legitimacy of a legal system is an accretion; it develops over time and is maintained only by adherence to the legal forms of justification. To the extent that these modalities are compromised or ignored, particular decisions are illegitimate, and, over time, the legitimacy of the system as a whole is undermined.

Bobbitt provides three illustrations of his approach to constitutional law. The first is an analysis of Justice Holmes' opinion in *Missouri v. Holland*,[82] a case concerning the constitutionality of a treaty of the United States enforcing a closed season on hunting certain game birds. The second illustration is the so-called "Iran-Contra Affair." Bobbitt discusses the matter in such a way that one can easily appreciate the constitutional issues raised by this most vexing of recent events. Finally, Bobbitt analyzes the failed nomination of Robert Bork for a seat on the United States Supreme Court. All three of these matters are interesting in themselves, and Bobbitt's analyses are among the most intelligent one is likely to find. The last of these, the Bork nomination, will be my focus. After reading his account of the hearings, one has, perhaps only for the first time, a clear sense of what it was all about.

B. *Application of the Modalities: The Bork Hearings*

Was Bork the victim of an unscrupulous media attack, or was his rejection a vote of "no confidence" in the originalism he so staunchly defended before, during, and after[83] the hearings on his confirmation? Bobbitt's answer is "both and neither." Bork clearly made more than a few after-dinner speeches and wrote a few articles arguing that the intent of the framers should be regarded as the sole criterion of constitutional interpretation, and many in the media indeed mischaracterized his views if not his person. But the dichotomy of arch-defender of the oracles of intent versus maligned media victim fails to capture the true picture. Let us take a closer look at what there is to be found.

A recurring issue in Supreme Court nomination hearings, one much discussed during the last half-dozen nominations, is the question of whether and to what extent the Senate Judiciary Committee may inquire into the so-called *political* views of the nominee. The terms within which this question is usually discussed are, to say the least, simplistic.[84] On the one hand there are the nominee's judicial abilities, candor, and judicial philosophy. On the other are the nominee's political views—his or her views about what the law on any given subject or topic might or ought to be. Bobbitt notes that, among recent nominees

82. 252 U.S. 416 (1920).

83. See Robert H. Bork, The Tempting of America: The Political Seduction of the Law, passim (1990).

84. An exception is Ronald Dworkin's recent essay on the Clarence Thomas nomination. See Ronald Dworkin, Justice for Clarence Thomas, N.Y. Rev. Books, Nov. 7, 1991, at 41, 42–45.

to the Court, there has developed a trend "of refusing to comment on matters that might come before the Court on which the nominee would sit if confirmed" (p. 83). Of course, history shows that Judge Bork, far more than anyone before or after him, was all too willing to discuss his views on almost any subject. But this is not what Bobbitt finds interesting in the hearings. Bobbitt is not interested in the question of whether Bork ought or ought not to have been confirmed, but rather in using the modalities as a way of understanding the confirmation hearings. His rather surprising conclusion is that Robert Bork does not understand his own judicial philosophy because he is not really an originalist, but rather a prudentialist. In his opening statement, Bork said the following about his own judicial philosophy:

> "The judge's authority derives entirely from the fact that he is applying the law and not his personal values.... How should a judge go about finding the law? The only legitimate way, in my opinion, is by attempting to discern what those who made the law intended. The intentions of the lawmakers [of the Constitution . . .] are those [of the persons] who ratified our Constitution and its various amendments.
>
> The judge's responsibility is to discern how the framers' values, defined in the context of the world they knew, apply in the world we know. If a judge abandons intention as his guide, there is no law available to him and he . . . goes beyond his legitimate power" (pp. 88–89).[85]

From the moment Bork finished his opening statement, the hearings never focussed on the question of the utmost importance: the nominee's conception of how a judge ought to decide cases. Both the nominee and the members of the Senate Judiciary Committee failed to see the important distinction between the substantive content of our constitutional rights and the *ways* in which courts decide cases regarding the question of what rights we have. The distinction is revealed in the following exchange between Senator Biden and Judge Bork:

> "*Senator* Judge, I agree with the rationale offered in the [*Griswold*] case. Let me just read it to you . . . I happen to agree with it. It said, in part, 'would we allow the police to search the sacred precincts of marital bedrooms for telltale signs of contraceptives? The very idea is repulsive to the notions of privacy surrounding the marriage relationship. We deal with the right of privacy older than the Bill of Rights. Marriage is a coming together for better or worse, hopefully enduring, and intimate to the degree of being sacred. The association promotes a way of life, no causes. A harmony of living, not political face. A bilateral loyalty, not a commercial or social project.'

85. Quoting from Nomination of Robert H. Bork to be Associate Justice of the Supreme Court of the United States: Hearings Before the Senate Comm. on the Judiciary, 100th Cong., 1st Sess. 104 (1987) [hereinafter Senate Hearings].

> *Bork* I could agree with . . . every word you read but that is not . . . the rationale of the case. That is the rhetoric at the end of the case. What I objected to was the way in which this right of privacy was created.
> *Senator* As I hear you, you do not believe that there is a general right of privacy that is in the Constitution.
> *Bork* Not one derived in *that* fashion" (p. 90).[86]

This exchange also illustrates the other fatal flaw in the hearings. Every time a question was put to Bork in the form of "Do you believe there is a constitutional right to 'x'?", Bork would respond in a manner consistent with his belief that the important question was not *what* rights we have but the *manner* in which those rights were derived. Repeatedly, "Bork tried to draw the obvious distinction between ways of deriving constitutional arguments and substantive decisions. His questioners typically did not accept the distinction, prompting him repeatedly to reassert it" (p. 212 n.23). When it came to discussing precedent, Bork sealed his fate with his own words:

> "[T]he role of precedent in constitutional law is less important than it is in a proper common law or statutory model . . . So if a constitutional judge comes to a firm conviction that the courts have misunderstood the intentions of the founders, he is freer than when acting in his capacity as an interpreter of the common law or of a statute to overturn a precedent . . . [A]n originalist judge would have no problem whatever in overruling a non-originalist precedent, because that precedent by the very basis of his judicial philosophy, has no legitimacy" (p. 93).[87]

Everyone understood what Bork meant by these words. If intention was to be the sole measure of legitimacy, Bork was stating forthrightly that the weight of precedent could be ignored and, if found wanting by the measure of an originalist yardstick, overturned. As Bobbitt explains,

> [i]t meant that decisions like *Roe v. Wade* (the abortion case), *Reynolds v. Sims* (the re-districting opinion that mandated one-man-one-vote), *Shelley v. Kramer* (outlawing racially restrictive real estate covenants), even *Brown* itself—all of which the nominee had criticized at one time or another—could be overturned even if the nominee was careful not to say he would do so. Bork's implicit demand that such holdings be re-examined for legitimate support was enough to cause an avalanche of public disapproval (id.).

What conclusions are we to draw? Is it the case that "in the end, the Senate rejected the nominee because it rejected the judicial philosophy of constitutional intentionalism with which Judge Bork had associated himself" (pp. 94–95)? The answer must be that the vote against Bork

86. Quoting id. at 117.
87. Quoting id. at 370.

was, indeed, a rejection of what was perceived as his particular brand of intentionalism. But was the perception accurate? "[W]as this really Bork's view?" (p. 95)

Before proceeding, it is important to ponder just what it is in the constitutional philosophy of intentionalism that many find troublesome. Like many other approaches to the interpretation of the Constitution, intentionalism is a theory of legitimacy: to the intentionalist, the very act of reading the Constitution cannot itself be legitimate unless that act is underwritten by something outside itself—legitimation flows from the recovery of the intentions of the drafters of the document. Correlatively—and this is the worrisome point—any precedent not so generated is illegitimate, and hence subject to being overruled. It is this last aspect of intentionalism that, in the end, was Judge Bork's undoing.

It did not have to be this way, for Bork is not a thoroughgoing intentionalist. In objecting to *Roe v. Wade*, Bork noted that the principal failing of the opinion is that it " 'does not have legal reasoning in it that roots the right to an abortion in constitutional materials' " (id.).[88] When Bork made this statement at his confirmation hearings, Senator Hatch queried: " 'I presume that your concerns about the reasoning of the . . . case do not necessarily mean that you would automatically reverse that case as a Justice of the Supreme Court?' " (id.).[89] Bork's answer to this question is most interesting. After rehearsing the line of questioning an intentionalist might take on the legitimacy of prior precedent and the right to privacy, Bork replied: " '[T]here are cases we look back on and say they were erroneous or they were not compatible with original intent, but we don't overrule them *for a variety of reasons*' " (id.) (emphasis added).[90]

What might be some of the reasons that would cut against overruling an illegitimately derived precedent? Bork offered a few to his senatorial questioners:

> "I suppose the passage of time by itself is not important. The only reason it is important is that if expectations and institutions and laws and so forth have grown up around the decision in that passage of time. That certainly weighs in favor of not overruling the decision" (p. 96).[91]
>
> "I will be glad to discuss my general approach to *stare decisis* and the kinds of factors I would consider . . . It has to be in the first place clear that the prior decision was erroneous. I mean, not just shaky but really wrong in terms of constitutional theory . . . But that is not sufficient to overrule. I have discussed these factors before . . . For example, the development of pri-

88. Quoting id. at 185.
89. Quoting id.
90. Quoting id.
91. Quoting id. at 264–65.

vate expectations on the part of the citizenry . . . The growth of institutions, governmental institutions, private institutions around a ruling . . . The need for continuity and stability in the law . . . The need for predictability in legal doctrine" (p. 97).[92]

Bork then put statements such as these together with his originalism. The mix made for a heady brew:

"From the beginning of these hearings, Senator, I have said that . . . the ultimate touchstone for a judge . . . in constitutional law . . . is the original understanding; that means what the ratifiers understood when they ratified the Constitution. But I have also said that the law has developed, and the nation has developed, and decisions have been made around which too much has been built, and around which too many expectations have clustered, for them to be overruled . . . . The commerce clause cases cannot be overruled. You cannot cut the commerce clause back . . . . The equal protection cases cannot be overruled . . . . I have mentioned some first amendment cases that cannot be overruled. I have mentioned a lot of cases that I think are now part of our law, and whatever theoretical challenges might be levelled at them, it is simply too late . . . for a judge to overrule them . . . . Incorporation doctrine [by which the Bill of Rights is applied to the States, the source for the principal due process decisions of the Warren Court] I mentioned . . . is also something that is now thoroughly established" (p. 99).[93]

What do these quotations really show? Could they not be read as yet another instance of "confirmation conversion"? Many choose so to read them, and there is nothing in the substance of Bork's remarks that rules out such a reading.[94] Yet this reading would miss the fact that even so ardent an intentionalist as Bork has a hard time maintaining allegiance to a single constitutional modality. Like his teacher and fellow prudentialist, Alexander Bickel, Bork realizes that constitutional

92. Quoting id. at 292–93.

93. Quoting id. at 465. Of course, one sees the same point of view at work in the plurality opinion of Justices O'Connor, Kennedy, and Souter in Planned Parenthood v. Casey, 112 S. Ct. 2791, 2804–16 (1992) (pointing out that for two decades people have relied on the availability of abortions in organizing their relationships and lives, and that the cost of upsetting these expectations cannot be dismissed in re-examining the abortion issue). For a different reading of the implications of the opinion, see Ronald Dworkin, The Center Holds!, N.Y. Rev. Books, Aug. 13, 1992, at 29, 31–33 (casting the opinion as an example of (what else?) law as integrity).

94. The following statement by Senator Thurmond is representative of the sort of opinion many Americans no doubt developed during the hearings: "[Y]ou have criticized certain . . . decisions, [but] you have also indicated that some of these decisions are accepted law, and should not be disturbed by the Supreme Court. This has been taken by some as change in your views, in order to enhance the probability of your confirmation" (p. 98) (quoting Senate Hearings, supra note 85, at 465). It is precisely to statements such as these that Bork had to respond, and respond well. He did not. The trick was to appear principled yet pragmatic. Bork had a far easier time with one task than the other.

law cannot be an axiomatic exercise in justification. But Bork, driven as he is by a narrow (but not irrelevant) conception of justification in constitutional law, manages to deceive even himself about the nature of his own theoretical commitments. In his testimony, Bork showed himself to be something more than the knee-jerk intentionalist many took him to be. Yet he seemed unable to put together his philosophical commitment to original intention with his quite pragmatic view of the role of entrenched precedent.[95] When read against the background of the modalities of constitutional justification, Bork's jurisprudence becomes as clear as it has ever been, and turns out to be more sophisticated than even Bork himself understands. It is perhaps this lack of self-knowledge that, in the end, cost Bork his place on the Court.

I have included Bobbitt's analysis of the Bork hearings in this Part as evidence supporting Bobbitt's claim that in the use of the modalities one can come to a deeper understanding of constitutional law. The Bork hearings were not just an opportunity to plumb the depths of the nominee's judicial philosophy, nor were the questions put to Bork mere lines from another episode of political theater. The hearings were a constitutional event and the modalities the means for understanding that event.

III. Modal Conflict and the Recursion to Conscience

Bobbitt's singular contribution to constitutional jurisprudence, in both *Constitutional Fate* and *Constitutional Interpretation*, is drawing attention to the ways in which arguments within the practice of constitutional law justify claims about the content of law. The six modalities are the ways in which propositions of constitutional law are shown to be true or false. They are not true *by virtue of* something outside the practice of argument that provides the practice's normative foundations. There is also no sublime logic to constitutional argument that theory might somehow disclose. There is only the practice and nothing more.

Moving beyond the recapitulation and expansion of the position first advanced in *Constitutional Fate*, Bobbitt in *Constitutional Interpretation* addresses himself to a matter he had not previously considered—the problem of modal conflict.[96] Richard Fallon, who shares Bobbitt's de-

---

95. See supra text accompanying note 93.

96. Bobbitt states: "What I did not see [when I wrote *Constitutional Fate*] was that the possibility of conflict between forms [modalities] would resuscitate the debate over legitimacy and encourage an eager resort to 'ideologizing' preferred modalities to provide the external referent that such legitimacy was, mistakenly, thought to require" (p. xiv). Bobbitt's failure to address this problem was a central criticism of *Constitutional Fate*. See Sanford Levinson, The Audience for Constitutional Meta-Theory (Or, Why, and to Whom, Do I Write the Things I Do?), 63 U. Colo. L. Rev. 389, 398 (1992).

> [I]t is a notorious truth about *Constitutional Fate* that it does not remotely offer a way of choosing among the six legal-grammatical modalities that Bobbitt discusses—text, history, structure, doctrine, prudence, and ethos. When, for example, one concludes that history and doctrine, or text and prudence lead to

scriptive approach to constitutional jurisprudence, analyzes the problem this way:

> Constitutional law has a commensurability problem. The problem arises from the variety of kinds of argument that now are almost universally accepted as legitimate in constitutional debate and interpretation.[97]
>
> [I]t is impossible to reason or argue about the correct decision in hard cases—cases made hard by the actual or apparent tendency of different kinds of arguments to point to divergent results—without a theory of how different kinds of constitutional argument appropriately contribute to a single decision.[98]

For Fallon, the problem of modal conflict—which he identifies as "the commensurability problem"—is "among the most important in constitutional law."[99] In sharp contrast to Fallon, Bobbitt not only does not see modal conflict as a problem, he regards it as a distinct virtue of constitutional law. He states:

> The space for moral reflection on our ideologies is created by the conflict among modalities, just as garden walls can create a space for a garden (p. 177).
>
> The recursion to conscience is the crucial activity on which the constitutional system of interpretation that I have described depends. It is the purpose of this book to remind the Reader of this fact. This particular sort of recollection is the very thing that the current commentary on constitutional decision-making seeks to dispense with by insisting on the illegitimacy of our practices and the need for a particular decision process (p. 184).[100]

These quotations contain the essentials of Bobbitt's solution to the problem of modal conflict, albeit in compressed form. The solution has two parts. The first is its negative aspect, which denies both the need for and the coherence of meta-theoretical legitimation of constitutional practice. The second, positive aspect of the position is the role of the six modalities in the practice of constitutional argument. As these quotations demonstrate, there are two components to the positive position: the modalities of argument and the recursion to conscience. The question is whether these two elements cohere. It is not at all clear that they do.

The central difficulty with the positive aspect of the position is the

---

> conflicting results, Bobbitt does not in fact present a hierarchy that allows resolution.

Id.

97. Richard H. Fallon, Jr., A Constructivist Coherence Theory of Constitutional Interpretation, 100 Harv. L. Rev. 1189, 1189 (1987).

98. Id. at 1191–92.

99. Id. at 1191.

100. The problem with the metaphor of the garden (p. 177) is that without a public practice of gardening, it is impossible to tell whether someone is gardening or merely moving plants around.

role Bobbitt assigns to the exercise of individual conscience. As mentioned, Bobbitt sees modal conflict as a distinct *virtue* of his approach. The reason this conflict is a virtue is that such conflict provides "[t]he space for moral reflection" (p. 177). For recursion to conscience to succeed as a solution to the problem of modal conflict, it must be possible to wed to the exercise of individual conscience an account of constitutional argument that relies so heavily on a public, intersubjective practice of justification.[101] It is far from clear that this is even possible.

Consider any proposition of constitutional law. To the question of how one settles the truth or falsity of a proposition of constitutional law, Bobbitt answers that one employs the modalities. The *use* of the modalities is a practice—they (and the ways they are used) are public, cultural property. This means that the truth of a constitutional proposition is not a function of what anyone *thinks* or *believes* about the proposition; rather, one uses the modalities of argument to show that the proposition is true. Since the modalities of constitutional interpretation are public coin, no private meanings are permitted.[102]

Recursion to the private realm of conscience is necessary only in the event of modal conflict. Because modal conflict is resolved by conscience, individuals—most importantly judges—must make moral choices. Thus, it is individual conscience that decides the truth and falsity of controversial propositions of constitutional law. The process of justification in easy constitutional cases (cases in which the modes do not conflict) will be public, but in "hard cases" (those of modal conflict), individual conscience is the only analytical apparatus at work.[103]

The philosophical inspiration for Bobbitt's position, Wittgenstein, himself inveighed against the possibility of a private language. The central tenet of Wittgenstein's writing after 1929 is that knowledge is not achieved by the individual subject's grasp of a connection between

---

101. The problem is that conscience, as Bobbitt describes it, is supremely private—"hidden from view," as it were. Interestingly, Ronald Dworkin's "interpretive" approach to legal practice suffers from precisely the same difficulty. See Postema, supra note 36, at 296–97.

> There is nothing in Dworkin's meta-theory of interpretation . . . that requires attention to the interpretive activities of fellow participants. Herein lies the strong "protestantism" of Dworkin's theory. Not only is each participant encouraged to take up the interpretive enterprise . . . but each individual participant also has access to the truth, as it were, about what the practice is and requires, through private interpretation of the practice-text. While Dworkin seems to recognize that the practice is common, he counsels participants to live as if each had a private understanding of his own.

Id.

102. Nor, as Wittgenstein demonstrated, are they possible. See Wittgenstein, supra note 51, at §§ 243–315, 348–412; Ludwig Wittgenstein, The Blue and Brown Books 46–74 (Basil Blackwell, 2d ed. 1960) (demonstrating the impossibility of a private language).

103. Of course, there is no public access to this inner realm, for by its very nature, conscience is a function of "individual moral sensibility" (p. 168).

word and object. Rather, knowledge turns out to be the grasp of the topography of a word's uses in activities into which language is woven. It is the task of philosophy not to theorize about what lies behind language, but to describe its grammar.[104] The bounds of sense, as it were, are all within language, and meaning is nowhere other than in the many activities in which human beings use their various languages.

The central lesson of much of twentieth-century analytic philosophy is that when it comes to our words, "it is *we* who fix a reference."[105] The legacy of philosophy from the middle of this century to the present has been the systematic replacement of foundationalist epistemology with holism,[106] referential theories of language with an emphasis on speech as action,[107] and a general movement away from the individual

---

104. See Barry Stroud, An End to Anxiety, London Rev. Books, July 18, 1985, at 13, 14 (1985).

> [I]f philosophy is not the search for philosophical truths or theories of some kind or other, what could it possibly be?
>
> Wittgenstein's later work embodies an answer to that question. It is easier to see it at work than it is to explain it in general terms. Philosophy is to be purely "descriptive", not explanatory. But the description is always offered with a certain point, or purpose, not simply for its own sake.

Id.

105. Henry Staten, The Secret Name of Cats, *in* Redrawing the Lines: Analytic Philosophy, Deconstruction, and Literary Theory 27, 43 (Reed W. Dasenbrook ed., 1989). This is a lesson Bobbitt himself completely endorses. My contention is that Bobbitt does not follow through on the implications of his argument.

> Twentieth century philosophy discredits many of the epistemological assumptions of natural law and positivism, of formalism and realism, but it does not replace these schools (which partly accounts for the curious isolation of political philosophy from the developments in logic and epistemology). The message of such philosophy is: you are on your own; we've done enough harm already (p. 175).

(citing Richard Rorty, Philosophy and the Mirror of Nature (1979)).

106. See generally Willard V.O. Quine, Two Dogmas of Empiricism, *in* From a Logical Point of View 20–46 (2d ed. 1961) (arguing against the analytic/synthetic distinction and urging a view of knowledge as embedded in "the whole of science"). One interesting feature of Bobbitt's position is that it is the best example in the current literature of a postmodern approach to legal justification. Many scholars, both in constitutional theory and elsewhere, identify postmodernism with deconstruction or some other version of arch-skepticism. This is a profound error. Nothing could be more modernist in character than Derridean skepticism (was Hume a postmodernist?); it is little more than the opposite of the "representationalism" that Wittgenstein had destroyed before Derrida even glimpsed the École Normale Supérieure. For discussion of deconstruction and postmodernism, see Nancey Murphy & James W. McClendon Jr., Distinguishing Modern and Postmodern Theologies, 5 Mod. Theology 191, 211–12 (1989) (discussing Mark Taylor's "Postmodern A/Theology"). For an equally profound misunderstanding of postmodernism from the perspective of the eternal verities, see Thomas L. Pangle, The Ennobling of Democracy 65–68 (1992) (reviewing Sanford Levinson, Constitutional Faith (1988)). For discussion of law and postmodernism, see Dennis Patterson, Postmodernism/Feminism/Law, 77 Cornell L. Rev. 254, 262–79 (1992).

107. See J.L. Austin, How To Do Things With Words passim (J.O. Urmson & Marina Sbisá eds., 2d ed. 1975); Wittgenstein, supra note 51.

as the locus of empirical, linguistic, and moral judgment. The nineteenth century's emphasis on the individual as the site of judgment has been replaced with various conceptions of "group" knowledge: the language-game,[108] the scientific community,[109] and the web of belief.[110] Having recognized this fundamental shift in our conceptions of knowledge, meaning, and truth, we confront the question of what we are to make of this topographical shift.

Were Bobbitt true to the force of his own argument, he would have to admit that the inevitable conflicts among the modalities can only be settled in the public sphere.[111] Conflicts among the modalities are resolved not by what individuals decide, but by what they ultimately accept as an adequate resolution of modal conflict.[112] No particular resolution of modal conflict springs forth from conscience as a fully formed resolution, since it is persuasion, not conscience, that ultimately

108. See Wittgenstein, supra note 51, at § 7 ("I shall call the whole, consisting of language and the actions into which it is woven, the 'language-game.' ").

109. See Thomas S. Kuhn, The Structure of Scientific Revolutions 163–64 (2d ed. 1970).

110. See Quine, supra note 106, at 42. For discussion of this point, see Peter Galison, History, Philosophy, and the Central Metaphor, 2 Sci. in Context 197, 203 (1988) ("Quine strongly opposed the total separation of observation from other forms of knowledge; for him, all were up for evaluation."); Nancey Murphy, Scientific Realism and Postmodern Philosophy, 41 Brit. J. Phil. Sci. 291, 294 (1990) ("Quine not only replaced the foundationalist theory of knowledge with a holist account, but also provided a new picture or metaphor—that of a web or network of beliefs—to replace the 'layer-cake' model.").

111. By way of contrast, Richard Fallon handles the problem of modal conflict by resort to a theory of coherence. See Fallon, supra note 97, at 1237–51. The problem with appeal to a general theory of coherence is that the form of the argument is prudential. Thus, modal conflict is eliminated but at the cost of reductionism: all modes of justification are reduced to one, the prudential. (For an analysis of this shortcoming, see Bobbitt, supra note 4, at 1301–02.) It is perhaps unfair to characterize Fallon's endeavor as reductionist, for he does not seek to bring all the modalities under control by resort to one. Rather, his effort is to identify "a decision calculus that assesses the rightness or wrongness of possible conclusions along more than one dimension." Fallon, supra note 97, at 1241 n.230. Fallon does not identify or produce such a calculus, instead claiming that "constructivist coherence theory assumes a decision calculus . . . ." Id. at 1240–41 n.230. Instead, Fallon advances a hierarchy of arguments, with arguments from text at the top of the list. His reason for giving pride of place to the textual modality "follows from the settled proposition that it is the Constitution we are interpreting." Id. at 1244. This states, rather than solves, the problems under consideration.

112. Bruno Latour makes a parallel observation in the sociology of science. See Bruno Latour, Science in Action 42 (1987).

> [A] fact is what is collectively stabilised from the midst of controversies when the activity of later papers [for our purposes, judicial opinions, law review articles, addresses, etc.] does not consist only of criticism or deformation but also of confirmation. The strength of the original statement does not lie in itself, but is derived from any of the papers that incorporate it.

Id.

drives choice.[113] Charles Taylor, the brilliant contemporary exponent of the hermeneutic tradition, puts the matter thus:

> What if someone does not "see" the adequacy of our interpretation, does not accept our reading? We try to show him how it makes sense of the original nonsense or partial sense [or, in Bobbitt's terms, modal conflict]. But for him to follow us he must read the original language as we do, he must recognize these expressions as puzzling in a certain way, and hence be looking for a solution to our problem. If he does not, what can we do? The answer, it would seem, can only be more of the same. We have to show him through the reading of other expressions why this expression must be read in the way we propose. But success here requires that he follow us in these other readings, and so on, it would seem, potentially forever. *We cannot escape an ultimate appeal to a common understanding of the expressions, of the "language" involved.*[114]

What is missing in Bobbitt's otherwise compelling account of the practice of constitutional law is some description of the practice of persuasion that is so much a part of constitutional law and law generally.[115] How is it that lawyers convince one another of a particular reading of the law when the meaning of law is put in question? Why is one rendering of a modal conflict followed by some courts or judges and not others? It is an obvious and important feature of law that the merits of a single judicial decision play no role in the wider discourse of law unless and until another judge or court finds the reasoning persuasive.[116] The cultural methods and resources for persuasion simply can-

113. See generally Brian Simpson, The Common Law and Legal Theory, *in* The Common Law and Legal Theory 14 (William Twining ed., 1986) ("[C]ommon law rules enjoy whatever status they possess not because of the circumstances of their origin, but because of their continued reception.").

114. Charles Taylor, Interpretation and the Sciences of Man, *in* 2 Philosophy and the Human Sciences (Philosophical Papers) 15, 17 (1985) (emphasis added). Compare Geertz's evaluation of the importance of persuasion in anthropological writing:

> This capacity to persuade readers (most of them academic, virtually all of them at least part-time participants in that peculiar form of existence evasively called "modern") that what they are reading is an authentic account by someone personally acquainted with how life proceeds in some place, at some time, among some group, is the basis upon which anything else ethnography seeks to do—analyze, explain, amuse, disconcert, celebrate, edify, excuse, astonish, subvert—finally rests.

Clifford Geertz, Works and Lives: The Anthropologist as Author 143–44 (1988).

115. To be quite specific, and to make the point on the same plane as Bobbitt's argument, one wants to know where a discussion or argument goes after the individual decision makers resolve a modal conflict differently. In the present formulation of his position, Bobbitt resorts to conscience as the next step in the process. For the reasons given, I think this move fails.

116. See generally Richard Bronaugh, Persuasive Precedent, *in* Precedent in Law 217, 217–47 (Lawrence Goldstein ed., 1987) (providing a philosophical account of persuasion in appeal to precedent).

not be ignored.[117] By leaving the resolution of modal conflict to the uncharted realm of conscience, Bobbitt leaves for another day further discussion of a central aspect of the practice of constitutional law that he has otherwise described so well.[118]

Conclusion

Notwithstanding the failure to reconcile justification and conscience, Bobbitt's book represents a major contribution to legal philosophy. In an age self-absorbed with frivolous and shallow assessments of law, Bobbitt's book provides not only a welcomed respite but a glimmer of hope. In prose both enlightening and poetic, Bobbitt demonstrates a passion for legal argument that is positively infectious. Better still, he communicates a genuine sense of how one marshals the power of legal argument, not as a mere tool but as a *Weltanschauung*. At a time when so many who stand as professors of the law can manage only to condemn or trivialize it, Bobbitt's book teaches us that law is, and will remain, a noble—and ennobling—endeavor.

117. For friendly criticism of Bobbitt's position from one who sees law as a particular form of argumentative (semiotic) culture, see J.M. Balkin, The Promise of Legal Semiotics, 69 Tex. L. Rev. 1831, 1842 n.38 (1991).

118. It may be the case that, from the legal point of view, there is nothing more to be said about justification in constitutional law. The modalities of justification are the ways in which propositions of law are shown to be true or false. When a judge decides a case, she employs the modalities. The decision may require resort to conscience, but conscience does not do any normative work (Bobbitt seems to say that it does, but he has not made a convincing case for this central claim). The reasoning is either persuasive or it is not. Conscience does not persuade, nor is it persuaded: only argument can do that.

[12]
Law's Pragmatism: A Theory of Law as Practice and Narrative

The more concrete the idea, the greater the probability. The more abstract the medium is, the less the probability; the more concrete, the more. But what does it mean that the medium is concrete except that it either is, or is seen in its approximation to, language, for language is the most concrete of all media.

-Kierkegaard[1]

Introduction

THE demise of foundationalism, the attempt to find an indubitable ground for claims to knowledge and truth, has been both charted and heralded.[2] Among the views that have been advanced to fill the void left in the wake of foundationalism's demise is pragmatism. Though pragmatism's roots lie in early twentieth century philosophical thought, it has in recent years undergone a renaissance that borders on a rebirth. Legal scholars have been among those in the forefront of that rebirth, championing the revival of pragmatism in the human sciences.[3] But what does it mean to be "pragmatic" about the law? This Article advances an answer to this question by providing an outline for a pragmatist theory of legal discourse.

---

* Associate Professor of Law, Rutgers University School of Law—Camden. This Article is part of a larger work in progress bearing the title Law, Language and Skepticism. I have benefitted greatly from comments received during a presentation of this paper at the University of Toronto, Legal Theory Workshop in November, 1988. I wish to thank the following people for their comments on drafts of this Article: Jay Austin, Bill Eskridge, S. Stephen Hilmy, Allan C. Hutchinson, Richard Hyland, Don Korobkin, Brian Langille, Tom Morawetz, Arthur Ripstein, Martin Stone, Jeff White, and Ernest Weinrib. This Article is dedicated, in friendship, to Bob Ackermann.

1 1 S. Kierkegaard, Either/Or 55 (H. Hong & E. Hong trans. 1987).

2 The demise of the varieties of *philosophical* foundationalism is described in R. Rorty, Philosophy and the Mirror of Nature (1979). For a critique of foundationalism in ethics, see B. Williams, Ethics and the Limits of Philosophy 1-70 (1985). For a broader view of the demise of modernism, see D. Harvey, The Condition of Postmodernity 3-118 (1989).

3 For a review of the literature, as well as the presentation of a substantive theory of pragmatic statutory interpretation, see Eskridge & Frickey, Statutory Interpretation as Practical Reasoning, 42 Stan. L. Rev. 321 (1990); see also Eskridge, Gadamer/Statutory Interpretation, 90 Colum. L. Rev. 609 (1990).

The demise of foundationalism in twentieth century philosophical thought is largely reflected in the questions philosophers now ask. In epistemology, for example, debate has shifted from questions regarding the indubitable grounds for knowledge to an attempt to specify the conditions under which one can rightly claim to have knowledge.[4] The inclination to ask, not for the grounds of knowledge, but for the conditions under which assertions of knowledge will be accepted is informed by a distinct view of the relationship between language and the world. This view sees language as constitutive, as the medium through which understanding occurs. Once one accepts this view of language, the investigation of the use of language becomes paramount. In other words, the recognition that cognition is a function of language, and not of reason, is the key to the abandonment of foundationalism. For if all understanding occurs in and through language, then only the study of language will bring us closer to truth.[5]

It is the thought of Ludwig Wittgenstein which is central to modern philosophy's turn to language. For Wittgenstein, all philosophical problems are ultimately problems of language. This approach is evident in his treatment of what it means to "follow a rule."[6] Consider, for example, the rule of "plus." "75" is the answer to the question "what is 50 + 25?" But how do we know that this answer is correct; what tells us that this is the rule of "plus"? A skeptic might claim that "plus" means "add the numbers up to seventy, but after 70, always add an additional 5." Thus for the skeptic, "80" would be the correct answer to the question "what is 50 + 25?" How do we prove the skeptic wrong? To what do we appeal; what counts as evidence for or against our, or the skeptic's, claim to correctness?

These are the questions that surround the now much discussed

---

4 As Keith Lehrer has stated:

> A theory of knowledge need not be a theory about the meaning of epistemic words any more than it need be a theory about how people come to know what they do. Instead, it may be one explaining what conditions must be satisfied and how they must be satisfied in order for a person to know something.

K. Lehrer, Theory of Knowledge 5 (1990).

5 The use of the word "truth" is always problematic. At this point, I understand truth to mean the conditions under which an assertion meets adequacy conditions established by some group or discourse.

6 The most recent mention of this problem in the law review literature is Radin, Reconsidering the Rule of Law, 69 B.U.L. Rev. 781 (1989).

problem of "the skeptical paradox" of rule-following.[7] Two distinct philosophical views of the rule-following paradox have emerged from the literature. The first of these is advanced by the principal English-language commentators on Wittgenstein, Peter Hacker and Gordon Baker. They argue that there exists an "internal relation" between a rule and what counts as acting in accordance with it. It is the rule, and nothing else, that determines what counts as a correct application of the rule. The opposing view is the "community consensus" perspective. According to this view, there is a "community consensus" that serves as a mediating device between a rule and what counts as acting in accordance with that rule. Thus, it is not the rule, per se, but the conduct of the requisite social group that determines what constitutes acting in accordance with the rule.

The debate between Baker and Hacker and the community consensus view parallels in many ways the contemporary dispute in legal theory over the indeterminacy of law. As such, the debate over rule-following in the later Wittgenstein may be used to illuminate the current conflict among legal theorists as to whether or not the law can yield "right" answers. Representative of one side of the legal debate is Ronald Dworkin's view that the law can in fact yield "right" answers.[8] Like Baker and Hacker, Dworkin believes that there is an objective, determinable answer for the question of whether or not the conduct accords with the rule (the law). In contrast to Dworkin's view, there are a number of Critical Legal Studies (CLS) scholars who claim that there are no determinate answers at all.[9] They, like adherents to the community consensus view, believe that the application of law is determined by societal constructs and is, thus, in an ultimate

[7] A recent, select survey of this literature is found in Boghossian, The Rule-Following Considerations, 98 Mind 507 (1989). By alluding to current Anglo-American debates about objectivity in the law, I do not intend to set up a parallel between law on the one hand (Dworkin/CLS) and Wittgenstein scholarship on the other (Baker & Hacker/Community Consensus). I am simply making the point that participants in the legal debates over the nature of objectivity would benefit from a look at the Wittgenstein literature. I have argued elsewhere that the terms of current Anglo-American debates over objectivity are a non-starter and ought to be abandoned. See Patterson, Interpretation in Law: Toward a Reconstruction of the Current Debate, 29 Vill. L. Rev. 671 (1984).

[8] R. Dworkin, Taking Rights Seriously, 279-90 (1977).

[9] For discussion, see Langille, Revolution Without Foundations: The Grammar of Scepticism and Law, 33 McGill L. J. 451 (1988).

sense, indeterminate.[10] I believe that both of these views are *philosophically* flawed, and I believe that Wittgenstein's arguments demonstrate the flaws in a powerful way.

I shall use the debate over the rule-following paradox as a springboard for the presentation of an original approach to the question of rule-following in law; a view of law as practice and narrative discourse.[11] The later Wittgenstein presents a compelling account of a conventionalist conception of practice.[12] He has, however, little to say about the problem of conceptual change within a practice. While it is an obvious truism that the law changes, the interesting question is whether or not a *philosophical* account of conceptual change can be given.

The account I offer builds upon the philosophy of the later Wittgenstein, in particular his claim that following a rule is a practice. I take that insight and develop it into a conception of law as discursive argument. My claim is that law is an interpretive enterprise whose participants engage in the production of, and debate about, explanatory narratives—narratives that account for the history of the practice and are produced in the service of argumentation about how to resolve legal problems. In short, law is an activity and not a thing. Its "being" is in the "doing" of the participants within the practice.

---

[10] By "indeterminate" I mean that there is no preexisting connection between a concept and individual judgments that a certain state of affairs is an instance or example of that which is picked out by the concept. Without a determinate link between concept and application, judgment is a species of violence. See H. Caygill, The Art of Judgment 395 (1989) ("The text bears witness to a binding which is prior to law—an act of binding which is also a realization—and which does not efface differences but congregates them in the furtherance of life evoked by the beautiful.")

[11] The present Article represents the development of an orientation begun in Patterson, Wittgenstein and the Code: A Theory of Good Faith Performance and Enforcement Under Article Nine, 137 U. Pa. L. Rev. 335 (1988). There, I assessed the concept of good faith from the perspective of Wittgenstein's account of meaning and understanding. Notwithstanding my best efforts to remain within the pure Wittgensteinian framework, I often found myself unable to retain a non-revisionist stance toward the Wittgenstein corpus. The present Article is an explicit attempt to move beyond Wittgenstein. It does, I suspect, demonstrate that, despite my best efforts, I have succumbed to the urge to do philosophy.

[12] By "conventionalism" I mean a group practice that revolves around standards of conduct and behavior that are appealed to by members of the group as a ground for conduct and criticism. Further, the meaning of the standards and *what the standards are* is subject to revision and question. For a full discussion of recent philosophical approaches to conventionalism, see Patterson, An Introduction to Conventionalism, 10 W. New Eng. L. Rev. 43, 51 n.36 (1988).

I begin, in Parts I-III, by presenting the details of the Baker and Hacker/community consensus debate over the nature of rule-following in the later Wittgenstein. In Part IV this philosophical debate is related to the law through the argument that there is *both* an internal and an external element to rule-following in law. I here assert one of the principal claims of my position; viz., that legal argument is directed at constructing the *point* of law.[13]

Part V introduces the distinction between the *formal* and the *material* elements of a concept. As I shall show in detail, form is a heuristic for illuminating conceptual understanding. The formal element of a notion is that which enables us to see a group of things as "the same" even though each item has features that make it unique. For example, chairs come in all different shapes and sizes. The different shapes and sizes are the material elements. Because we understand that, despite their differences, each of these items is a chair, there must be something that enables us to recognize them as such. That "something" is the formal element of the concept "chair." Form determines matter in that the needs, wants, desires, and reasons of the community of rule-followers are the sources for the point (form) of law. As those needs, wants, desires, and reasons change (or are reconceptualized) so does the point (form) of law. In Part VI, I move on to provide several examples in support of the form/matter distinction. Part VI also provides arguments in support of the proposition that understanding is internal to a practice and thus not necessarily coextensive with regularity in behavior.

Part VII takes up some much ignored remarks of Wittgenstein about the relationship between rules and their application. These remarks suggest that there is more to rule-following than the internal connection recognized by Baker and Hacker. Further, these remarks strongly suggest that Wittgenstein himself also recognized that there was an additional element to rule-following beyond a rule's internal connection.

13 On the idea of the point of law, see Morawetz, The Rules of Law and the Point of Law, 121 U. Pa. L. Rev. 859, 869 (1973) ("The possibility is that at all levels of the on-going practice participants have recourse not only to rules but to relevant purposes and goals of the practice.").

Part VIII presents Wittgenstein's views on the relationship of language to reality. Like Gadamer[14] and the early Heidegger,[15] Wittgenstein believed that all representation occurs in language and that there is no way to "step outside" of language in order to survey its connection with reality.[16] In essence, reality is a social process of conventions which are not "agreed to" but shared.

Part IX explores the implications for law of Wittgenstein's remarks on rule-following and the view that all representation occurs in language. I argue that law is a social product of reason mediated through language. Part X sketches the parameters of the claim that legal argument consists of, and takes the form of, narrative accounts (histories) of the practice advanced in support of arguments about how to "go on" (forward) with the practice. Finally, Part XI provides an illustration of the narrative approach to legal discourse through the "duty to read" doctrine in contract law.

I. The Problem of Rule-Following in the Later Wittgenstein

No topic in the philosophy of the later Wittgenstein has generated more scholarly debate than Wittgenstein's remarks on rule-following. One problem for scholars attempting to find a unitary thesis on rule-following in the later Wittgenstein is that his remarks on the topic are both varied[17] and widely scattered. His most sustained treatment of the problem of rule-following is found in sections 185-242 of

---

[14] See H. Gadamer, Truth and Method (J. Weinsheimer & D. Marshall trans. rev. ed. 1988).

[15] See M. Okrent, Heidegger's Pragmatism: Understanding, Being and the Critique of Metaphysics (1988).

[16] The intralinguistic nature of truth is a central component of Richard Rorty's pragmatism. Rorty writes that "[t]he pragmatist has no notion of truth which would enable him to make sense of the claim that if we achieved everything we ever hoped to achieve by making assertions we might still be making *false* assertions, failing to 'correspond' to something." R. Rorty, Consequences of Pragmatism xxiv (1982).

[17] In their recent book, the Hintikkas advance the argument that rules are only one stop along the way in the development of Wittgenstein's thought from an emphasis on ostensive definitions to language games as the central element in his philosophy. Thus, they write:

> it is the idea of language-game that in Wittgenstein's later philosophy replaces the role of rules that he relied on during his middle period. Language-games are Wittgenstein's definitive solution to the problems he could not handle by means of the concept of rule. They are characteristic of Wittgenstein's last period in contradistinction to his middle period, in so far as the two can really be told apart.

M. Hintikka & J. Hintikka, Investigating Wittgenstein 190 (1986).

Philosophical Investigations.[18] No account of Wittgenstein's position(s) on rule-following is complete without paying serious attention to his sustained treatment of the topic in these sections.

The problem of rule-following is really two problems. First, there is what Saul Kripke labels Wittgenstein's "sceptical paradox":[19] one can never know whether one's current use of a word coheres with one's past use, for one's current use of a word (or calculation of a sum) can always be shown to be in accord with any number of different rules.[20] Thus:

> [t]here can be no such thing as meaning anything by any word. Each new application we make is a leap in the dark; any present intention could be interpreted so as to accord with anything we may choose to do. So there can be neither accord, nor conflict. This is what Wittgenstein said in § 202.[21]

I shall label the thesis for this problem, which Kripke finds in Wittgenstein, the "overdetermination thesis."[22] The problem can be articulated in general terms as the relationship between acts and possible descriptions of them. Any practice is a finite set of behavioral moves (acts). For example, the practice of gardening is a complex repertoire of behavioral sequences that involve constant repetition and variation (e.g., watering, pruning, etc.). The overdetermination thesis posits that any given act, say watering the garden, need not necessarily be described as being in conformance with a rule of gardening (e.g., "water the vegetables regularly"). Rather, it might also be explained as behavior in accordance with a host of other rules which are part of wholly different practices (e.g., in a collectivized state, watering a private garden could be a political act).[23]

---

[18] L. Wittgenstein, Philosophical Investigations §§ 185-242 (G. Anscombe trans. 3d ed. 1968). A complete understanding of Wittgenstein's remarks on rule-following and private language requires an analysis of at least two other major portions of the text, §§ 143-84 and §§ 243-315 (this latter group being the remarks on private language).

[19] S. Kripke, Wittgenstein on Rules and Private Language 4 (1982).

[20] Id. at 7.

[21] Id. at 55.

[22] I borrow the overdetermination/underdetermination distinction from Michael Rosen. Rosen, Critical Theory: Between Ideology and Philosophy, *in* The Need for Interpretation: Contemporary Conceptions of the Philosopher's Task 90, 111-13 (S. Mitchell & M. Rosen eds. 1983).

[23] It is important to see that the overdetermination thesis is a *logical* one. That is, it need not be the case *in fact* that there is available to an agent another repertoire of behavior in

The second problem of rule-following is the question of whether or not any system of rules is, by itself, capacious enough to both determine, and allow the participants in a practice to know, when and under what circumstances they are acting in conformity with a given rule. This problem of "underdetermination" is a familiar one in law,[24] and one which reaches its expressive zenith in the claim of certain CLS adherents that law is "indeterminate."[25]

The scholarly literature has yielded two "solutions" to the "problems"[26] of underdetermination and overdetermination. The first solution is posited by Gordon Baker and Peter Hacker in their book, *Scepticism, Rules & Language*.[27] Baker and Hacker argue that a rule and its applications are internally related through the medium of grammar.[28] Understanding a rule means understanding its grammar. There is no "interpretation" that "mediate[s] between a rule and its application."[29] Rather, reality and grammar are coextensive.[30]

The second solution is offered in the community consensus reading of Wittgenstein's remarks on rule-following. This view is well represented in the comments of Norman Malcolm: "[F]or Wittgenstein the concept of a rule presupposes a community within which a common agreement in actions fixes the meaning of a rule."[31] Thus, "[o]nly someone who had been a member of a community in which there was the *institution* of sign posts, could be said to *take his direction* from a sign post."[32] This view is supported by a number of

which the agent might be engaged. All that is required is that there exist an *in principle* possibility of some other explanatory framework.

24 H.L.A. Hart describes the "underdetermination" problem as precipitating "something in the nature of a crisis in communication." H. Hart, The Concept of Law 123 (1961).

25 See, e.g., Singer, The Player and the Cards: Nihilism and Legal Theory, 94 Yale L.J. 1, 61 (1984) (law is indeterminate because it cannot mechanically yield answers to interpretive questions). For a discussion of the relationship between the indeterminacy thesis and wider trends in post-modern theory, see C. Norris, Paul deMan: Deconstruction and the Critique of Aesthetic Ideology 125-48 (1988).

26 The words "solution" and "problem" are in quotes to indicate that, for some, these are only pseudo-problems yielding pseudo-solutions.

27 G. Baker & P. Hacker, Scepticism, Rules & Language (1984).

28 Id. at 123-24.

29 Id. at 128.

30 Id. at 135.

31 N. Malcolm, Nothing Is Hidden: Wittgenstein's Criticism of His Early Thought 175 (1986); see also, Malcolm, Wittgenstein on Language and Rules, 64 Phil. 5, 8 (1989) (arguing that "community consensus" is what determines how to "go on" with a practice or a rule.).

32 Id. at 172.

passages in which "Wittgenstein stresses the point that a language can exist only if there is *agreement* between persons in their applications of the language."[33]

Baker and Hacker believe the community consensus reading of Wittgenstein is incorrect because it exploits the social aspects of rule-following at the expense of the internal relation between a rule and its applications. As they put it:

> The pivotal point in Wittgenstein's remarks on following rules is that a rule is *internally* related to acts which accord with it. The rule and nothing but the rule determines what is correct (PI § 189). This idea is incompatible with defining 'correct' in terms of what is normal or standard practice in a community. To take the behavior of the majority to be the criterion of correctness in applying rules is to abrogate the internal relation of a rule to acts in accord with it.[34]

The choice between the two readings of Wittgenstein has important implications for legal jurisprudence. If a judicial decision cannot be said to be a necessary result of the application of a preexisting rule, then the decision can be attacked, at least prima facie, as a subjective choice having nothing to do with the rule. An example of such an attack can be seen in Dworkin's persistent critique of positivism; viz., his claim that the judicial phenomenology of positivism commits its proponents to the view that judges exercise strong discretion in deciding novel cases at law. In its latest formulation, Dworkin criticizes positivism as necessitating a system in which

> [j]udges must decide . . . novel cases as best they can, but by hypothesis no party has any right to win flowing from past collective decisions—no party has a *legal* right to win—because the only rights of that character are those established by convention. So the decision a judge must make in hard cases is discretionary in this strong sense: it is left open by the correct understanding of past decisions.[35]

This is precisely the sort of charge Baker and Hacker level against the community consensus interpreters of Wittgenstein: "On this account [the community consensus view], there is, in effect, *no* explanation of what it is to apply a rule correctly. That would require pinning down a single interpretation of the rule over the entire (infinite) range of its

---

[33] Id. at 173.

[34] G. Baker & P. Hacker, Wittgenstein: Rules, Grammar and Necessity 171-72 (1985).

[35] R. Dworkin, Law's Empire 115 (1986).

application, and this, it is argued, is impossible."[36] Further, Baker and Hacker are strident in their criticism of the community consensus view regarding objectivity: "[I]ndependently of a given rule it is unclear how to determine in advance what the community disposition is in respect of hitherto unencountered cases. Although both views aim to establish an objective standard of correctness in the face of sceptical doubts, the form of objectivity looks distinctly flaccid."[37]

Read from a jurisprudential perspective, I hope to show that it is possible to fuse the discordant voices in this debate. The community consensus reading of Wittgenstein does suffer from some critical weaknesses that the "internal relations" thesis highlights. On the other hand, Baker and Hacker's claim that "[t]he rule and *nothing but* the rule determines what is correct"[38] cannot, at least in law, be sustained. First, I shall detail the claims each side makes for its reading of Wittgenstein. I shall then seek to enrich the view of each by incorporating Wittgenstein's remarks on practices. It is Wittgenstein's pragmatism with respect to practices that will, I hope, prove to be the fibre that links these now discordant voices.

II. The Community Consensus View

The paradox to which the community consensus interpretation responds is found in section 201 of *Philosophical Investigations*:

> This was our paradox: no course of action could be determined by a rule, because every course of action can be made out to accord with the rule. The answer was: if everything can be made out to accord with the rule, then it can also be made out to conflict with it. And so there would be neither accord nor conflict here.[39]

The community consensus reading of section 201 is rooted in the claim that, for Wittgenstein, "there are always, on the basis of any normal training in and exposure to others' applications of the concepts involved, indefinitely many equally viable interpretations of which rule it is that we are intended to follow."[40] Consider, for example, Wittgenstein's discussion of how one would continue the series

---

[36] G. Baker & P. Hacker, supra note 27, at 69.
[37] Id. at 71.
[38] G. Baker & P. Hacker, supra note 34, at 172 (emphasis added).
[39] L. Wittgenstein, supra note 18, § 201.
[40] C. Wright, Wittgenstein on the Foundations of Mathematics 23 (1980).

"0, 1, 2, 3, 4, 5 . . . ."[41] The pupil is instructed to continue the series by adding by 1 until he reaches 1000 and then adding by 2 thereafter. If he continues the series after 1000 with 1004, 1008, 1012, we say that he has gotten it wrong; he has failed to follow the rule we gave him. But, "[s]ince the pupil's answers are compatible with myriad possible rules, how can we ever be certain that a pupil has grasped the rule we meant?"[42]

Following a rule correctly requires that it be performed in a manner consistent with that of any other similarly situated member of the community. As Christopher Peacocke puts it, "what it is for a person to be following a rule, even individually, cannot ultimately be explained without reference to some community."[43] Rule-following is a matter of habit insofar as behavior (or the requirement to act or refrain from acting) in accordance with a rule is a process of being socialized (trained) to act a certain way.[44] From this perspective, rules cannot be understood acontextually; the social, or contextual, element is central to the community consensus view.

How then, if there is no internal means for fixing the meaning of a rule, is its meaning determined? The community consensus readers of Wittgenstein point to section 202 and Wittgenstein's assertion that " 'obeying a rule' is a practice."[45] It is only in practices (established ways of acting) that the common ways of "going on" with rules get settled. Knowing what a rule requires in a given case is a matter of assessing the function of the rule within a practice. Mastering a rule is part of mastering "a technique—a technique is part of a social practice, institution or custom."[46]

Malcolm develops this aspect of the community consensus reading in his analysis of Wittgenstein's remarks in section 198 of *Philosophical Investigations*. Wittgenstein writes that "a person goes by a sign post only in so far as there exists a regular use of sign posts, a custom."[47] In other words, in order for there to be rules about sign

[41] L. Wittgenstein, supra note 18, §§ 143, 185.

[42] S. Shanker, Wittgenstein and the Turning-Point in the Philosophy of Mathematics 15 (1987).

[43] Peacocke, Reply: Rule Following: The Nature of Wittgenstein's Arguments, *in* Wittgenstein: To Follow a Rule 73 (S. Holtzman & C. Leach eds. 1981).

[44] See C. McGinn, Wittgenstein on Meaning 24 (1984).

[45] L. Wittgenstein, supra note 18, § 202.

[46] R. Fogelin, Wittgenstein 162 (1976).

[47] L. Wittgenstein, supra note 18, § 198.

posts, there must first be a community in which there is an institution of sign posts.[48] To react to the sign post in the "normal" or "required" way, there must be a response to sign posts that is consistent with some social training. Without the training, there would no "normal" response: the training is the embodiment of normalcy, its genesis. This point is affirmed by Wittgenstein in his statement that "[f]ollowing a rule is analogous to obeying an order."[49] What constitutes a correct response to the order must be assessed against the background of the training that supplies the contextual foreground for the meaning of the order. For example, unless one was trained in military tactics, the order "soften the beachhead before deployment of troops" would be open to any number of interpretations: the order and its many possible meanings would "hang[] in the air."[50]

The community consensus reading of the alleged skeptical paradox of section 201 of *Philosophical Investigations* is consistent with much that Wittgenstein has to say about related notions such as practice, custom, and institution. Despite its plausibility, however, Baker and Hacker present powerful objections to this "social gloss" on Wittgenstein's position. It is to these objections that we now turn.

III. Rules and Internal Relations

Baker and Hacker uncharitably describe the community consensus reading of section 201 as a "caricature" of Wittgenstein's remarks on rule-following.[51] The reason for their disparaging characterization lies in their belief that, for Wittgenstein, there must be an *internal* relation between a rule and acts that accord with the rule.[52] By their view, only *the rule itself* can be a source for its meaning: "To take the behavior of the majority to be the criterion of correctness in applying rules is to abrogate the internal relation of a rule to acts in accord with it."[53] In short, the fact that the majority acts in a certain way does not constitute the standard for acting in accord with the dictates

---

48 N. Malcolm, supra note 31, at 172.
49 L. Wittgenstein, supra note 18, § 206.
50 Id. § 198.
51 G. Baker & P. Hacker, supra note 34, at 171.
52 Id. at 117-72.
53 Id. at 172.

of a rule. At most, it merely serves to show that most people, most of the time, act in accordance with the rule.[54]

On this view, the notion of "correctness" is logically unrelated to the behavior of any member of the community. The justification for any application of a rule is the internal relation exemplified by the grammar of the rule. Applying the rule correctly is a matter of grammar; correct application means no more than applying a rule in accordance with its grammar. Thus, there cannot be, and need not be, any external (social) *justification* for a claim that a particular extension of the rule is mandated or warranted. The "justification" is in applying the rule correctly:

> What *justifies* calling rubies 'red'? Red is this ↑ colour; and rubies are this ↑ colour, i.e. red! Saying 'rubies are red' is a correct application of this rule for the use of 'red'. What *makes* it correct? Nothing. That is what we call 'applying "red" correctly.' There is no room for justification.[55]

It is not true, as the community consensus view asserts, that correctness in rule-application is reducible to, or is no more than, "a notion of assertion-conditions for correctness and incorrectness . . . ."[56] It is simply not enough to say that one "acts as everyone else does" in applying a rule. Such a claim misses the internal relation between a rule and its extension. Knowing what a rule requires and what accords with it is "akin to intending and knowing what will fulfil one's intention . . . ."[57]

Examples of what counts as following a rule "are no more *applications* of the rule explained than is an ostensive definition of 'red' (by pointing at a tomato) an application (predication) of 'red.' "[58] There must be a "canon of correct use,"[59] which is made manifest in the applications of a rule. For example, no explanation of a rule containing the phrase "one metre" can be correct unless some *further* explanation is given of the uses to which measuring rods are put. The rule, coupled with the teaching or instruction in its application, makes manifest the internal relation between the rule and its extension. The

---

[54] Id.

[55] G. Baker & P. Hacker, supra note 27, at 83.

[56] Id. at 72.

[57] Id.

[58] Id. at 73.

[59] Id.

fact that rules for the use of measuring rods are "used in justifying, correcting, and sometimes even in applications. . . is not a matter of collective dispositions, but of a normative practice, which may be collective, but need not be."[60]

One particular objection Baker and Hacker level against the community consensus view is significant, at least for present purposes; the problem of objectivity. The power of this objection lies in its simplicity, as an example will illustrate:

> If the leader of the community instructed his people to sacrifice to the gods on midsummer's day, they may well miscalculate the day, and later discover that they had misapplied the law (equally, just one of them might make this discovery, and despite his being right, be disbelieved by the rest).[61]

Simply stated, the problem of objectivity is what to count as correct application of a rule if the rule is to be judged *solely* by reference to what the community takes the rule to be. If that is the reference point, then is there not an unstable link (the community's consensus) between a rule and its extension? Baker and Hacker are correct to press their claim that interposing a notion of community consensus between a rule and its applications severs the internal relation between a rule and its extension. As they put it:

> In place of that internal relation the community view substitutes the notion of community *agreement*, which is not an *internal property* of the rule. Community agreement shows that the members of the community are all playing the same game, as it were, but that they should agree in applying the rules of the game is not itself one of the rules of the game. It is a framework condition within which the community game is possible. But that acting thus-and-so *is* acting in accord with *this* rule is no more a matter of what people are disposed to do than the fact that *p* is the fact that makes the proposition that *p* true is a matter of what people are disposed to believe.[62]

If the community consensus view is correct, then it is human agreement that decides what is true and false and not the world. As Baker and Hacker see it, such a formulation of the relationship between a rule and what accords with it collapses the distinction between mean-

---

60 Id. at 73-74.

61 Id. at 74.

62 Id. at 75.

ing (which humans create) and truth (which is determined by the world).[63] Maintaining the distinction between meaning and truth requires that there be "a certain constancy in the results of following a rule . . . ."[64] There can be no such constancy unless the internal relation between a rule and what accords with it remains unsevered. This is precisely what the community consensus view fails to do. By interposing consensus between a rule and its extension, both objectivity and the truth/meaning dichotomy are destroyed.

What the community consensus reading fails to account for is the "stipulative" nature of the relationship between a rule and its extension. A rule stipulates, in itself, its own content: the content (the extension) is "fixed (not open)."[65] One does not discover that "2 + 2 = 4." Getting "4" is "a *criterion* for following the rule of [plus]."[66] To do otherwise is, quite simply, to make a mistake.

For Baker and Hacker, past applications of a rule, (one source of content for the community's view of what a rule requires), do not count in any future judgment of correctness in rule application. They write:

> The suggestion that my past *applications* of a rule are the evidence that *I* must go on to 'discover' or 'determine' what I mean by 'W' (or what 'W' means), what I understand by 'W', or what a rule for the use of 'W' I am now following, is surely absurd.[67]

The thrust of this last shot at the community consensus view is that rule-following is not a matter of "*Praxis*."[68] Past applications do not in any way constrain present contexts. What the rule requires now is the same as what it always required, that is, application of *the rule*. Only "[t]he rule-sceptic thinks that what counts as doing the same thing is determined here by precedent."[69] Again, "[t]he rule and

---

63 Id.

64 Id. at 76.

65 Id. at 79.

66 Id. at 77.

67 Id. at 79.

68 While Baker and Hacker state that "[f]ollowing a rule is a *Praxis*," id. at 88, it is difficult to make sense of their claim. They deny that there is *any* necessarily social element to rule-following, stating that "[the community consensus view] wrongly takes Wittgenstein's conception of a practice to be necessarily a *social* practice (as if 'social practice' were a pleonasm)." G. Baker & P. Hacker, supra note 34, at 164.

69 G. Baker & P. Hacker, supra note 27, at 87.

nothing but the rule determines what is correct."[70] Rule-following is not social; it is grammatical. The internal relation between a rule and what accords with it is isomorphic and closed. Precedent teaches us nothing about what a rule does or does not require. Only the rule can do that. Precedent is nothing more than the history of correct and incorrect applications of what the rule requires; it is merely illustrative and not determinative of correct application.

IV. Law, Rules, and Interpretation: An Overview of the Argument

Reduced to its simplest terms, the argument between Baker and Hacker and proponents of the community consensus view is over the appropriate criterion of choice for how to "go on" with a rule; i.e., apply a rule in the future. If Baker and Hacker are correct in their claim that the rule and only the rule determines what will count as "acting in accordance with the rule," then assessing the propriety of any claim for what a rule requires in a given case that resorts to a source of authority outside the parameters of the rule itself constitutes an unwarranted undermining of the internal, normative force of the rule.[71]

In contraposition to Baker and Hacker, the community consensus position locates the interpretive criterion for correct application of rules outside the canonical form of the rule. The community of rule-followers determines *both* what its rules are (the answer to overdetermination) and what their content will be (the answer to underdetermination). The community consensus view is problematic, however. While the content of the rules, what they require in particular cases, is set in advance, it is always subject to revision. It is this aspect of the community consensus view with which Baker and Hacker take issue: if what is required by rules is always subject to revision, then the purveyors of the community consensus approach do not know the meaning of the word "rule." Rules require or prohibit actions *in advance*; they are not retrospective. It is inherent in the concept "rule" that what is permitted or mandated be known in

[70] G. Baker & P. Hacker, supra note 34, at 172.

[71] Cf. Raz, Authority, Law and Morality, 68 The Monist 295 (1985) (arguing that the authoritative nature of law is undermined by appeals to evaluative arguments beyond the "source" of the law).

advance so that actors can conform their conduct to what the rules require. It will not suffice to decide, after the fact, what the rules *ought to be read* as requiring. For Baker and Hacker, it must be the case that ex post facto determinations of what is required for conduct to count as "following a rule" are illegitimate (beyond the bounds of consideration). This makes a great deal of logical sense. How can it be said that "X was following A" when we only know what A requires after X has acted? If this were the state of affairs, then the best that could be said is that X acted in a manner that, after the fact, can be described as having been in accord with A. X could not, however, *really* have been "following A" at the time he acted because, prior to acting, we could not have known what A required.

These are strong arguments indeed for the necessity of recognizing the internal relation between a rule and its extension. I shall demonstrate, however, that while it is true that there is an internal relation between a rule and its extension in law, it is not the case that what a rule requires can be determined solely by reference to that internal relation. For, as the community consensus view makes clear, determining what a rule requires in a given case is essentially a *social* question, though in a manner distinct from that described by the proponents of the community consensus view. In brief, I will argue that the determination of what a legal rule requires is arrived at through the disclosure of the *point* of the rule in a legal system, a "disclosure" that is essentially a matter of social anthropology.[72] In order to follow a rule, we must know the reasons why the rule exists as part of the normative structure of law. The point of the rule, which is socially determined, constitutes the internal relation that links together the divergent factual contexts that comprise the extension of a rule. Community consensus does not, by itself, determine what constitutes acting in accordance with a rule. Rather, what constitutes acting in accordance with a rule is determined by the point of the rule and is analytically and socially specifiable apart from the rule. Thus, it is indeed true that there is necessarily a social element to rule-following, but it is not true that community consensus alone decides what constitutes acting in accordance with a rule.

---

[72] Recognition of this fact is perhaps the greatest contribution of Peter Winch to the importance of Wittgenstein's thought to social theory. See P. Winch, The Idea of a Social Science and Its Relation to Philosophy 62 (1958).

The claim that the meaning of a legal rule is determined by the point or purpose of the rule begins with the notion of a "practice." Following Rawls, practice may be defined as "any form of activity specified by a system of rules which defines offices, roles, moves, penalties, defenses, and so on, and which gives the activity its structure."[73] While it is true that games and law are both rule-governed practices, there is an important difference between the two that is not often recognized.[74] The difference is in the nature of the rules governing each. For example, chess is a game comprised solely of rules for the movement of the pieces. There is nothing to chess qua game that is not stated in the rules. In other words, the game is identical and coextensive with the sum of its rules. This is so because all the rules of chess are constitutive rules.[75]

Unlike games, however, law is comprised of prescriptive as well as constitutive rules.[76] While it makes no sense (it is a category mistake) to say, vis-à-vis chess, that "the rule of castle has negative consequences," it makes perfect sense in law to say "stealing from your neighbor is wrong." The difference lies in what Hart describes as "the critical reflective attitude" that is a necessary element of social rules.[77] The critical reflective attitude constitutes the "internal point of view"[78] that participants in a legal system have toward their own conduct and that of others. When conduct is criticized, appeal is made to a rule for justification of the criticism. But the character of the appeal in the practice of law is different from a claim for violation of a rule in a game. In chess, when one says "X has violated the rule for moving the bishop diagonally," no appeal beyond the rule need be made. The rule is the sole justification for the claim of violation. The only justification necessary or possible is the comment, "That's how the game is played."

In contrast to games, normative practices like law provide for the evaluation of conduct by reference to norms that are analytically ante-

---

[73] Rawls, Two Concepts of Rules, 64 Phil. Rev. 3, 3 n.1 (1955).

[74] In the analysis that follows, I have profited from the insights of T. Morawetz, Wittgenstein & Knowledge: The Importance of On Certainty 53-58 (1978).

[75] Morawetz, The Concept of a Practice, 24 Phil. Stud. 209, 209-10 (1973).

[76] The rule "no will is valid without the testator's signature" is a constitutive rule. Constitutive rules state conditions for something being what it is, e.g., a valid will. Prescriptive rules state "ought" requirements, e.g., the rule prohibiting assault.

[77] See H. Hart, supra note 24, at 56.

[78] Id. at 86-96.

cedent to the rules that embody them. Norms are embodied in legal rules that are comprised of concepts having the character of "open texture."[79] This marks the essential difference between games as practices and law as a practice. In law, claims of justification for what counts as "acting in accordance with a rule" must necessarily go beyond (behind) the rules to the norms that are the ground of justification for the rule. It is the norm, the *point* (reason) of the rule, that serves as the criterion for what does and does not count as acting in accordance with the rule. As J. L. Austin showed that it is proper to ask after the *point* of an utterance,[80] it is likewise constitutive of the practice of law to ask the interpretive question "What is the point of the rule?"

These considerations suggest that something is missing in the debate between Baker and Hacker and the community consensus view on the nature of following rules. It *is* true, as Baker and Hacker maintain, that there is an internal relation between a rule and its extension, but this relation is not, as Baker and Hacker suggest, *in* the rule itself.[81] It is not the case that there is no conceptual space within which community consensus, or anything else, can do work. Grammar does not completely fill the conceptual space of understanding; understanding the rule is not accomplished simply by understanding its grammar. Baker and Hacker claim that: "In so far as grammar is shared among the speakers of a single language, reality will be a public and community-wide creation of grammar. But in so far as grammar is a collection of decisions or stipulations, reality will depend upon us."[82] This characterization of the relationship between grammar and understanding creates a false dichotomy that serves as a rhetorical ploy in the argument for an unseverable internal relation between a rule and its applications. It is *not* the case, however, that a community consensus reading of the relationship between a rule and its applications need reduce rule-following *solely* to community consensus. In other words, the community consensus view need not be a thorough-going reductionist argument for rule-following. Rather, what "relates" the instances that can be said to fall under a rule with

79 See Waismann, Verifiability, *in* Logic and Language 122, 125-30 (A. Flew ed. 1965).

80 J. Austin, How to Do Things with Words 94-131 (1962).

81 G. Baker & P. Hacker, supra note 34, at 172 (stating that "[t]he rule and nothing but the rule determines what is correct (PI § 189)").

82 G. Baker & P. Hacker, supra note 27, at 135.

the rule itself is the norm that is the *point* of the rule in the practice of law.

For their part, the community consensus theorists are right to claim that rule-following is essentially a social enterprise. But, as Baker and Hacker suggest, it is conceptually untoward to reduce rule-following to mere consensus. Rather, the point of the rule is a social construct without which the rule would have no point and would be unintelligible.

Thus, with respect to law, there is a relationship between the grammar of rules and community consensus that is dialectical. The grammar of the rule enables us to understand what counts as "following the rule"; however, the grammar is erected upon an edifice of social practice which is itself subject to criticism and reconceptualization.

All of this is perfectly consistent with Wittgenstein's remarks about practices and rule-following. In section 43 of Philosophical Investigations, Wittgenstein remarks that "the meaning of a word is its use in the language."[83] This remark serves as an invitation to see language not merely as *expression* but *action*: the idea that we use words to *do* things.[84] Language games are activities comprised *both* of words and of acts. Understanding language requires attention to the point of its use(s) in context. Only by giving our attention to the *reasons* why norms are part of discourse, including legal discourse, can we make any sense of what they require when they are applied in concrete cases.

This would appear to be what Wittgenstein himself envisaged when he took up the question of doubt: "If you tried to doubt everything you would not get as far as doubting anything. The game of doubting itself presupposes certainty."[85] To doubt means to raise questions from a perspective within the practice; it is to ask questions about

---

[83] L. Wittgenstein, supra note 18, § 43.

[84] Strawson makes this point in his review of Philosophical Investigations where he writes:

> Variants on 'use' in Wittgenstein are 'purpose' 'function' 'role' 'part' 'application' . . . . The general aim is clear enough: to get us away from our fascination with the dubious relation of naming, of meaning, and to make us look at the speaking and writing of language as one human activity among others, interacting with others; and so to make us notice the different parts that words and sentences play in this activity.

Strawson, Review of Wittgenstein's Philosophical Investigations, *in* Wittgenstein: The Philosophical Investigations 22, 25 (G. Pitcher ed. 1966).

[85] L. Wittgenstein, On Certainty § 115 (G. Anscombe & G. von Wright eds., D. Paul & G. Anscombe trans. 1969).

what is going on (e.g., claims of knowledge) from within a shared perspective. Without (some) agreement in judgments, there would be no communication and no critique.[86] But the possibility of critique, and thus the reformulation of grammar, is inherent in all social practices. To deny this, as Baker and Hacker seem to, is unwarranted.

V. Purpose, Meaning, and Interpretation in Law

In the previous Section, I advanced the claim that discerning the meaning of a legal rule is a matter of seeing the purpose of the rule within the practice of law. I should now like to defend that claim through the use of several examples.[87] My goal is to choose relatively simple examples to support the general descriptive claim that legal argument is always directed at constructing a purpose or rationale for law. Without this rationale, law would be unintelligible. It is the effort to clarify the point of legal norms that drives legal argument.

A. *Form and Matter*

Many concepts, and certainly all social and political concepts, have a formal and a material element. By formal element I mean that which makes something what it is and not something else. As stated in the Introduction to this Article, the distinction between formal and material elements is heuristic. My use of these terms implies no metaphysical claims about the nature of reality *sub specie aetermitatis*.[88] The distinction serves merely to highlight certain aspects of conceptual understanding.

The distinction can be illustrated with a simple rule. For example, "All automobiles, bicycles and other wheeled vehicles must stop at red lights."[89] Let us suppose that, when the rule was promulgated, it

---

[86] L. Wittgenstein, supra note 18, §§ 241-42.

[87] Absent from this Part is any discussion of the conflict of interpretations. I will, however, address this subject in Part IX.

[88] In contrast to my view, see Weinrib, Legal Formalism: On The Immanent Rationality of Law, 97 Yale L.J. 949, 957-66 (1988). In Weinrib's view, "[f]orm is not separate from content but is the ensemble of characteristics that marks the content as determinate, and therefore marks the content as content." Id. at 958. Unlike the view advanced here, Weinrib's concept of "law" as form and content is *distinctly* metaphysical. Law has "juridical significance" (immanent *metaphysical* rationality) of which "positive law may provide only a *defective* [relative to its metaphysical form] rendering of the juridical [form] . . . ." Id. at 957 (emphasis added). See also Weinrib, The Intelligibility of Law, *in* The Rule of Law: Ideal or Ideology? 59-84 (A. Hutchinson & P. Monahan eds. 1987).

[89] This example is taken from E. Hirsch, Jr., Validity in Interpretation 124-25 (1967).

was empirically the case that all "vehicles" had wheels which, in normal use, touched the ground. Suppose that one day a "vehicle" is designed which rides not on rubber tires but on a cushion of air. Does the rule cover such a "vehicle"?

By resort to the formal element of the rule, we know that the point of the rule is the regulation of traffic in the interests of safety and the like. The *reason* for the rule, which arises in a particular way of life, is the basis upon which we make the judgment that this object is a "vehicle" for the purpose of this rule. Without the formal element, we could not make such a judgment.[90]

Whether a concept is moral or non-moral will depend upon differences in the formal element. My reason for this assertion is not to argue that there is no distinction between description and evaluation, but rather to argue that the relationship between the formal and the material elements of both descriptive and normative concepts is the same. Form determines matter.

A favorite philosophical example of this point is the table. What makes a table a table? Tables serve a multiplicity of functions and are the subjects of various language games. Tables are used for eating, for meetings, for piling things, for writing, etc. The language games of tables include stacking, counting, comparing, and selling. All of these activities are what we do with objects called "tables." The reasons we have tables are, "as it were, the guiding principle for deciding what are tables and what are not, or what new constructions will be accepted as tables."[91]

Language games are the practical activities into which and out of which we weave the concept of a table. Taken together, these language games exemplify the grammar of the word "table." The unity of the things we do with tables (e.g., eating, sitting, setting, stacking, etc.) is exemplified by the grammar of the word "table." That is why "[g]rammar tells us what kind of object anything is."[92]

---

90 Notice that what is common to these vehicles is not their *empirical* similarities (criteria), but the fact that the point of view from which they are collected is the *single* thing that brings them together. The *point* of collocation is the formal element.

91 J. Kovesi, Moral Notions 3 (1967); see also S. Cavell, The Claim of Reason: Wittgenstein, Skepticism, Morality, and Tragedy 71 (1979) (discussing the grammar of "chair"); Sellars, Aristotle's Metaphysics: An Interpretation, *in* W. Sellars, Philosophical Perspectives 73-124 (1967).

92 L. Wittgenstein, supra note 18, § 373.

One important feature of the form/matter distinction is the fact that there is no necessary or entailment relation between formal and material elements. Wittgenstein recognized this fact and evinced his recognition in the concept of "family resemblance."[93] But Wittgenstein did not go far enough in recognizing that essence is in grammar and not, as Aristotle thought, in the world.[94] The formal element of "table" does not require that a table be a particular height, depth, or shape in order to be a table. Such a requirement may arise in the course of a particular language game (e.g., choosing a table for a specific purpose), but there is nothing in the formal element itself that selects one group of characteristics over another *for a specific purpose*. All that is required is that the material elements belonging to the proffered "table" satisfy the social need for tables.

One might object, asking: "But can't a chair serve as a table? Can't it perform the function of a table and, thus, 'be' a table?" The very form of the question contains its own answer. Surely it is possible to treat a chair *as a* table, or a table *as a* chair. But, as Stanley Cavell reminds us, "[w]hat can *serve as a chair* is not a chair, and nothing would (be said to) serve as a chair if there were no (were nothing we called) (orthodox) chairs. We could say: It is part of the grammar of the word 'chair' that *this* is what we call 'to serve as a chair'."[95]

B. Form, Matter, and Rule-Following

Conceptual form determines what will and will not count as an example of the form. Form determines matter, but not ontologically. The position advanced here does not advocate looking for formal properties *in the object*. Such an approach fails to recognize that form is an object of reason, not the senses.[96] We no more sense with our

93 Id. § 67 (stating that the features of things that bear the same name will have no *one* thing in common, but will exhibit a variety of shared or overlapping features).

94 The mistake Wittgenstein makes is to locate similarity recognition at the level of criteria. The concept of "family resemblance" is an expression of the view that we see things as "the same" because they share certain features in common. This view is mistaken. In my opinion, we see things as "the same" because they have the same role in a situation or language game. The key to similarity recognition is the formal element and not, as Wittgenstein thought, criteria.

95 S. Cavell, supra note 91.

96 Hume made the same mistake, in a different way, when he complained that vice was not a "matter of fact." D. Hume, A Treatise of Human Nature 468 (L. Selby-Bigge ed. 1888). Hume's mistake was his failure to recognize that vice is an object of reason and not the senses. We "know" what vice is because we know its formal element.

minds than we reason with our fingers.[97] The making of one or the other of these regrettable moves engenders bad metaphysics.

This Part expands upon the argument for the conceptual distinction between the formal and the material elements of concepts by tying that dichotomy to the issue of rule-following. The connection lies in the fact that it is by virtue of the formal element of a concept that a rule can be followed. As previously stated, the "point" of a rule is a crucial element in understanding what conduct can be considered to fall within the rule. To take this inquiry a step further, it is important to realize that the point of a rule is the reason underlying the formal element in the concept as it is expressed by or contained in the rule under question. Thus, the meaning of a rule is a function of the formal element which is itself the verbal formulation of the reason underlying the rule. In short, a rule is a verbal formulation of a reason, and the reason is the formal element of the rule. For the moment, I shall concentrate on the concept of the point of a rule, as opposed to a group of rules, with an eye toward developing the relationship between the formal element in rule-following. Again, my claim is that, without a formal element, no rule can be followed. A correlative point is that the meaning of a rule is a function of its point or purpose and that this point is coextensive with the formal element.

To make my point, I can do no better than return to H.L.A. Hart's famous example of the "vehicle" in the park.[98] As you may recall, Hart's focus was on the interpretation of the rule: "No vehicles are allowed in the park."[99] In his debate with Lon Fuller,[100] Hart maintained that words have a settled or "core" meaning and that it is by virtue of this core of settled meaning that communication is made possible. If the meaning of the concept in question were debatable, then judicial discretion would resolve questions of "penumbral" meaning.[101]

---

[97] See J. Kovesi, supra note 91, at 19 ("We do *not* perceive with our reason any more than we know with our fingers . . . .").

[98] Hart's argument was first advanced in a debate with Lon Fuller in the Harvard Law Review. Hart, Positivism and the Separation of Law and Morals, 71 Harv. L. Rev. 593 (1958), *reprinted in* H. Hart, Essays in Jurisprudence and Philosophy 49 (1983).

[99] Id. at 607.

[100] Fuller responded to Hart in Fuller, Fidelity to Law, 71 Harv. L. Rev. 630 (1958).

[101] Hart, supra note 98, at 606-15.

For his part, Fuller disputed the core/penumbra distinction. Fuller claimed that meaning was a function of the purpose of the rule. His position is captured by his rhetorical question: "[I]s it really ever possible to interpret a word without knowing the aim of the statute?"[102] Without knowledge of purpose, no understanding of a statute is possible. In Fuller's view, statutory meaning is coextensive with legislative purpose.

Within the context of the form/matter distinction, it is easy to reconcile the seemingly incommensurable positions of Hart and Fuller. Hart's "core meaning" is nothing more than a function of the formal element in standard contexts. The reason we understand the meaning of the word "vehicle" is because, in hearing it, we attribute to it (it calls to mind) the contexts in which the word is used.[103] Use means context, and core meaning is nothing more than contextual, standard use.

Fuller's interpretive purposiveness exposes the Benthamite element in Hart's thought.[104] Hart seems to say that when the core of settled meaning runs out, a judge is inexorably forced to create meaning where none existed before (judicial legislation). Fuller objects to this move. The judicial obligation, according to Fuller, is to discern meaning from the point of view of the statute. Hart's rejoinder, though direct, is somewhat curious. He states:

> We are invited to include in the "rule" the various aims and policies in the light of which its penumbral cases are decided on the ground that these aims have, because of their importance, as much right to be called law as the core of legal rules whose meaning is settled. But though an invitation cannot be refuted, it may be refused and I would proffer two reasons for refusing this invitation. First, everything we have learned about the judicial process can be expressed in other less mysterious ways. We can say laws are incurably incomplete and we must decide the penumbral cases rationally by reference to social aims. I think Holmes, who had such a vivid appreciation of the fact that "gentle propositions do not decide concrete cases," would have put it that way. Second, to insist on the utilitarian distinction is to

---

102 Fuller, supra note 100, at 664.

103 See L. Wittgenstein, supra note 18, § 43 (stating that "the meaning of a word is its use in the language").

104 For an insightful discussion of the pragmatic and ontological presuppositions of Bentham's view of the common law, see Simpson, The Common Law and Legal Theory, *in* Legal Theory and Common Law 8, 16-18 (W. Twining ed. 1986).

> emphasize that the hard core of settled meaning is law in some centrally important sense and that even if there are borderlines, there must first be lines.[105]

What Hart fails to see, and Fuller sees all too well, is that settled meaning is settled because contexts of use are regular. Without settled contexts of use, there would be no such thing as core meaning. We can agree with Hart that "laws are incurably incomplete"[106] without rejecting as "mysterious" Fuller's claim that meaning is a function of purpose. Secondly, Hart is correct in asserting that there must be lines in law. Fuller would not dispute this. His complaint is not with the drawing of lines per se, but rather with Hart's analysis of how lines should be drawn.

My purpose in discussing this debate is not to take sides, for I find merit in both positions. The interesting point, however, is that these apparently conflicting positions are both reconcilable and explicable within the framework of formal and material elements. Hart's "core meaning" and Fuller's "purpose" both exemplify the logic of the formal element. Core meaning is a function of settled contexts of use. "Vehicle" means a car because the point of many rules isolates this configuration of (material) elements as "vehicle" (e.g., automobile registration and inspection, the auto club, autobahn, autoglass, auto tire, auto fuel, etc.). Likewise, the point of having vehicle inspections is to keep the road and other drivers safe from the hazards of dilapidated vehicles. The concept of a "vehicle inspection" is unintelligible apart from a way of life where vehicles are driven on roads by persons who have some interest in their own safety and the safety of others. What *counts* as a proper inspection can only be discerned from the point of view of these (conventional) interests.[107]

---

105 Hart, supra note 98, at 614.

106 Id.

107 D.W. Hamlyn presents a strong case for this view in the context of perception. The very idea of visual discrimination presupposes a scheme of concepts. Without concepts, "whatever information is available in the stimulus array . . . will not be available *to the perceiver* unless he has the concepts necessary to make that possible." D. Hamlyn, In and Out of the Black Box: On the Philosophy of Cognition 98 (1989). Perception is a function of knowledge and knowledge is a matter of concepts.

> [T]he perception of something as F cannot, logically, take place without the knowledge of what it is for something to be an F.
>
> But to have that understanding is to have the concept of F, and it is put to use in some way in perceiving whatever it is as F. To put the matter in a slightly different way—to have a concept of F is to know what it is for something to be an F. To know

Thus, in answering the question "May a statue of a vehicle be placed in the park?" appeal must be made to the formal element of the rule. It is proper to ask what *the point* of the rule is, why the legislature has promulgated it, and what reason(s) there is for making this rule part of the law. To ask these questions is to ask for the formal element. A preliminary answer to the question may be found in settled contexts of use, Hart's core meaning. But the better answer, the complete answer, is found in the purpose of the rule. Without knowledge of the formal element, a court asked to apply the rule can only guess at its meaning.

C. Examples of Form, Matter, and Rule-Following

These general remarks on rule-following can be amplified through a further legal example. Take the common law rule of contract, the idea that no contract is enforceable absent consideration. How does one comprehend the meaning of "consideration"? To begin, we might offer a definition or state a rule; better still, we might look at some examples of what has, in the past, "counted" as consideration. As we go through the examples, it is important to note how they are united, i.e., what it is that brings them all under the rubric "consideration."

A and B each have children in the Happy Trails Nursery School. Each morning A and B take their children to school prior to the commencement of classes at 8:00 a.m. From there, they both proceed to their respective jobs at the same office. One day at their office, A offers to pick up B's child the next morning and take him to school. B is thankful and tells A that he appreciates the favor. A's promise to B is unenforceable because B did not give A anything in return for A's promise. There has been no reciprocal offer of *value* by B, i.e., B has not offered *consideration*.

Jones is interested in purchasing a lawn tractor and goes to the Acme Tractor Co. for that purpose. After haggling with a salesman for an hour, the salesman promises to sell Jones the top-of-the-line

> what it is for something to be F involves knowing that an indeterminate list of things are so—things such as that being F involves being . . ., or that such and such range of things are F. But it is important that that list is indeterminate. One cannot lay down a determinate set of knowings—that which are necessary and sufficient for knowing what it is for something to be F. To perceive something as F nevertheless entails having that knowledge.

Id. at 92.

model for ten percent off the list price. Jones promises to pay that amount and signs a contract to that effect. The contract is enforceable because, among other things, each side has offered the other consideration.

An initiate into the practice of contract law would, at this point, be able to say at least two things about consideration:

1. consideration is something of value given in exchange for a promised performance; and
2. each side of a bargain must offer consideration in order for the contract to be enforceable.

With these two attributes of consideration in mind, can we decide whether or not the following agreement is enforceable as a contract?[108]

> A widow promises to repay a debt owed by her deceased husband in exchange for the creditor bank's cancelling the estate's debt. The husband's estate is without assets, and no part of the cancelled debt could ever have been collected.[109]

The obvious question is whether or not the widow's promise to pay her deceased husband's debt is an example of "consideration." Can we elaborate on the meaning of consideration by describing its predicates? How do we know which of its predicates are accidental and which are essential? A view that the widow's promise of repayment is consideration is only intelligible within the context of a theory of contract which has at its core a concept of contract as bargain. Only in recognizing the practice of contract as a system of rules with bargain theory at its center can we decide whether or not the widow's promise serves as consideration.[110]

---

[108] C. Fried, Contract as Promise 28-31 (1981).

[109] Id. at 31.

[110] Notice that I said *a* concept of contract as bargain and not *the* concept of contract as bargain. Compare the concept of contract as bargain with the benefit/detriment test of consideration employed in Hamer v. Sidway, 124 N.Y. 538, 27 N.E. 256 (1891). In *Hamer*, the New York Court of Appeals decided the question of whether or not an uncle's promise to pay his nephew $5,000 if the young man refrained from alcohol and tobacco until his 21st birthday was enforceable against the uncle's estate.

The court found that the "detriment" imposed upon the nephew (his abstention from conduct he had a right to pursue) was sufficient to support a determination that the promise was enforceable. The point is not that the New York Court of Appeals *called* "consideration" something different than did the Restatement test of a bargain. Rather, the point is that the conception of contract as bargain makes the concept of consideration intelligible. The

Let me return to my general claim that the meaning of a legal rule is a function of the point or purpose of the rule. The rule that no contract is enforceable without consideration cannot, on its own or in conjunction with a definition of consideration, tell us whether or not a contract is enforceable.[111] The constituent components of consideration are determinable only when we have elaborated the point of the rule requiring consideration. The rule of consideration is unintelligible until one realizes that it is "grounded" in a particular conception of contract law—the bargain theory. It is only against the background of the bargain theory that we can make sense of the question of whether or not "X" is consideration. The answer will be determinable only after we recognize the purpose of consideration and its role in contract law.

VI. All Justification Must Come to an End—But Only Temporarily

If anything is central to the later philosophy of Wittgenstein, it is the distinction between reasons and causes. Of the former, he had much to say. Of the latter, he could not disparage enough the psychological theories of his day, particularly their proponents' wish to explain meaning as a mental phenomenon.[112] For Wittgenstein, meaning is a public process, a socially created phenomenon. To know the meaning of a word is to give a correct linguistic performance in appropriate contexts.

In this Part, I will elaborate upon the claim that the meaning of a legal rule is a function of its point or purpose. What I offer will, in some quarters, be seen as a sociology of law—and in a sense it is, if one understands sociology as the description of what participants in

---

meaning of consideration is a function of the conceptual presupposition of contract as bargain. The very intelligibility of consideration is tied to *this* (as opposed to some *other*) conception of contract.

111 In other words, contra Hegel, the idea of contract cannot be understood in itself, for itself. See G. Hegel, The Philosophy of Right § 80 (T. Knox trans. 1977) (stating that "[t]he classification of contracts and an intelligent treatment of their various species once classified is not here to be derived from external circumstances but from distinctions lying in the very nature of contract").

112 For an extensive and extremely well-informed treatment of this topic, see generally S. Hilmy, The Later Wittgenstein 190-226 (1987) (noting Wittgenstein's rejection of meaning as a mental phenomenon).

legal discourse actually do.[113] In another sense, what I offer is a phenomenology of legal practice. I will describe, first in general terms and then by way of example, the *constructive* aspects of purpose. In addition to illustrating that the phenomenology of judging is more a *collective* than an *individual* enterprise, I will illustrate how that collective enterprise contributes to the construction of legal meaning. In short, attribution of purpose is constructive and dialogical; constructive in the sense that the source of purpose is multiple, not unitary, and in the sense that legal meaning is produced through dialogical encounter among participants in legal discourse.

The general philosophical claim that lies at the center of the theory of law as narrative discourse is that the meaning of the activities of rational agents cannot be understood apart from the agents' own perceptions and self-descriptions of the activity under question. In other words, the meaning of a practice is an *internal* phenomenon. It is within the practice, and by virtue of the acts of the participants in the practice, that the practice has meaning. Without purposeful activity, there would be no practices. Practices are creatures of reason and function as conventions. It is, therefore, against the specifics of a practice that claims for actions consistent with the practice are validated. Our perception of the objectivity of any particular decision is a function of the degree to which the act in question is in conformity with the demands of the practice as understood by the participants.

It is perhaps paradoxical to assert that a practice has standards against which claims of conformity are measured and, at the same time, to claim that those standards are a function of the needs, wants, desires, and purposes of the participants. This is precisely my claim, however. Claims of consistency with the practice are measured against the practice, but the participants in the practice determine what those standards are and will be. I shall now present arguments in support of each of these claims.

Concepts are not theories.[114] The relationship between concepts

---

113 For a discussion of the connection between Wittgenstein and Karl Llewellyn on the central role of description in jurisprudence, see Patterson, Law's Practice (Book Review), 90 Colum. L. Rev. 575 (1990).

114 See Hacker, Language, Rules and Pseudo-Rules, 8 Lang. & Commun. 159, 170 (1988) ("Understanding a language does not involve constructing a theory of any kind, but mastery of an array of skills or techniques in the use of words."). A recently influential example of an attempt to equate (and reduce) understanding to a (posited) inner structure is the work of

and actions is one of reasons and justifications. Purposeless activity is unintelligible as action, for no action is intelligible apart from some

---

some psychological linguists. See, e.g., M. Johnson, The Body in the Mind: The Bodily Basis of Meaning, Imagination, and Reason (1987); G. Lakoff, Women, Fire, and Dangerous Things: What Catagories Reveal About the Mind (1987).

In resorting to this corner of the structuralist literature, Steven Winter has sought to understand law from what he describes as a "cognitive" perspective. See, e.g., Winter, "The Cognitive Dimension of the *Agon* Between Legal Power and Narrative Meaning," 87 Mich. L. Rev. 2225 (1989). The following is representative of his view:

> [T]he human mind constructs meaning "from the ground up," bootstrapping from its own basic experience in the world and imaginatively elaborating those thought structures or *schemata* in its further interactions with its physical and social environment.
>
> ....
>
> Each of these quite basic interactions with the world is generalizable, and each is in fact generalized across a series of other domains. Each of these generalizations is a mental construct by which the human mind creates meaning, a "recurring structure" or "repeatable pattern" that is "a chief means for achieving order in our experience so that we can comprehend and reason about it".... These schemata are... powerful aspects of human rationality because their operation is automatic and unreflexive—that is, without conscious awareness, reflection, or control.

Id. at 2231-32 (citing and quoting M. Johnson, supra).

Perhaps the best way to be clear about just what claims are being made is to ask the questions "What is it that is under investigation?" and "What is the phenomenon to be explained?" The answer is plain to see—the understanding of language. What is the theory advanced for the phenomenon of human linguistic understanding?—That learning a (first) language is a matter of (the mind's) creating a "recurring structure" that is generalized across an infinite domain of experience which the structure organizes. There are many reasons to doubt the plausibility of such a view of human understanding. We shall focus on two.

Take the claim that "the human mind constructs meaning." Think about the presuppositions of such a claim. The most obvious one is that the human mind can construct meaning *before it has language*. (Remember, it is language *learning* (understanding) that is being explained.) What Winter is claiming is that the human mind first creates a (recursive) structure and then proceeds to use it in the organization of experience. And the mind is doing all of this without first having learned a language!

The second claim is that these thought structures or *schemata* operate "without [our] conscious awareness, reflection, or control." Id. at 2232. Thus, the meaning of words is not a function of use; rather, it is a function of acting in accordance with the right (unconscious) structure. The patently suspect character of such an approach to understanding is apparent the moment one reflects upon what such an account of understanding renders superfluous—the normative dimension of understanding. If understanding were the mysterious, unconscious process so described, then all "the normative activities of teaching and training, guiding conduct by reference to [extant] rules, justifying, explaining, evaluating [would play no role in understanding]." Hacker, supra at 164. Knowing that a driver, who stops at a stop sign is acting in accordance with the rule for the use of stop signs is a matter of resort to the rule for stop signs. Explanations of such matters by resort to the mysteries of unconscious structures are science fiction and nothing more. It is no more helpful to explain human understanding by reason or justification for the act undertaken.[115] But not just *any* concept will explain the meaning of an agent's action. If the explanation is not one the agent would accept, at least in principle, then the explanation must be rejected, for it fails to capture the meaning of the act in question.

But why insist that any proffered explanation of action be one the agent would, in principle, accept as a rationale for her action? Let me return to the notion rejected at the outset; the idea of concepts as theories. I am *not* saying that actions are not to be *causally* explained by concepts. My claim is that there exists no set of concepts that explain an agent's activity better than those in which the agent finds her activity intelligible.[116] Regularity or pattern in behavior, coupled with a hypothesis about what the regularity could amount to, is not understanding. No theory of regularity can hope to make sense of behavior until and unless its proponent is willing to construct the theory in a manner consistent with a subject's self-understanding. Of course, when this is done, the need for an explanatory theory disappears.

---

resort to mythical devices like "recursive structures" than it is to suggest that opium puts one to sleep because it possesses "dormative powers."

For a more thorough refutation, see G. Baker & P. Hacker, Language, Sense & Nonsense (1984); Wright, Wittgenstein's Rule-following Considerations and the Central Project of Theoretical Linguistics, *in* Reflections on Chomsky 233-64 (A. George ed. 1989).

[115] As Alasdair MacIntyre has stated:

> Unintelligible actions are failed candidates for the status of intelligible action; and to lump unintelligible actions and intelligible actions together in a single class of actions and then to characterize action in terms of what items of both sets have in common is to make the mistake of ignoring this. It is also to neglect the central importance of the concept of intelligibility.

A. MacIntyre, After Virtue: A Study in Moral Theory 195 (1st ed. 1981)

[116] I do not deny that texts can be read in contexts that create meanings unknown to the authors of those texts or beyond the cultural milieu out of which those texts were produced. What I do claim, however, is that it is a fundamental mistake to fail to consider the self-understanding of the participants in a discourse. The limitation here is one of representation: if the framework within which a practice is redescribed is not *in principle* cognizable by the subjects of the description, it must be rejected as meaningless. Why? Because meaning is neither in the text nor in the head (of the described participants). Meaning is what the discursive participants do with their texts. Compare C. Altieri, Act & Quality: A Theory of Literary Meaning and Humanistic Understanding 155-56 (1981) (stating that meaning is the intention an author can accept on redescription) with Ricouer, The Model of The Text: Meaningful Action Considered as a Text, *in* P. Ricouer, Hermeneutics and the Human Sciences 218 (J. Thompson ed. & trans. 1981) ("The depth semantics of the text is not what the author intended to say, but what the text is about, i.e., the non-ostensive reference of the text.").

Consider the cancellation of debts and gift-giving. If A loans money to B and then decides not to demand payment, what are the observed regularities? A gives a pile of paper (money) to B; B acquires material objects by giving the paper to third parties; and B never returns the paper or its equivalent to A. Without knowing more, four possible explanations of these behavioral regularities are possible:

1. A made a gift of money to B, which B then spent;
2. A loaned money to B and they orally agreed that B would pay it back to A at 10 percent interest per annum, and B has refused to repay the loan;
3. Same as 2 except that A has forgiven B's obligation; or
4. A was repaying a debt to B which required no further action on B's part.

In order to determine which of these four possible explanations is appropriate in relation to the activity of A and B, an observer must understand the concepts of loan, gift, repayment, contract, breach, etc. The meaning of the actions of A and B are unintelligible apart from these terms. They are, as it were, merely "brute facts." It is the practice of lending money or making a gift that makes the action intelligible. But, and this is important, if A and B had no notion of gift-giving and explained their behavior relative to the practice of lending money with a promise of repayment, it would be a *misunderstanding* of their actions to explain it in any other terms, e.g., gift-giving. Money-lending is not a *theory* that explains the actions of A and B. Rather, it is the framework within which these actions are intelligible. To describe the actions of A and B in any other terms is to misconstrue *the meaning* of their actions. Understanding a practice and understanding the concepts that comprise the practice are one and the same thing.

One possible objection to my general philosophical claim that the meaning of legal rules is unintelligible apart from contexts of use (wherein the point of the rule is made manifest) is the fact that words can often be understood apart from context.[117] In short, the claim is that literal semantic meaning is a feature of linguistic practice, and thus of legal practice as well.

---

[117] See, e.g., Schauer, Formalism, 97 Yale L.J. 509, 527-28 (1988).

The fact that words can be understood apart from context in no way impairs the substance of my argument. I do not dispute, for example, the claim that Lord Russell's famous sentence, "the present King of France is bald," is understandable by a competent speaker of English. But understanding is not enough. The statement must also be *intelligible*. If I called upon a student for the facts of *Hadley v. Baxendale* and she responded with Lord Russell's famous sentence, I would not know what to say, how to respond to her statement. I would understand her utterance, but it would not be intelligible; I would not know what *she* meant by it.[118]

It simply will not do, as proponents of semantic formalism maintain, to make the obvious point that words and sentences have meaning apart from their contexts of use. No one would dispute this. What is disputed is the claim that one can build a theory of law (formalism) on such an edifice. Bare semantic meaning exists as a feature of linguistic practice because the contexts in which the words were first learned provide the background necessary for the recognition of meaning by the listener. The meaning of words is a function of training in the contexts of use.[119] The training provides the foundation for meaning and makes meaning possible. Without training in contexts of use, words would have no meaning. Thus, when a sentence is uttered in an inappropriate context, the *sentence* is understood because the listener associates the sentence with the contexts in which it was learned.[120] The reason the sentence is unintelligible is because, in the situation in which the listener finds himself, he cannot find anything with which to link the utterance. In answer to the question, "[o]n what occasion, for what purpose, do we say this,"[121] the listener is forced to say "none." Thus, the statement may be understandable and yet still be unintelligible.

---

118 This, I take it, is the point Wittgenstein makes when he says: "If a lion could talk, we could not understand [verstehen] *him*." L. Wittgenstein, supra note 18, at 223e (emphasis added). We would understand the utterance, but not what the lion meant by it.

119 L. Wittgenstein, Zettel § 419 (G. Anscombe & G. von Wright eds., G. Anscombe trans. 1967) (stating that "[a]ny explanation has its foundation in training").

120 Rorty, How to Interpret Actions, *in* Rationality, Relativism and the Human Sciences 81 (J. Margolis, M. Krausz & R. Burian eds. 1986) ("But when we interpret isolated sentences and events, we supply the standard contexts in which they occur.").

121 L. Wittgenstein, supra note 18, § 489.

VII. Wittgenstein's Tailor

It is now time to return to the dispute between Baker and Hacker and the community consensus readers of Wittgenstein's remarks on rule-following. Recall, if you will, that the basic disagreement between these two readings of Wittgenstein is over the extent to which the conduct of the community of rule-followers contributes to the meaning of the rules. For Baker and Hacker, *no* contribution is allowed. As they put it, "the rule and only the rule determines what counts as 'following the rule.' "[122] In other words, the extension of a rule is a function of its internal relation.

For their part, the community consensus readers of Wittgenstein claim that it is *only* in a community of rule-followers that the extension of a rule comes to light. The community consensus readers take the position, exemplified by Malcolm, that "the concept of following a rule implies the concept of a *community* of rule-followers."[123] In short, far from agreeing with Baker and Hacker that the rule and only the rule determines what will count as part of its extension, the community consensus reading indicates that, without a *community* that follows the rule, the notion of "following" the rule makes no sense at all.

Can there be an internal relation between a rule and its applications that is socially determined? I think this is possible and I believe Wittgenstein thought so as well. In his *Lectures on Aesthetics*,[124] Wittgenstein discusses several practices that are governed by rules,

---

122 G. Baker & P. Hacker, supra note 34, at 172.

123 M. Malcolm, supra note 31, at 156.

124 L. Wittgenstein, Lectures and Conversations on Aesthetics, Psychology and Religious Belief (C. Barrett ed. 1972). I should note that while I refer to what Wittgenstein *said*, he wrote none of the words in this book. The book is a compilation of notes taken by some of Wittgenstein's students. Nevertheless, there is little or no reason to doubt the accuracy of what is written.

For the sake of accuracy, I should reaffirm that my primary interest in discussing Wittgenstein's thoughts on rule-following is *not* in rendering an authoritative interpretation of Wittgenstein. Wittgenstein's texts are rich enough for most to find in them one's own Wittgenstein. Apropos of this, I wish to point out that the material from *Lectures on Aesthetics* was dictated by Wittgenstein in the summer of 1938. The remarks on rule-following in *Philosophical Investigations* comes from the first part of the text, which Wittgenstein completed in 1945. One might wish to make the case that Wittgenstein abandoned the line of though set out in the summer of 1938 in favor of that advanced in the later work. I take no position on such a claim.

including tailoring. Wittgenstein's remarks on the practice of tailoring reveal much about the relationship between rules and practices.

> In the case of the word 'correct' you have a variety of related cases. There is first the case in which you learn the rules. The cutter learns how long a coat is to be, how wide the sleeve must be, etc. He learns rules—he is drilled—as in music you are drilled in harmony and counterpoint. Suppose I went in for tailoring and I first learnt all the rules, I might have, on the whole, two sorts of attitude. (1) Lewy says: 'This is too short.' I say: 'No. It is right. It is according to the rules.' (2) I develop a feeling for the rules. I interpret the rules. I might say: 'No. It isn't right. It isn't according to the rules.' Here I would be making an aesthetic judgement about the thing which is according to the rules in sense (1). On the other hand, if I hadn't learnt the rules, I wouldn't be able to make the aesthetic judgement. In learning the rules you get a more and more refined judgement. Learning the rules actually changes your judgement.[125]

In considering these remarks, one cannot help but notice that Wittgenstein's emphasis on the relationship between a rule and its interpretation is compatible with, yet in an important way different than, his comments in *Philosophical Investigations*. In *Philosophical Investigations*, he says that "[i]nterpretations by themselves do not determine meaning."[126] The reason for this is clear: interpretations of rules only make sense in practices where there is an established way of "going on" with the rule such that the interpretations of a rule will have something that will moor them to the practice.

Different types of practices, however, have different rules and, more importantly, different criteria for what does and does not constitute "following the rule." Wittgenstein comments:

> On the other hand we can contrast different kinds of formula, and the different kinds of use (different kinds of training) appropriate to them. Then we *call* formulae of a particular kind (with the appropriate methods of use) "formulae which determine a number y for a given value of x", and formulae of another kind, ones which "do not determine the number y for a given value of x". ($y = x^2$ would be of the first kind, $y \neq x^2$ of the second.) The proposition "The formula .... determines a number y" will then be a statement about the form of the formula—and now we must distinguish such a proposition as

[125] Id. § 15.

[126] L. Wittgenstein, supra note 18, § 198.

> "The formula which I have written down determines y", or "Here is a formula which determines y", from one of the following kind: "The formula $y = x^2$ determines the number y for a given value of x". The question "Is the formula written down there one that determines y?" will then mean the same as "Is what is there a formula of this kind or that?"—but it is not clear off-hand what we are to make of the question "Is $y = x^2$ a formula which determines y for a given value of x?" One might address this question to a pupil in order to test whether he understands the use of the word "to determine"; or it might be a mathematical problem to prove in a particular system that x has only one square.[127]

The discussion of rules in *Philosophical Investigations* is addressed to the emptiness of skepticism and is aimed at showing that rules make sense in practices and that only through use is the meaning of a rule made manifest. In his remarks on tailoring in *Lectures on Aesthetics,* Wittgenstein seems to have a different point in mind. Instead of focusing on which rule to apply, Wittgenstein draws our attention to the *application* of rules that participants in the practice agree are the rules of the enterprise. There is a distinction between knowing the rules of a practice and being a competent practitioner; a practitioner exercises "aesthetic judgement" whereas a nonparticipant does not. Although learning the rules is *necessary* to having aesthetic judgment, *knowing the rules* of tailoring is not enough to make someone a competent tailor.

As I hope to show in the next Part, there is, indeed, a close connection between community consensus and judgment about what counts as "following a rule," but it is the nature of the enterprise, the practice, that makes the role of community consensus more prominent than it is in practices such as tailoring or mathematics. I hope to show that law is by nature, and as a practice, fundamentally different from tailoring, and that, because of the difference, the analysis of rule-following must also necessarily be fundamentally different.

VIII. Representation and Language

A. *The Universal Medium*

One of the most prevalent metaphors in the later Wittgenstein is the idea that the use of words is comparable to the employment of

127 Id. § 189.

tools to perform some task. For example, in an early section of *Philosophical Investigations*, Wittgenstein writes: "Think of the tools in a tool-box: there is a hammer, pliers, a saw, a screw-driver, a rule, a glue-pot, glue, nails and screws.—The functions of words are as diverse as the functions of these objects."[128] Words are tools employed to satisfy purposes. They function in language games that combine to form the constellations of activities we refer to as "practices." What practices we choose to create, and how we wish to construe them, is a function of our needs, desires, and common ways of life (forms of life). The organization of our concepts and ideas is a function not only of the broad features of our natural history,[129] but of the things we *do* with language, the activities into which it is woven. It is in and through language that we achieve self-understanding. Put another way, our way of life is intelligible only through language.

The relationship between words and things (activities) is a function of social relations. As Wittgenstein observes: "[H]ow we group words into kinds will depend on the aim of the classification,—and on our own inclination."[130] Inclination, in turn, is a function of training. Thus, even for Wittgenstein's builders, ostensive definition is not enough for there to be meaning.[131] The meaning of the activity is a function of "a particular training."[132] If the training were different, "the same ostensive teaching of these words would have effected a quite different understanding."[133]

For Wittgenstein, concepts are intelligible only in and through language.[134] In other words, language is the universal medium of understanding. There is no Archimedean perspective from which to survey the relationship of language to the world, because it is only in and through language that we have a world at all.

---

128 L. Wittgenstein, supra note 18, § 11.

129 Cf. J. Kovesi, supra note 91, at 3 ("Owing to the construction of our body . . . we find it convenient to sit by bending our knees at something like a right angle."); L. Wittgenstein, supra note 18, at 230e ("Our interest certainly includes the correspondence between concepts and very general facts of nature.").

130 L. Wittgenstein, supra note 18, § 17.

131 Id. § 6.

132 Id.

133 Id.

134 L. Wittgenstein, Tractatus Logico-Philosophicus 5.6 (D. Pears & B. McGuinness trans. 1961) ("*The limits of my language* mean the limits of my world.").

Implicit in this account of meaning is a rejection of all forms of transcendence. Unlike positivists who claim that we can have direct, non-linguistic contact with the world, Wittgenstein maintains that knowledge is a function of linguistic categories. A "fact" is, as Rorty puts it, a "hybrid" entity.[135] Facts are the product of physical stimuli in conjunction with as many organizing schemes or language games as are then available.

Wittgenstein's belief that all understanding occurs in and through language also stands in opposition to all forms of rationalism, of which Kant's transcendental idealism is a prime example. For Kant, judgments about the world require experience of the world, but experience alone is insufficient for knowledge. Understanding is a product of reason, which is conditioned upon formal or a priori concepts or categories. It is by bringing experience under concepts of judgment (subsumption) that we have knowledge.[136] In other words, for Kant, our ideas are not genuine (determined) unless they comport with the appropriate a priori concept.

Wittgenstein's rejoinder to this scheme of representation would be that Kant has gone beyond the bounds of sense. In order to posit a realm of ideas separate from language, there must be some non-linguistic way to get at that realm. Yet, anything that can be said must be expressible in language. If the Kantian realm of ideas is linguistic, then one would, by necessity, be attempting to understand a medium through itself. In other words, there is no way for Kant to show that what we claim is "fair" corresponds with the "Idea of Fair."[137] The

---

135 Rorty, Texts and Lumps, 17 New. Literary Hist. 1, 4 (1986).

136 See I. Kant, Critique of Pure Reason A313/B370 (N. Smith trans. 1965).

137 Or as Rorty states, though in a slightly different context, the Kantian cannot demonstrate "whether our language cuts reality at the joints." Rorty, supra note 135, at 3.

For an excellent discussion of the full range of arguments surrounding Rorty's claims for the edifying character of (post) philosophy, see C. Prado, The Limits of Pragmatism (1987). In that discussion, Prado gives a perspicuous summary of the Rorty's reading of Gadamer on the question of the extent to which the noumenal can be represented in language (and, thus, at all):

> The noumenal must be eradicated as an idea; no philosophical contrast should be tolerated if it allows room for skeptical doubts *within* the linguistic, which exhausts what there is though somehow not in an ontological sense. . . . Philosophical *theory* can only attempt to get beyond the linguistic through transcendental arguments. But if there is *nothing* beyond language—and we cannot even say nothing intelligible—then efforts at such theorizing must be pointless, and truth cannot be any sort of faithful mirroring. The last thing truth can be is correspondence between ideas and sentences and states of affairs as extralinguistic. To the tradition all of this naturally looks like idealism; the Kantian distinction, or something like it, persists.

metaphor of truth as correspondence is exhausted. All we have is our language and our practices. Truth is local and pragmatic.

The Kantian noumenal self is the self that gives itself the law. The noumenal self is a subject given prior to and independent of its (particular) ends. As such, the transcendental subject is not constituted by its having any *particular* ends; it is a subject capable of the exercise of an autonomous will. As pure deontological subjects, each citizen comes before the law, not as an individual personality, but as a pure and equal subject. No adjustment is made for disparities in wealth, status, natural talent, or other fortuitous externalities.[138]

Kant's noumenal self is paradoxical at several levels. First, it can be nothing other than an odd conception of a self that has no ends but is capable of choosing ends for itself.[139] In other words, there must be a self that can choose ends but has not exercised the choice (this is the sense in which the self is "prior" to its ends). From whence does this "self" arise? What "form of life" does it inhabit? Can there ever be a self that does not have some wants and desires? How does the concept of "will" even make sense apart from a language game in which willing occurs?

It must also be questioned whether Kant's conception of "equality" is simply one among several conceptions. Kant wants to level all the differences between persons in order to make them "equal." Kant assumes that similarity and equality are coextensive. But how does the refusal to take wealth, power, and status into account achieve equality? One does not diminish the effects of differences by refusing

---

Id. at 75 (emphasis added); see also R. Bernstein, Beyond Objectivism and Relativism: Science, Hermeneutics and Praxis 168 (1983).

[138] As Kant writes:

> This uniform equality of human beings as subjects of a state is, however, perfectly consistent with the utmost inequality of the mass in the degree of its possessions, whether these take the form of physical or mental superiority over others, or of fortuitous external property and of particular rights (of which there may be many) with respect to others. Thus the welfare of the one depends very much on the will of the other (the poor depending on the rich), the one must obey the other (as the child its parents or the wife her husband), the one serves (the labourer) while the other pays, etc. Nevertheless, they are all equal as subjects *before the law*, which, as the pronouncement of the general will, can only be single in form, and which concerns the form of right and not the material or object in relation to which I possess rights.

Kant, Theory and Practice (On The Relationship of Theory to Practice in Political Right), *in* I. Kant, Kant's Political Writings 75 (H. Reiss ed., H. Nisbet trans. 1970).

[139] See M. Sandel, Liberalism and the Limits of Justice 19 (1982) ("[B]efore an end can be chosen, there must be a self around to choose it.").

to acknowledge them.[140] But that is all that Kant's conception of equality achieves.

If the transcendence in Kant's position is sacrificed in favor of a more local, pragmatic conception of the role of reason, what are the consequences? Is a pragmatic conception of reason "historicist"?[141] The answer can only be in the affirmative if one conceives of historicism as the view that "thinking is no longer detached nor fully detachable from the situation and must inevitably carry within it some stance toward or interpretation of the situation."[142] But this will not satisfy the unpersuaded, for the pragmatist has not yet justified her intralinguistic claim; she has not demonstrated the *truth* of historicism. In short, historicism's claims for its own truth are self-refuting.[143] The following is representative:

> On the one hand, Nietzsche sees the possibility of an artistic contemplation of the world carried out with scholarly tools but in an antimetaphysical, antiromantic, pessimistic, and sceptical attitude. Because it serves the philosophy of the will to power, a historical science of this kind is supposed to be able to escape the illusion of the belief in truth. Then, of course, the validity of that philosophy would have to be presupposed. That is why Nietzsche must, on the other hand, assert the possibility of a critique of metaphysics that digs up the roots of metaphysical thought without, however, itself giving up philosophy.[144]

This argument is a kind of fake because it presupposes the very question at issue—whether reason has a unitary form. To put it differently, the claim that historicism is itself caught in the vicious circle

---

140 For an argument that goes further than the present suggestions, see E. Wolgast, Equality and the Rights of Women 92 (1980) ("True equality is safe only where there is uniformity.").

141 An excellent discussion of the concept of historicism is found in G. Iggers, The German Conception of History: The National Tradition of Historical Thought from Herder to the Present 295-98 (rev. ed. 1983).

142 Sullivan, After Foundationalism: The Return to Practical Philosophy, *in* Antifoundationalism & Practical Reasoning 29 (E. Simpson ed. 1987).

143 A version of this argument appears in Habermas' recent critique of French post-structuralism. See J. Habermas, The Philosophical Discourse of Modernity: Twelve Lectures (F. Lawrence trans. 1987).

144 Id. at 96-97. For a reading of Nietzsche that sees him not as *anti*-rational but open to multiple rationalities, see A. Nehamas, Nietzsche: Life as Literature 65 (1985) ("If there are different interpretations of the world, it is not because the world has an indeterminate number of characters but because there are many kinds of people, not all of whom can live by the same views and values.").

of relativism presupposes the truth of the foundationalist's claim that "there *must* be ahistorical, 'objective' foundations for judgment, and therefore that pragmatism (or historicism) can only be relativistic if it denies those foundations."[145] Objectivism and relativism are not the only alternatives, however. While the historicist affirms the intralinguistic nature of truth, she denies the pernicious consequences of relativism. The question whether or not a judgment is true or correct is jettisoned in favor of the evaluation of beliefs by "seeing how they cohere with our other beliefs, how they connect up with views we are reasonably confident of . . . ."[146] As von Wright says of Wittgenstein:

> A world-picture, therefore, is neither true nor false (cf. [Philosophical Investigations §§ 162 & 205]). Disputes about truth are possible only inside its frame. The presupposition then is that the disputants share the same culture or form of life, play *the same* language-games. They must, for example, *mean* the same by the words they use. But sameness or difference of meaning is possible only if there is already a certain amount of agreement about facts.[147]

B. Wittgenstein's Conventionalism

The view that reason admits of more than one form is a type of conventionalism—standards are a function of local, defeasible conditions. Wittgenstein was indeed a conventionalist, but one cannot begin to appreciate the subtlety of his conventionalism without due attention to his remarks on the relationship between rules and practices. It is well-known that Wittgenstein's broadest construal of the relationship between rules and practices is his remark that " 'obeying a rule' is a practice."[148] Consider, for instance, his comments on the relationship between a rule and a sign post:

> [W]hat has the expression of a rule—say a sign-post—got to do with my actions? What sort of connexion is there here?— Well, perhaps this one: I have been trained to react to this sign in a particular way, and now I do so react to it.

---

[145] C. Prado, supra note 137, at 95. See also S. Cavell, supra note 91, at 307 ("[R]ules are themselves binding only subject to our commitment.").

[146] D. Herzog, Without Foundations: Justification in Political Theory 223 (1985).

[147] G. von Wright, Wittgenstein 178 (1982).

[148] L. Wittgenstein, supra note 18, § 202.

> . . . [A] person goes by a sign-post only in so far as there exists a regular use of sign-posts, a custom.[149]

The rule "stop at the red light" exists only in so far as there is a signifier (the light) signifying a signified (the rule) through the medium of the practice. The practice is the medium that grounds the signifier and the signified. The rule (the signified) does not tell one how (not) to go on any more than the signifier (the sign) can. The understanding is *in the medium* (the practice) that makes or creates the link between the signifier and the signified.

The unique nature of Wittgenstein's conventionalism is crystallized in the distinction he articulates between "agreement in opinion" and "agreement in judgment."[150] For example, if one thinks that a presidential candidate's selection of a running mate is a poor one, that is something about which people can disagree and still communicate. But in order to have that agreement (or disagreement) *in opinion*, it is first necessary that there be "agreement in judgments," such as what constitutes a government, what are free elections, what is the role and function of the office of President, etc. Unless these language games are first understood, no opinion can be intelligible and there can be neither agreement nor disagreement.

There is a different side to Wittgenstein's conventionalism that must be mentioned as well; his rejection of Cartesianism.[151] In Wittgenstein's view, "action is, on the whole, an unreflective reaction to the meaningfulness of the situation in which one is engrossed."[152] This view leads Wittgenstein to say that obeying a rule is not a matter of choice but is done blindly.[153]

This is not to suggest that one is an automaton in following a rule, nor that one proceeds with absolute certainty.[154] Rather, language, behavior, and understanding are interwoven in the day-to-day routines which have meaning and to which we react (participate) in unre-

[149] Id. § 198.

[150] L. Wittgenstein, supra note 18, §§ 241-42.

[151] I rely here on the discussion of this issue in Schatzki, The Prescription is Description: Wittgenstein's View of the Human Sciences, *in* The Need for Interpretation: Contemporary Conceptions of the Philosopher's Task 132-34 (S. Mitchell & M. Rosen eds. 1983).

[152] Id. at 133.

[153] L. Wittgenstein, supra note 18, § 219.

[154] Compare R. Baker & P. Hacker, supra note 34, at 214 ("So I follow the rule blindly; not like a machine, but with the blindness of complete certitude.").

flective but meaningful ways. We go to the market and buy food (participate in the language game of buying and selling) without engaging the butcher in substantive moral debate about the rightness of the institution (commerce) which is the cornerstone of the medium (the language game of buying and selling) upon which his enterprise (capitalism) is built. We agree in our judgment that he is entitled to be paid for the meat we receive from him. We do not reach this agreement through discussion in judgments that makes our behavior meaningful (intelligible) to one another, but, rather, it is developed out of shared contexts (practices, language games).

It is the locus of linguistic practice and the regularity with which it is practiced that makes agreement in judgments possible. The possibility begins with training: "understanding and training are not distinct; the two processes merge—there is only one."[155] Only in practices,[156] the *loci* of linguistic engagement, can there be meaning:

> What we in a complicated surrounding [*Umgebung*] call 'to follow a rule', we would surely not call it that if it stood there in isolation. Language [i.e. a verbal or written sign] I might say is based on a *way* of life [*Lebenweise*]. In order to describe the phenomenon of language one must describe a practice [*Praxis*], not an isolated event, of *whichever kind* it is. This is a very difficult insight.[157]

IX. Law as Practice

A. *Law as Thing, Law as Activity*

The implications of Wittgenstein's description of the relationship between language and reality for law are significant. To the extent there is law, we can only know it relative to our practices; the activities we identify as "law." "Law" is not law merely because we call it "law," nor is what we call "law" law because it comports with an a

---

[155] E. Wolgast, The Grammar of Justice 196 (1987).

[156] Joseph Margolis distills these considerations as follows:

> The point is that Wittgenstein's thesis identifies the conceptual space (a) within which, *holistically*, all our determinate, socially formed practices (including thinking) obtain; and (b) within which, in virtue of our having been introduced, in a natural way, to the particular forms of life it manifests in our society, we achieve a certain normal "praxical" aptitude.

J. Margolis, Texts Without Referents: Reconciling Science and Narrative 343 (1989).

[157] 6 L. Wittgenstein, Schriften 335-36 (1960) (quoted and translated S. Hilmy, supra note 112, at 291).

priori Idea of Law.[158] What we call "law" is law because it is that activity by which we institutionally organize collective argument about how we should live. Law is a medium of intelligibility; it is a way of making sense of our collective and individual experience.

As an institution, law gives meaning to utterances which they would not have, but for the institution.[159] In other words, the meaning of the law cannot be separated from the institution of law. Consider John Canfield's discussion of this concept in connection with the simple declaration "he can swim the river."

> In the case of "He can swim the river," the background "institutions" of warfare, a chief assigning battle roles or tasks, and so on, are parts of the surroundings necessary for the making of the assertion in that language game. One might be inclined to deny this. For couldn't we imagine that these cultural patterns or roles are absent, and yet the assertion "He can swim the river" is made sensibly, and made, moreover, as governed by exactly the same criterion as governed it in the original example? For instance, "He can swim the river" might be said in the "narration circumstances" mentioned above. But, to argue the other side, "He can swim the river" as uttered in the narration circumstances does not make the same assertion as it does when uttered in the preparing for warfare circumstances. "He can swim the river," in the warfare use makes the assertion it makes because it is said in a particular cultural surrounds, and because it has, therefore, certain implications and a certain portent. It engages in a certain way with the life of the people. Hence, it seems these particular cultural surrounds, or at least quite similar ones, are a necessary condition for the utterance to be the move it is in that language game.[160]

Canfield's example effectively demonstrates the Wittgensteinian antipathy to generalization. Like the sentences that express them, there is no unitary, singular meaning to concepts.[161] Language use

---

158 For a discussion of this distinction in the context of Wittgenstein's position vis-a-vis nominalism and realism, see Bambrough, Universals and Family Resemblances, *in* Wittgenstein: The Philosophical Investigations 186 (G. Pitcher ed. 1968).

159 It should be noted, however, that the same can be said of all institutions.

160 J. Canfield, Wittgenstein: Language and World 55 (1981).

161 As Wittgenstein put it in *The Blue Book*:

> The idea that in order to get clear about the meaning of a general term one had to find the common element in all its applications has shackled philosophical investigation; for it has not only led to no result, but also made the philosopher dismiss as irrelevant the concrete cases, which alone could have helped him to understand the usage of the

occurs in situations (contexts); it is in and through these activities that understanding occurs.

Generalization abounds in contemporary jurisprudence. For example, in A Theory of Law,[162] Philip Soper advances the claim that legal theory is at a "dead end" because it continues to ask the sterile question "What is law?"[163] To eradicate the sterility of modern legal theory, Soper recommends that we change the question from "What is law?" to "What is law that I should obey it?"[164] One reason to change the question, according to Soper, is that no modern legal theorist holds the view that "law is somehow 'out there' with a unique essence awaiting discovery."[165]

Soper is wrong on both counts. The question "What is law?" remains viable because legal theory has yet to advance an adequate conception of law as an activity and not a thing. In addition, if anyone in modern legal theory advances an "essentialist" conception of law, it is Ronald Dworkin. Dworkin's distinction between concepts and conceptions, first advanced in Taking Rights Seriously and reemphasized in Law's Empire, can only be read as an attempt to promote the Kantian distinction between an Idea and its representations. It is hard to see how else passages like the following can be read:

> Suppose I tell my children simply that I expect them not to treat others unfairly. I no doubt have in mind examples of the conduct I mean to discourage, but I would not accept that my 'meaning' was limited to these examples, for two reasons. First I would expect my children to apply my instructions to situations I had not and could not have thought about. Second, I stand ready to admit that some particular act I had thought was fair when I spoke was in fact unfair, or vice versa, if one of my children is able to convince me of that later; in that case I should want to say that my instructions covered the case he cited, not that I had changed my instructions. I might say that I meant the family to be guided by the *concept* of fairness, not by any specific *conception* of fairness I might have had in mind.[166]

> general term. When Socrates asks the question, "what is knowledge?" he does not even regard it as a *preliminary* answer to enumerate cases of knowledge.

L. Wittgenstein, The Blue and Brown Books 19-20 (1958).

162 P. Soper, A Theory of Law (1984).

163 Id. at 1.

164 Id. at 7.

165 Id.

166 R. Dworkin, supra note 8, at 134 (1977).

If law does not have some Archimedean perspective from which to assess competing claims, then how is there ever objectivity in law? To put the point differently, if the point of law is not imposed from without,[167] then from whence does it arise?

B. Law As Narrative

To conceive of law as an activity and not as a thing is to approach law as a way of making sense of the world; that is, as a medium of understanding. James Boyd White's characterization of law as "a continuing and collective process of conversation and judgment"[168] is a powerful metaphor. Its power lies in its ability to picture law as a process of becoming. Law is more like painting than archaeology; it is more a process of creation than pure discovery. But what is it that is painted in this conversation?

Let us return to the idea of the form of law. I said that to understand the point of a legal concept it is necessary to know its form. As I described it, the form of a legal notion is that which makes it intelligible. Thus, knowing the meaning of a legal notion means understanding or "grasping the *point* or *meaning* of what is being done or said"[169] by someone employing the concept. Law is a form of social relations: we associate with others through the medium of law. It is a means of ideational expression. Like all cultural forms, law has a history or, to put it better, histories. It is to these that we appeal when we engage in the practice of law.

1. Easy Cases

But must we always appeal to legal history in support of a claim in law? Surely not. And therein lies the distinction between hard and easy cases. The easy case is the one which can be decided by reference to a rule, the extension of which clearly covers the case and against the application of which no good reason can be advanced. Examples of such cases abound in the reporters; one might mention going against a red light, a promissory note signed by the maker, and dozens, nay thousands, of others.

---

167 For example, Dworkin's "best" interpretation of the practice of law.

168 J. White, When Words Lose Their Meaning 264 (1984).

169 P. Winch, supra note 72, at 115 (1958).

It is in these easy cases that Baker & Hacker's reading of Wittgenstein's rule-following provides a complete description both of what rule-following is like in actual practice and what Wittgenstein likely would have said about easy cases in law, had he thought about law.[170] There *is* an internal relation between a rule and its applications, but contra Baker and Hacker, that relation is in and through the concept embodied in the rule.

For example, consider the rule, "[a]n offeree's power of acceptance is terminated when the offeree receives from the offeror a manifestation of an intention not to enter into the proposed contract."[171] What is the meaning of the word "receive"? Does the rule require that the offeror personally communicate the revocation to the offeree? Is it sufficient that an agent of the offeree perform the act of communication? Need the notice be in writing? What if the offeree gets the news from a third party unrelated to the transaction?

The point of the rule generates the form of the concept of "receive" and provides the internal relation between the rule and what will count as "receiving notice." The point of the notice requirement is to prevent a detrimental change of position on the part of the offeree in reliance upon the offer which, if accepted before notice of revocation, could lead to injurious reliance upon the (withdrawn) offer.[172]

I wish to stress that the concept of "receipt" as used in the rule is unintelligible apart from its relation to the (institutional) practice of law. As Peter Winch puts it: "[t]o give an account of the meaning of [the] word is to describe how it is used; and to describe how it is used

---

170 Wittgenstein had little to say about law. The only remarks I know of are in L. Wittgenstein, Remarks on the Foundations of Mathematics I at 116-18, III at 65 (G. von Wright, R. Rhees & G. Anscombe eds., G. Anscombe trans. rev. ed. 1978). This reference was brought to my attention by Roger Shiner. See Shiner, Precedent, Discretion and Fairness, *in* Law, Morality and Rights 127 n.74, 136 n.85 (M. Stewart ed. 1983). Another remark is found in L. Wittgenstein, supra note 119, § 350:

> So what I am saying comes to *this*: A law is given for human beings, and a jurisprudent may well be capable of drawing consequences for any case that ordinarily comes his way; thus the law evidently has its use, makes sense. Nevertheless its validity presupposes all sorts of things, and if the being that he is to judge is quite deviant from ordinary human beings, then e.g. the decision whether he has done the deed with evil intent will not become difficult but (simply) impossible.

171 Restatement (Second) of Contracts § 42 (1981).

172 See Dickinson v. Dodds, 2 Ch. D. 463 (C.A. 1876).

is to describe the social intercourse into which it enters."[173] The "fact" that someone in any given case received notice of revocation is the result of interaction between the institution of contract and doings in the world. The "fact" that " 'x' received notice of revocation" is what Anscombe and Searle refer to as an "institutional fact."[174] Without the social practice of contract, there would be no "notice" to be "received."

2. *Hard Cases*

Not all cases are easy cases, and it is in distinguishing easy from hard cases that the role of community consensus in legal argument will be clarified. Consider *Riggs v. Palmer*.[175] Elmer Palmer's grandfather, Francis Palmer, executed a will in which he left his estate to three persons: his grandson Elmer and Elmer's two aunts, Mrs. Riggs and Mrs. Preston.[176] When Elmer's grandfather remarried, Elmer feared his grandfather might change his will and, to preclude this possibility, murdered his grandfather.[177] Elmer was convicted of murder and sent to prison.[178]

Elmer's aunts sued in New York to prevent Elmer from taking anything under his late grandfather's will.[179] The New York Statute of Wills said nothing about devisees being precluded from inheriting because they murdered the testator. On the basis of that silence, a New York trial court dismissed the aunts' complaint.[180] On appeal, the New York Court of Appeals held, in a split decision, that the principle, "no man shall profit by his own wrong," precluded the enforcement of the will in Elmer's favor.[181] In dissent, Judge Gray argued that, because Elmer had received the punishment for murder and was duly incarcerated, it would be unjust to impose additional

[173] P. Winch, supra note 72, at 123. For a different view of "internal," see L. Wittgenstein, supra note 134, § 4.123 ("A property is internal if it is unthinkable that its object should not possess it.").

[174] See Anscombe, On Brute Facts, *in* G. Anscombe, 3 Collected Papers (Ethics, Religion and Politics) 22-25 (1981); J. Searle, Speech Acts 50-53 (1969).

[175] 115 N.Y. 506, 22 N.E. 188 (1889).

[176] Id. at 508, 22 N.E. at 188.

[177] Id. at 508, 22 N.E. at 189.

[178] Id. at 515, 22 N.E. at 191 (Gray, J., dissenting).

[179] Id. at 508, 22 N.E. at 188.

[180] Id. at 515, 22 N.E. at 191 (Gray, J., dissenting).

[181] Id. at 513, 22 N.E. at 190.

punishment upon him.[182] In short, Judge Gray advanced the principle, "no man shall be punished unjustly," in order to contend that Elmer should receive his inheritance just as if his grandfather had died of natural causes.[183]

It seems to defy practical legal experience to say that there is one "right" way to answer the question posed by the *Riggs* case. Instead, most participants in the practice of law, the group Brian Simpson refers to as the "caste of lawyers,"[184] would say that each reading of the appropriate legal materials[185] in *Riggs* is plausible and that there is no way to decide which reading is "the best." And yet, pace CLS, if the community of lawyers cannot agree on which reading of the legal materials is "right," doesn't that mean that the law is "indeterminate"?[186]

The position of these CLS theorists is reminiscent of the "outsider" of which Alasdair MacIntyre speaks.[187] With no Archimedean point from which to judge the adequacy of legal arguments, all we can do is appeal to the history of our collective practice and make sense of where we are going by reference to our understanding of where we have been. If law is an activity, and the caste of lawyers a community, then the two readings of the legal materials advanced in *Riggs* should be seen as two plausible narratives of the point of our practice, each pointing in a different direction.

---

[182] Id. at 519, 22 N.E. at 129 (Grey, J., dissenting).

[183] Id. at 519.

[184] Simpson, supra note 104, at 20.

[185] One can only agree with Charles Silver that Dworkin is simply incorrect in his contention that " 'the dispute about Elmer was not about whether judges should follow the law or adjust it in the interests of justice. . . . It was a dispute about what the law was, about what the real statute the legislators enacted really said.' " Silver, Elmer's Case: A Positivist Replies to Dworkin, 6 Law &. Phil. 382 (1987) (quoting R. Dworkin, supra note 35, at 20).

[186] As Joseph Singer puts it:

> For a theory to generate answers, it must be mechanical, yet no mechanical theory can render an adequate account of our experience of legitimate moral choice. We cannot even escape the dilemma by trying to make some of our choices (the "core") mechanical and some (the "periphery") open-ended: *No* mechanical choices appear to be unequivocally valid. Moreover, the history of legal thought has repeatedly demonstrated that *any* indeterminacy in a theory fatally undermines the appearance of determinacy elsewhere; if the theory really contains indeterminate principles, someone who opposes a rule or an outcome within the supposedly determinate, objective core will inevitably use an open-ended standard to reopen an issue that was supposed to have been laid permanently to rest, and the theory itself will enable her to do this.

Singer, supra note 25, at 61.

[187] A. MacIntyre, Short History of Ethics 266 (1966).

The direction chosen will be the result of dialogue among the members of the community: courts, lawyers, and scholars. It is out of this dialogical encounter among the participants in the discursive practice of law that the point of law is determined.[188] The great debates in law, debates about the point or purpose of the law, are collective arguments about where we ought to take the law. As collective argument, law is the premier activity, for it affords us the opportunity to shape our collective future. As such, the activity of law is charged with the utmost opportunity and, more importantly, responsibility.

X. Tradition, Practice, and Narrative

T.S. Eliot believed that the appreciation of a poet "is the appreciation of his relation to the dead poets and artists."[189] Clearly, tradition is at the center of Eliot's view of poetry. Tradition plays a similar role within a conception of law as narrative.[190] As with poetry and art, the law reproduces itself through the participants in the practice. The question then becomes how it is that law reproduces itself.

The understanding of the practice of law as narrative is internal. Understanding the practice means knowing how to "go on" with the repertoire of behaviors identified as the practice. "Going on" means taking the existing world of the practice and absorbing "new items in

---

188 This is not to say that all applications of law require such a dialogical encounter. What counts as "following a rule" is often a relatively simple matter. If this were not the case, then ordinary citizens having little or no knowledge of legal materials would live in a Kafkaesque nightmare. This is not an apt description of our condition.

On a different plane, it reaffirms the truth of Llewellyn's insight that legal knowledge is not reducible to a structure constitutive of law. See Patterson, Law's Practice, supra note 113, at 592-600. Since the time of Hobbes, legal theorists have maintained that the validity of law was a function of structure or source. For Hobbes and Austin this could be traced to the command of the sovereign; for H.L.A. Hart, to the Rule of Recognition; for Hans Kelsen, to the *Grundnorm*; and for Dworkin, to a structure of embedded principle. See Postema, "Protestant" Interpretations and Social Practices, 6 Law & Phil. 283, 317-18 (1987) (discussing Dworkin's theory of interpretation of the nature and practice of law).

189 Eliot, Tradition and the Individual Talent, *in* T.S. Eliot, Selected Prose of T.S. Eliot 38 (1975); see also, R. Shusterman, T.S. Eliot and the Philosophy of Criticism 83-85 (1988) (discussing Eliot's "literary constellation" theory, according to which new authors build on the tradition of old authors, thus augmenting the body of art and criticism).

190 For a general discussion on the importance of tradition to law, see Krygier, The Traditionality of Statutes, 1 Ratio Juris 20 (1988); Krygier, Law as Tradition, 5 Law & Phil. 237 (1986).

that world, to move around with a certain ease in the web of relationships created by it."[191]

Narrative is the nerve of historical reason. The key to a narrative account of law is not to reveal a preordained pattern in law's past, but to create a discursive intelligibility out of temporal unity. In short, accounting for the coherence of law "primarily involves narrating the process of its development, highlighting the rhyme and reason therein."[192]

Practices carry their own internal standards and rules. To become an initiate into a practice means accepting the authority of the standards articulated and adhered to by the practitioners at the time of initiation.[193] That initial acceptance, however, does not preclude subsequent critique of the practice. As Amelie Rorty has recently noted, "[R]easons do not end with embededness."[194].

So what does narrative provide in the way of illuminating legal argument? It suggests that the way law changes is through the advancement of stories or accounts of the practice that have an internal unity that captures the significant elements of the practice while pointing in a direction different from the current understanding of the enterprise.[195] For instance, can there be any doubt that Fuller and Perdue's essay on the reliance interest in contract suggests a radical

---

191 Postema, supra note 188, at 304.

192 Carroll, Art, Practice and Narrative, 71 The Monist 140, 150 (1988).

193 See A. MacIntyre, supra note 187, at 177.

194 A. Rorty, Mind In Action: Essays in the Philosophy of Mind 288 (1988).

195 This will, of course, necessitate that narrative accounts of law begin with existing legal categories. In a fuller account of the constitutive role of narrative in legal argument, I intend to develop the idea that, in law, there are essentially three forms of narrative argumentation. They are:

1. RECONSTRUCTIVE NARRATIVE. A narrative that rewrites our understanding of existing legal categories or doctrine through the invention of a new vocabulary. An example is Karl Llewellyn's concept of "Agreement" in the Uniform Commercial Code.

2. INTERROGATIVE NARRATIVE. This type of narrative is pressed into service to resolve a dispute over which of several legal categories is the correct or appropriate one. An example is the concept of "alien" in Church of the Holy Trinity v. United States, 143 U.S. 457 (1892).

3. DISCRIMINATORY NARRATIVE. Here narration serves to resolve a dispute over which of several legal categories is the correct or appropriate one. An example of such a dispute is the conflict over the distinction between a transaction as a "true lease" or one "intended for security" (and, hence, secured transaction in disguise).

reinterpretation of the practice of contract law?[196] Their "story" was and is a powerful narrative because it takes all of the "elements" that the participants agree to be what we refer to as "contract" and casts them in a new light. The power of the narrative is a direct function of its ability to conceptualize the subject matter in a way previously unseen by the participants, yet in a form that most agree still captures the point of the practice.

My suggestion is that the whole of law is the production of one narrative after another. Every innovative case, law review article, and judicial opinion is an account of the past practice of the law and the advancement of reasons and arguments in support of a claim for the point (form) of law. Of course, each individual focus (a constitution, a statute, the common law) will have unique features that set it apart. Nevertheless, the unity of law as a discursive enterprise will be the primary element of narrative and will lie at the center of arguments over the point of law.

XI. A Representative Narrative

One of the classic rules of contract law is that there is a duty to read.[197] The doctrine generally states that, regardless of whether or not one reads the contract, the affixing of one's signature has the legal effect of binding one to the terms contained in the agreement.[198] This rule has been applied to a variety of cases including standardized form contracts[199] and contracts written in a language which the signer was unable to read.[200]

In this Part, I focus attention on standardized form contracts or, as

---

196 Fuller & Perdue, The Reliance Interest in Contract Damages: 1, 46 Yale L.J. 52 (1936); Fuller & Perdue, The Reliance Interest in Contract Damages: 2, 46 Yale L.J. 373 (1937).

197 See generally Calamari, Duty to Read—A Changing Concept, 43 Fordham L. Rev. 341 (1974) (overview and analysis of the duty to read doctrine).

198 See, e.g., National Bank v. Equity Inv., 81 Wash. 2d 886, 506 P.2d 20 (1973) ("The whole panoply of contract law rests on the principle that one is bound by the contract which he voluntarily and knowingly signs.").

199 See, e.g., Lewis v. Great W. Ry., 157 Eng. Rep. 1427 (Ex. 1860) (denying a claim for bailee's loss of the parcel because bailor failed to file a claim within the narrow window allowed by a written contract which bailor had neglected to read).

200 See, e.g., Landry Loan Co. v. Avie, 147 So. 2d 725 (La. Ct. App. 1962) (binding a French-speaking illiterate as co-signer on a promissory note despite the fact that he had made his 'X' without understanding the nature of the liability undertaken).

they have come to be known, "contracts of adhesion."[201] The law on contracts of adhesion is particularly useful for assessing the cogency of a conception of law as narrative. I say this because the question of the enforceability of contracts of adhesion has been the subject of much academic writing.[202] Yet no consensus exists as to the extent to which these contracts should be enforced.

A contract of adhesion is one that is presented to a party on a take-it-or-leave-it basis. The contract usually consists of a form, composed in various print sizes, and containing an excess of what has euphemistically come to be known as "boilerplate." Much of this boilerplate is never read by the parties who sign these contracts. This is largely due to the fact that there is simply no reason to read the contract. Even if one were to take the time to read the contract, it is almost always the case that the party proffering the document will either simply refuse to alter, or will lack the requisite authority to alter, the terms of the contract.[203]

The traditional common law of contracts reveres the sanctity of the written agreement.[204] A natural consequence of such reverence is the emergence of a duty to read rule: "one having the capacity to understand a written document who reads it, or, without reading it or having it read to him, signs it, is bound by his signature."[205] The reason, or at least one reason, for the rule is clear: "no one could rely on a signed document if the other party could avoid the transaction by

---

201 The term "contrats d'ahesion" has been traced to R. Saleilles, De la Declaration de Volonte 229 (1901), and was introduced into American jurisprudence in Patterson, The Delivery of a Life-Insurance Policy, 33 Harv. L. Rev. 198, 222 (1919).

202 See, e.g., Rakoff, Contracts of Adhesion: An Essay in Reconstruction, 96 Harv. L. Rev. 1174 (1983) (arguing that standardized form terms, because of the balance of power between commercial organizations and individuals, should be presumptively unenforceable).

203 See Farnsworth, Contracts § 4.26 (1982). This happens frequently with national franchisees, and the courts generally enforce the standardized contract. See Zapatha v. Dairy Mart, 381 Mass. 284, 408 N.E.2d 1370 (1980) (court declines to find franchise agreement unconscionable).

204 Several commentators describe the historical embrace of the writing by describing the sanctity of the written contract as *inviolate*. See, e.g., Birnhaum, Stahl & West, Standardized Agreements and the Parol Evidence Rule: Defining and Applying the Expectations Principle, 26 Ariz. L. Rev. 793, 793 (1984).

205 Rossi v. Douglas, 203 Md. 190, 199, 100 A.2d 3, 7 (1953). The rule in the first Restatement is that: "One who makes a written offer which is accepted, or who manifests acceptance of the terms of a writing which he should reasonably understand to be an offer or proposed contract, is bound by the contract, though ignorant of the terms of the writing or of its proper interpretation." Restatement (First) of Contracts § 70 (1932).

saying that he had not read or did not understand the writing."[206]

When parties enter into a contract, each has certain individual motivations and expectations. As a general matter, the law does not guarantee a party to a contract a remedy in the event the other party's performance fails to live up to the expectations of a hopeful contractual partner. Contract law does not guarantee results; it simply provides a vehicle whereby two parties can strike a deal on mutually agreed terms with the ability to engage the state's power of enforcement (or to award damages) in the event one of the parties fails to live up to the *terms* of that bargain (as opposed to one party's subjective expectations).

The form contract ("contract of adhesion") has altered the classical view of contract, or so it would seem. Insurance contracts, loan agreements, and retail installment sales contracts are everyday, familiar examples of a contract of adhesion. Nothing remotely recognizable as "bargaining" enters into the picture. The form contract is presented by the seller-drafter on terms that are the product, not of the party presenting the document, but of an industry that circulates model forms that impose a unitary structure on a corner of commerce.[207] Should adhesion contracts be treated differently than "normal," contracts? If so, how far should the courts go in policing the terms of the agreements and on what basis?

These and other questions are raised by *C & J Fertilizer, Inc. v. Allied Mutual Insurance Company*.[208] The plaintiff in *C & J Fertilizer* was a 37-year-old farmer who owned and managed a fertilizer plant.[209] The plaintiff had two insurance contracts with the defendant insurance company, Allied Mutual, which covered him for losses resulting from, among other things, burglary.[210] In each policy, "burglary" was defined as follows:

> [T]he felonious abstraction of insured property (1) from within the premises by a person making felonious entry therein by actual force and violence, *of which force and violence there are visible marks made by tools, explosives, electricity or chemicals upon, or physical damages*

206 J. Calamari & J. Perillo, The Law of Contracts 410 (3d ed. 1987).

207 See Rakoff, supra note 202, at 1222-48.

208 227 N.W.2d 169 (Iowa 1975).

209 Id. at 171-72.

210 Id. at 171.

to, the exterior of the premises at the place of such entry . . . .[211]

One Monday morning, after a weekend when the premises were checked and found to be secure, the plaintiff discovered that his building had been burglarized and that a quantum of chemicals had been removed.[212] The trial court found that the burglar had gained entrance to the area where the fertilizer was stored by breaking the lock on the *interior* door.[213] Any perplexity on the part of the plaintiff as to how a burglar could gain entrance without leaving any marks on the exterior door was dispelled by an investigator who demonstrated how the *exterior* door could be opened without damaging the door, or even leaving any marks.[214]

The insurance company, however, refused to pay the claim, arguing that the break-in did not meet the definition of "burglary" in the policies.[215] The case was tried to the bench and a judgment entered for the defendant insurance company, the judge holding that the definition of "burglary" in the policies was "unambiguous" and thus binding on the parties.[216] There being nothing in the record to support a finding of "felonious entry" as defined in the contract, the trial court's ruling was, in its view, inexorable.[217]

In reversing the trial court's judgment in favor of the insurance company, the Iowa Supreme Court moved first to consider evidence extrinsic to the contract, evidence which it claimed "throws light on the situation of the parties."[218] The evidence is exactly what one would expect. The insured never looked at the policies after he got them; he expected that he was covered for all break-ins that were not "inside jobs." Further, the plaintiff and the agent who sold him the policy never discussed any details of coverage, and the agent who sold him the policy expressed shock at the company's denial of the claim.[219]

---

211 Id.

212 Id.

213 Id. at 172.

214 Id. at 171.

215 Id.

216 Id.

217 Id.

218 Id. at 172.

219 Id. at 172-73.

The majority's entire opinion, and the reasons it adduces in support of its conclusion that adhesion contracts are not enforceable if they are inconsistent with the reasonable expectations of the insured, is built upon the assumption that adhesion contracts should be specially treated. In support of this claim the court marshalled the following (material) elements:

1. it is generally recognized that insureds do not read their contracts;[220]
2. assent is a fundamental element of contract;[221]
3. the law of contracts attempts the realization of reasonable expectations;[222]
4. mass advertising creates an expectation of "protection";[223]
5. the principles of (classical) contract law were formulated at an early time when parties were of equal bargaining strength and negotiated on a face-to-face basis.[224]

The majority's opinion is built on the claim that, because empirical reality (the reality of the world of insurance) has changed, the law must be responsive to that fact. This is a fundamentally different conception of law than that advanced by the dissent in *C & J Fertilizer.* The dissent never gets past the problem of contractual (linguistic) ambiguity. As the dissent sizes up the case, the fact that the language was unambiguous means that the contract should be enforced according to its terms.[225] Further, according to the dissent, "Once this indisputable fact is recognized, plaintiff's arguments virtually collapse."[226]

More important than the details of the two opinions is the fact that the majority opinion reflects the triumph of legal realism and the death of the orthodox view of contract (if not the orthodox view of law).[227] In support of the argument that form determines matter, it is important to see that what counts as an enforceable clause in a con-

220 Id. at 174.
221 Id.
222 Id. at 176.
223 Id. at 178.
224 Id. at 173.
225 Id. at 183.
226 Id.
227 See generally Grey, Langdell's Orthodoxy, 45 U. Pitt. L. Rev. 1 (1983) (discussing, in detail, orthodoxy and contrasting views of Legal Realism). See also Patterson, Good Faith, Lender Liability, and Discretionary Acceleration: Of Llewellyn, Wittgenstein, and the

tract is a function of divergent conceptions of the "point" of contract law. If the point of contract law is to enforce an agreement that one had an opportunity to read but chose not to (the *First Restatement* view),[228] then parol evidence should be barred when offered to explain an unambiguous term, and it should be of no consequence that one had certain expectations with respect to any particular agreement.[229]

At the global level, the majority opinion supports the view that the individual circumstances and persona of the parties is critical to the adjudication of their claims. This presupposition dominates the majority's view of the form of contract law as the enforcement of the agreement of the parties in a manner consistent with the reasonable expectations of the (economically) weaker party. According to this view, the point of contract law is, in part, paternalistic—the protection of the (informationally, economically, etc.) disadvantaged party.

Which is the "better" view? Which view is more (less) "just"? What is the "right answer" to the question posed by *C & J Fertilizer*? What is the "best constructive interpretation" of the issues at stake in *C & J Fertilizer*? Isn't the case really just the expression of two diametrically opposed political visions?

For different reasons, I don't believe that any of these questions are at all useful in accounting for what lawyers *do*. There are no "right" (single) answers in law. The materials out of which arguments are fashioned are themselves multivocal, that is, capable of a multitude of readings, both individually and collectively. As I have said, lawyers take the (historical) materials and articulate a narrative that participants in the discourse recognize as having a coherence, an internal rhythm. It is the task of the lawyer to articulate that narrative and render clear both its internal coherence and relevance to present problems.

The power of a narrative, however, is contingent upon the extent to which it figures in other narratives. As Bruno Latour says of scientific "facts":

Uniform Commercial Code, 68 Tex. L. Rev. 169, 186-211 (1989) (discussing Llewellyn's Code jurisprudence in light of the classical (Langdellian/Willistonian) conception of contract).

228 Restatement (First) of Contracts § 70 (1932).

229 See Restatement (Second) of Contracts § 215 (1979). This section, which states the current common law rule, prohibits the introduction in evidence of just the sort the majority uses in *C & J Fertilizer*.

> [A] fact is what is collectively stabilised from the midst of controversies when the activity of later papers [for our purposes, judicial opinions, law review articles, addresses, etc.] does not consist only of criticism or deformation but also of confirmation. The strength of the original statement does not lie in itself, but is derived from any of the papers that incorporate it.[230]

If no form of representation (narrative) is privileged, then isn't one story as good as another?[231] There can be no doubt that many legal narratives are "politically" motivated in the sense that they represent a particular vision of social life. But that is what I have been arguing all along: law is an institutional forum for the advancement of arguments (narratives) about how we are to live. The judgments of the participants in the discourse are the product of arguments which occur "within an institutionally defined structure of opportunities and possibilities."[232] The task of the committed discursive participant is to make of the institutionally defined possibilities for argument what she will. The denser the institutional history, the greater the possibilities for argument. In the words of Jean-François Lyotard:

> [T]he people are only that which actualizes the narratives: once again. They do this not only by recounting them, but also by listening to them and recounting themselves through them; in other words, by putting them into "play" in their institutions—thus by assigning themselves the posts of narratee and diegesis as well as the post of narrator.[233]

---

230 B. Latour, Science in Action 42 (1987).

231 Further, the persuasiveness of a particular story is in part dependent on the talent of the teller—i.e., the storyteller's storytelling abilities. Lawrence Friedman puts the point this way:

> There are of course good judges and bad ones; the terms are applied to the technical skill or elegance with which a judge may structure or write his opinion. The great judges of the common-law countries—Oliver Wendell Holmes, Jr. or Lord Mansfield—are great either because of their style, their self-awareness or their social vision or all of these. The greater the judge, the less he can be described as an "interpreter" in any literal sense. His greatness does not usually depend on his ability to shed light on the meaning or original understanding of some legal text; indeed, the greater he is, the more likely he is to obfuscate, twist, extend or manipulate the text, though the way he does it is of course crucial to his reputation.

Friedman, Some Comments On Legal Interpretation, 9 Poetics Today 95, 99 (1988).

232 R. Beiner, Political Judgment 148 (1983).

233 J. Lyotard, The Postmodern Condition 23 (G. Bennington & B. Massumi trans. 1984).

CONCLUSION

What are the implications for legal pragmatism of a narrative conception of legal discourse? Perhaps the clearest implication is that vocabulary—the categories with which we make sense of experience—must be the primary focus of attention. One cannot reject the false dichotomy of objectivism and relativism yet retain the notion that the ways in which we divide up the world can somehow be compared along a neutral continuum of measurement. The success or failure of our conceptual schemes must be judged, not relative to "the world" or "reality" (moral or otherwise), but with respect to the degree to which problems are solved (or dissolved), efficacious doctrinal schemes identified, or, at the level of political action, "by providing piecemeal nudges and cautions in respect to particular projects at particular times."[234]

Pragmatism of the sort argued for here is surely to be criticized for the seeming lack of grandeur in its hopes for the power of theory. While not advocating a position "against theory," the perspective advanced here is humble with respect to the possibilities of "grand narratives."[235] It would be a mistake to attack pragmatism at the level of humility, however, for the position is itself a realistic expression of the recognition that metatheoretical claims to truth are philosophically indefensible. Pragmatism's merit lies the recognition that our collective energies are better spent working within the limits of the possible rather than attempting to transcend the infinite.

---

234 Rorty, Philosophy as Science, as Metaphor, and as Politics, *in* The Institution of Philosophy 27 (A. Cohen & M. Dascal eds. 1989).

235 For discussion of the demise of grand narratives in postmodernity, see J. Lyotard, supra note 233.

[13]
Law's Practice
(reviewing Karl N. Llewellyn, *The Case Law System in America*)

There may yet be a way out of the nineteenth century.[1]
[T]here is no knowledge which is not "know how."[2]

In 1919, Ludwig Wittgenstein spent the last days of the First World War in an Italian prisoner of war camp. There he put the finishing touches on one of the greatest works of twentieth-century philosophy, *Tractatus Logico-Philosophicus*.[3] Believing he had solved the problems of philosophy,[4] Wittgenstein returned to his native Austria to

---

* Assistant Professor of Law, Western New England College, School of Law. For comments on drafts of this essay, I wish to thank Jay Austin, Charles Collier, Anne Goldstein, Richard Hyland, Don Korobkin, Tom Morawetz, Jeff White and Zipporah Wiseman. Thanks are also extended to Professor Michael Ansaldi for providing me with a copy of his translation of the German text of *The Case Law System in America*. I should like to take this opportunity to comment upon Professor Ansaldi's translation. This is the first English translation of this work. Only small portions have previously appeared in English and the German edition has been out of print for many years. The difficulties of Llewellyn's English language prose are well known. His style in German, while more accessible, reflects Llewellyn's unique mode of expression. Professor Ansaldi's rendering of Llewellyn's German text does, I believe, improve upon the expression of Llewellyn's ideas. In fact, I think it safe to say that the road from German-language expression to English translation has had a salutary impact upon the articulation of Llewellyn's thought.

1. Gilmore, The Good Faith Purchase Idea and the Uniform Commercial Code: Confessions of a Repentant Draftsman, 15 Ga. L. Rev. 605, 629 (1981).

2. M. Oakeshott, Rationalism in Politics, *in* Rationalism in Politics and Other Essays 9 (1962).

3. L. Wittgenstein, Tractatus Logico-Philosophicus (D. Pears & B. McGuinness trans. 1961).

4. The central claim of the *Tractatus* is that the structure of the world is mirrored in the logical structure of language. How Wittgenstein might have come to this idea is described in the following passage by one of his literary executors:

> There is a story of how the idea of language as a picture of reality occurred to Wittgenstein. It was in the autumn of 1914, on the eastern front. Wittgenstein was reading in a magazine about a lawsuit in Paris concerning an automobile accident. At the trial a miniature model of the accident was presented before the court. The model here served as a proposition; that is, as a description of a possible state of affairs. It has this function owing to a correspondence between the parts of the model (the miniature-houses, -cars, -people) and things

become a primary school teacher.[5] His abandonment of philosophy was short-lived. In 1929, Wittgenstein returned to the Cambridge of Bertrand Russell and G.E. Moore. He returned disavowing the central claim of the *Tractatus*: that philosophy can reveal the logical structure of language's relation to the world. The returning Wittgenstein now compared the workings of language to "an ancient city: a maze of little streets and squares . . . ."[6] The task of philosophy was no longer theoretical but practical, "to bring words back from their metaphysical to their everyday use."[7]

As important as the year 1929 might have been for philosophy, it was a propitious one for law as well; for it was in that year that a young American law professor named Karl Nickerson Llewellyn could be found in Germany giving a series of lectures on the subject of the case law system in America (p. ix).[8] In itself, the idea of an American academic lecturing to Germans in their (but not his) native tongue is perhaps out of the ordinary but otherwise unremarkable. Its uniqueness can only be appreciated against the background of subsequent events in intellectual history. Just at the moment Wittgenstein was back at Cambridge laying the foundation for a second revolution in philosophy,[9] Llewellyn was in Germany delivering lectures that prefigured much of what Wittgenstein would ultimately be credited with having achieved.[10] In short, the series of lectures that became the book *Präjudizienrecht und Rechtsprechung in Amerika*[11] contains many of the cen-

---

> (houses, cars, people) in reality. It now occurred to Wittgenstein that one might reverse the analogy and say that a *proposition* serves as a model or *picture*, by virtue of a similar correspondence between *its* parts and the world. The way in which the parts of the proposition are combined—the *structure* of the proposition—depicts a possible combination of elements in reality, a possible state of affairs.

G. von Wright, Wittgenstein 20–21 (1982).

5. See W. Bartley, Wittgenstein 15 (2d ed. 1985).

6. L. Wittgenstein, Philosophical Investigations § 18 (G. Anscombe trans. 1958).

7. Id. § 116.

8. At the time, Llewellyn was on a leave of absence from the Columbia Law School, having joined the faculty in 1924 (p. ix & n.1).

9. The question whether there is one Wittgenstein or two is endlessly debated. Compare R. Ackermann, Wittgenstein 7 (1988) (one Wittgenstein) with N. Malcolm, Nothing Is Hidden: Wittgenstein's Criticism of his Early Thought ix (1986) (the earlier thought is "purged" by the later). Perhaps the only agreement among scholars is that in his "first phase," Wittgenstein argued that language mirrored reality. Thus, the study of language could be a way of uncovering the logical structure of the world. In his "second phase," which began when he returned to Cambridge in 1929, Wittgenstein took up a whole new approach to philosophy. In this phase of his thought Wittgenstein concerned himself with the question of how language acts as a constitutive medium of understanding. Put succinctly, in his first phase, Wittgenstein believed that language pictured the world. In his second phase, Wittgenstein believed that language gave us a world.

10. The most important idea anticipated by Llewellyn is that all understanding occurs in language. See infra Part I.

11. K. Llewellyn, Präjudizienrecht und Rechtsprechung in Amerika (1933).

tral notions now identified with the "linguistic turn" in philosophical thought.[12] Far from being limited to an important contribution to the legal theory of his day, Llewellyn's *The Case Law System in America* represents what can only be regarded as one of the most significant advances in the development of legal thought since the abandonment of formalism.

But what is the advance that Llewellyn wrought? In a sentence, it is this: Llewellyn recast the notion of legal epistemology. In other words, Llewellyn fundamentally altered the very idea of understanding in law. The centerpiece of Llewellyn's discursive advance[13] is his account of legal "practice," for it is the practice that is the ultimate source of legal meaning. Practice or "way of acting" (p. 77), not rule or principle, is primary. Thus, "to know" is knowing how to "go on" with the practice.[14] Llewellyn demonstrated the limits of theoretical accounts of legal discourse. In this, Llewellyn prefigures not only Wittgenstein, but much of recent thought in the social sciences[15] and philosophy.[16]

---

12. See generally The Linguistic Turn: Recent Essays in Philosophical Method (R. Rorty ed. 1967) (collection of important philosophical essays representing the turn to critique of language as an alternative to more traditional modes of philosophy, namely, the construction of metaphysical systems).

13. I refer to Llewellyn's contribution as an "advance" because he developed a new way of thinking about the law. In other words, he advanced a completely new way of thinking about "understanding." Is this an "advance"? Consider the following comment on the present state of empirical social science:

> Any given set of tools both enables and constrains. It facilitates certain lines of action while restricting others. Advancement in understanding largely derives, then, from the development of new forms of discourse. With the emergence of new language frames, the potential for effective human action is augmented. To view social life as an exchange of reinforcements is both fascinating and rich in evocative potential—but ultimately delimited. Greater efficacy can be achieved if one has at one's disposal lenses through which social life may be seen as sets of rituals, theatrical presentations, economically determined patterns, power dynamics, dialectic transformations, and so on. In effect, the socio-behavioral sciences stand in an optimal position to contribute to the symbolic resources of the culture.

Gergen, Correspondence versus Autonomy in the Language of Understanding Human Action, *in* Metatheory in Social Science 157 (D. Fiske & R. Shweder eds. 1986).

14. In any practice, the ultimate question is how the participants decide what counts as the proper way to "go on" with the practice. For a review of current disagreements over how to read the later Wittgenstein on this point, see Malcolm, Wittgenstein on Language and Rules, 64 Phil. 5, 6–9 (1989) ("community consensus" is what determines how to "go on" with a practice or rule).

15. The relationship of the mental to the social is decidedly problematic.

> Ideas are not an instance separate from social relations; they are not merely appearances, nor are they deformed and deforming reflections in social consciousness. Rather, they are an integral part of social relations as soon as the latter begin to take shape, and they are one of the conditions for their formation. But, whilst there is an element of the mental everywhere, this in no way implies that everything that is (socially) real is mental.

M. Godelier, The Mental and the Material 129 (M. Thom trans. 1986).

16. I have in mind the many recent arguments directed against theory.

The Case Law System in America is so rich with ideas upon which one might choose to focus attention that any discussion of it must, of necessity, assume a focus that leaves out much of importance. This essay emphasizes the broadly philosophical notions implicated by Llewellyn's discussion of case law as a "system." Of utmost importance in this connection is the role of language in conditioning our understanding of reality. Read against the background of nineteenth and early twentieth-century thought, Llewellyn's text is simply remarkable in its prescience. While Llewellyn wrote and thought against the general background of a wide American revolt against formalism,[17] there is no one else in the first three decades of this century to approach questions of knowledge, understanding and law in the way Llewellyn does in this book.

The connection between Llewellyn and Wittgenstein is one that has been noted previously.[18] While surely not a focal point for the present essay, Llewellyn's ideas on the relationship between language and the world are so close in inspiration—if not some detail—to the later thought of Wittgenstein that the parallel must be further explored. Lawyers are often seen to follow philosophers in the development of their thought. To be sure, the relationship between Llewellyn and Wittgenstein is not causal: Wittgenstein never read Llewellyn. However, there can be little doubt that the insight that all understanding occurs in language *and* that understanding is a function of linguistic practices is one that Llewellyn could not have gotten directly from anyone else,[19] and Wittgenstein did not think of it until well after Llewel-

---

> [T]here are two ways of thinking about theory. The first way would see it as developing out of particular cases of practice but then necessarily ordering and informing subsequent practice. Once a theory is arrived at, it is "proved" by showing how many cases it can fit. And the aim of the theoretical enterprise is to build a system in the old philosophical sense. . . . The other way of thinking about theory would suggest that there is no automatic, already given relationship in force between reading a specific text and mulling over a general question that crops up again and again. Nonetheless, such general questions are interesting and worth spending time on, just as the antitheoreticians do.

Dasenbrock, Redrawing the Lines: An Introduction, *in* Redrawing The Lines: Analytic Philosophy, Deconstruction, and Literary Theory 22 (R. Dasenbrock ed. 1989).

17. See generally M. White, Pragmatism and the American Mind 41–67 (1973) (the attack on formalism led to the advancement of historicism); Horwitz, The Rise of Legal Formalism, 19 Am. J. Legal Hist. 251 (1975) (describing sources of legal formalism). For an especially important critique of legal formalism, see Dewey, Logical Method and Law, 10 Cornell L.Q. 17, 24–27 (1924).

18. See, e.g., Patterson, Wittgenstein and the Code: A Theory of Good Faith Performance and Enforcement Under Article Nine, 137 U. Pa. L. Rev. 335, 352–78 (1988) (describing Wittgensteinian account of meaning).

19. This claim is somewhat complicated. The complications cohere around the question of just what Llewellyn read and how he understood it. Llewellyn read a number of German sociologists both before, during and after his first visit to Leipzig in 1928–29. The work of Max Weber ultimately became the most significant influence on Llewellyn. The academic year 1931–32 saw Llewellyn return to Leipzig to deliver the lectures that became Recht, Rechtsleben und Gesellschaft (1977) (Law, Life of the Law,

lyn made his guest appearance in Leipzig. Hence, as a matter of intellectual history, Llewellyn came to the ideas first.

---

and Society). This book, which is explicitly concerned with Weber's thought (as well as that of Eugene Ehrlich), is Llewellyn's first sustained effort at a legal sociology. The ultimate influence of Weber is evinced in the following:

> I also agree completely with Max Weber in emphasizing the importance of action over norms; whereas Ehrlich, in his Rules for Conduct, confuses the two, sometimes invariable regularities of conduct, sometimes as norms for action, and sometimes not drawing a distinction between them.

Id. at 45 (translation is my own).

So what does all this amount to for the question of intellectual influence? Let us take Weber as an example. What did Llewellyn take from Weber when he was writing *The Case Law System in America*? This enormously complicated question can be given a tentative answer. Start with the lectures that became *The Bramble Bush*. These were written *before* Llewellyn made his first trip to Leipzig. There he wrote:

> No language stands alone. It draws life from its background. Technical terms used in a statute, undefined, must draw their meaning from the law which brought them forth. Only the background of the case teaches what the law was which the statute-maker sought to clarify or change. Against that background, then, his meaning must be sought.

K. Llewellyn, The Bramble Bush 79 (1960). In Weber's great work *Economy and Society*, he describes "explanatory understanding" in the following way:

> [W]e understand in terms of *motive* the meaning an actor attaches to the proposition twice two equals four, when he states it or writes it down, in that we understand what makes him do this at precisely this moment and in these circumstances. Understanding in this sense is attained if we know that he is engaged in balancing a ledger or in making a scientific demonstration, or is engaged in some other task of which this particular act would be an appropriate part. This is rational understanding of motivation, which consists in placing the act in an intelligible and more inclusive context of meaning.

M. Weber, Economy and Society: An Outline of Interpretive Sociology 8 (G. Roth & C. Wittich eds. 1978). Llewellyn cites the 1925 (second) edition of *Economy and Society* in *The Case Law System in America* (p. 82). Did Llewellyn get the idea that "interpretation" must be from the "inside" (that is from the perspective of the actor in an activity) from reading Weber? The answer is not clear at two levels. One level is that of derivation. Do the two quoted passages express the same idea? Put another way, is the same reading appropriate to both? Secondly, it must be remembered that the legacy of Weber is itself less than clear. Many think Weber a positivist (that is, one who believes that "knowledge" can come directly from "experience"). For a discussion of this point, see P. Halfpenny, Positivism and Sociology: Explaining Social Life 84–85 (1982) (focusing attention on Weber's theory of "causal" explanation). Toby Huff suggests that the positivistic reading of Weber's corpus is incorrect. What he says about Weber will, I believe, prove useful in reading Llewellyn:

> It is one thing to speak of the "meaning" of some object or process, but it is quite another possibility to speak of the *motive* or *intention* of somebody. One can talk of the "meaning" of "nature" or whatever, but one cannot refer to the "motive" of "nature", or of some inanimate process. Furthermore, this is another aspect of Weber's altered conception of "causal *interpretation*." To explain or interpret some human action is to interpret the "meaning" by supplying a "motive". The motive in this sense would be constituted by a set of "reasons" and/or "purposes" for the action. As we shall see, this results in Weber's conception of "teleologically rational behaviour."
>
> In brief, the trajectory of Weber's critique of his predecessors, Roscher and Knies, has led him to fashion a "qualitatively" distinct criterion which char-

This essay is divided into three sections. In Part I, I discuss Llewellyn's views on language's connection with reality because it is central to his most far-reaching claim: that the law's relationship to the world is fundamentally a linguistic one. What this means is that for Llewellyn, "the world" is not a reality independent of language but exists only in and through the categories that comprise language.

Once one accepts the view, as Llewellyn did, that all understanding occurs in language, then one is inexorably compelled to a "pragmatic" view of understanding in legal practice.[20] Part II examines Llewellyn's practical approach to legal understanding. Llewellyn's conception of law is perhaps best characterized as dynamic and problem-solving.[21] He saw legal categories as perpetually changing in response to the constant pressure of litigation and social change. He believed deeply that legal theory must account for law as essentially a sociological, discursive phenomenon. Hence, his view of law as a practice is articulated more in the language of the social than the strictly philosophical.

This brings us to the third and most important category, that of legal certainty, discussed in Part III of this essay. It has been the bane of American Legal Realism to find itself cast in a lineage with the view of law as fundamentally indeterminate.[22] As argued here, this view is not only false but a caricature of Realism. Llewellyn never said that the

---

> acterizes "causal" explanation in the sociocultural sciences. By insisting that there must be a "meaningful interpretation" (*sinnvollen Deutung*) in terms of *motives* and *intentions*, Weber has drastically modified the "positivist" covering-law model of scientific explanation. And he adamantly rejected the possibility of using "an empirical-statistical demonstration of the strictest sort" as a *substitute* for a meaningful interpretation which would reveal the connection between the actor's conduct and his "intentions and beliefs".

T. Huff, Max Weber and the Methodology of the Social Sciences 48 (1984) (footnotes omitted).

Here we see many of the same ideas that are commonly associated with Llewellyn. Chief among these are intentions, purposes and reason (as in "singing reason"). Perhaps the best way to characterize this is to say that if Llewellyn read Weber the way Toby Huff reads Weber, then one can see in Weber the genesis of some of Llewellyn's key ideas. For a different reading of the German sources of Llewellyn's thought, see Whitman, Commercial Law and the American *Volk*: A Note on Llewellyn's German Sources for the Uniform Commercial Code, 97 Yale L.J. 156, 166–173 (1987) (influence on Llewellyn of German Romantic thought).

20. Here Llewellyn's specific contribution follows the general tenor of Realism. See Singer, Legal Realism Now (Book Review), 76 Calif. L. Rev. 465, 474 (1988) ("The legal realists wanted to replace formalism with a pragmatic attitude toward law generally.").

21. For a similar view, see N. Luhmann, A Sociological Theory of Law (E. King & M. Albrow trans. 1985) (articulating a general theory of the social system and law's role within it as a means for the resolution of fundamental social problems).

22. I refer, of course, to the Critical Legal Studies movement. There is, now, some question whether the thesis of strong indeterminacy is still maintained. For a discussion of the thesis, see Fiss, The Death of the Law?, 72 Cornell L. Rev. 1, 9–13 (1986). The continuing efficacy of the strong indeterminacy thesis is discussed in Gabel & Kennedy, Roll Over Beethoven, 36 Stan. L. Rev. 1 (1984).

law is indeterminate. He did, however, believe that the law was not determinate in the ways legal formalists believed it to be. The certainty of law lies, Llewellyn argued, not in abstract categories but in the practice itself, properly understood. The importance of *The Case Law System in America* is that it provides us another occasion to assess the significance of Llewellyn's contribution to our ongoing thinking on these matters.

I. Language

Llewellyn's account of law as a practice is rooted in his approach to language. For it is in his approach to the relationship between language and understanding that one finds the driving force behind his account of such key concepts as legal change, legal certainty, interpretation and legal validity. For Llewellyn, the world is a function of the linguistic categories which we use to make sense of it. Put more strongly, he believes that the legal world exists only in and through language.[23] Legal certainty, then, is a function of current semantic networks; it "concerns the world of What Already Exists" (p. 74 n.1). But what exists "can never extend beyond the symbol's . . . content at a given time" (id.). Thus, meaning is a function of signs and the meaning of a sign at any given point is a function of the particular historical context within which it is employed.[24]

Because words are mere symbols, they do not by themselves convey meaning. Yet how is it that the symbol can function as "a means of *referring* to things or mental constructs?" (p. 74). The answer lies in the network of connections between symbols and the "things or mental constructs" for which they are proxies.

The movement from established meaning to new understandings occurs in a subtle and not completely discernible manner. Every legal category possesses what Llewellyn refers to as a "latent content which has an unambiguous and predictable (along with an ambiguous and not fully predictable) capacity *for expanding*" (p. 74). The expansion of the existing content of a legal category reflects this double aspect of understanding. The new and different is not immediately recognized as such but is first "felt to fit within existing categories" (id.).

Some expansions of a rule appear clear—almost uncontroversial—for "every lawyer would expand the rules in the same way" (id.). Despite "the language of legal analysis [which] assumes that the applica-

23. As a general matter, this is as true in fiction as it is in real life. See M. Riffaterre, Fictional Truth xiii-xv (1990) ("The narrative need not be judged true because it corresponds to an external image of the world, but because it is consistent with the linguistic usages current in a given social context, at a given moment in time.").

24. One might go even further and argue that the very *instrument* of the production of meaning is itself constitutive of what is produced. See A. Ronnell, The Telephone Book (1989) (a deconstruction of the telephone as a technological presence in discourse).

bility of legal categories is uncontestable" (p. 76), subliminal restructuring of the content of legal categories—their "immanent expansive capacity" (p. 74)—is always in process. In the moment of decision the innovation is not recognized. It is only later, after one "works over a *line* of cases *in retrospect* [that one] recognizes that something new has *been* created" (p. 76).

The dialectic of understanding and expansion that Llewellyn speaks of occurs within the realm of language, specifically the language of legal categories. However—and this is Llewellyn's unique orientation to the Realist enterprise—this process is one that is *situated.* When Llewellyn states that "every category in fact has an immanent expansive capacity" (p. 74) which is "*sociologically* immanent" (p. 74 n.1) the point of emphasis is the sociological. "[L]egal certainty means calculability in advance of the actual rendering of a decision" (id.), not in the crude statistical sense but in the sense of sensitivity to and appreciation for the way in which language—the language of legal discourse—creates a world. The object of prediction is the *use* to which a word is being put in the discourse. Thus, Llewellyn urges that which would become the centerpiece of Wittgenstein's later thought: the meaning of a word is its use in a language. Llewellyn's orientation to the problem of the accommodation of troubled cases is toward a theory of coherence. The existing discourse or vocabulary of law is in a "constant process of reformulation, in the light of having to work through concrete fact situations. . . ." (p. 63). Of course, what is being made to cohere are the linguistic categories that themselves are the heart of the system. When the "social conditions may have fundamentally changed" (p. 75) for example, there is a need to reformulate the rule.

> If the new case is brought under an old category, the category thereafter is broader than it had been. But if the new case is excluded, the category has acquired a more determinate boundary where earlier its boundary was uncertain and there was still the possibility of its extending to cover this or a similar case (id.). [25]

One can see more clearly Llewellyn's view of language as a constitutive medium by considering the intellectual background against which he developed his views.[26] Legal formalism, as propounded by Langdell, was a favorite Realist target and Llewellyn, following Corbin, made it the focus of his later work on the Uniform Commercial Code

25. For an excellent discussion of this aspect of interpretation see Eskridge, Dynamic Statutory Interpretation, 135 U. Pa. L. Rev. 1479, 1488–94 (1987) (discussing United Steelworkers v. Weber, 443 U.S. 193 (1979)).

26. The widest possible vantage point is that of the Enlightenment. Broadly speaking, the Enlightenment approach to rationality presumes that there is "only one possible answer to any question." D. Harvey, The Condition of Postmodernity 27 (1989). In answer to the question, "What is contract?" Llewellyn answered "many things." This response, which evinces Llewellyn's overall intellectual perspective, represents a distinct break with the ideology of the Enlightenment.

("U.C.C.").[27] The dream of Langdell was, as far as possible, to make law like science.[28] Formalist in aspiration, Langdell took it as his task to reduce law, specifically contract law, to a few abstract principles. In the language of schema, "the heart of classical theory was its aspiration that the legal system be made complete through universal formality, and universally formal through conceptual order."[29]

The establishment of legal principles is only the first step to a complete legal method. Application—the employment of principles to decide cases—is equally important. The formalist method, of course, was deduction. The formula was as follows:

1. Legal principle
2. Facts
3. Conclusion[30]

It is important to emphasize that Llewellyn did not reject deduction as a form of legal method.[31] What he questioned was the formalist's assumption that the language of legal categories is always and everywhere sufficiently stable such that "the existing categories are *the only ones possible*" (p. 96). What Llewellyn challenged was the notion that from the perspective of law (as a putative "science") the world could be divided into "the legal" and "the nonlegal." That is, Llewellyn put into question legal formalism's *picture* of the relationship of language to the world. In the course of doing so, he was the first in jurisprudence to advance the pragmatist position. The currency of Llewellyn's view of the matter is confirmed in the following from Richard Rorty, perhaps the most visible academic to claim a lineage with pragmatism:

> Pragmatists say that the traditional notion that "truth is correspondence to reality" is an uncashable and outworn metaphor. Some true statements—like "the cat is on the mat"—can be paired off with other chunks of reality so as to associate parts of the statement with parts of the chosen chunk. Most true statements—like "the cat is *not* on the mat" and "there are transfinite numbers" and "pleasure is better than pain"—cannot. Furthermore, we will be no better off even if we construct a metaphysical scheme which pairs off something in the world with each part of *every* true statement. . . . For we should still

27. For the specifics of Llewellyn's critique of the classical theory of contract, see Patterson, Good Faith, Lender Liability, and Discretionary Acceleration: Of Llewellyn, Wittgenstein, and the Uniform Commercial Code, 68 Tex. L. Rev. 169, 186–91 (1989).

28. By "science" I mean the nineteenth-century view of scientific practice, the ground of which is "[t]he rule (or belief) that there is an 'essential unity of scientific method.' " D. Oldroyd, The Arch of Knowledge 169 (1986) (citing L. Kolukowski, The Alienation of Reason: A History of Positivist Thought 8 (N. Guterman trans. 1968)).

29. Grey, Langdell's Orthodoxy, 45 U. Pitt. L. Rev. 1, 11 (1983).

30. For discussion of the continuing importance (and limitations) of deductive justification in law, see N. MacCormick, Legal Reasoning and Legal Theory 19–72 (1978).

31. "I too believe that *much* in the process is in fact to be explained as deduction—at least where a situation is on all fours with a previously decided case or had explicitly been taken into consideration when a norm was established" (p. 56 n.11).

> be faced with the question of whether the . . . language we use *itself* "corresponds to reality." That is, we should still wonder whether talk of cats or numbers or goodness is the right way to break up the universe into chunks, whether our language cuts reality at the joints. The pragmatists conclude that the intuition that truth is correspondence should be extirpated rather than explicated.[32]

Llewellyn anticipates the current assault on "Truth" with his position that there can be no law without language because the law exists, if it exists at all, in and through the categories that give it expression.[33] The symbol "is a means of *referring* to things" (p. 74). The relationship of words to things is never static, because meaning is a function not only of currently accepted usage but of historical circumstances.[34] Whichever way a legal decision goes, "the symbol thus acquires a new content" (p. 75): "the new illuminates and *at the same time changes* the old" (p. 79). The changes wrought upon our linguistic categories are not the result of "interpretation"; for the process of application "does not involve any interpretation of legal rules" (p. 80). Legal categories touch base with "the experiential basis and the approved direction for developing norms, and thus the foundations of existing law" (id.). We often fail to appreciate the utter contingency of our fundamentally linguistic relation to the world: "the world" is not "out there" waiting to be found but is "made" in language.[35]

---

32. Rorty, Texts and Lumps, 17 New Literary Hist. 1, 2–3 (1986).

33. Thus, Llewellyn is one of the earliest proponents of the noncognitive, antirealist orientation. Llewellyn's views about the realm of value are properly described as noncognitivist because of his assent to the thesis that "there is no such thing as moral cognition or knowledge." S. Lovibond, Realism and Imagination in Ethics 1 (1983); see also W. Twining, Karl Llewellyn and the Realist Movement 186 (1973) ("As an ethical relativist Llewellyn maintained that 'every man of conscience must hold his own perceptions of Justice to be the basic ones.' "). On the relationship between noncognitivism and antirealism, see Sayre-McCord, The Many Moral Realisms, 24 S.J. Phil. 1, 3 (Supp. 1986) ("[One way to be] an antirealist [is to] embrace a non-cognitivist analysis of [ethical] claims . . . .").

34. This point has been much discussed in recent literature, particularly in the context of statutory interpretation. See Eskridge, supra note 25, at 1479 ("The dialectic of statutory interpretation is the process of understanding a text created in the past and applying it to a present problem.").

35. As the following passage suggests, Llewellyn's thought would anticipate the current preoccupation with jettisoning the idea of language as a picture or representation and replace it with the notion of a network of linguistic practices.

> To drop the idea of languages as representations, and to be thoroughly Wittgensteinian in our approach to language, would be to de-divinize the world. Only if we do that can we fully accept the argument . . . that since truth is a property of sentences, since sentences are dependent for their existence upon vocabularies, and since vocabularies are made by human beings, so are truths. For as long as we think that "the world" names something we ought to respect as well as cope with, something personlike in that it has a preferred description of itself, we shall insist that any philosophical account of truth save the "intuition" that truth is "out there." This intuition amounts to the vague

Llewellyn's response to nineteenth-century formalism starts on the best-known front: the level of method. He attacks the formalist "belief in the availability of a deductive or quasi-deductive method capable of giving determinate solutions to particular problems of legal choice"[36] as unhelpful to saying "anything certain about how a lawsuit will turn out when the law is in doubt" (p. 9). At the level of critique of language, Llewellyn is not content with pointing out the obvious shortcomings of the formalist approach to language, which sees words as if they were "things with fixed content" (p. 75). Beyond words are "facts," which are themselves linguistic entities.[37] Facts are hybrid entities, for they are as much a product of "us" as what is "out there":

> A case comes out one way or the other depending on how the fact situation is treated. Without needing a separate opinion to prove it, a scholar might already have suspected that the facts of the case undergo reshaping as the decision is being made, but especially as the opinion is being written. He knows that it is impossible for anyone to have objective knowledge of the facts as they really are. Out of one and the same mass of facts, each of us, based on individual experience, decides what "the" facts are. (pp. 52–53)

For Llewellyn, a "fact" is a composite of "raw factual matter" (p. 53) together with a category that gives it meaning.[38] Llewellyn's objec-

---

> sense that it would be *hubris* on our part to abandon the traditional language of "respect for fact" and "objectivity"—that it would be risky, and blasphemous, not to see the scientist (or the philosopher, or the poet, or *somebody*) as having a priestly function, as putting us in touch with a realm which transcends the human.

R. Rorty, Contingency, Irony, and Solidarity 21 (1989).

36. R. Unger, The Critical Legal Studies Movement 1 (1986).

37. For a discussion of the role of the classification of "facts" in the use of precedent, see Collier, Precedent and Legal Authority: A Critical History, 1988 Wis. L. Rev. 771, 796–98.

38. This approach to "facts" is an important element in the pragmatism of Richard Rorty.

> The pragmatist . . . agrees that there is such a thing as brute physical resistance—the pressure of light waves on Galileo's eyeball, or of the stone on Dr. Johnson's boot. But he sees no way of transferring this brutality to *facts*, to the truth of sentences. The way in which a blank takes on the form of the die which stamps it has no analogy to the relation between the truth of a sentence and the event which the sentence is about. When the die hits the blank something causal happens, but as many *facts* are brought into the world as there are languages for describing that causal transaction. As Donald Davidson says, causation is not under a description, but explanation is. Facts are hybrid entities; that is, the causes of the assertibility of sentences include both physical stimuli and our antecedent choice of response to such stimuli. To say that we must have respect for facts is just to say that we must, if we are to play a certain language game, play by the rules. To say that we must have respect for unmediated causal forces is pointless. It is like saying the blank must have respect for the impressed die. The blank has no choice, nor do we.

Rorty, supra note 32, at 4.

tive here is not only to get us away from the notion that there is "just one possible way to classify facts, but also that *the particular classification made* in a specific lawsuit has something necessary, something foreordained about it" (p. 53).[39] There is no "fact of the matter" in the law any more than there is a fact of the matter in science, literature, criticism or philosophy. The meaning of the law in any given case is a function neither of what is "out there" in the world nor the "meaning" of a text (e.g., common-law rule, statute or regulation). The "facts" and the "law" are both texts: their meaning is a function of the way they are related not just to one another but "to the other texts . . . mentioned in or presupposed by the propositions which we use to describe them."[40] As Llewellyn puts it: "Legal history makes it clear that these creative innovations and adaptions, these fact-shaped reinterpretations of legal institutions, constitute the life-blood of the law" (p. 97).

Llewellyn's view that all understanding occurs within linguistic categories, and that all such categories are the product of particular historical circumstances, would today be labelled "historicism."[41] Elsewhere described as "the recognition of the historical and cultural contingency of law,"[42] historicism's chief sin, at least as its detractors see it, is that it is a form of relativism.[43] While more a rhetorical than a substantive term, relativism[44] acts as a foil for the critic of historicism only if certain

39. Some in contemporary philosophy of science take the same view of scientific "facts." See B. Latour, Science in Action 42 (1987) (when reading the quotation, substitute "judicial opinion" for "[scientific] papers" and the parallel will be clear):

> This rare event is what people usually have in mind when they talk of a "fact." I hope it is clear by now that this event does not make it qualitatively different from fiction; a fact is whatever is collectively stabilised from the midst of controversies when the activity of later [scientific] papers does not consist only of criticism or deformation but also of confirmation. The strength of the original statement does not lie in itself, but is derived from any of the papers that incorporate it.

40. Rorty, supra note 32, at 12. The most thorough treatment of the notion of social "fact" is M. Gilbert, On Social Facts (1989) (assessing the theories of, among others, Winch, Weber and Wittgenstein).

41. See generally, R. D'Amico, Historicism and Knowledge (1989) (discussing historicist position that human understanding is determined by historical circumstances). For an assessment of the theological implications of historicism, see W. Dean, History Making History: The New Historicism in American Religious Thought 1–22 (1988).

42. Gordon, Historicism in Legal Scholarship, 90 Yale L.J. 1017, 1017 (1981).

43. For a general discussion of the relativistic implications of historicism in the context of recent developments in Weberian social theory, see C. Lloyd, Explanation in Social History 300–04 (1986). A wider discussion of the relativistic implications of historicism in twentieth-century thought is D. Roberts, Benedetto Croce and the Uses of Historicism 117–67 (1987).

44. Richard Rorty argues that relativism is

> the view that every belief on a certain topic, or perhaps about *any* topic, is as good as every other. However, no one holds this view. Except for the occassional cooperative freshman, one cannot find anybody who says that two incompatible opinions on an important topic are equally good. The philosophers who get *called* "relativists" are those who say that the grounds for choosing

presuppositions are granted. Not surprisingly, these suppositions turn out to be rationalist or objectivist in nature.[45]

The most fervent critic of historicism is the objectivist that has science as her model of the best law can be.[46] The objectivist begins with the supposition that there is a real world "out there" and that it is the business of science to describe it. Philosophy, the handmaiden of science, is thus cast in the role of tool-sharpener, refining the language of scientific discourse in order to bring us closer to reality.

It is here that the objectivist and the historicist part company. To the objectivist, it is the job of philosophy to make clear the relationship between "language" and "the world." The way to do this is to clarify the way language hooks up with or corresponds to reality. But it is at this juncture that the objectivist makes the most important of her assumptions. (Important, if for no other reason than the rhetorical power it provides her.) The assumption is that there is a world "out there" that we can know apart from some form of representation.[47] Put

---

> between such opinions are less algorithmic than had been thought. . . . The position in question is criticized for not having done what philosophers are employed to do: explain why our framework, or culture, or interests, or language, or whatever, is at least on the right track—in touch with physical reality, or the moral law, or the real numbers, or some other sort of object patiently waiting about to be copied. So the real issue is not between people who think one view is good as another and people who do not. It is between those who think our culture, or purpose, or intuitions cannot be supported except conversationally, and people who still hope for other sorts of support.

R. Rorty, Consequences of Pragmatism 166–67 (1982).

45. By "objectivist" I mean belief in the possibility or actuality of some permanent, ahistorical framework for knowledge. A "rationalist" framework is objectivist in that the frame is provided by reason. For discussion of the impact on current legal theory of the objective-subjective dichotomy, see Patterson, Interpretation in Law—Toward A Reconstruction of the Current Debate, 29 Vill. L. Rev. 671, 674–82 (1984).

46. Thus, Langdell argued that,

> Law, considered as a science, consists of certain principles or doctrines. . . . [T]he number of fundamental legal doctrines is much less than is commonly supposed; the many different guises in which the same doctrine is constantly making its appearance, and the great extent to which legal treatises are a repetition of each other, being the cause of much misapprehension. . . . It seemed to me, therefore, to be possible to take such a branch of the law as Contracts, for example, and, without exceeding comparatively moderate limits, to select, classify, and arrange all the cases which had contributed in any important degree to the growth, development, or establishment of any of its essential doctrines. . . .

1 C. Langdell, A Selection of Cases on the Law of Contracts viii–ix (1879).

47. An additional problem is the question of the *hierarchy* among competing forms of representation. Clark provides a Marxist, materialist treatment of this problem in another context:

> [A]ny social order consists primarily of classifications. What else do we usually mean by the word "society" but a means for solidarity, distance, belonging, and exclusion? These things are needed pre-eminently to enable the production of material life—to fix an order in which men and women can make their living and have some confidence that they will continue to do so. Orders of this sort

another way, there is an independent reality against which we can test the truth or falsity of our linguistic claims about the world. If law, the most primordial of humanistic enterprises, was like science, the promises of method could be harnessed in the way they are in the empirical sciences.[48]

Alas, the assumptions the objectivist makes prove to be too much for the account of the representation-reality model she advances. The account of representation the objectivist would have us follow is one in which language "pictures" reality. To see if the picture is correct, we need to compare it to reality. In science, we would do this through experimentation. If the results of the experiment match our expectations, then the picture is accurate.[49] If not, then the picture is false and we must rework it and try again. But as Quine has shown, even so simple an exercise as translating a word such as "gavagai" from one language to another is fraught with ineradicable indeterminacy.[50] Thus, if certainty cannot be grounded in "reality," it is a function of our conceptual systems. The presence of multiple conceptual schemes for organizing "reality" means that absolute certainty, assuming it is an intelligible idea,[51] can never be achieved.

> appear to be established most potently by representations or systems of signs, and it does not seem to me to trivialize the concept of "social formation"—or necessarily to give it an idealist as opposed to a materialist gloss—to describe it as a hierarchy of representations.

T. Clark, The Painting of Modern Life: Paris in the Art of Manet and His Followers 6 (1984). The problem identified here is one of interest: *whose* interests are to count as underwriting our conception of reality? Systems of classification cannot choose between themselves for dominance, for that is a matter of politics.

48. For criticism of humanistic preoccupation with the (false) promises of method, see H. Gadamer, Truth and Method 491 (J. Weinsheimer & D. Marshall trans. 2d rev. ed. 1989) ("[W]hat the tool of method does not achieve must—and really can—be achieved by a discipline of questioning and inquiring, a discipline that guarantees truth.").

49. These expectations, as well as the answer to the question of what counts as confirmation, are a function of the operative discursive formations of scientific practice. The best way to know what is "true" from the scientific point of view is to undertake an ethnography of scientific discourse (those who bemoan the lack of empirical work in law would do well to undertake such investigations). For a recent example, see M. Mulkay, The Word and the World: Explorations in the Form of Sociological Analysis (1985) (analyzing the discourse of biochemistry).

50. See W. Quine, Word and Object 29–35 (1960) (language alone cannot isolate *what* in an event is the focus of a word). Even greater problems stem from the recognition that "theories about the world transcend all possible observations of the world, and, further, that different, competing theories can be developed on the same observational basis. In a word, theories can be shown to be logically incompatible with one another, yet empirically equivalent." R. Gibson, Enlightened Empiricism: An Examination of W.V. Quine's Theory of Knowledge 11–12 (1988).

51. It is not at all clear that such a notion is intelligible. The problem with such theories is that "[t]hey cannot be tested like scientific theories because they do not make contact with the phenomena . . . ." 2 D. Pears, The False Prison: A Study of the Development of Wittgenstein's Philosophy 499 (1988).

If philosophy cannot provide certainty for science, then what hope have we that it can contribute anything to the development of legal analysis? One way of answering this question, that is at the level of philosophical theory,[52] is resoundingly rejected by Llewellyn.[53] Throughout *The Case Law System in America*, indeed throughout the entirety of his work (both jurisprudential and practical),[54] Llewellyn shared the view that theory cannot resolve problems of practice.[55] As Wittgenstein would later come to say, philosophy "leaves everything as it is."[56] And so it does.

Llewellyn's approach to adjudication is broader than his account of the linguistic nature of facts. Anticipating later developments in hermeneutical theory, Llewellyn argues that "understanding" of the law stops not with the construction of linguistic categories but continues as those categories are employed in legal discourse.[57] In the moment of "the 'application' of the legal rule" (p. 54) the legal category is "ad-

52. By "philosophical theory" I mean any approach to knowledge that seeks solutions to problems of thought at the level of a general, abstract theory without regard to the interplay between theory and practice in the production of understanding.

53. William Twining recounts a Llewellyn outburst in response to a student (not Twining) submission on the subject of "is" and "ought" in Kant. See W. Twining, The Karl Llewellyn Papers 9 (1968) ("What the hell . . . has Kant to do with *my* course on Jurisprudence?"). This story is reproduced in W. Twining, supra note 33, at 117.

54. For an assessment of the impact of Llewellyn's jurisprudential ideas on the Uniform Commercial Code, see Patterson, supra note 27.

55. In this vein, Paul Gewirtz's otherwise helpful and interesting introduction to *The Case Law System in America* is unnecessarily complicated by his comparison of Llewellyn's views on the relationship of theory to practice with those of the scholar of seventeenth-century English literature, Stanley Fish (pp. xviii-xix). In making his comparison of Llewellyn's views with those of Fish, Professor Gewirtz highlights Llewellyn's emphasis on the primacy of practice with his observation that "Fish, who celebrates the role of the reader in giving meaning to texts, is invigorated by the possibility that a powerful, ambitious individual might be able to recreate the community of interpretation in his own image" (p. xx). The contrast of Fish to Llewellyn underscores the subtlety of Llewellyn's fusion of training, tradition and knowledge: for Llewellyn (as for Wittgenstein) it is impossible for one individual to "recreate the community of interpretation in his own image" (p. 20). The very idea makes no sense, for all ideas *about* the community of interpretation are already *embedded in* the community.

Fish's observations about the internal dynamics of practice cannot be sustained at even the most basic level, that is the self-understanding of the participants, for in Fish's view the participants *never reflect upon the point of the practice*. See S. Fish, Doing What Comes Naturally ix (1989) ("I intend it to refer to the unreflective actions that follow from being embedded in a context of practice. This kind of action—*and in my argument there is no other* . . . .") (emphasis added). Fish denies what Llewellyn regards as central to law as a practice—self-consciousness. (In fact, it is not at all clear that, for Fish, the notion of a "self" makes any sense at all. But that issue is beyond the scope of the point under discussion.).

56. L. Wittgenstein, supra note 6, § 124.

57. Here Llewellyn anticipates Gadamer's recovery of the moment of *applicatio* in hermeneutical understanding. Briefly, Gadamer's claim is that no understanding is complete without application. See H. Gadamer, supra note 48, at 311 ("To interpret the law's will or the promises of God is clearly not a form of domination but of service.

just[ed]" (p. 53).[58] Thus, the distinction between the law "as it is" and "the law as it ought to be" cannot be maintained.[59] Every application of the law involves change in the existing category. There is no "in principle" distinction between "hard" and "easy" cases, or relative degrees of alteration.

It is here that we see most clearly the anticipatory character of Llewellyn's thought. Our relationship to the world is through "a nexus of linguistic symbols" (p. 74). But these symbols are not all that enable us to understand, for "[i]n itself the symbol is nothing" (id.). But what more is there to understanding than the word? Understanding requires that our vocabulary for dividing up the world be made to cohere with our continuing experiences. But this is paradoxical: if all understanding occurs in language, and language is the only means by which we understand, then what is the point of looking at words when they themselves have no inherent meaning (when they are a necessary but insufficient means for understanding)?

Wittgenstein's approach to this question can illuminate the problem Llewellyn is attempting to articulate. The answer to the question of the relationship of language to the world was, Wittgenstein recommended, in the study of simple uses of words.[60] Words, and the activities of which they are a part, constitute the basic unit of meaning, which is the "language-game."[61] To understand a language-game, we must

---

They are interpretations—which includes application—in the service of what is considered valid.").

58. The importance of "application" in understanding is a central feature of debate between Gadamer and E.D. Hirsch, Jr., the most persistent advocate of the "authorial intent" school of interpretation. The particulars of this debate are discussed in Patterson, supra note 18, at 369 n.109. For a Gadamerian "response" to Hirsch, see G. Madison, The Hermeneutics of Postmodernity: Figures and Themes 3–24 (1988).

59. On "Is" and "Ought" in the thought of Llewellyn, see Casebeer, Escape From Liberalism: Fact and Value in Karl Llewellyn, 1977 Duke L.J. 671.

60. Wittgenstein's claim is that "[i]t disperses the fog to study the phenomena of language in primitive kinds of application in which one can command a clear view of the aim and functioning of the words." L. Wittgenstein, supra note 6, § 5.

61. See id. § 43 ("[T]he meaning of a word is its use in the language."). The claim that the thought of the later Wittgenstein culminates in the view that we are always inside language and cannot critique the relationship of language to the world is perspicuously sustained in M. Hintikka & J. Hintikka, Investigating Wittgenstein 20–21 (1986) ("Wittgenstein's doctrine of meaning as use was based on his belief in language as the universal medium."). For further extension of this argument, and discussion of its implications for forms of argument, see Kusch, Husserl and Heidegger on Meaning, 77 Synthese 99 (1988). Kusch, after summarizing the Hintikkas's reading of Wittgenstein, states:

> The corollaries of this general point can be summarized in the following argument—here I follow more the spirit than the letter of *Investigating Wittgenstein*:
> 1. Semantical relations are inaccessible; therefore
> 2. we cannot imagine different semantical relations; therefore
> 3. model theory (and talk of possible worlds) is impossible (since model theory is based on the systematical variation of meaning relations); and

grasp its point,[62] for "how we group words into kinds will depend on the aim of the classification,—and on our own inclination."[63] We get a clear sense of Wittgenstein's point in this connection by considering his remarks on rule-following. By themselves, rules—and their interpretations—"do not determine meaning,"[64] for that is a matter of custom, use and intuition.[65] Following rules, legal or otherwise, "is a practice."[66] Because it is "a labyrinth of paths,"[67] language is something in which one learns one's way about.[68] Both Wittgenstein and Llewellyn look at understanding as a gradual process of initiation. Whether the activity is law, gardening or cooking, understanding the process of each is a dawning that comes only after one has found one's feet in the enterprise. Understanding, then, is a matter of know-how.

In asking after the meaning of words, it is unproductive to ask after the relationship of language to the world, for understanding only occurs in and through language: "[y]ou can never get outside it."[69] Being inside language means only that instead of responding to the philosophical urge to lay bare language's point of contact with reality, we would do better to discern the point of the language-game or rule.[70]

> 4. linguistic relativism is inevitable (we are trapped in our language); for (due to 1 & 2)
> 5. we cannot grasp reality without linguistic (distorting) interference; and (due to 1)
> 6. the construction of a metalanguage is impossible; therefore
> 7. truth as correspondence is inexpressible, therefore (and due to 1)
> 8. we have to limit ourselves to syntax, i.e., formalism.

Id. at 99–100.

62. See generally J. Kovesi, Moral Notions 46–49 (1967) (arguing by example for the proposition that concepts are forged against the background of intersubjective social experience).

63. L. Wittgenstein, supra note 6, § 17. Llewellyn expresses the same idea in the wider context of judicial response to changing factual circumstances:

> If one observes a new fact situation *and is sensitive to its real-life meaning*, then there is a sudden and (so to speak) ex post facto change in the meaning of one's prior life experience in that area, and thus a change of content in the words used to describe and regulate the area (p. 79).

64. L. Wittgenstein, supra note 6 § 198. Llewellyn makes the point this way:

> I would like to start off with a hypothetical case that no one has any doubt about how to handle, but that no one had in mind when the rule was created. Nonetheless, anyone who looked at the case and the rule at the same time would "recognize" that the case *must* be governed by the rule. Here I maintain that no real "interpretation" of the rule is taking place. Rather, there is an extension, a reformulation, a reading of something new into the rule (p. 74).

65. See L. Wittgenstein, supra note 6, § 199.

66. Id. § 202.

67. Id. § 203.

68. For a superb discussion of this point in the context of the limitations of Dworkin's theory of interpretation, see Postema, "Protestant" Interpretation and Social Practices, 6 Law & Phil. 283 (1987).

69. L. Wittgenstein, supra note 6, § 103.

70. Llewellyn argued that "[an] interpretation either does or does not further a particular purpose. . . ." (p. 53).

But how is one purpose settled on? What are the criteria for choice? To answer these questions, we must consider Llewellyn's account of law as a practice. More than on any other subject, this is where Llewellyn is truly ahead of his time.

The analysis of the fundamentally linguistic nature of understanding shows that legal knowledge cannot be modelled along the lines suggested by legal formalists. Legal understanding is not a "top down" affair: the subsumption of "facts" and "rules" by broader principles is incompatible with the holistic structure of understanding. For Llewellyn, legal knowledge is a function of linguistic networks that are worked and reworked in the course of legal practice. It is to this aspect of his thought that we now turn.

II. Practice

From its earliest pages, Llewellyn describes *The Case Law System in America* as "anthropological" (p. xxxv).[71] The project is "descriptive": "to *show how the doctrine of precedent actually works*, and to provide an insight into the nature of case law adjudication, and judicial decision-making more generally" (p. xxxiii). As he describes it, "the primary aim of this work is to observe and to describe what it observes . . . ." (p. xxxv). But what of legal method and legal norm; are these not of interest? They are, Llewellyn tells us, but only to the extent of "their actual *effects* on the outcome of cases . . . ." (id.).

The anthropology of which Llewellyn speaks has as its object the conduct of officials for it is "*[w]hat these officials do about disputes [that is] the law itself*."[72] This famous, perhaps infamous, remark of Llewellyn's is usually taken to exemplify the extreme element in Realism, that is, the view that judicial activity is little more than an occasion for the expression of subjective *ought* and a disregard of the law as it actually exists. Of course, this view is a caricature. The extent of the caricature must not obscure what is really at stake in Llewellyn's claims for the primacy of practice over theory.[73] If there is no understanding outside of language, and understanding is always relative to historical circumstance, then what is the ground for the adjudication of legal disputes? Stated

71. For an example of Llewellyn's talents as an anthropologist, see K. Llewellyn & E. Hoebel, The Cheyenne Way (1941).

72. K. Llewellyn, The Bramble Bush, supra note 19, at 3.

73. Compare Llewellyn's conception of practice with the following commentary on the view of practice articulated by Wittgenstein in his last work. L. Wittgenstein, On Certainty (G. Anscombe & G. von Wright eds. D. Paul & G. Anscombe trans. 1969). Johannessen argues that Wittgenstein

> is mostly trying to make his reader realize the complexity of the interrelationship between our language and the world. It is fairly well recognized that this is a problem that is fundamental to *all* of Wittgenstein's thinking. But until now it has not been looked into with the concept of practice at the very centre.

Johannessen, The Concept of Practice in Wittgenstein's Later Philosophy, 31 Inquiry 357, 357–58 (1988).

in the language of Critical Legal Studies, is the law not reducible to, or merely another form of, politics?

Llewellyn's answer to this question is his theory of legal practice.[74] Truth, that is legal truth, is the product neither of the correspondence of sentences with "the world" (objectivism) nor is it simply what judges decide it will be (relativism). Truth in law is a function of three elements: training,[75] tradition[76] and creativity.[77]

Llewellyn illustrates the importance of training[78] by inviting the reader to contemplate "the different results a layman and a trained lawyer derive from identical legal rules, even if one hands the layman every rule that the lawyer intends to use in solving the problem" (p. 77). What is it that structures the lawyer's intuition that is absent for the layperson? It is none other than "the *operating technique* of the trained lawyer as passed down to him . . . ." (id.). It is the "practice, not norm; way of acting, not verbal formula" (id.) that shapes the intuitive reaction to fact-situations.[79] There can be no appeal beyond the confines

---

74. The following statement is a nice summary of his position, the full implications of which would be worked out in all of Llewellyn's later work:

> Practice, again, is the bony structure of a legal system. Yet practice is no part of *law* except as it becomes wrapped in and is measured constantly against the held norm or felt ideal. Men are the lifeblood of a legal system, yet men are not even of it, save as bedded in the context of tradition, both existent and becoming, which shapes the men even as it is being shaped by them.

Llewellyn, My Philosophy of Law, *in* My Philosophy of Law 187–88 (1941). One is struck by Llewellyn's identification of "the practice" apart from the participants, while at the same time recognizing that it is the participants in the practice that "shape and are shaped by it." It is by virtue of remarks such as these that one sees clearly that, for Llewellyn, both "radical skepticism" and "determinacy" have to be rejected not merely as wrong but simplistic.

75. "The sort of legal certainty that does exist is to be found in the predictable reaction of a trained lawyer . . . ." (p. 80).

76. "But no less important is the trained, tradition-determined manner of handling the material" (p. 77). Here, Llewellyn follows Cardozo. See B. Cardozo, The Nature of the Judicial Process 151 (1921) (discussing the relationship between history and the proper understanding of precedent).

77. Llewellyn believed that the greatest credit for creativity must go to the practising bar (p. 98). For a discussion of "creativity" see infra page 599.

78. The idea of training as a basis for explanation is widely accepted by those advocating a "strong" approach to the sociology of knowledge. The following, from one of the leading proponents of the "strong" approach is illustrative:

> The social component [of knowledge] is clear and irreducible. Processes such as education and training must be invoked to explain the enplanting [sic] and the distributing of the states of prior belief. They are absolutely necessary if experience is to have a determinate effect. These processes are also necessary for an understanding of how the resultant beliefs are sustained and to account for the patterns of relevance that connect experiences to some beliefs rather than others. Although this view incorporates some of the insights of empiricism it entails that no belief falls outside the sociologist's purview. There is a social component in all knowledge.

D. Bloor, Knowledge and Social Imagery 28 (1976).

79. See also, L. Wittgenstein, supra note 73, § 204 ("Giving grounds, however, jus-

of existing practice for a justification as to how to "go on" with the practice.[80] Unlike the layman, "the lawyer's experience . . . [coupled with] the trained, tradition-determined manner of handling the material" (id.) is the ground of legal justification.

We get a clearer sense of Llewellyn's conception of the role of training in constituting a practice if we compare it not to what goes on in the constitution of the scientific community,[81] but in what the Germans call "*Bildung*" or culture. The concept of *Bildung* has close affinities with the notion of taste in aesthetics.[82] The qualities that enable an individual to appreciate the beauty of a painting are there not so much as the result of training but of cultivation. Sensibility, the knack of being able to separate the wheat from the chaff in art, is not learned but imparted.[83] And one learns how to do this, that is one learns what constitutes good legal argument, by engaging in legal argument. As J.B. White puts it so well, "[t]o learn law, one must do law."[84]

It is in the course of the "doing" of law that *Bildung* is at work. The reference of the term means more than simply imparting skills, for *Bildung* results in a fashioning, which

> describes more the result of the process of becoming than the process itself. The transition is especially clear here because the result of Bildung is not achieved in the manner of a technical construction, but grows out of an inner process of formation and cultivation, and therefore constantly remains in a state of continual Bildung. It is not accidental that in this respect the word Bildung resembles the Greek word physis. Like nature, Bildung has no goals outside itself. . . . In having no goals outside itself, the concept of Bildung transcends that of the mere cultivation of given talents, from which concept it is derived. The cultivation of a talent is the development of something that is given, so that practicing and cultivating it is a mere means to an end. Thus the educational content of a grammar book is simply a means and not itself an end. Assim-

tifying the evidence, comes to an end;—but at the end it is not certain propositions striking us immediately as true, i.e., it is not a kind of *seeing* on our part; it is our *acting*, which lies at the bottom of the language-game.").

80. See also L. Wittgenstein, supra note 6, § 154 ("If there has to be anything 'behind the utterance of the formula' it is *particular circumstances*, which justify me in saying I can go on—when the formula occurs to me.").

81. See generally, B. Latour & S. Woolgar, Laboratory Life: The Construction of Scientific Facts (1986) (analyzing the role of scientific practice in the construction of scientific "facts").

82. See I. Kant, The Critique of Judgment § 60 (W. Pluhar trans. 1987) ("It seems that for all fine art, insofar as we aim at its highest degree of perfection, the propaedeutic does not consist in [following] precepts but in cultivating our mental powers by exposing ourselves beforehand to what we call *humaniora*. . . .").

83. In this regard, law and virtue are the same. See Eisele, Must Virtue be Taught?, 37 J. Legal Educ. 495 (1987).

84. J. White, Heracles' Bow: Essays on the Rhetoric and Poetics of the Law 53 (1985).

> ilating it simply improves one's linguistic ability. In Bildung, by contrast, that by which and through which one is formed becomes completely one's own.[85]

To envision legal training along the lines of *Bildung* enables us to approach the role of tradition in the formation and transformation of legal practice in ways which might otherwise be precluded. Tradition is the ground for training and practice. Like other historicists, Llewellyn believes that it is tradition that frames our intuitions regarding the application of existing rules to new circumstances. Understanding, Llewellyn tells us, is "immanent" to existing legal practice (p. 74 n.1). That is, the practitioner's[86] understanding of the practice cannot be separated from the categories she uses to make sense of the enterprise. For example, in order to understand the meaning of the "merchant" exception to the Statute of Frauds in Section 2-201(2) of the U.C.C., one needs to grasp the point of the rule itself.[87] Outside the contexts within which the rule is "at home" or has a use, the rule (and its exception) can have no meaning.[88]

Understanding that is "*sociologically* immanent" (id.) is directed at grasping the meaning of legal categories from within lived experience. It is within this lived experience that the "sociologically immanent *and predictable* capacity of linguistic symbols or legal rules [is forced] to expand" (p. 77 n.1). Expansion occurs when a judge "observes a new fact situation *and is sensitive to its real-life meaning* . . . the new illuminates and *at the same time changes* the old" (p. 79).[89] What is it that enables this adjustment of category to a (new) experience? It is none other than judicial intuition which "lies in the judge's subconsciously using his prior experience and his sensitivity to the meaning of new fact situations" (id.). Thus, it is through tradition that the question posed in a given case is understood. Like the questions, the answers come from tradition coupled with sensitivity to the facts and the relationship of the legal categories to the facts. Legal concepts lie not in the realm of the theoretical but are instead the product of a pragmatic understanding. As tradition-bound, historical conceptions are forced to cohere with new factual contexts, they must of necessity be reformulated: correct results will often occur where existing rules are "reinterpreted with the maximum insight into evolving social norms . . . ." (p. 84). It is the case method that guarantees the orderly character of this evolution.

85. H. Gadamer, supra note 48, at 11.

86. By "practitioner" I mean any legal actor, be she judge, lawyer or academic.

87. This example is discussed by Llewellyn in Uniform Revised Sales Act, § 7, comment illustration 2 (Proposed Final Draft No. 1, 1944), reprinted in II Uniform Commercial Code Drafts 104–05 (1984) (compiled by E. Kelly).

88. See Patterson, supra note 18, at 374–75.

89. Gadamer makes precisely the same point with his argument that application is a necessary component of understanding. See H. Gadamer, supra note 48, at 311.

III. Legal Certainty

Llewellyn's conception of the relationship between language, practice and tradition reaches a synthesis in his approach to the problem of legal certainty. It has been the burden of legal theory since the demise of formalism to seek a foundation for legal argument.[90] This craving after certainty manifests itself in current parlance as the search for "objectivity," for it is with an objective criterion that claims for the autonomy of law and legal method can be sustained. What hangs in the balance, of course, is the idea of law as a neutral forum for the adjudication of contested claims. In short, the question is whether law is just another name for politics.[91]

In answering this question, Llewellyn takes a very pragmatic stance. In fact, he rejects the question altogether because he does not share the presuppositions that make the question possible. The question presumes a well-defined dichotomy between familiar categories: first, "politics" which, following Professor Unger, we might define as arguments over "the basic conditions of social existence,"[92] and second, law or legal method, which can generate answers to legal questions in a deductive, algorithmic or mechanical[93] fashion. While often read to be on the "radical" side of this version of the objectivism-relativism dichotomy, Llewellyn's position is much more sophisticated than either side of the divide. Of the possibility of objectivity in hard cases, he says that "this kind of legal certainty has never existed and never will exist" (p. 73). On the other hand, Llewellyn does say that "the law is predictable to a truly amazing degree, and for that reason the law is (descriptively) certain" (p. 76–77).

Can these two claims be reconciled? We are helped in answering this question by expanding our earlier consideration of Wittgenstein's remarks on what it means to "follow a rule." Much in Wittgenstein's remarks in this connection is negative: that is, he spends a fair amount of time telling us what following a rule does *not* consist in. Possible candidates that are now all too familiar are rejected one after the other:

---

90. See R. Unger, Knowledge and Politics 94 (1975) ("The history of modern jurisprudence may be characterized as a continuing attempt to find an adequate alternative to formalism as a basis for legal justice.").

91. See Bobbitt, Is Law Politics? (Book Review), 41 Stan. L. Rev. 1233 (1989).

92. "Formalism . . . is a commitment to, and therefore also a belief in the possibility of, a method of legal justification that contrasts with open-ended disputes about the basic terms of social life, disputes that people call ideological, philosophical, or visionary." R. Unger, supra note 36, at 1.

93. For a theory to generate answers, it must be mechanical, yet no mechanical theory can render an adequate account of our experience of legitimate moral choice. We cannot even escape the dilemma by trying to make some of our choices (the "core") mechanical and some (the "periphery") open-ended: *No* mechanical choices appear to be unequivocally valid.

Singer, The Player and the Cards: Nihilism and Legal Theory, 94 Yale L.J. 1, 61 (1984).

a mental process, a formula, interpretations, rails instead of a rule.[94] Why do none of these satisfy the criterion for what it means to "follow" a rule? What is missing?

Wittgenstein's answer is that what is missing is the correct *form* of explanation. Explanations of the connection between a rule and its applications take one of two forms: causal or normative. Causal explanations explain *why* one responds to a rule as one does.[95] An explanation of the form "his breaking the record for the 100 yard dash was drug induced" is a claim that calls for scientific or experimental validation.[96] Normative explanations of what a rule requires (e.g., the correct start of a race) explain not *why* a response occurs but what it is that makes the response correct. "Correctness" is a function of criteria (i.e., the proper performance of the activity in question). What the rule requires is found not in that which causes one to go one way rather than another, for one can go on or follow the rule either correctly or incorrectly. In short, "correctness" in rule application is a matter of reasons and not causes. Mistaking a causal explanation for a normative one confuses empirical truth with grammatical truth.[97]

So whence come the criteria for determining whether one has followed a rule correctly? Wittgenstein's answer is as simple as it is controversial:[98] the criteria come from the community that employs the rule. Rules themselves show us nothing, for they are just a form of words. Likewise, interpretations of rules cannot be the ground of appeal, for "[i]nterpretations by themselves do not determine meaning."[99] It is custom, usage,[100] way of acting or "practice"[101] that determines what counts as "following the rule." The normativity in rule-following is a function *not* of the rule but of the group. The group—those that use the rule—determines what is "correct" and "incorrect." In other words, there is no court of appeals beyond the practice.

---

94. See L. Wittgenstein, supra note 6, § 154 (mental process); id. § 189 (formula); id. § 198 (interpretations); id. § 218 (rails).

95. If one is a behaviorist, for example, one will say that the response to a Rule is a response to a stimulus. A sociological explanation could be an appeal to the political values of the rule-follower. For example, the socio-causal explanation could be "she responded in that way because she is a liberal judge."

96. See A. Kenny, Wittgenstein 175 (1973) (distinguishing causal from normative explanation).

97. See G. Baker & P. Hacker, Wittgenstein: Rules, Grammar and Necessity, *in* 2 Analytical Commentary on the Philosophical Investigations 107 (1985) ("That a given formula does (or does not) determine a value for each argument is a statement about the type of formula; not an empirical truth about behaviour, but a truth of grammar.").

98. For a presentation of a wide range of views on the implications of Wittgenstein's remarks on rule-following, see L. Wittgenstein: To Follow a Rule (S. Holtzman & C. Leich eds. 1981).

99. L. Wittgenstein, supra note 6, § 198.

100. Id.

101. Id. § 202 ("[O]beying a rule is a practice.").

Citing Weber, and anticipating Wittgenstein, Llewellyn finds certainty not in a heaven of concepts but "in the world," the "world of 'What Is' " (p. 82).[102] This world is that of the layman, for whom "legal certainty . . . does not consist in a lawyer's ability to predict the outcome of a lawsuit or the legal consequences of some action" (id.) but in "knowing that some dealing of his will be treated—*if* matters ever came to litigation—in a manner that a reasonable man (i.e., a reasonable layman in the circumstances) might have anticipated, had *he* thought about the then-unforeseen dispute at the start" (id.). But why take *this* perspective? What is the merit in "grounding" an account of law in the perspective of nonlegal actors? In this lies the genius of Llewellyn's account of legal practice.

The great error of formalism was the belief that the meaning of legal terms such as offer, acceptance or contract, can be delineated apart from the real-life contexts[103] within which those terms are at home. Like Wittgenstein, Llewellyn saw the task of legal theory not as the specification of the grounds for the possibility of legal understanding,[104] but as a *description* of the meaning of understanding. For Llewellyn, certainty means knowing how to move within a network of linguistic relations.[105] "Understanding" means grasping the point of a real-life activity that is regulated by law.[106] But in order for law to regulate the activity, judges must make themselves cognizant of the point of the activity and, thus, the role of law within it. As changes occur in the historical conditions within which real-life practices are conducted, it devolves on the judge to "make the direction and degree of semantic change in a legal rule (or verbal symbol used by the rule) keep up with the corresponding change in the real-life situation" (p. 83).[107] Cer-

102. Citing M. Weber, Wirtschaft und Gesellschaft 493 (2d ed. 1925).

103. Here Wittgenstein would use the phrase "language-game" for "real-life context."

104. Such is the project of legal formalism. For a powerful defense of legal formalism, see Weinrib, Legal Formalism: On the Immanent Rationality of Law, 97 Yale L.J. 949 (1988) (the understanding of law is a matter of immanent intelligibility).

105. It also means prediction. "[L]egal certainty in the American sense . . . [is] the prediction of the outcome of a lawsuit. . . ." (p. 76). Compare H. Gadamer, supra note 48, at 329–30 ("Every lawyer and every counsel is able, in principle, to give correct advice—i.e., he can accurately predict the judge's decision on the basis of the existing laws.").

106. This dovetails with Llewellyn's claim that "where reason stops there stops the rule." K. Llewellyn, Jurisprudence: Realism in Theory and Practice 217 (1962). For a discussion of the importance of the purpose of rules in Llewellyn's jurisprudence with particular attention to the jurisprudence of the U.C.C., see Wiseman, The Limits of Vision: Karl Llewellyn and the Merchant Rules, 100 Harv. L. Rev. 465, 495–97 (1987).

107. The very lifeblood of tradition depends upon its being open to critique.

> [T]radition admits of immanent critique. Even the most unified tradition will contain inner tensions or gaps which in the face of new circumstances would yield conflicting responses or troubling indecision as to how to behave. Such situations compel tradition to reflect critically on itself and to adjust or redefine itself to resolve them, where competing reconstructive interpretations of tradi-

tainty consists in the judicial proclivity to achieve congruence between norm and fact, for "if the rule is reinterpreted with the maximum insight into evolving social norms, there is a strong possibility, even a likelihood, that the outcome will be right" (p. 84).

In this connection, we must emphasize the importance of the particular and its relationship to the case method. Rules stand to cases as universals to particulars. The art of "case law technique is the art of dealing with fluidly worded rules of law" (p. 87). Judges must resist the tendency "to let themselves be trapped by the verbal form of the borrowed concept . . . ." (p. 88). Concepts exist to the extent that they serve human purposes and goals: apart from those contexts, concepts are lifeless. Their validity is a matter not of *logic* but of sociology. The gravamen of litigation, then, is in forcing the rethinking of existing categories for the organization of experience. It is "these creative innovations and adaptions, these fact-shaped reinterpretations of legal institutions, [that] constitute the lifeblood of the law" (p. 97).

But one can accept everything Llewellyn says and still ask from whose perspective are these retoolings of legal categories valid? Llewellyn's answer is sure not to satisfy:

> [I]f the same fact situation can be analyzed by learned judges in a variety of ways, it is only a matter of chance that the analyses eventuate in the same result, *if* the legal analysis is really the decisive factor in the decision. It is hard to avoid concluding that, to a large extent, legal analysis is not a means for coming to a *conclusion*, but rather a means for *justifying*—justifying as lawyer, justifying as craftsman—a conclusion reached on other grounds (p. 55).

Well there it is. That tired Realist refrain: the law decides nothing, for it is little more than an aggregate of *ad hoc* justifications for a decision reached, as Llewellyn himself says, "on other grounds." Is this the true legacy of Realism, as some would have us believe? Does Llewellyn celebrate uncertainty in legal discourse? Not at all.[108] While often tied to the caricatured legacy of Realism as a skeptical jurisprudence, Llewellyn in no way rejects the notion that the law is certain. What he does do, however, is locate that certainty in a place few have thought to place it.

Like Wittgenstein, Llewellyn believed that we can never escape the realm of linguistic understanding. What this means for the critique of

---

> tion stimulate further critical reflection. To suppose that tradition contains no possibility for internal conflict or different future projections is to conceive of it as a fully programmed and uniformly closed system, rather than the roughly fashioned, open-structed scheme of divergent elements which we know it to be.

R. Shusterman, T.S. Eliot and the Philosophy of Criticism 161 (1988).

108. But see Sunstein, Interpreting Statutes in the Regulatory State, 103 Harv. L. Rev. 405, 452 (1989) ("Llewellyn, like many of the realists attempted to liberate legal thought from flawed structures by denying the need for structures altogether, but structures are inevitably present.").

law is that the *ground* of critique must be *internal* to legal practice itself.[109] The impossibility of transcending the (linguistic) limits of the practice and reaching a point outside the practice from which to critique it[110] leaves only those within the practice as sources—and evaluators—of criticism. From the perspective of a judge, an opinion is "authoritative" because it is a *judicial* product. Its *validity* is a function of its acceptance by the discursive community, that is, the "caste of lawyers."[111] As Brian Simpson argues, "[T]he relative value of formulated propositions of the common law depends upon the degree to which such propositions are accepted as accurate statements of received ideas or practice, and one must add the degree to which the practice is consistent with them."[112]

Conclusion

Lawyers make the law. This is certainly one of the central messages of Realism, and it is the principal focus of this early attempt on the part of Llewellyn to articulate the theoretical parameters within which this statement is best understood. Law is found and made in the same place: the practice. When all the shouts and vitriols have been exhausted we are left with what we have always had: the practice. We can neither get outside it nor can we damn it for being what it is not.

Sounding a note that is often echoed today, but not much listened to, is the role of legal academics in changing the law. Llewellyn told his German audience that it is the task of law professors "to develop *new* concepts and methods in response to changing circumstances" (p. 105). Of course, Llewellyn went on to do just that when he jettisoned a plethora of useless conceptual schemes and replaced them with the fluid structures found in the Uniform Commercial Code.[113] Perhaps Llewellyn's greatest legacy to the legal academy is his example: he showed better than anyone that theory and practice are one.

---

109. "[I]deas cannot be torn out of their context . . . the relation between idea and context is an internal one. The idea gets its sense from the role it plays in the system." P. Winch, The Idea of a Social Science and its Relation to Society 107 (1958). For criticism of the primacy of internal understanding, see Gellner, Winch's Ideas of a Social Science, *in* The Concept of Kinship 18–46 (1987).

110. Candidates include the Kantian noumenal self, clear and distinct ideas, philosophical essences, original intentions and natural kinds.

111. Simpson, The Common Law and Legal Theory, *in* Legal Theory and Common Law 20 (W. Twining ed. 1986).

112. Id. at 21.

113. For example, the notion of "title" in Sales was completely eliminated by the architecture of Article Two, and the concept of "security interest" in Article Nine replaced a motley aggregate of security devices.

[14]
Realist Semantics and Legal Theory

1. Introduction

In "Legal Theory, Legal Interpretation, and Judicial Review",[1] David O. Brink advocates a central role in legal interpretation for considerations of human purpose. He states:

> It is important to remember that the primary objects of legal interpretation – statutes, constitutional provisions, and precedents – like most objects of interpretation, are human artifacts, the products of purposeful activity. In interpreting the products of purposeful activity, we must appeal to the purposes which prompted and guided the activity whose product we are trying to understand.[2]

The view that the meaning of human activities is best discerned from the point of view of the participants in the activity is one that is shared by philosophers from both the analytic and continental traditions.[3] Like others who argue for consideration of purpose in the interpretation of law,[4] Brink recognizes that no account of the purposive nature of law as a human activity can be complete without considering problems of meaning. In jurisprudence, this recognition finds specific focus in the problem of legal indeterminacy. Given the 'open texture' of legal norms, no theory of law can be adequate without some account of how problems of contextual indeterminacy are to be resolved. Indeed, without such an account, we cannot even make sense of the notion of 'disagreement' in law.[5]

As Brink reads its history, contemporary jurisprudence has attempted to solve problems of indeterminacy with an inadequate tool, that being an empiricist semantic theory.[6] As Brink sees it, proponents of this theory make the following two claims:

> (i) the meaning of a word or phrase is the set of (identifying) properties or descriptions which speakers associate with it, and
>
> (ii) the meaning of a word determines its reference.[7]

1. David O. Brink, "Legal Theory, Legal Interpretation, and Judicial Review, (1988), 17 *Philosophy and Public Affairs* 105 [hereinafter referred to by page number alone].
2. p. 125.
3. See Hans-Georg Gadamer, *Truth and Method*, translation ed. Garrett Barden and John Cumming (New York: Crossroad, 1975): Alasdair MacIntyre, "The Intelligibility of Action", repr. in J. Margolis M. Krausz & R.M. Burian eds., *Rationality, Relativism and The Human Science* (Dordecht: Martinus Nijhoff, 1986): 63-80.
4. This theme is illustrated in the work of, for example, both H.L.A. Hart and Ronald Dworkin. See H.L.A. Hart, *The Concept of Law* (New York: Oxford University Press, 1961): 121-32. Ronald Dworkin, *Law's Empire* (Cambridge: Harvard University Press, 1986) (hereinafter LE), 54-55, 64-65, 71.
5. p. 114.
6. p. 112. H.L.A. Hart is identified as a proponent of this view. *Id.*, 113.
7. p. 113.

Brink believes that traditional empiricist semantic theory[8] is flawed.[9] The nature of the flaw can be simply stated: empiricist semantic theory fails to draw a distinction between the meaning of a term and anyone's belief about its meaning.[10] By confusing meaning with belief, so Brink argues, legal theorists who embrace traditional semantic theory cannot account for the phenomenon of conceptual disagreement nor can they illuminate the connection between meaning and reference.[11]

The inadequacies of traditional semantic theory can be avoided, so Brink argues, by a realist semantics. Following Saul Kripke[12] and Hilary Putnam,[13] Brink urges legal theorists to adopt a semantics of natural kinds,[14] whereby the meaning of general terms is determined not by anyone's beliefs about their meaning but by reference to properties in the world. As he puts it: "natural kind terms . . . are general terms which refer to properties."[15]

Brink's programme is grounded in a metaethics of moral realism.[16] As he states: "[d]etermination of the meaning and reference of legal standards will often require reliance on theoretical considerations [the metaethics of moral realism] about the real nature of the referents of language in the law . . . ."[17] This is potentially a powerful claim if true, for it means that disputes over the meaning of general legal terms are irresolvable by traditional legal methods, which are clearly institutional.[18]

Despite the appeal of the argument, I think legal theorists would do well to avoid Brink's call to develop a general program of interpretation grounded in a realist semantics.[19] The meaning and reference of legal terms is not reducible to a natural kinds analysis because law is an institutional and not a scientific practice. Contrary to Brink's claims for the felicity of a natural kinds analysis, the meaning of general legal terms cannot be divorced from the beliefs of institutional participants in legal discourse nor can the meaning of general

---

8. Brink describes two versions of traditional semantic theory. He states the following:

   An individualistic theory makes the meaning of a word depend upon the criteria which *the speaker* associates with the word, while the conventionalistic theory makes the meaning of the word depend upon the criteria with which the word is *conventionally* associated or with which it is associated by a *majority*. p. 113.

9. As he describes it, I think he is right. But the strength of Brink's critique of the theory he identifies as 'traditional' depends upon the degree to which it is shared by linguistic philosophers as a whole. I don't believe the theory Brink denominates 'traditional' is the sort of theory advocated by, for example, Wittgenstein (Kripke's claims to the contrary notwithstanding).

   Therefore, I believe that the claims made against the theory Brink labels 'traditional' leave untouched positions that challenge the claims he makes for a realist semantics. Brink admits as much in his statement that his "discussion of these semantic issues will, of necessity, ride roughshod over many interesting details". p. 113.

   Given the focus of this critique of Brink's argument, I will not here defend a traditional theory that avoids the criticisms Brink advances. I have done that elsewhere. See Dennis M. Patterson, "Interpretation in Law: Toward a Reconstruction of the Current Debate," (1984), 29 *Villanova Law Review* 671; Dennis M. Patterson, "Wittgenstein and the Code: A Theory of Good Faith Performance and Enforcement Under Article Nine of the Uniform Commercial Code", (1988), 137 *University of Pennsylvania Law Review* 335. The cogency of my remarks on the semantic theory advanced by Brink do not depend on any alternative semantic theory I may hold.

10. pp. 117, 118, 121. Brink argues that legal theorists give up the claim of traditional semantic theory that meaning determines reference and follow a realist semantics whereby reference determines a meaning. *Ibid.*, 117.
11. p. 113.
12. See Saul Kripke, *Naming and Necessity* (Cambridge: Harvard University Press, 1980).
13. Hilary Putnam, "Meaning and Reference, repr. in *Naming, Necessity, and Natural Kinds*, ed. S. Schwartz (Ithaca: Cornell University Press, 1977), and "The Meaning of 'Meaning,'" repr. in Hilary Putnam, *Mind, Language and Reality* (New York: Cambridge University Press, 1975). It is not entirely clear that Putnam can still be classified as a realist. See Ian Hacking, *Representing and Intervening: Introductory Topics in the Philosophy of Natural Science* (New York: Cambridge University Press, 1983), 95-96.
14. p. 118.
15. p. 120.
16. Brink's metaethical program does not figure directly in his arguments for the assimilation of general legal terms into a natural kinds analysis. The arguments in support of a metaethics of moral realism are advanced in David O. Brink, *Moral Realism and The Foundation of Ethics* (New York: Cambridge University Press, 1989).
17. p. 121.
18. These include appeals to legislative intent, common law principles, and the like. It would also rule out methodological proposals such as Dworkin's model of "constructive interpretation" (LE, 52-53).
19. pp. 147-148.

legal terms be discerned without reference to the beliefs and purposes embodied in legal institutions.

2. Not All General Terms are Natural Kind Terms

Brink asserts that the realist semantics of Kripke and Putnam advance "claims for the semantics of both proper names and general terms, such as natural kind terms."[20] As Brink reads Kripke and Putnam, there is no *in principle* distinction between natural kinds and artificial kinds. As with scientific terms, the meaning and reference of legal terms "is given by the way the world is."[21] Like 'atom,' 'neutrino,' and 'mass,' "'[f]air' and 'cruel' are natural kind terms . . . they are general terms which refer to properties."[22] Therefore, the meaning of, say, constitutional terms is not 'created,' it is discovered.[23]

The meaning of a natural kind term is fixed in the following way; "the substance is defined as the kind instantiated by (almost all of) a given sample. . . . the identity fixes a reference: it therefore is *a priori*."[24] As mentioned previously, Brink does not limit his realism to the domain of science or natural (as opposed to artificial) kinds. His semantic realism is presented in the form of a general argument for the meaning of all general terms.

To demonstrate the shortcomings of Brink's wide-ranging claims for realism, it is not necessary that one prove false the claim of Kripke and Putnam that there are natural kinds: it is only necessary to show that not *all* general terms refer in the way Kripke and Putnam claim that natural kind terms refer.[25]

Consider the meaning of the general legal term 'negotiable instrument.' This term is central to the conventions of drawing, assigning, and paying what are ordinarily referred to as 'checks.'[26] What counts as a check, the legal rights and obligations of the parties to a check, and the manner by which checks are processed for collection are all known by virtue of human conventions. If there were no human beings, or no interest in a system of payment by means other than gold and silver, there would be no negotiable instruments.

Like the vast majority of general legal terms, 'negotiable instrument' is an artifact, a creature of convention. The meaning of 'negotiable instrument' is not "given by the way the world is";[27] there is no "real nature"[28] of a negotiable instrument. We do not "discover"[29] the meaning of 'negotiable instrument' by discerning objects in the world having rigidly designated natural properties. It is only in and through the institutional conventions of commerce that 'negotiable instrument' has its meaning. To know the meaning of this general legal term, one must consult the conventions for its use, for it is solely against that background that participants in legal discourse frame interpretive arguments. Those arguments are shaped through and through by institutional conventions that are constitutive of the discursive practice of law.

20. p. 118. Brink also states that "Kripke and Putnam have defended these semantic claims for the semantics of general terms, such as natural kind terms." *Id.*, 120.
21. p. 123.
22. p. 120.
23. p. 123.
24. Saul Kripke, *supra*, note 12 at 136.
25. For a fuller demonstration of this claim, see T.E. Wilkerson, "Natural Kinds", (1988), 63 *Philosophy* 29-42.
26. The rules governing negotiable instruments are found in Articles Three and Four of the Uniform Commercial Code (hereafter U.C.C.).
27. p. 123.
28. p. 121.
29. p. 123.

3. Natural Kinds and Statutory Intent

I shall maintain my neutrality on the question of the possible existence of natural kinds, for that neutrality is convenient to the argument I wish to advance here.

One of Brink's central claims about interpretation is that the meaning and reference of legal terms is a function of the way the world is and is not dependent upon the beliefs of anyone.[30] When this claim is brought to bear on the question of how far, and to what extent, legislative purpose determines statutory meaning, the results are problematic.

According to traditional semantic theory, close attention must be paid to the intentions of constitutional or statutory framers[31] because "their intentions place constraints upon constitutional interpretation independently of the plausibility of the framer's moral or political beliefs."[32] But proponents of traditional semantic theory fail to distinguish between specific and abstract intent. An abstract intent takes the form of a policy or principle that is the impetus for particular legislation.[33] Specific intent reduces the extension of abstract intent to "certain actions and not others."[34]

Brink claims that specific intent is less important than proponents of traditional semantic theory take it to be.[35] The nub of his argument is that the meaning of statutory terms should not be tied to the intentions of their authors but is properly determined by our best current theory of the meaning of those terms.

Brink's example is a statute passed in 1945 imposing "strict standards of due care"[36] in the handling of toxic substances. If a court is today to decide a case under the statute involving a substance that, according to the best available theory in 1945, would not be considered toxic, is the court to decide the case on the basis of the best theory in 1945 or today's best theory? According to Brink, if one follows the traditional semantic theory, the court must decide the issue on the basis of the best theory in 1945.[37] On a realist semantics, the court's obligation is to decide the question of toxicity relative to our current best theory of the matter.

A realist semantics runs into trouble when we alter the facts of the hypothetical. Consider a statute written in 1945 that prohibited all fishing within fifty miles of shore. Assume that at the time the statute was promulgated, Congress mistakenly believed that whales and dolphins were fish. In the preamble to the text of the statute Congress announced that the statute was passed to prevent the extinction of all forms of fish "including whales and dolphins." Our best current theory shows that whales and dolphins are not fish but mammals. Is it now the case that the clear meaning of the statute is to be ignored because Congress mistakenly classified whales and dolphins as fish?

30. p. 123. ("The meaning and reference of our terms is given by the way the world is ...."); p. 117 ("Beliefs do not determine reference.")
31. Brink explicitly rejects a 'global' distinction between constitutional and statutory interpretation. See p. 119, n. 20.
32. p. 123.
33. p. 122. An example would be the U.C.C.'s purpose to simplify, clarify, and modernize the law governing commercial transactions. See U.C.C. 1-102(2)(a).
34. To continue with the U.C.C., an example of a specific intention is the drafters' particular desire to repeal the common law that firm offers are not enforceable without consideration. See U.C.C. 2-205 (firm offers need not be supported by consideration).
35. p. 122. ("Proponents [of traditional semantic theory] ... insist that the correct interpretation of any legal provision must be guided by, or at least violate, the framers' (specific) intentions.")
36. p. 122.
37. I must confess that the cogency of this claim escapes me, but I will not pursue the matter here. For a powerful argument to the effect that statutory meaning is a function of changing social conditions, see William N. Eskridge, Jr., "Dynamic Statutory Interpretation," (1987), 136 *University of Pennsylvania Law Review* 1479.

The problem for a realist semantics is plain: ignoring Congress' 'mistake' in classifying animals comes at the price of direct frustration of Congress' power to regulate 'fishing.' Obviously, Congress intended to include whales and dolphins within the purview of the statute and did so on the basis of a mistaken theory of classification. But if the court applies the statute to preclude the fishing of whales and dolphins, it can only do so on the basis of an inadequate semantic theory (the traditional theory). The meaning of 'fish' is not determined "by the way the world is":[38] it is determined on the basis of the way Congress then thought the world was. In other words, it is the *belief* of Congress, not natural kind predicates, that determines the interpretive obligations of the court.

4. Conclusion

In this article I have argued for two claims. The first is that Brink's claim that all general terms are natural kind terms cannot be sustained. Institutional practices such as law are replete with general terms the meaning of which can only be discerned by investigation of the beliefs and attitudes of participants in the practice.

My second claim is that a realist semantics is itself not free from difficulty when we are invited to adopt it as an exclusive semantic theory for legal interpretation. It is frequently the case that the meaning of a statute in a present context cannot be determined by direct consultation of the specific intentions of the drafters of a statute. But it is sometimes the case that to do otherwise would be to elide the distinction between legislation and adjudication. Disregard of the limitations of a realist semantics leads to just such undesirable outcomes.

38. p. 123.

[15]
Interpretation in Law: Toward a Reconstruction of the Current Debate

> Only if we implicitly accept some version of Cartesianism does the exclusive disjunction of objectivism or relativism become intelligible.[1]

I. INTRODUCTION

RECENT SCHOLARSHIP on interpretive problems in law has evidenced a struggle between two competing conceptions of linguistic meaning.[2] Those arguing for the possibility of "objective" interpretation of juridical concepts see their task as saving law from the clutches of nihilism. Specifically, theorists of objectivity maintain that an interpreter of legal materials is not free to fashion meaning out of whole cloth, but is constrained by interpretive rules constitutive of the interpretive process. Those discounting the possibility of objective interpretation point to the radical indeterminancy of legal texts; for them the interpretation of legal concepts is little more than the imposition of power under the guise of "neutral interpretation."

I shall argue that the dichotomy between objective and subjective interpretation of legal texts is a false one. If the analysis of interpretive problems in law is to advance, we must jettison our preoccupation with labels borrowed from the natural sciences[3] and begin anew the search for meaning. In reconstructing the terms of the current debate, I endeavor to show how the objective/subjective

---

† Partner, Loyd, Bumgardner, Field, Patterson & Kennedy, Brunswick, Maine. B.A., 1976, M.A., 1978, J.D., 1980, Ph.D. 1980, State University of New York at Buffalo. I wish to thank John R. Troll, Esq. for his critique of earlier drafts of this article and for his continuing support of the analysis of ideas with which he disagrees.

1. R. BERNSTEIN, BEYOND OBJECTIVISM AND RELATIVISM: SCIENCE, HERMENEUTICS, AND PRAXIS 19 (1983).

2. *See generally Law as Literature*, 60 TEX. L. REV. 1 (1982). *See also* Dworkin, *My Reply to Stanley Fish (and Walter Benn Michaels): Please Don't Talk About Objectivity Anymore*, in THE POLITICS OF INTERPRETATION 287-313 (W. Mitchell ed. 1982, 1983); Dworkin, *Law as Interpretation*, 9 CRITICAL INQUIRY 169 (1982); Fish, *Wrong Again*, 62 TEX. L. REV. 299 (1983); Fish, *Working on the Chain Gang: Interpretation in Law and Literature*, 9 CRITICAL INQUIRY 201 (1982); McIntosh, *Legal Hermeneutics: A Philosophical Critique*, 35 OKLA. L. REV. 1 (1982).

3. For an insightful analysis of the problem of systematic unpredictability in human affairs, see generally A. MACINTYRE, AFTER VIRTUE: A STUDY IN MORAL THEORY 84-102 (1982).

dichotomy can be avoided and to reorder the priorities of the discourse on meaning. After all, meaning is the central focus of current concerns; that is as it should be. But we must not lose sight of the fact that the investigation of meaning in law is, at bottom, a *descriptive* one. That is, what we are concerned with is the means by which the language of the law comes to have significance for those who use it. This concern, in my view, is best addressed by a theory that describes how we in fact employ words in legal contexts and how those words come to have significance for us as participants in a discourse. In this way we will come to see not only that the objective/subjective dichotomy is unnecessary, but further that it impedes our ability to render intelligible the very idea of legal discourse.

The first of two positions currently taken to be exhaustive of the realm of interpretive choice, the objectivist position,[4] is best expressed by Professor Owen Fiss, who has been a staunch critic of what he describes as "the new nihilism."[5] As he sees it, the views of the new nihilists undermine the activity of adjudication by denying, *a priori*, the possibility of objective interpretation in law.[6] Professor Fiss sets forth an interpretive theory designed to counter the nihilists' argument that interpreters of legal texts are given, by virtue of the nature of language, absolute interpretive freedom to "create" the meaning of a legal text. The gravamen of Professor Fiss' argument is that objective interpretation of legal norms is possible, but only within an "interpretive community."[7] It is by virtue of membership in such a community and allegiance to its interpretive principles, that a judge

4. For discussions of one version of objectivism, that of interpretivism, see generally Bennett, *Objectivity in Constitutional Law*, 132 U. PA. L. REV. 445 (1983); *Judicial Review And The Constitution — The Text And Beyond*, 8 U. DAYTON L. REV. 1 (1983). *See also* J. ELY, DEMOCRACY AND DISTRUST (1980); Berger, *Mark Tushnet's Critique of Interpretivism*, 51 GEO. WASH. L. REV. 532 (1983); Brest, *The Misconceived Quest For The Original Understanding*, 60 B.U.L. REV. 204 (1980); Schauer, *An Essay on Constitutional Language*, 29 U.C.L.A. L. REV. 797 (1982); Tushnet, *Following the Rules Laid Down: A Critique of Interpretivism and Neutral Principles*, 96 HARV. L. REV. 781 (1983).

Gary Jacobsohn has recently advanced a "middle position" between strict interpretivism and what he terms "free-wheeling judicial review." Briefly, his contention is that the framers' conception of the constitution as a "document" included ideas of "natural justice," which ideas are part of "higher law" reflected in the document. *See* Jacobsohn, *E.T.: The Extra-Textual in Constitutional Interpretation*, 1 CONST. COMM. 21 (1984).

5. *See* Fiss, *Objectivity and Interpretation*, 34 STAN. L. REV. 739 (1982).

6. *Id.* at 742.

7. *Id.* at 745. Fiss' conception of objectivity is somewhat different than what the bare semantic sense of the concept implies. While imparting a notion of impersonality, the idea of objectivity need not require the presence of an interpretive standard wholly external to a judge. All that is connoted is that interpretation is an act that takes place under certain constraints. *See* text accompanying notes 26-33 *infra*.

can render decisions faithful to the ideal of the rule of law.[8]

Critics of the objectivist approach regard the lack of any "essential characteristics" in legal texts as proof positive of the futility of the objectivist line of thought.[9] Since legal concepts lack any "intelligible essence,"[10] intersubjective verification of their meaning is impossible. Indeed, to the subjectivist,[11] the ideal of judicial neutrality is an unattainable goal simply by virtue of the linguistic indeterminancy of the legal text. In short, law is power masquerading as neutral decisionmaking.[12]

In this article I do not purport to resolve all the issues raised by commentators on the interpretive strategy known as "interpretivism" or "originalism." Rather, I address the limited question of how, if at all, legal discourse is free from ideological construct. However, I do hope to add a dimension to the debate that has been conspicuously absent: the perspective of the philosophy of language. As I see it, the

8. *See* Fiss, *supra* note 5, at 744-47.

9. *See, e.g.*, Levinson, *Law as Literature*, 60 TEX. L. REV. 373, 385 (1982).

10. The phrase was first used by Roberto Unger, who defined it in this way: "The theory of intelligible essences states that there are a limited number of classes of things in the world, that each thing has characteristics that determine the class to which it belongs, and that these characteristics can be known directly by the mind." R. UNGER, KNOWLEDGE AND POLITICS 79 (1975).

11. Levinson's interpretive pluralism is but one strand of the subjectivism identified by Fiss. The dominant movement is that of Deconstruction, "which expands the idea of text to embrace all the world and at the same time proclaims the freedom of the interpreter." Fiss, *supra* note 5, at 741. The doyen of Deconstruction is the French philosopher, Jacques Derrida. An excellent introduction to the thought of Derrida is found in Garver, *Preface* to J. DERRIDA, SPEECH AND PHENOMENA at ix (1973). For a basic introduction to Deconstruction and the New Criticism school of literary thought, see C. NORRIS, THE DECONSTRUCTIVE TURN: ESSAYS IN THE RHETORIC OF PHILOSOPHY (1983). *See also* J. CULLER, ON DECONSTRUCTION: THEORY AND CRITICISM AFTER STRUCTURALISM (1982); C. NORRIS, DECONSTRUCTION: THEORY AND PRACTICE (1982). A recent sympathetic treatment of Deconstruction from an analytic point of view is found in Fuller, *A French Science (With English Subtitles)*, 7 PHIL. & LIT. 1 (1983). *But see* Searle, *The Word Turned Upside Down*, N.Y. REV. BOOKS, Oct. 27, 1983, at 74-79 (reviewing J. CULLER, *supra*).

12. Describing Friedrich Nietzsche as the "patron saint of all strong textualists," Levinson ascribes to him the view that it is not the text that exerts power over the interpreter, but just the opposite: all interpretation is, to use Nietzsche's phrase, "will-to-power." Levinson, *supra* note 9, at 381-83.

Neitzsche's own writings suggest that his views on language are far different from the irrationalist reading given them by Levinson. In fact, Nietzsche himself suggests that we are everywhere constrained by language: "*We cease to think when we refuse to do so under the constraint of language*; we barely reach the doubt that sees this limitation as limitation. Rational thought is interpretation according to a scheme we cannot throw off." F. NIETZSCHE, THE WILL TO POWER 283 (W. Kaufmann & R. Hollingdale trans., W. Kaufmann ed. 1967) (emphasis in original).

An excellent treatment of Nietzsche's remarks on language in the context of the will-to-power is found in B. MAGNUS, NIETZSCHE'S EXISTENTIAL IMPERATIVE 30-32 (1978). For a similar view, see R. HAYMAN, NIETZSCHE 162-65 (1980).

merits of interpretivism as a hermeneutic strategy cannot be assessed without taking a position on linguistic meaning. Arguments such as those over whether the values of the framers are ours, or should be ours, cannot even begin until those values are reasonably accessible. This problem of accessibility is overtly linguistic and hermeneutic in nature.

I will first describe the nature and terms of the argument between the rival camps of nihilism and objectivism, and then turn to the later work of the linguistic philosopher Ludwig Wittgenstein as the source of a philosophical position on meaning that undercuts the dichotomy of objectivism and subjectivism. After confronting a possible objection to the weight and importance of Wittgensteinian theory in meeting the claims of nihilism, I conclude with some observations on the limits of linguistic theory as a heuristic tool in solving the riddles of legal theory.

II. THE TERMS OF THE CURRENT DEBATE

Professor Fiss points to Professor Sanford Levinson as one who avows the new nihilism.[13] In a recent article, Professor Levinson proferred the view that "truthful" or "correct" interpretation of authoritative texts is not possible for, at best, an interpreter of textually situated legal norms "simply beats the text into a shape which will serve his own purpose."[14] The craft of interpretation, Professor Levinson instructs us, is in no real sense an intersubjective enterprise, for there exists "a genuine plurality of ways of seeing the world,"[15] each of which is no more "correct" or "true" than another.[16]

To put the matter formally, Professor Levinson's argument is that because there is no inner essence of a legal (or literary) text capable of public disclosure by a reader/interpreter, then "anything is permitted."[17] Further, "what eventually gets construed as the correct

13. Fiss, *supra* note 5, at 740 n.3. Professor Fiss locates Paul Brest in the nihilist camp, in addition to Levinson. *Id. See* Brest, *The Fundamental Rights Controversy: The Essential Contradictions of Normative Constitutional Scholarship*, 90 YALE L.J. 1063 (1981). For Brest's response to Fiss' arguments for objectivity in law, see Brest, *Interpretation and Interest*, 34 STAN. L. REV. 765 (1982).

14. Levinson, *supra* note 9, at 385 (quoting R. RORTY, *Nineteenth Century Idealism and Twentieth-Century Textualism*, in CONSEQUENCES OF PRAGMATISM 151 (1982)). The initial focus of Levinson's remarks is on the interpretation of constitutional norms, but he in no way intimates that his view is limited to this particular doctrinal area, and I see no reason for reading him as so limiting the scope of his argument.

15. Levinson, *supra* note 9, at 386.

16. *Id.*

17. *Id.* at 388. Definitionally, "inner essence" is synonymous with "intelligible essence."

interpretation in any given instance is a function merely of the institutional fiat or 'coerciveness' of the interpreter."[18]

Professor Fiss will have no part of Professor Levinson's textualist nightmare. Fiss' criticism of the new nihilists is so far-reaching that he accuses them of having "turned their backs on adjudication [and] begun a romance with politics."[19] Despite the stinging tone of his characterization, Professor Fiss does concede a basic premise of the nihilists: adjudication is by no means a mechanical process and does, by its nature, reflect the "freedom" of the interpreter.[20] However, Professor Fiss insists that we can have subjectivity without inexorably committing ourselves to Professor Levinson's brand of interpretive pluralism.

Fiss' argument for "bounded objectivity"[21] in legal interpreta-

18. Graff, *"Keep off The Grass," "Drop Dead," and Other Indeterminancies: A Response to Sanford Levinson*, 60 TEX. L. REV. 406 (1982) (citing Levinson, *supra* note 9, at 386). In theory, no reason exists for limiting Levinson's argument to language alone. In fact, much in modern social thought centers on the problem of essences, linguistic or otherwise. In his magesterial *Knowledge and Politics*, Roberto Unger identifies the problem of intelligible essences as central to liberal thought. R. UNGER, *supra* note 10, at 79-81. In the realm of moral values, the lack of intelligible essences renders all values subjective; in every sense, choice is arbitrary.

Facts are no less immune than values to the deleterious effects of the absence of essence. As Unger puts the matter,

> Because facts have no intrinsic identity, everything depends on the names we give them. The conventions of meaning rather than any perceived quality of 'tableness' will determine whether an object is to count as a table. In the same way, convention rather than nature will dictate whether a particular bargain is to be treated as contract.

Id. at 80.

Not surprisingly, the abandonment of the doctrine of intelligible essences leads to the fetishization of language; Unger comments that language is then worshipped as "the demiurge of the world." *Id.*

The turmoil that ensues from the rejection of any sort of recognizable objectivity all but destroys the principal element of legalism: the classification of facts under legal rules. Without intelligible essences, Unger states, there exist "no obvious criteria for defining general categories of acts and persons when we make the rules . . . . Nor are there clear standards by which to classify the particular instances under rules when we come to the stage of applying the rules we have made." *Id.* Hence law is power, for the power to name a thing is the power to decide what it is. Lacking objective standards for classification, judges are vested with unbridled power to develop their own normative metaphysics and, most importantly, to impose their private vision on litigants.

19. Fiss, *supra* note 5, at 740.

20. Of course, the extent of this freedom is the gravamen of the debate.

21. The concept of bounded objectivity "is suggested by the idea of the hermeneutic circle, which denotes the parameters within which an interpretation achieves its validity and is based on the assumption that, at some point, an interpretation must make an intuitive appeal to common understandings." Fiss, *supra* note 5, at 745 n.12. *See also* D. HOY, THE CRITICAL CIRCLE: LITERATURE, HISTORY AND PHILOSOPHICAL HERMENEUTICS (1978); Taylor, *Interpretation and the Sciences of Man*, 25 REV. METAPHYSICS 3, 6-13(1971). *See generally* H. GADAMER, TRUTH AND METHOD (1975). In similar vein, Wittgenstein remarks, "Justification by experience comes to

tion is made by way of contrast with the interpretation of literary texts.[22] A literary critic who casts about for authority and support for an interpretation of the meaning of a text may well find an alliance only with those who share the same interpretive premises (e.g., psychoanalysis, Marxism or historicism). Being a member of an interpretive literary community means that one is committed to a set of underlying premises through which the meaning of texts is disclosed. In a real sense, texts are "out there" waiting to have their meaning distilled by a set of assumptions which the interpreter and others sharing like views have validated by agreement. Of course, where one is always free to abandon one set of premises for another, the literary community will have no hold over its members, save a continuing belief in the efficacy of its premises. Thus, interpretations of texts are "true" or "correct" only within each interpretive community. Correlatively, the most that can be said of another community's interpretive work by way of criticism is that the premises taken as basic are misapplied, or that a given interpretation is internally inconsistent. With no common ground from which to speak, literary critics can only talk to "their own kind."[23]

---

an end. If it did not it would not be justification." L. WITTGENSTEIN, PHILOSOPHICAL INVESTIGATIONS § 485 (G. Anscombe trans. 1958).

Ronald Beiner has recently argued, following Gadamer, that disputants must necessarily "share" a concept before disputing the criteria for its application. "Even divergent judgments of the most deep-seated and fundamental kind are rooted in some relation of community, otherwise one would lack the concepts with which to disagree." R. BEINER, POLITICAL JUDGMENT 141 (1983). *See also* T. SEUNG, STRUCTURALISM AND HERMENEUTICS 210-12 (1982). *See generally* R. BERNSTEIN, *supra* note 1.

22. Fiss, *supra* note 5, at 745-46. For a recent survey of the treatment given the idea of an "autonomous text" by the New Criticism school of literary thought, see T. SEUNG, SEMIOTICS AND THEMATICS IN HERMENEUTICS 1-16 (1982). An excellent bibliography of works by, among others, the New Criticism school is found in READER-RESPONSE CRITICISM: FROM FORMALISM TO POST-STRUCTURALISM 233-72 (J. Tompkins ed. 1980).

23. For a similar view of the current state of literary criticism, see Crews, *Criticism Without Constraint*, COMMENTARY, Jan. 1982, at 65. *See also* T. SEUNG, *supra* note 21, at 183-212.

The tendency of much contemporary literary criticism to embrace nihilism has not gone uncriticized. *See, e.g.*, T. EAGLETON, LITERARY THEORY (1983).

> The claim that we can make a literary text mean whatever we like is in one sense quite justified. What after all is there to stop us? There is literally no end to the number of contexts we might invent for its words in order to make them signify differently. In another sense, the idea is a simple fantasy bred in the minds of those who have spent too long in the classroom. For such texts belong to language as a whole, have intricate relations to other linguistic practices, however much they might also subvert and violate them; and language is not in fact something we are free to do what we like with. If I cannot read the word "nightingale" without imagining how blissful it would be to retreat from urban society to the solace of Nature, then the word has a certain power for me, or over me, which does not magically

While this interpretive pluralism may win the day in literary criticism, Professor Fiss maintains that nothing of the sort exists in the legal interpretive community—nor can it. Unlike literary critics, judges "do not belong to an interpretive community as a result of shared views about particular issues or interpretations but belong by virtue of the commitment to uphold and advance the rule of law itself. . . .[I]n legal interpretation there is only one school and attendance is mandatory."[24] Only through allegiance to the ideal of the rule of law can a judge properly exercise authority: the power to speak with the authority of law and to coerce citizen compliance with it stems from participation in, and allegiance to, the norms of the community of legal interpreters. To command authority, however, judges must demonstrate more than mere membership in an authoritative interpretive community; they must show that their decisions are objective and not, as the nihilists charge, the imposition of ideology under the guise of judicial neutrality. The main point of Professor Fiss' response to the nihilists is not only that objective interpretation by judges is possible, but moreover, that this possibility is a clear demonstration of the unique character of interpretation in the juridical community.[25]

The conception of objectivity advanced by Professor Fiss does not require that a judge's interpretive act be the product of a source totally external to the judge.[26] In other words, Professor Fiss does not maintain that interpretation in law is possible without human intervention; he simply denies that it is *totally* a product of human choice.[27] As discussed above, the first aspect of legal interpretation that Professor Fiss points to as differentiating it from literary interpretation is the idea of a single interpretive community, of which one either is or is not a member. Unlike literary criticism, where interpretive communities abound, law admits of only one interpretive group having the requisite authority to declare the meaning of the law. One cannot rightly be said to be a "member" of the legal interpretive community; one either discharges the duties of the judicial office or one

> evaporate when I encounter it in a poem. This is part of what is meant by saying that the literary work constrains our interpretations of it, or that its meaning is to some extent "immanent" in it. Language is a field of social forces which shape us to our roots, and it is an academicist delusion to see the literary work as an arena of infinite possibility which escapes it.

Id. at 87-88. *See also* D. Bleich, *Subjective Criticism* (1978).

24. Fiss, *supra* note 5, at 746.

25. *Id.* at 746-47.

26. *See id.* at 744.

27. *See id.*

does not.[28]

The primary constitutive element of the interpretive legal community, according to Professor Fiss, is that of *disciplining rules*, "which constrain the interpreter and constitute the standards by which the correctness of the interpretation is to be judged."[29] Disciplining rules preclude judges as interpreters of legal texts from assigning to those texts any meaning they wish. While Professor Fiss does not dispute the nihilist's claim that the meaning of a legal text does not reside in the text itself,[30] he does reject the nihilist's apparent conclusion that without a demonstrable textual essence the interpreter is free to assign any meaning to it. In short, Professor Fiss finds limits on the subjectivity of the interpreter in the set of disciplining rules that constitute the fabric of the interpretive community of judges.

Disciplining rules constrain interpretive license by specifying "the relevance and weight to be assigned to the material (e.g. words, history, intention, consequence)"[31] and by defining the basic conceptual apparatus and procedures by which interpretation must proceed. While interpretive rules may vary—for example, from contractual interpretation to statutory interpretation—their function or purpose remains unchanged: "they constrain the interpreter, thus transforming the interpretive process from a subjective to an objective one, and they furnish the standards by which the correctness of the interpretation can be judged."[32] In other words, the disciplining rules provide an "interpretive grammar" that regulates the discourse of the interpretive community. To deny their presence, Professor Fiss claims, is to preclude both intersubjective recognition of meaning[33] and the possibility of critique from within the interpretive community.

Nothing in Professor Fiss' position denies the possibility of disagreement within the interpretive community.[34] However, that disagreement can take either of two forms, only one of which poses any serious threat to the stability of the interpretive legal community. The less onerous form of disagreement is over the application of disciplining rules. As an example, Professor Fiss considers the problem of the proper approach to interpreting the history of the fourteenth amendment. He asks whether it is more plausible, as a matter of history, to suggest that in promulgating the amendment, the framers'

28. *See id.* at 746.
29. *Id.* at 744.
30. *See id.*
31. *Id.*
32. *Id.* at 745.
33. *See id.* at 750.
34. *See id.* at 747-50.

focus was on desegregation of schools or on the elimination of the caste system.[35] Disputes of this sort do not challenge the basic premise of the disputants that history is pertinent to a proper understanding of the drafters' intendment;[36] they merely pose the issue of the proper application of history to an understanding of that intendment.

A more serious problem arises when the challenge comes not to the proper application of history, but to the need to consult history at all in fashioning intendment. Here the *application* of history is not in question, but the *relevance* of history to constitutional interpretation.[37] This disagreement challenges the very basis of objectivity in interpretation: the validity of the disciplining rules themselves. However, according to Professor Fiss, such a dispute is ameliorated, if not eliminated, by the hierarchy of judicial authority.[38] Once a determination of the validity of an interpretive rule is made by the highest court, its inherent authority mandates the acquiescence of lower tribunals to that interpretive choice. The juridical community overcomes challenges to the authority of its interpretive rules by virtue of the hierarchy of interpretive prerogative. No such hierarchy exists in literary criticism and, for that reason, disputes over the validity of interpretive rules remain intractable.

We are now in a position to summarize the status of the current debate between the nihilists and their objectivist counterparts. To the nihilist, interpretive choice is tantamount to license. Lacking anything that can be denominated linguistic essence, interpretive choice is little more than absolute freedom to create a metaphysics of justice fashioned out of a private vision of moral reality.[39] In a sense, the nihilist is a moral/legal skeptic *tout court*. The nihilist, seeing nothing in legal discourse on which participants can agree, concludes that the power to assign meaning is absolute.

Although the bounded objectivists admit the lack of intelligible

35. *See id.* at 747.

36. I use the word "intendment" here as a more accurate substitute for what is usually denominated "legislative intent." Since I argue words do not derive their meaning from a speaker's intention but from linguistic conventions, sentence meaning is not reducible to the intentions of a "speaker" (e.g., a legislature). See notes 47-50 and accompanying text *infra*. *See also* Patterson, *The Decline of the Privity Rule in the Maine Law of Tort Products Liability: A Conceptual History*, 35 ME. L. REV. 1, 11 n.49 (1983). For a different view, see E. HIRSCH, VALIDITY IN INTERPRETATION (1967) (authorial intent as determinative of textual meaning). Hirsch has recently recanted much of his earlier position. *See* Hirsch, *Past Intentions and Present Meanings*, 23 ESSAYS IN CRITICISM 79 (1983). *See also* J. SEARLE, *Literal Meaning*, in EXPRESSION AND MEANING: STUDIES IN THE THEORY OF SPEECH ACTS 117 (1979).

37. Fiss, *supra* note 5, at 747.

38. *See id.*

39. *See* note 10 and accompanying text *supra*.

essences, they do not concede that the lack of such essences mandates interpretive abandon. Particularly in law, the interpretive community, with its disciplinary rules, saves the legal text from the untrammeled whims of the interpreter. Objectivity, we are told, is not only attainable but mandatory. To deny the limits placed on interpretive freedom by the interpretive legal community is to deny both the possibility of intersubjective discourse and the authority of law. In short, meaning is the product of both the interpretive act (subjectivity) and the constraints of the interpretive community with its disciplining rules (objectivity).[40]

Both the objectivist and subjectivist appear to have the same objective: to explain the status of meaning in legal interpretation. To the objectivist, "interpretation . . . is neither a wholly discretionary nor a wholly mechanical activity."[41] Meaning is neither the product of a speaker nor does it reside "out there" in legal texts waiting to be disclosed; rather, it is the product of "a dynamic interaction between reader and text."[42] The nihilist, on the other hand, sees the objectivist as foreover damned to chasing the chimera of objectivity. Meaning, the nihilist asserts, "is created rather than discovered";[43] and it is created within rival interpretive communities, none of which countenances the point of view of the other.[44]

Fortunately, we need not enter the objectivist/subjectivist debate to see that the argument has gone awry. In a sense, the fault for this lies with those who, like Professor Fiss, attempt to meet the nihilist on

40. *See* Fiss, *supra* note 5, at 744.

41. *Id.* at 749.

42. *Id.*

43. Levinson, *supra* note 9, at 383.

44. *See* S. FISH, IS THERE A TEXT IN THIS CLASS? (1980). For a similar view in the philosophy of science, arguing that scientific "communities" are demarcated along the lines of rival "paradigms," see T. KUHN, THE STRUCTURE OF SCIENTIFIC REVOLUTIONS (1962).

It is indeed regretable that Levinson puts Thomas Kuhn in the "subjectivist" camp. *See* Levinson, *supra* note 9, at 384 n.40, 394 n.85. More than any other philosopher of science, Kuhn has sought to dissolve the false dichotomy between subjectivism and objectivism.

> When my critics say I deprive theory choice of objectivity, they must, therefore, have recourse to some very different sense of subjective, presumably the one in which bias and personal likes or dislikes function instead of, or in the face of, the actual facts. But that sense of subjective does not fit the process I have been describing any better than the first. . . . Objectivity ought to be analyzable in terms of criteria like accuracy and consistency. If these criteria do not supply all the guidance that we have customarily expected of them, then it may be the meaning rather than the limits of objectivity that my argument shows.

T. Kuhn, *Objectivity, Value Judgment, And Theory Choice*, in THE ESSENTIAL TENSION 337-38 (1977). *See also* R. BERNSTEIN, *supra* note 1, at 51-93.

his own ground;[45] for the nihilist is much like the radical skeptic in morals who, when presented with an otherwise cogent argument, will respond. "That is merely *your* point of view!"[46] Rather than try and find fault with the nihilist's shaky syllogism that because there are no intelligible essences, everything is permitted, opposition to nihilism is best advanced not by argument but by demonstration. Let me explain.

The nihilist avers that meaning is solely the product of one's private vision of linguistic truth. Interpretation of legal concepts is, the nihilist urges, wholly dependent upon the interpretive subject. The words of the speaker have no meaning *in themselves* but only in relation to the intent and understanding of the speaker or reader. Again, the meaning of a word is, *ceteris paribus*, simply "what you say it is."

This view of meaning is not only nihilistic; it is a "red herring." Meaning neither resides in a text nor with a speaker. To coin a phrase, it is a matter of convention.[47] To know the meaning of a word is to know how that word functions in a discourse.[48] To know a language or technical discourse (the law, for example) is to possess the demonstrable ability to participate in an intersubjective enterprise (speaking) in which the participants are engaged in an ongoing practice.[49] Being a participant in a practice means that one knows or can recognize when concepts are employed correctly, when they are not,

45. The direct nature of Fiss' attack on nihilism is clear:

> The nihilism that I have addressed is based on the premise that for any text there are any number of possible meanings and the interpreter creates a meaning by choosing one. I have accepted this premise; but have tried to deny the nihilism by showing why the freedom is not absolute.

Fiss, *supra* note 5, at 762.

46. For an exacting critique of the problems of skepticism in morals, see J. MACKIE, ETHICS 15-49 (1977). *See also* Moore, *Moral Reality*, 1982 WIS. L. REV. 1061 (assessing the role of moral choice in legal decisionmaking).

47. Readers familiar with the literature in the philosophy of language will no doubt recognize the breadth of the Wittgensteinian perspective drawn upon here. For an excellent general introduction to Wittgenstein's thought, the reader is directed to A. KENNY, WITTGENSTEIN (1973). The best short introduction I know of is Kavka, Book Review, 26 STAN. L. REV. 1455 (1974) (reviewing H. PITKIN, WITTGENSTEIN AND JUSTICE (1972)).

48. *See* Stone, *From a Language Perspective*, 90 YALE L.J. 1149, 1158 (1981).

49. R. FLATHMAN, THE PRACTICE OF RIGHTS 12 (1976). Flathman has noted that "the notion of a practice is most commonly applied to *sets* of actions that recur over time and that are thought to be interrelated or to cohere together in some significant degree." *Id.* For a more technical, but no less important discussion of the concept of "practice," see Morawetz, *The Concept of a Practice*, 24 PHIL. STUD. 210 (1973). *See also* R. BEINER, *supra* note 21, at 130-35; F. DALLMAYER, LANGUAGE AND POLITICS 86-95 (1984); R. FLATHMAN, THE PRACTICE OF POLITICAL AUTHORITY (1980); M. OAKESHOTT, ON HUMAN CONDUCT 55-60 (1975).

and when their use can rightly be called into question.[50] To understand the role and function of language we must look not to subjectivity, nor to objectivity, but for meaning.

In advocating an approach to meaning different from the views of Professors Fiss and Levinson, I will draw on the later philosophy of Wittgenstein.[51] My purpose is to advance a theory of meaning that is both superior in its explanatory power to that offered by Professor Levinson and, at the same time, responsive to the need for "objectivity" so important to Professor Fiss' account of the interpretive legal community. Unlike my necessarily critical discussion of the subjectivist position, my analysis will show the objectivist arguments to be not so much wrong as beside the point. We simply do not need the idea of an interpretive legal community to fashion an adequate response to nihilism; for the latter, I hope to show, is a form of skepticism that contains within itself the seeds of its own demise.

III. WITTGENSTEIN'S THEORY OF MEANING

Wittgenstein's account of linguistic meaning, as developed in his later writings, provides the analytical framework needed to undercut the skeptical claims of nihilism. In fact, the nihilist critique of legal discourse, with its roots in Deconstructionist literary theory, is precisely the sort of criticism that "reveals the significance of the model of philosophical thinking projected by Wittgenstein's later writings."[52] While Wittgenstein did indeed repudiate the analysis of language into logical simples evident in his youthful writing,[53] he ultimately opted not for indeterminacy but for a theory of grammatical competence produced by education in a linguistic culture. This

50. *See* S. KRIPKE, WITTGENSTEIN ON RULES AND PRIVATE LANGUAGE 74 (1982).

51. Wittgenstein is a unique figure in the history of philosophy, for he managed to develop two distinct approaches to philosophical problems of meaning. In his "earlier" work, Wittgenstein maintained that the structure of reality determined the structure of language. This approach is best represented in WITTGENSTEIN, TRACTATUS LOGICO-PHILOSOPHICUS (D. Pears and B. McGuinness trans. 1961), which appeared in 1921. In his "later" thought, reposed most systematically in PHILOSOPHICAL INVESTIGATIONS, *supra* note 21, Wittgenstein reversed his earlier view, arguing that language determines our view of reality. *See generally* D. PEARS, LUDWIG WITTGENSTEIN (1969).

There are some Wittgenstein scholars who dispute the degree to which there are "two Wittgensteins." *See, e.g.*, A. KENNY, *supra* note 47, at 219-32.

52. C. ALTIERI, ACT & QUALITY 39 (1981). Altieri's book is perhaps the most thoroughgoing Wittgensteinian response to the full range of Deconstructionist claims. *See also* T. SEUNG, *supra* note 21, at 241-79.

53. *See* L. WITTGENSTEIN, TRACTATUS LOGICO-PHILOSOPHICUS, *supra* note 51. *See also* M. BLACK, A COMPANION TO WITTGENSTEIN'S TRACTATUS 58-61, 206-07 (1964); J. GRIFFIN, WITTGENSTEIN'S LOGICAL ATOMISM (1964).

education (training) enables a subject "to establish criteria for appropriateness [of concept application] and then to rely on practical considerations for defining degrees of probable relevance in hypotheses about meaning."[54]

Concepts derive their linguistic significance from the social wholes of which they are a part.[55] The principal analytical device for elucidating how meaning is derived from context is that of the "language-game," which Wittgenstein obliquely describes as "the whole, consisting of language and the actions into which it is woven."[56] The meaning of words and concepts is woven into the activities of which they are a part: their meaning is disclosed by all the language-games of which they are (or could be) a part. Since language-games have many purposes, so do the words contained within them. Understanding the part

> . . . requires some grasp of the whole of which it is a part. In the case of a language-game, this entails understanding what that human activity is, what it is for, why it is played. Words—at least many words—are used in many different activities. To understand the full meaning of a word requires some grasp of all the activities, the social wholes, in which the word plays a part.
>
> The meanings of words can only be understood if we understand the purpose or ends of the human activities of which they are a part. Ignoring the different language-games and their ends or purposes when seeking the meaning of a word is like trying to understand the brake lever in a locomotive without understanding what a locomotive does, or what it is for.[57]

Wittgenstein's urging to look for meaning in the uses to which words are put in a discursive practice is best expressed by the following deceptively simple statement: "For a *large* class of cases—though not for all—in which we employ the word 'meaning' it can be defined

54. C. ALTIERI, *supra* note 52, at 40. *See also* Hacker, *Wittgenstein On Ostensive Definition*, 18 INQUIRY 267, 276-78, (1975).

55. *See* Brest, *supra* note 4, at 206.

56. L. WITTGENSTEIN, *supra* note 21, § 7. For a complete analysis of the role of language-games in Wittgenstein's later philosophy, see A. KENNY, *supra* note 47, at 159-77. *See also* G. HALLETT, A COMPANION TO WITTGENSTEIN'S PHILOSOPHICAL INVESTIGATIONS 81-82 (1977). A recent treatment of the sociological implications of Wittgenstein's later thought is D. BLOOR, WITTGENSTEIN: A SOCIAL THEORY OF KNOWLEDGE (1983).

57. J. DANFORD, WITTGENSTEIN AND POLITICAL PHILOSOPHY 85 (1978).

thus: the meaning of a word is its use in the language."[58] On its face, this definitional statement entreats us to look for meaning not in an inchoate intelligible essence, but in the use to which words are put in a discourse.

Earlier, in *The Blue Book*,[59] Wittgenstein decried the nihilist premise that the meaning of a concept could be found only in an "essence" shared by its multifarious applications.

> The idea that in order to get clear about the meaning of a general term one had to find the common element in all its applications has shackled philosophical investigation; for it has not only led to no result, but has also made the philosopher dismiss as irrelevant the concrete cases which alone could have helped him to understand the usage of the general term.[60]

To illustrate this point, Wittgenstein directs our attention to Socrates' attempt in Plato's *Theaetetus*[61] to answer the question, "what is knowledge?" There, as in other Platonic dialogues, Socrates presses his interlocutor for a definition of knowledge that will crystallize an essence present in all its uses. But why look for an essence? Why, Wittgenstein asks, does Socrates "not even regard it as a *preliminary* answer to enumerate cases of knowledge?"[62]

The point of Wittgenstein's remarks is to dissolve the false dichotomy between meaning as interpretive license and meaning as determined by an objective extra-linguistic source.[63] The concrete cases that offer clues to meaning do not have a life outside the discourse of which they are a part. That is why Wittgenstein regards it as error for philosophers to dismiss as irrelevant the concrete cases that can elucidate the meaning of a general term. Concrete cases are important not because of their unilateral enjoyment of some essential element, but rather by virtue of their unique role in a discourse.[64] In short, the solution to problems of meaning lies not in the correspondence between word and object but in the established ways in which concepts are employed in a discourse. As a substitute for the essen-

58. L. WITTGENSTEIN, *supra* note 21, § 43 (emphasis in original).

59. L. WITTGENSTEIN, THE BLUE AND BROWN BOOKS (1968).

60. *Id.* at 19-20.

61. PLATO, *Theaetetus*, in THE COLLECTED DIALOGUES OF PLATO 845-919 (F. Cornford trans., E. Hamilton & H. Cairns eds. 1961).

62. L. WITTGENSTEIN, *supra* note 59, at 20 (citing *id.* at 1460-7C) (emphasis in original).

63. *See* P. HACKER, INSIGHT AND ILLUSION: WITTGENSTEIN ON PHILOSOPHY AND THE METAPHYSICS OF EXPERIENCE 166-84 (1982).

64. *See* T. MORAWETZ, WITTGENSTEIN AND KNOWLEDGE 58-61 (1978).

tialist rendering of linguistic meaning, Wittgenstein invites us to view the instances to which a word or concept applies as connected not by a common property but by "relevant resemblances." In the course of demonstrating his analysis by reference to the concept of a "game," Wittgenstein introduces the central notion of "family resemblance,"[65] the principal elements of which can be summarized as follows:

(1) The activities we call "games" have no common properties in virtue of which we apply the same word to them all. If we look carefully at various games, we see that the dogma of essentialism — that they *must* have something in common — is false;
(2) Consequently, there is no correct essentialist definition of "game";
(3) Consequently, too, the ability to give an essentialist definition of a word is not a necessary condition of understanding it;
(4) Various activities are "games" because of a complicated network of similarities; that is, a large number of relationships between these different activities. This concept resembles a long rope twisted out of many shorter fibers. It is held together by the overlapping of many similarities;
(5) The network of overlapping similarities constituting the concept of a game is compared with the various resemblances between members of a family. These may be of very different kinds: resemblance in build, facial features, color of eyes or hair, gait, temperament, manner of speaking, attitude, or manners. In specifying respects of resemblance between people recognizably of the same family, we speak of such things as the Churchillian manner or the Hapsburg chin. Although we can make such respects of resemblance precise, it is not by virtue of their all having some set of common properties that we group together members of an extended family; no single property is sufficient for membership in the group, nor is any one necessary. This is what makes the metaphor of family resemblance so illuminating when applied to such concepts as that of a game;
(6) The explanation of what a game is primarily consists of giving examples. Examples used to explain "game" are meant to be taken and used in a particular way, viz, as paradigmatic examples. They are, as it were, "centers of variation." One who takes them as an exhaustive list of (possible) games, would not understand the explanation correctly. *Multiplicity* of examples is an important feature of explaining such a concept;
(7) Consequently, "game" can be *explained*, though it cannot be

65. L. WITTGENSTEIN, *supra* note 21, §§ 65-71.

given an essentialist definition. It is a fallacy to think that an indefinable expression cannot be explained;
(8) The adducing of relevant similarities justifies applications of "game" since it is on account of the relationships among games, especially on account of those between activities and the paradigmatic examples of games, that we correctly call games "games." Presence of similarities justifies our using the same word for all these activities; we call something "a game" because it is very similar to other activities that are properly called "games";
(9) All games form a *single* family. What holds them together and gives them a unity is the overlapping of the many similarities among games. In view of this unity, it is appropriate to speak of *the* concept of a game, *the* concept of a number, etc.;
(10) The concept of a game has no sharp boundaries. Since it is not explained by an essentialist definition, there is no rigid, precise circumscription of its extension. Instead, the explanation is by paradigms; and even if it includes a similarity-clause, it does not specify the range or degree of similarities within the paradigms required for an activity to fall under the concept of a game. Explanations by examples are comparable to indicating a place by pointing, not to demarcating it by drawing a boundary;
(11) For special purposes we can draw boundaries around the concept of a game. But whether we should draw it here or there depends only on what facilitates achieving these purposes.[66]

Through regularity of application, in light of a consistent purpose, the multifarious applications of a concept come to be seen as constitutive of its meaning. A speaker who comes to the point of knowing the conditions under which the use of a word is appropriate demonstrates an understanding of the word's grammar, which "includes all of the various verbal expressions in which that word is characteristically used."[67] As Wittgenstein puts it: "grammar tells us what kind of object anything is."[68] In short, essence is no part of the word-object relationship, for it "is expressed by grammar."[69]

These considerations bring us back to the central contention of the nihilist that without a grounding in linguistic essences, the act of interpretation is surrendered to a privileged subject: the judge. The

66. G. BAKER & P. HACKER, WITTGENSTEIN: UNDERSTANDING AND MEANING 325-27 (1980).

67. H. PITKIN, WITTGENSTEIN AND JUSTICE 117 (1972).

68. L. WITTGENSTEIN, *supra* note 21, § 372.

69. *Id.* § 371. *See* J. CANFIELD, WITTGENSTEIN: LANGUAGE AND WORLD 151-211 (1981); J. RICHARDSON, THE GRAMMAR OF JUSTIFICATION 106-30 (1976).

nihilist seeks a beginning—an object standing outside the bounds of discourse free from the clutches of the knowing subject.[70] Only in this way can meaning be certain, for without such grounding no forum exists for the resolution of doubt and uncertainty in the interpretive community. In his quest for absolute interpretive truth, the nihilist has not only denied himself a viable ground for meaning, but has set himself a goal unattainable *even on his own terms*. To deny the possibility of certainty without essence requires that there be some ground for doubt that stands *outside language*. But if essence is to be denied, what grounds do we have for resolving doubt? All that remains is faith.

There is a deeper issue, however, for the nihilist's "doubt" that concepts can have objective meaning is in no real sense a defensible questioning of objectivist certainty. For a doubt to make any real sense at all, "it must itself accept its second-order status as a move within an established system for testing and confirming. Doubt only makes sense where certitude is possible; doubting the possibility of certitude is a doubt with no possible resolution, and hence not a doubt but an ungrounded metaphysical statement."[71] Consider the following:

> What would it be like to doubt now whether I have two hands? Why can't I imagine it at all? What would I believe if I didn't believe that? So far I have no system at all within which this doubt might exist.[72]

Doubt is a matter of giving grounds. When I am asked by a judge, "Why does this claim sound in tort?," I am called upon to give reasons why an avowed cause of action should stand alongside those that have traditionally been regarded as such. But if I am asked by a nihilist judge to elucidate the concept "tort," and am further required to do so with no reference to legal discourse, I am mute. What is it that I am being asked to supply? What possible "explanation" could be offered to assuage this kind of "doubt"? Without reference to the shared forms of legal discourse, I am reduced to silence.

This shows not that the nihilist has demonstrated that my analysis of doubt is wrongheaded, but only that doubt, as he understands

70. Kant's "noumena" are an example of such an object. *See* I. KANT, CRITIQUE OF PURE REASON 266-75, 291-95 (N. Kemp Smith trans. 1929).

71. C. ALTIERI, *supra* note 52, at 49.

72. L. WITTGENSTEIN, ON CERTAINTY § 247 (D. Paul & G. Anscombe trans., G. Anscombe & G. von Wright eds. 1969). *See also* G. GRAFF, LITERATURE AGAINST ITSELF 195 (1979). The most thorough and philosophically astute analysis of Wittgenstein's remarks on the concept of certainty is T. MORAWETZ, WITTGENSTEIN AND KNOWLEDGE (1978).

it, precludes the use of the shared experience upon which the language-game of doubting depends. Does this mean that the concept is in some way defective? I think not. What it illustrates is that the concept of doubt depends upon the shared forms of human experience upon which legal discourse is based. Without intelligible essences, the only ground (and a wholly sufficient one) available for the justification of conceptual claims is that of discursive experience.

The most salient aspect of Wittgenstein's argument is that insistence on linguistic essence as a ground for meaning leads one to dismiss as irrelevant the general forms of language that provide the public basis of meaning. The practical significance of this is to demonstrate the misguided nature of the nihilist's claim that it is impossible to have meaning without essence. Wittgenstein's account of meaning demonstrates that discourse rests upon shared linguistic practices that are, as he says, part of natural history.[73]

IV. OBJECTIONS AND REPLIES

Some readers may object that I have not completely rebutted the nihilist's claim that there cannot be objective word meanings because the theory of linguistic practices fails to account for conceptual change. In other words, the account of meaning advanced thus far might be found inadequate, for it does not offer a direct solution to the interpretive dilemmas to which nihilists point as evidence of the incommensurability of rival interpretive paradigms. To persuade the nihilist that things are not as bad as they seem to be, my alternative account of meaning must do more than explain the *stability* of meaning: I must show how arguments over the application of disputed concepts can move toward resolution.

My alternative account of meaning does not provide such a methodological tool; but that has not been my purpose. To this point, I have endeavored to show only that the theory of meaning proferred by Professor Levinson is fundamentally unsound, based as it is upon a fallacious argument. I think it best to restate the nihilist argument in the following skeletal form:

(a) There can be no objective justification for the application of a general term to its instances unless those instances have *something* in common (e.g., an "essential characteristic" or "inner essence");

(b) There *is* no such element;

(c) THEREFORE, there can be no objective justification for the

73. L. WITTGENSTEIN, *supra* note 21, § 415.

application of any general term. In short, "[m]eaning is created rather than discovered."[74]

At the same moment that Professor Levinson advances this argument, he also admits that "our ordinary speech acts are full of meanings instantly grasped by listeners, given the standard contexts in which they occur."[75] Taken together, the argument above and the claim that there exist "meanings instantly grasped by listeners" result in a contradiction. If there are no intelligible essences, and "[m]eaning is created rather than discovered,"[76] then not even in cases of ordinary speech acts can there be anything in the way of objectivity; yet Professor Levinson says that there is. What goes unexplained in his account of meaning is why, given the existence of shared linguistic practices, there can be "no uniformity of rules of interpretation"[77] and hence, no methodology for resolving conceptual conflict.

In responding to Professor Levinson's skepticism, I will advance an outline for the resolution of the conflicts he deems intractable by building upon the argument advanced earlier: that meaning is the product of shared linguistic practices that provide a basis for the interpretive strategy I propose. The nub of this strategy is contained in the idea that in resolving what are now often referred to as "hard cases,"[78] the obligation of a judge is to look for "relevant similarities" between undisputed examples of a concept's meaning and a proposed analogue.[79] The continuing importance of this methodology was recently demonstrated by Joseph Raz who, in *The Authority of Law*,[80] provides the needed extension of Wittgenstein's theory of meaning in a manner that illustrates the important role of analogical argument in legal reasoning.[81]

74. Levinson, *supra* note 9, at 383.

75. *Id.* at 382 n.33.

76. *Id.* at 383.

77. *Id.* at 394.

78. The phrase "hard cases" is Ronald Dworkin's. He describes a hard case as one where "no settled rule dictates a decision either way." R. DWORKIN, TAKING RIGHTS SERIOUSLY 83 (1977, 1978).

I use the phrase somewhat differently than Dworkin to refer to those instances where a concept's application is in question or otherwise challenged. I should like to have used the phrase "contested concepts," but that refers to a broad body of literature to which my argument is only partially directed. *See* Gaille, *Essentially Contested Concepts*, 56 PROC. ARISTOTELIAN SOC'Y 167 (1965). *See also* W. CONNOLLY, THE TERMS OF POLITICAL DISCOURSE 10-44 (1974).

79. *See* H. HART, THE CONCEPT OF LAW 121-37 (1961).

80. J. RAZ, THE AUTHORITY OF LAW (1979).

81. *Id.* at 201-06. *See also* Murray, *The Role of Analogy In Legal Reasoning*, 29 U.C.L.A. L. REV., 833, 850-58 (1982).

To avoid initial confusion over the point of his remarks, Raz urges that in making an analogical argument, it is not at all helpful to look for the *extent* (in terms of raw numbers) of similarities between the concrete case and the proposed analogue.[82] As he puts the matter, "it is not the number of differences [or similarities] but their importance which counts. What, however, is the test of importance?"[83] In commenting on this point, James Murray notes correctly that "[t]wo analogues can be similar in many respects, and yet one difference between them may destroy the value of the analogy."[84] In deciding the strength of an analogy, one must not look to raw numbers, but must adduce reasons why a proposed analogue ought or ought not to be brought within the ambit of a rule containing the unchallenged case.

The strength of any proposed analogy is a function of the degree to which the addition of the new analogue, and thus a new legal rule, will advance "the underlying justification of the rule which forms the basis of the analogy."[85] In short, "if a given reason is good enough to justify one rule, then it is equally able to justify another that can be derived from it in a similar way."[86]

An example may prove helpful. In *Davis v. Colonial Securities Corp.*,[87] the defendant corporation leased a house to the plaintiff for a monthly rental of $150.00. The written lease provided that the plaintiff was to pay all taxes assessed against the property, make repairs at her own expense, pay water and sewerage charges, insurance, plus interest on the unpaid balance at the rate of 11 3/4%. The lease further provided that it was for a one month period, renewable monthly and terminable by either party on ten days notice. At the expiration of ten years, the plaintiff was to receive a deed to the property upon payment of the sum of $1.00. The sole issue in the case was whether this arrangement constituted a "credit sale" under the provisions of the Federal Truth-In-Lending Act (the Act) and the regulations promulgated under it by the Federal Reserve Board.[88]

82. J. RAZ, *supra* note 80, at 203.

83. *Id.*

84. Murray, *supra* note 81, at 852 (Murray's use of an analogy between man and ape is helpful in making his point).

85. J. RAZ, *supra* note 80, at 204.

86. Murray, *supra* note 81, at 852 (quoting J. RAZ, *supra* note 80, at 208-09).

87. 541 F. Supp. 302 (E.D. Pa. 1982).

88. *Id.* at 303. *See* 15 U.S.C. § 1602(g) (1983). Section 1602(g) provides:

> The term "credit sale" refers to any sale with respect to which credit is extended or arranged by the seller. The term includes any contract in the form of a bailment or lease if the bailee or lessee contracts to pay as compensation for use a sum substantially equivalent to or in excess of the aggre-

Despite the contrary holdings of many courts that had previously considered the question,[89] Judge Giles of the Eastern District of Pennsylvania held that the transaction was a credit sale within the purview of the Act. The court dismissed defendant's argument that the lease could not fit within the meaning of "credit sale" where both parties had the right to terminate it on ten days notice. The court's analysis in reaching its conclusion is exemplary.

First, the court discerned the Act's legislative purpose to be that "of benefiting the consumer by eliminating unscrupulous and predatory credit practices."[90] Further, the legislative history of the Act revealed a genuine concern on the part of its drafters to distinguish between "true leases," which are not covered, and disguised credit sales:

> The definition of credit sale is also limited to include leases only if they are, in essence, disguised sale arrangements. The language covering disguised leases is nearly identical to the language used in the Uniform Conditional Sales Act and in many state retail installment sales acts to distinguish between "true leases" and other leases.[91]

Additionally, the court noted that in drawing the distinction between disguised credit sales and true leases, the meaning of each concept is in part determined by state commercial law, for "congress intended to employ language already in use in state commercial law when it included leases in the Section 1602 (g) definition of a credit sale."[92]

> gate value of the property and services involved and it is agreed that the bailee or lessee will become, or for no other or a nominal consideration has the option to become, the owner of the property upon full compliance with his obligations under the contract.

Id. For the regulations enacted under the Act, see Regulation Z, 12 C.F.R. §§ 226.1-15.

89. *See* 541 F. Supp. at 302, 304 and the cases cited therein. For a complete analysis of the conflicting interpretations of the meaning of "credit sale," see Note, *The Applicability of The Federal Truth In Lending Act to Rental Purchase Agreements*, 66 CORNELL L. REV. 118 (1980).

90. 541 F. Supp. at 302, 305 (citing Johnson v. McCrackin-Sturman Ford Inc., 527 F.2d. 257, 262 (3d Cir. 1975)).

91. 541 F. Supp. at 305 (quoting H. R. REP. NO. 1040, 90th Cong., 2nd Sess., *reprinted in* 1968 U.S. CODE CONG. & AD. NEWS 1962, 1980).

92. 541 F. Supp. at 306 (citing H. R. REP. NO. 1040, 90th Cong., 2nd Sess., *reprinted in* 1968 U.S. CODE CONG. & AD. NEWS 1962, 1980). The relevant Pennsylvania statute provides in part as follows:

> Whether a lease is intended as security is to be determined by the facts of each case; however:
>
> (1) The inclusion of an option to purchase does not of itself make the lease one intended for security; and
>
> (2) an agreement that upon compliance with the terms of the lease

In light of these considerations, the court discerned the following relevant resemblances between the "lease" in question and a credit sale:

(a) The lessee was granted an option to purchase for little or no consideration;
(b) Monthly rentals were credited toward the purchase price;
(c) Thus, the plaintiff acquired an equity interest in the property as the payments were made;
(d) The rental fees of $150.00 per month for ten years totaled $18,000.00, an amount far in excess of the property's fair market value of $2,000.00;
(e) The incidents of ownership shifted to the lessee under the agreement (e.g., responsibility for making repairs).[93]

The only attribute of a sale transaction absent between the parties to this agreement was that the "lessee" was never obligated to pay the aggregate value of the property or its substantial equivalent. Yet, in light of the purposes of the Act this difference, standing alone, is insufficient to outweigh the importance of the five similarities between this agreement and a credit sale.

Unilateral focus on the absence of an obligation to pay an outstanding balance is precisely the sort of essentialist reasoning Wittgenstein's analysis is designed to prevent. Advancement of the underlying purpose of the Act—distinguishing between true leases and disguised credit sales—counts as the reason (justification) for finding this agreement to be an instance of the meaning of "credit sale." By virtue of the purpose of the Act, these resemblances are relevant and, perhaps, overwhelming.

This solution to the problems of interpretive choice is hardly a panacea for all interpretive dilemmas. Much jurisprudential ink has been spilled over the proper justification or choice of reasons for extending a primary analogue;[94] but that ink has not been wasted, for

---

> the lessee shall become or has the option to become the owner of the property for no additional consideration or for a nominal consideration does make the lease one intended for security.

13 PA. CONS. STAT. ANN. § 1201 (Purdon 1984).

93. 541 F. Supp. at 306.

94. For example, Dworkin's contention that principles are morally antecedent to policies as a source of justification for judicial decisions is hotly contested. Dworkin's arguments for the axiological superiority of principles are contained in R. DWORKIN, *supra* note 78. Kent Greenawalt disputes the priority of principles in Greenawalt, *Policy, Rights and Judicial Decision*, 11 GA. L. REV. 991 (1972). For Dworkin's response to Greenawalt (and others), see R. DWORKIN, *supra* note 78, at 294-330. *See also* RONALD DWORKIN AND CONTEMPORARY JURISPRUDENCE 247-300 (M. Cohen ed. 1983).

these arguments contain an implicit justification of the Wittgensteinian approach to meaning and discourse. If no common ground exists for arguments over the proper choice of *reasons* for analogical extension of unchallenged cases, then there can be no argument at all that one reason is to be preferred over another.[95] Normative claims for the superiority of any given form of justification cannot even begin until some agreement exists as to the meaning of primary analogues. To deny, as the nihilist does, any common ground of meaning is to preclude resolution of these larger jurisprudential inquiries into the nature of justification in legal argument. Were this the condition on contemporary legal discourse, it would indeed be unfortunate. Thankfully, it is not.

V. CONCLUSION

The limited nature of my characterization of the argument between nihilism and objectivism stems in large part from the radical nature of Professor Levinson's claims concerning linguistic meaning. As I understand his argument, Professor Levinson reposes absolute interpretive power in judges; they are, in a real sense, the lone keepers of the law.[96] This is the claim to which my disputation has been directed.

In opposing Levinson's position, I have sought to justify the claim that legal discourse enjoys a modicum of stability that is not mere fodder for judicial ideology, but something from which judges fashion fresh legal arguments as they go about the business of adjudicating novel lawsuits involving claims that pull at the fiber of legal discourse. Argument by analogy is proposed as a possible tool to relieve this conceptual tension. Admittedly, as a form of argument, it is by no means free from abuse.[97]

95. Jurgen Habermas makes the same point with respect to the understanding of "forms of life" other than our own (or earlier stages of our own social development). An interpreter of an alien culture must have the ability to isolate reasons for actions taken by the participants. A judgment that a validity claim has been made does not inexorably entail the conclusion that the claim is supported by good or bad reasons. *See generally* R. BERNSTEIN, *supra* note 1, at 182.

96. For a similar understanding of Professor Levinson's position, see Graff, *supra* note 17, at 405-06.

97. *See* Kairys, *Legal Reasoning*, in THE POLITICS OF LAW: A PROGRESSIVE CRITIQUE 11-17 (D. Kairys ed. 1982) (criticizing the U.S. Supreme Court's disingenous use of reasoning by analogy in certain of its labor law opinions). Unfortunately, Kairys jumps from this lone demonstration of a *misuse* of analogical reasoning to the extravagant conclusion that

> [j]udicial decisions ultimately depend on judgments based on values and priorities that vary with particular judges (and even with the same judge, depending on the context) and are the result of a composite of social, political, institutional, experiential, and personal factors.

The relative stability of legal discourse affords us the opportunity to assess competing arguments for the expansion (and contraction) of the doctrinal sphere. When we consider the relative worth of the claims these arguments make upon us,[98] we have moved from the realm of the (linguistic) given to that of political choice. That is the business of social and political theory. If anything is clear in my argument, I hope it is this: without the relative stability of legal discourse, the possibility of normative choice in law is absolutely precluded. As an interpretive strategy, nihilism's greatest sin is not to render us mute, but to persuade us that the role of politics in law is utterly transparent.

Id. at 14. For a similar view, see generally J. FRANK, LAW AND THE MODERN MIND (1930).

The analytic tradition of philosophical thought is itself not entirely free from irrationalist tendencies. Owing to his perception that it leaves the determination of "relevant resemblance" to the imagination, the arch-empiricist David Hume found an irreducible element of irrationality in reasoning by analogy. See J. HARRISON, HUME'S THEORY OF JUSTICE 226-28 (1981).

98. *See* P. BOBBITT, CONSTITUTIONAL FATE (1982).

Name Index

For Product Safety Concerns and Information please contact our EU representative GPSR@taylorandfrancis.com
Taylor & Francis Verlag GmbH, Kaufingerstraße 24, 80331 München, Germany

www.ingramcontent.com/pod-product-compliance
Ingram Content Group UK Ltd.
Pitfield, Milton Keynes, MK11 3LW, UK
UKHW050800180926
475701UK00008B/1161

* 9 7 8 1 1 3 8 3 8 3 5 5 5 *